BUSDRIVERS NEVER GET ANYWHERE

Also by the Author

The Tax Climate for Philanthropy

World Changing Through Life Changing

The Spirit of Charles Lindbergh

BUSDRIVERS NEVER GET ANYWHERE

A Rendezvous With the Twentieth Century

T. Willard Hunter

Regina Books
Claremont, California

Editor: Alice Blake Chaffee
Typesetting: Peggy Zappen, Ives Community Office
Publishing Consultant: Richard D. Burns
Photographs: Richard D. Burns / Mark M. Dodge
Cover Production: Clinton Wade Graphic Design

Library of Congress Cataloging-in-Publication Data

Hunter, T. Willard, 1915-   **Busdrivers Never Get Anywhere:**
A rendezvous with the twentieth century / T. Willard Hunter.
p. cm.
ISBN 1-930053-15-0 (alk. paper)
1. Hunter, T. Willard, 1915- 2. Moral Re-armament
(Organization)–Officials and employees. 3. Clergy–United
States–Biography. 4. United States–Social life and customs. I.
Title
CT275.H75565 A3 2002
277.3'082'092–dc21

2002012099

Regina Books
Post Office Box 280
Claremont, California 91711
(909) 624-8466 Fax (909) 626-1345

Manufactured in the United States of America

To

Walter H. Judd

Missionary-Statesman

who more than anyone outside my family

triggered this journey

Table of Contents

Author's Note

Growing up in Northfield, Minnesota, in the 1920s, I went through the customary childhood career aims like firefighter and cowboy. Creeping maturity brought another goal—busdriver. Now we were talking power. Especially when the airbrake went HHCHCHSSSSSS. Awesome white motor coaches descended from the Twin Cities, thirty-five miles to the north. These low-slung white Fageol carriages (not the tall ones of today) were on their way to Iowa, and in Northfield they pulled up on Division Street across from the Stuart Hotel. When buses arrived, the ancient inn's Victorian lobby turned into an instant terminal. It claimed to be the nation's oldest bus depot. The name has since been changed to Archer House and it bills itself as "one of Minnesota's oldest river inns."

When the bus rolled to a stop, the dashing driver—moustache, leather gauntlets, puttees—came around and opened a half dozen right-hand doors onto the sidewalk. There was no center aisle, and each row of seats had its own exit. The fleet was owned and operated by the Jefferson Transportation Company, so named because its main routes ran from Minnesota to Louisiana along the north-south Jefferson Highway, a sister thoroughfare to the Lincoln Highway east and west.

Some of the buses' destination signs said MASON CITY, a precinct that sounded glamorous and far away. Actually it was just below the Iowa border, a scant hundred miles. In later years I made an after-dinner talk there (on Will Rogers) and learned that it was the hometown of Meredith Willson, whose River City in *The Music Man* was based on Mason City.

The passage of time cooled my zeal for busdriving. I noticed each driver had to bring that big rig to a complete stop at every railroad crossing, even though it might be a streak of rust on a siding long unused. In the dead of winter at ten below zero he had to open the door to make sure he could both hear and see the train that was not coming. These people went round and round, day after day, thousands of miles in the same ruts.

At length I told my father I had decided against being a busdriver.

"Why is that?" he asked.

"Well, they have to stop all the time, and they go back and forth and back and forth. They don't get anywhere."

With his wise smile full of years he said,

"Busdrivers **never** get anywhere."

Come to think of it, they are paid not to get anywhere.

Such a fate was not for me. As a young man I wanted to get somewhere. In a hurry. Or know the reason why. Being rich did not hold much appeal. Being famous had a lot to be said for it.

Then a funny thing happened on my way to the White House. John Lennon has been quoted as saying, "Life is what happens to us while we are busy making other plans." Somehow the whole thing changed around for me. Maybe getting somewhere was not what I was really about. A new purpose began when I tried to focus less on myself and more on others.

Busdrivers never get anywhere. But they help other people get somewhere.

I've never been all that good with others. But a different focus arose, so this story is more about focus than about achievement. The Alcoholics Anonymous folks say the way to help people is to "tell them what happened to you." I would be pleased if this account of one journeyman busdriver's itinerary might help some wayfarer get somewhere.

The Value of Stories

Everybody has a defining story. Garrison Keillor, after bouncing through Denmark and Brooklyn, brought his career back home to Minnesota, saying, "When you lose your story, you lose something you shouldn't lose."

There is a whiff of narcissism about autobiographies. Some make the disclaimer that they are putting it down for the grandchildren. In the mother of all autobiographies Benjamin Franklin writes, "My posterity may like to know," and adds,

> . . .I shall indulge the inclination so natural to old men, to
> be talking of themselves and their own past actions. . . .And (I

may as well confess it, since my denial of it will be believed by nobody), perhaps I shall a good deal gratify my own **vanity**. Indeed, I scarce ever heard or saw the introductory words **"Without vanity I may say, &c"** but some vain thing immediately followed.

There is another impetus. I wish I understood more than I do about my grandparents. I knew three of them, but we never talked about their prime time lives. And the fourth, Matthew Chambers Willard, a Galesburg Illinois merchant, died before our century began, so he is a blank, and I wish he were not. Matthew's widow, my grandmother Willard, lived with us for years during my boyhood. But we communicated only about immediate concerns like food and church, plus the occasional sharing of a missionary relative's letter from Korea. I wish I had asked her not only what kind of person her husband was, but also what life was like raising a family on the Illinois prairie as the nineteenth century wound down. If in the future, some one is curious about **our** generation, I hope these pages will fill some gaps.

People who have worked in the White House or on Capitol Hill can justify their accounts by an obligation to the historical record.

My motivations for producing this volume include all of the above—grandchildren, family annals, the historical record, encouraging a few others along the way, and personal vanity. The reader will soon discover that the stories in this book are designed to make the writer look good. I am really like the opponent of whom Winston Churchill said, "He is a humble man, and he has a great deal to be humble about."

I Was "Before" Quite a Lot

The year I was born, 1915, Woodrow Wilson was president of the United States. World War I had started but America was not yet in it. Battleships used the Panama Canal for the first time that year en route to San Diego. Ty Cobb set a major league record for stolen bases in one season, 86 (829 lifetime). War songs, "Keep the Home Fires Burning" (the first popular song I remember singing) and "Pack Up Your Troubles" were everywhere. Douglas Fairbanks and Charlie Chaplin were comers on the silent screen. In 1915 Henry Ford sold his millionth Model T, and Alexander Graham Bell made the first transcontinental phone call. Thomas Edison received the Nobel Prize for physics. Norman Rockwell had started drawing popular illustrations for the *Saturday Evening Post*. Chautauqua's tent programs were bringing top-quality lectures and concerts by famous performers to the small towns of the West.

I was "before" all the things Nardi Reeder Campion wrote about in her 1983 *Boston Globe* essay "Class of 1938 B.C.—Before Computers" for the forty-fifth reunion of her class at Wellesley—an essay that has been quoted more than anything since "The Message to Garcia."

Like everyone else of my generation, I respond to her litany:

> We were before television, penicillin, polio shots, antibiotics, Frisbees...frozen food, nylon, Xerox...radar...fluorescent lights...credit cards and ball point pens...*Grapes of Wrath*...Snoopy...Frank Sinatra...DDT...vitamin pills...Scotch tape...zippers...the automatic shift...tape recorders...electric typewriters...computers...jet aircraft...electric blankets...freezers...clothes dryers.

Culturally, I suppose you would call me middle-brow. My favorite music is George Gershwin; favorite artist, Charles M.

Russell. In books I prefer biography and history to novels, which don't give me anything I can write. I'm a slow reader, and I can get the gist of a novel's screen version which only takes a couple of hours.

A golfing buddy of Dwight D. Eisenhower, George Allen, wrote the ultimate name-dropping book, *Presidents Who Have Met Me*. Some may see the following report as another of those. But I have decided to take that chance. After all, names however dropped make news.

This book owes much to Alice Blake Chaffee of Carpinteria, the astute editor of this and other quality volumes. She was particularly helpful in giving the work form and flow. On the typesetting side, Peggy Zappen of the Ives Community Office in Claremont has been not only a whiz at her computer keyboard, but also has been most patient through many drafts with the author's maddening additions and corrections. Richard Burns, publisher of Regina Books in Claremont, has provided inestimable counsel, supplied out of his more than twenty years of publishing excellence.

Making the Formations

In World War II infantry training, central to the daily routine was falling out in formation in front of the barracks at the beginning of each day. From then on until sundown we did what we were told. The only decision ever required was to keep making those formations. It was what Woody Allen caught in his famous comment, "Ninety percent of life is just showing up."

For most of the twentieth century I usually showed up when and where I was supposed to. In the process I was led through four varied careers, and came close to some important events and eminent movers.

John Wayne sometimes asked, "Where you trottin' off to, pilgrim?" This book tries to answer for one pilgrim.

Harry Truman liked the epitaph he saw in Tombstone, Arizona:

"He done his damnedest."

I hope I have done mine.

Foreword

Tom Hunter

The title of this book is not altogether true, of course. Busdrivers do get somewhere. They just don't get somewhere of their own choosing. They follow prescribed routes and schedules, getting other people to places they want to get—to work, for example, or to school, or shopping, or home. They take people across the country too, or to the airport, or on charter tours, sometimes doubling as tour guides full of offbeat historical anecdotes. Often, when people don't know how to get somewhere, they ask busdrivers for directions.

My father has never been a busdriver, at least not that I know. Still, the metaphor works. For one thing, it connects him to his own father, and it's an important connection (which he'll tell you about later). For another, it suggests his role in helping quite a few other people get places they either wanted to go or agreed to go when he started driving, and how he sees that role as such a mixed blessing.

The truth is he wishes he had gotten more places himself—more accomplishments, more positions of influence. He's not unique in that wish, but what's also true is that many who 'rode his bus' are deeply grateful they did. Some have simply enjoyed spending time with him: he's a fascinating person to ride along with. Others are grateful because where his driving got them was into life-changing experiences—rehab programs, a deeper faith, a closer relationship with spouse or friend or colleague; with some the connection has been more distant.

He's driven well, through intense highs and lows—highs and lows that no one should have to experience—through the kind of personal pain and loss that might have done in someone with less spine or less faith, and through the mind-boggling changes of almost all of the twentieth century. He's driven with humor, many jokes, much celebration, and with tears too, sometimes from a heart broken or touched and sometimes from a belly convulsed with laughter.

And always, as he's driven, he's communicated. He sees himself as a communicator, and it's true. All along the way, he's tried to find ways to express faith, how God must have a plan, how lives can change, how education needs support, how the stories of history are interesting and instructive. He's communicated in writing and speaking, often looking with his words to find a deeper word—what spiritual energies drove Charles Lindbergh, or what sense of providence and heroism influenced the framers of the Constitution, or what's the morality of taxes and the federal debt? The journey has been filled with family and fun, passion and prayer, and much wrestling in the soul.

This busdriver may not have gotten some places he would have liked to get. But don't be fooled—this bus has traveled a long way, with many people aboard, and there are wonderful stories to tell. It's been quite a ride. And now it's quite a read.

> *Tom Hunter, a minstrel to children*
> *and their teachers, is the*
> *author's oldest of three sons.*

- 1 -

GROWING UP IN JESSE JAMES COUNTRY

What Northfield Did to Jesse James
What Jesse James Does for Northfield

On September 7, 1876, my hometown, Northfield, Minnesota, stormed its way into American mythology. In seven minutes Jesse James and his highly professional gang were stopped cold by aroused Northfield citizens who were prepared to defend to the death what they had and what they were. They rang down the curtain on the career of America's most famous criminal. Their shots were heard 'round the world.

Northfield, a quiet farming and college town thirty-five miles south of Minneapolis / Saint Paul, was targeted that fall by the notorious Missouri brigand and his brother Frank. With them were the Younger brothers, Cole, Jim, and Bob, plus three more desperados—Bill Stiles, Clell Miller, and Charlie Pitts. The eight had developed a highly successful and well-publicized strategy for looting banks and railroads. Jesse, with a fifteen-year run of unanswered crime behind him, had turned only twenty-nine two days before the Northfield raid.

Although the renowned visitors were feared in the middle states to the south, the Northfield storekeepers, hundreds of miles from the robbers' Missouri base, would have no way of knowing who these strangers were, dressed like cattle buyers in their long gray linen dusters. Whoever they were, it was soon clear that the invaders were robbing their bank.

The alarm was sounded, rifles materialized, and a fierce battle followed. It lasted no longer than it takes to cook a hard-boiled egg, but the small town heroes had foiled the nation's most celebrated outlaws. Stiles and Miller lay lifeless in the street. Also a local Swedish immigrant, Nicholas Gustafson, who spoke no English and could not understand the robbers' orders. Inside the bank the cashier, Joseph Lee Heywood, had been shot dead, probably by Frank James, for refusing to open the safe.

The gang had to flee with no take. The James brothers would soon be in South Dakota and then safely back home in Missouri, but they never robbed another bank. The three Younger brothers were captured, tried in nearby Faribault, the seat of Rice County, and sentenced to imprisonment for life in Minnesota's Stillwater penitentiary on the Saint Croix River.

As soon as word went out that the brigands had been resisted and had fled, a thousand people turned up from everywhere, hoping to join a real live western posse. The fugitives slogged westward through the wetlands during the long days and nights, and the footing was so bad they had to let their horses go. It was in Hanska Slough near Madelia, sixty miles west of Northfield, that the posses closed in to dispatch Pitts and apprehend the Youngers.

The town was famous overnight. It still is. Of the many Hollywood versions of the Jesse James story, one of the best is entitled *The Great Northfield Minnesota Bank Raid.*

The folks in Northfield have reenacted the raid every year since 1948. During the first week of each September crowds pour through the town to celebrate what at first was called Jesse James Days. Not wishing to be seen as glorifying a criminal, they soon changed the name to The Defeat of Jesse James Days. The theme of the festival is the courageous strength of the forces of righteousness rallying to defeat the legions of evil. Increasing emphasis is given to the hero-martyr, Joseph Lee Heywood, who resisted the demand of the robbers and laid down his life, as memorialized to this day on the wall of the bank:

IN THIS ROOM
JOSEPH LEE HEYWOOD
REFUSING TO BETRAY HIS TRUST
WAS SHOT BY BANK ROBBERS
SEPTEMBER 7, 1876
FAITHFUL UNTO DEATH

The expanding annual gala during the week after Labor Day brings an estimated 100,000 to the city, where they see not only numerous reenactments of the bank raid, but also a major outdoor art festival, a professional rodeo, and a celebrity parade. Jesse James did not take a dime out of Northfield but he has pumped millions into it.

The story of Jesse James was part of the upbringing of all us Northfield kids. We were proud of the town's Old West legacy—real shoot-em-up with horses, riders, guns, robbers, and, in the end, good overcoming evil.

One of our neighbors, H. A. Bert Whittier, had been an eyewitness to the raid. One of Northfield's most notable sons, he went into railroading with Empire Builder James J. Hill and later constructed the Minneapolis, Northfield, and Southern line, then went on to mining lignite coal in North Dakota. His family lived in one of the town's fine houses, across Nevada Street from us. On the day of the James-Younger raid, Bert was thirteen years old and working in a blacksmith shop across the square from the bank. He and his friend were of course riveted, and after the raid and the escape of the robbers, they saw Bob Younger's dead horse lying in the street. They ran out, cut the saddle off the horse, and took it to the Whittier home.

The saddle was inherited by Bert's daughter Gladys (Petie), a horsewoman married to movie cowboy Don Coleman. For years the Colemans kept it in their home in Willits, California. After Petie's death, a northern California cowboy friend, Charles

Benbow, in 1988 brought the saddle back to Northfield, and it is displayed under glass in the room of the raid.

Some Missouri people saw Jesse as a kind of Robin Hood, using crime to help the poor. But most scholars agree with author John Ernst in *Jesse James* (New York: Prentice Hall, 1976), "There is no solid evidence that he used his illegal gains to benefit anyone but himself."

He did, however, earn quasi-hero status in southern-sympathizing Missouri. During the Civil War he and his brother had been trained by the ruthless pro-Southern guerilla, William Clarke Quantrill. They cultivated the aura of Confederate champions, carrying on the War Between the States, avenging the North's humiliation of the South. Since the banks and railroads represented eastern yankee money, robbing them was only frontier justice. In fifteen years of major crime the James brothers never spent a day in jail. Hundreds of farm homes were available to them for hiding out, protected by well wishers.

Their aim in Northfield was to expropriate the substantial deposits they heard had been made in the local bank by two Union Army officers, General William Butler of Massachusetts and his son-in-law, Adelbert Ames. Ames was hated in the South as he had served during the reconstruction as a carpet-bagger governor of Mississippi.

It was this North-South aspect of the 1876 raid that led Carl Weicht, editor of the *Northfield News*, to surmise, "The final shots of the Civil War may have been fired on the streets of Northfield, Minnesota."

Cows, Colleges, and Contentment

The roads leading into Northfield have at times displayed highway signs proclaiming it to be a city of "COWS, COLLEGES, AND CONTENTMENT." For a while that sentiment proved too corny for the academics of Northfield's two colleges. So the friendly signs were replaced with a stuffier legend, "A Special Place." In recent times, however, the three "Cs" have come back.

The "Cows" theme arose from Northfield's onetime position as center of the Holstein dairy cattle industry. When I was a boy, this distinction was symbolized by newspaperman turned cattleman W. F. Schilling, who managed a large Holstein herd southwest of town. He was also a member of President Herbert Hoover's five-person Farm Board.

The "Colleges" element, featuring Carleton and Saint Olaf colleges, made Northfield even better known, developed by two distinct strains of immigrants to southern Minnesota. The Cannon River divides Northfield east and west. The Anglo-Saxons clustered mainly on the east side, where dwells Carleton College, founded by New England Congregationalists in 1866. A substantial Congregational church grew up alongside, which our family attended.

Scandinavians settled on the west side. The Norwegian Lutherans established Saint Olaf College in 1874 on the city's western hill, known as Manitou Heights. During its first century, the school held as its chief mission the preservation in the New World of the Norwegian Lutheran culture. Saint John's Lutheran Church was their spiritual anchor. The Saint Olaf Choir, founded by F. Melius Christiansen, burst on the world scene at New York's Carnegie Hall in 1920, and ever since has made international impact. Its Christmas program has been telecast annually by Public Broadcasting Service (PBS). Christiansen (pronounced "Krist-Johnson") composed or arranged over 250 musical selections, including the choir's popular signature anthem "Beautiful Savior."

Incidentally, Christiansen's son Paul and I were classmates at Northfield High School He went on to clone his father's experience at Concordia College in Minnesota for fifty years. The other Saint Olaf icon in our day was Norwegian novelist O. E. Rolvaag, who wrote a national bestseller about the hardship of Scandinavian immigrants entitled *Giants in the Earth* (New York: Harper 1927). His son Fritz and I ran on the high school track team, and he became governor of Minnesota.

The story of our journey to Northfield is the story of my father bridging two careers and my mother's gifted and loving support. The two careers were education and the church, and the journey was from Idaho to Minnesota with a stop on the Missouri River in Nebraska.

Our family moved in 1917 from Emmett, Idaho, where I was born, to Bellevue, Nebraska, south of Omaha, where we lived for two years. Dad had graduated from Bellevue College in 1905, studied theology in Omaha and Princeton, and in 1908 received two degrees in Princeton—one a Bachelor of Divinity degree from Princeton Theological Seminary, and the other a Master of Arts degree in English literature from Princeton University. The diploma from the latter carries in fading ink the signature of Woodrow Wilson, Princeton's president at the time.

My father was ordained in Omaha in 1908 and then taught in Florida 1908-10 at the Presbyterian College in Eustis. Health problems prompted him to seek a drier climate in the West, being later diagnosed as having recovered from incipient tuberculosis. His father, the Rev. Thomas K. Hunter, who was a kind of star in frontier Presbyterianism in the early twentieth century, helped him find a position as a Presbyterian home missionary in three small Idaho towns. He served there from 1911 to 1917, spending the last of those years in Emmett, a Payette Valley agricultural center twenty-five miles northwest of Boise.

In the fall of 1914, following her graduation from Knox

College, my father married Louise Willard of Galesburg, Illinois. They had met in Omaha where her stepfather, theology professor Joseph J. Lampe, had organized a new Presbyterian church in suburban Dundee and had retained Dad's father, T. K., as pastor for its first four years.

My father had already served three years in Idaho home missionary churches when he was married, and his bride joined him for the next three in Emmett. I was born there September 22, 1915, in a house, now torn down, at 503 Washington.

Dad used to express warm appreciation for my mother's uncomplaining adjustment from a well-to-do upbringing in a successful businessman's home in Galesburg to the rather crude amenities on the Idaho frontier. "She was used to all the comforts and luxuries," he said, "yet entered into home mission life in primitive country with zest, winning hearts. With few conveniences and small means, she showed the utmost cheerfulness and helpfulness."

My mother's grandfather, Silas Willard (1814-57), was a pioneering business power in Galesburg, Illinois. When he was twenty, he left Barré, Vermont, to move his tubercular brother to a healthier climate. The attempt to save his brother's life was not successful, but Silas, a harness-maker, stayed on to become a merchant, joining the business of another transplant, Matthew Chambers, who had made the trek to Illinois in 1836 from Bridport, Vermont. A Chambers daughter, Cordelia, became Mrs. Silas Willard, and thus my mother's grandmother. Family records indicate the Willards are descended from Stephen Hopkins, a signer of the Mayflower Compact. The Chambers had been stirred by the Second Great Awakening to move west and build with others an ideal college, church, and community at Galesburg. Matthew Chambers held the first Knox College trustees' meeting in his log store. He was also a leader of Illinois' aggressive anti-slavery movement. Cordelia was a member of the first student class at Knox. Her husband, Silas Willard, lived in Galesburg only eight years, but during that time he started the first flour mill, was a heavy investor in routing the Burlington Railroad through Galesburg, served as a Burlington director for life, was honored by having the city's premier grade school named for him, and built one of Galesburg's fine old homes. The dwelling was later taken over by his son Matthew Chambers Willard, and Matthew's three children were born there, one of them being my mother (1892). In the 1990s this home was renovated as a bed and breakfast inn.

In Idaho where I was born, they tell me I was taken in a basket to the Emmett church every Sunday. I've been going to church most Sundays ever since. For a baby-sitter, the folks sometimes retained thirty-something Daisy Chandler, known as an outstanding teacher, who fifty years later showed us around Emmett when I took my own family back to explore.

Among the happy memories the folks had of Emmett was the friendship and support of the family of Andrew Little, the "sheep king" of Idaho. He and his wife Agnes were immigrants from Scotland and made it big in the Western sheep business. According to biographer Louis Shadduck, Agnes was "the moving force behind the building of the Presbyterian Church in Emmett."

In addition to his church work, my father dabbled in growing prunes on forty acres on the Bench, a low mesa north of town. The fruit business did not pan out for him. Apparently the ministry, at that location, was not all that great either. He wrote:

> To this community, then in my inexperienced enthusiasm, I brought my beautiful, college-bred bride; and with high hopes we entered upon our work. . . . After three years of heartbreak and futile effort I left that field, my spirit well nigh broken and my self-sacrificing, splendid Christian wife in tears.

Bellevue on the Missouri River

They left the Idaho frontier in the summer of 1917 so poor, according to Dad, they had to borrow thirty dollars to pay their freight east. They were off for what turned out to be a two-year hitch in Bellevue, Nebraska. My father had a dual assignment. He was dean of Bellevue College (now Bellevue University) and also helped out with the local Presbyterian congregation, the oldest church in Nebraska, organized by missionaries in 1856. The city lies on a bluff above the Missouri River, south of Omaha. In 1838 John Jacob Astor's American Fur Company established a trading post here.

In contrast to the Emmett period, Dad called the Bellevue time a happy two years.

My experience is that most people's memories begin around age three (although Dad insisted throughout his life that he could remember seeing a bird being killed when he was eight months). At any rate my first memories are of Bellevue when I was three. In my mind's eye I have pictures of the old gray church, and looking up at the pulpit where Dad was preaching. Also of my wagon that I drove up and down the sidewalk. Behind the church was a spreading tree, great for climbing. One afternoon I fell out of it, and the thud knocked the wind out of me. Recovering, I started to yell, and it took Dad a while to find where the hollering was coming from. I also remember the streetcar and its efficient conductor on the ride from Bellevue up to Omaha. For some reason I have often pictured in my mind stretches of the ride when repeating the different parts of the Twenty-Third Psalm. We took that streetcar to visit Mother and my new baby brother Stuart. They say I went looking for him under her hospital bed. He was born March 4, 1919, and Belle-vue College closed for the day in honor of the dean's family's blessed event.

In the summer of 1919 the Presbyterians folded the college. They believed they could not support two schools of this type and decided to merge Bellevue into Hastings College out in the middle of the state. Dad believed this to be an error and that it would be better to consolidate at Bellevue, nearer sources of support in metropolitan Omaha. He thought he had the board's approval of his plan to raise funds for continuing the Bellevue site. But they changed their minds and in the end decided on Hastings.

When the final decision to terminate was made, it was summer and a new academic year barely two months away. Dad was, in his words, "exhausted and out of a job." He also had two youngsters to feed. He applied to the Teacher's Exchange in Chicago for a college classroom position. It so happened that at the very moment his application arrived, late in August, Dr. Donald J. Cowling, president of Carleton College, was at the agency looking for an English professor. Cowling was dedicated to the college's church traditions, and it probably did not hurt that Dad was a minister-teacher as well as a former college dean. At any rate he was off to Northfield, the rest of us not far behind.

It was, as they say, a defining moment for our family. Nothing was ever again the same. All three of us children (sister Helen was to come along seven years later) grew up and were educated in Northfield. Mother was to live her remaining fifteen years there, and Dad would remain, remarry, and live and teach in the community for a total of thirty-three years.

-2-

SMALLTOWN USA

I have vivid memories of arriving in Northfield that fall of 1919. Dad came on ahead, while Mother, my brother Stu (six months) and I (four years) followed. We landed in Northfield's tiny Milwaukee railroad station and waited for Dad to come and get us. On the waiting room wall was a terrifying safety-poster picture of a family being crushed in their auto by a speeding train. Sitting around were some old codgers from the hot stove league. One of them asked my name, and I gave my standard, four-year-old answer, "Thomas Willard Hunter, but they call me Willard."

"Hunter, eh?" he responded, "What are you hunting?" Heh, heh, heh. He thought that was a good one.

That depot was to be important to us for a long time. It linked us with the Twin Cities and Chicago. As a college student, I went from there to Kansas City both for a summer job and for a winter national student meeting. There in 1957 we offloaded Dad's casket at the end of his journey home from California to be buried beside our mother.

A small, Midwestern community is a great place to grow up. During our first years in Northfield, starting in the fall of 1919, we lived in four houses on Nevada Street. One night during our first winter, the snow that piled up on the roof was so heavy that the front porch caved in. That summer we had a big hailstorm. Fifty years later, next-door neighbor Grace Whittier, Bert's older daughter, told me that she had been amused at my father parsimoniously gathering hailstones for our icebox.

One of our Nevada Street homes was called Sperry Lodge, a large residence converted to a dormitory for Carleton freshman girls. We lived there because my mother was named resident head, for the students to have someone to talk to and someone to encourage friendly compliance with college standards. At the tender age of eight I was sometimes included in the residents' dramatic productions, once playing a singing seed in an enlarged watermelon mock-up. In the 1920 May Fete I was a butterfly.

The Hunter apartment at Sperry Lodge was on the ground floor, and there was a low-positioned airflow register in the wall between our quarters and the next room occupied by two of the girls. One day they reported to my mother that I was peeking through the register. That took care of that. When I became a college student myself and addressed a homecoming convocation, I could brag that I was the only male student at Carleton who had ever lived four years in a women's dormitory. It was a good line at the time, but that was before coed living.

Our mother was beautiful in every way, both a loving and a diligent parent. I still remember the times around her knee memorizing the Beatitudes and the Ten Commandments, the latter including the explanatory fine print. She put a chart on the kitchen wall, with a column for each day of the week. A color-coded star was placed for each activity she deemed important for our physical and spiritual health—hair combed, teeth brushed, bowels moved, and Bible verses memorized.

Mother's knee was the locale of my first reading experience also. I was about four, and she had me repeat the word B-E-S-T from a Pillsbury flour sack. We acquired our flour in cotton bags, which later became dishtowels. Also we bought coffee in the natural bean, and a Saturday chore of mine was to sit on a stool with an old-fashioned, Armstrong (my arm) coffee grinder and reel the handle for what seemed like hours. In the process I got to chew some of the beans, and they tasted great.

Mother was careful with the family finances, and at month's end she would at times stay up most of the night tracking down a discrepancy in the bank balance.

I recall an early lesson in honesty. Coming home late one afternoon, I claimed I had to stay after school. Mother reported that a friend of hers had seen me downtown instead. I was in trouble on two counts: I had not let my parents know of reasons for modifying normal movements, and I had lied about the nature of the modification. The episode made a big impression on me.

My father, Stuart McKlveen Hunter (five consonants in a row) (1883-1957) was slightly smaller in stature than mother. He was born in Griswold, Iowa, the son of a Presbyterian minister. He had a huge spirit and a somewhat wizened psyche. His repression may have been due to his mother having given preferred treatment to his sister. He was impressed that I was able, with people, as he said, to put my "best foot forward." His father, Thomas K. Hunter (1852-1923), was of a different stripe—cheerful and outgoing, a leader in church and community. As I reviewed his dates, I was startled to realize how much history three generations can cover. Here was my grandfather, a person I knew and talked with in my lifetime, who was already a teenager when Abraham Lincoln was assassinated. Like Harry S. Truman, his middle initial stood for nothing. Grandpa Hunter's great contribution was to bring a whole string of Iowa, Nebraska, and Idaho Presbyterian churches from "Home Missionary" class to self-supporting status. He was the only one of seven brothers to receive an education, as he had been, as the first born, "dedicated to the Lord" by his parents. He attended Wooster College and Danville Seminary. He was tall and grizzled, yet cultured and well-read. My mother called him a saint. The severity of his bushy moustache was topped by twinkly eyes. When he visited us in Northfield, he hoisted me on his knee and with great gusto belted out:

> How much wood could a woodchuck chuck
> If a woodchuck could chuck wood?
> He could chuck as much wood as a woodchuck would
> If a woodchuck could chuck wood!

Grandpa Hunter died in 1923 in Kimball, Nebraska, his last parish, almost on the Wyoming border. Dad and my brother and I went down for the services in Kimball and Omaha. Mother stayed in Northfield, and it was my first excruciatingly painful experience of homesickness. Another first for me on this trip was in an Omaha school to sit with black boys and girls in a classroom. I had not seen people like that in Minnesota, but I was not there long enough to make friends.

As the Minnesota snow began to melt each year, we went through not only "mud season," but also a convulsion called "spring cleaning." Everything got moved around and dusted and vacuumed. Women's heads and brooms were wrapped in dishtowels while cobwebs were brushed down from upper corners.

Spring, of course, has special delights in Minnesota, such a contrast to the heavy winter. The robin was our particular friend, and the children vied with each other at school over who would be the first to tell the teacher they saw one. The Minnesota state bird is the common loon, but birds of that feather flock together only up north. Our bond was with Robin Red Breast.

Around the age of ten, I contracted a case of ringworm in my scalp. The doctor prescribed shaving my head, applying an ointment, and wrapping it in a cap down to my eyes and ears. My mother made fresh dressings daily from old bedsheets. This of course gave me quite a lot of notoriety. It may have gone on for six months. When it appeared that no progress was being made, I was taken to a specialist in Saint Paul, who put me through an x-ray treatment. That cleared it up—except for lifelong bouts with another ringworm condition, athlete's foot.

Our family physician, Dr. Haskins, a wheezy, red-faced, genial type, made house calls in the old style. One time I had soreness in one of the "family jewels," and I recall Mother being happy that boys as well as girls had problems in the reproductive area. The condition may have been a harbinger of the hydrocelectomy that would later interrupt my army training in World War II.

We sang together as a family, not only Sunday evening hymns, but also Stephen Foster and a wide variety. Mother would sing to us her sorority pep song from Knox College days, "Pi Phi's will shine tonight, Pi Phi's will shine . . . When the sun goes down and the moon comes up, Pi Phi's will shine!" The Broadway tune she especially liked came from *No, No Nannette*: "I want to be happy, but I can't be happy, till I make you happy too!" "That's such a wonderful philosophy," she would say.

When we had the wedding at our house in Northfield for a friend from Emmett days, Jessie McCauley, to Summer Whitney, I was an attendant and wore what my father called "ice cream pants." I believe it was shortly after this occasion that my mother explained to my brother and me that we were going to have a little brother or sister before long. My father said they were praying for a girl.

Mrs. Bertha Vestling, across the street, was due ahead of Mother, and when her time came, all of us on the street could hear her cries of pain from the bedroom in their house. Sadly, her baby was stillborn.

For our event, Mother moved to Northfield's make-do hospital, a large house on Water Street near the river. On June 23, 1926, seven years after my brother arrived, our sister Helen was born. Of course everyone was delighted and has been ever since.

After Helen's birth Mother developed something that was

then called "milk leg," a not uncommon postpartum condition. However, it seemed to develop into something more, affecting her motor nerves and making her stagger. Sometimes she could not lift her arms high enough to fix her hair. At other times, she was better. We went everywhere where we heard of a wisp of hope, including one time when we waited for a day on a South Dakota farm where a semi-faith healer was attracting crowds of cure-seekers. Sadly, our parents' ten minutes with him resulted in no change. The problem was later diagnosed as multiple sclerosis, and few had ever heard of it. Now it is known as "MS," and the search for its cure is one of today's popular multi-million-dollar causes.

My mother had a keen sense of history and was involved with the Daughters of the American Revolution (DAR). She spurred the family to drive thirty-five miles north to Mendota, at the confluence of the Mississippi and Minnesota Rivers, and tour with others from around the state the home of Henry Hastings Sibley, the first governor of Minnesota. My mother and her mother, Ideletta Willard Lampe, traced their lineage to the American Revolution through William Faris (1734-1818), a three-year Continental army private who fought at the Battle of Yorktown. Mother could also have made the claim through her great-great-grandfather, Matthew Chambers, Sr., who served as a captain in the Revolutionary Army, was commanding officer at West Point, and a confidant of George Washington.

The Northfield DAR never had a more active member than my mother. In Washington's 200th birthday year, May 1932, the local DAR ladies planted on the lawn of our Carnegie Library a "Washington Elm," derived from the tree in Cambridge, Massachusetts, under which George Washington in 1775 took command of the Continental Army. The mayor and a dozen or so civic types were on hand for the dedication. Mother was in charge of the program, and enlisted me to deliver the Washington Bicentennial oration I had presented in high-school circles that year. Unhappily, perhaps from too much hot air, the little tree soon died. However, all was not lost. The ladies obtained another planting from Cambridge; it grew to sixty feet and was later removed to make way for a library addition.

Siblings

My sister Helen, eleven years younger than I, made her way with everybody. She inherited her mother's beauty and developed an upbeat, classy personality, concerned with the well-being of everyone she met. When she was twelve, she was chosen official flower girl to present, at a ceremony in Northfield's Bridge Square, a bouquet to the visiting Norwegian royal couple, Crown Prince Olav and Crown Princess Martha, duly photographed in the *Minneapolis Tribune*. She never knew why she was selected ahead of someone from the local Norwegian community, but speculates they might have been avoiding possible jealousies among their own.

My younger brother Stu (Stuart McKlveen Hunter II), being nearer my age, was a closer friend in the growing-up days. Although we were separated in age by only three and a half years, class scheduling put us five school years apart. One result was that our five-year class reunions at Carleton have coincided.

Stu was the humorist of the family. I'm the kind of person who can *remember* funny things. He *thought* funny. Dad always got a big boot out of Stu's antics and the twist he put on things. When we were camping in Yellowstone Park, and had been warned against familiarity with the bears, we were startled one evening by heavy clawing on the outside of our tent. When Dad went out to investigate, he was relieved and delighted it was Stu making like a bear. Stu's quotes would fill a pamphlet. For example:

"I've made a sap out of myself a hundred times already. I guess I can stand it once more."

He was larger and taller than I, but with the age differential we came out pretty even in the fights. One summer a neighbor across the lake looked at Stu, and then at Dad, a fairly small man, and said, "Well, I see you're improving the breed." Although my football career was only about as successful as Richard Nixon's, Stu was a regular starting lineman on the Northfield High School squad and was selected for the all-regional team. When Northfield met Faribault, he played opposite Faribault's Bruce Smith, who went on to become an All-American back at the University of Minnesota.

My brother was a notable student citizen. In 1936 he was tapped for the honor of giving Lincoln's Gettysburg Address at the Northfield Memorial Day ceremonies. In World War II, he was a Transportation Corps officer in Europe, receiving a medal from General Patton for his critique of the Transportation Corps. On his last assignment he was commander of Hermann Goering's former personal train. Then for twenty-three years he was personnel director of Northfield's Sheldahl Company, plastic bag making machinery, and was called by the company's president the "consummate human relations expert."

The House on Second Street

Around 1930, we finally left Nevada Street and moved a block and a half west to 407 East Second Street, another dwelling owned by the college. The depression was rough, but our experience of it was better than that of many. Dad's salary for years never went above $2,800 a year, part of it paid in scrip, some of it subject to an agreed faculty cut of ten percent. Over against that, we paid rent of but $45 a month and enjoyed the upkeep skills of college maintenance personnel.

The Second Street house was a two-story, square box, with a screened half-porch on the front right. The outside walls were of synthetic siding. Inside, on the first floor back, was our parents' bedroom. To the west was the dining room, and to the east a book-lined study with a fireplace. The living room in front had a bay window looking out onto Second Street. A switchback stairway led to three upstairs bedrooms and a bathroom, the gabled roof descending here and there to cut into the space. In the basement there was a coal bin, coal furnace, and a water storage cistern to catch rain run-off, and this was used for washing. We also kept "eggs in glass" through the winter by means of a huge crockery cask in the basement. The "glass" was a gelatinous, liquid preservative.

My father had a reference book entitled *8000 Words Often Mispronounced.* I asked him why he wanted a book with so many mistakes? He laughed and said, "I guess you think the title ought to read, '8000 Words Pronounced As Well As They Possibly Could Be'."

Our garage in back was an old barn from the horse and buggy era, with a second-floor reminder of the hay-dispensing days. Between the barn and the neighbor's fence was a narrow strip where we buried our garbage every day with a spade-fork. While disposing of kitchen wastes, the exercise also fertilized what garden was possible in the small space. Dad usually arranged for a larger gardening area in another neighborhood, as he was good at growing tomatoes, corn, and beans. He would go out and bring back what he called a "mess" of peas, enough for the family's evening meal. I recalled this word when in the war I ate in army mess halls. In harvesting corn, the deal was that mother would put the water on to boil only when dad came into view with the fresh ears. No good having any taste-deadening time between picking and eating.

We got through the Minnesota winters with a furnace that

burned soft coal. A truck would come up alongside the house, a metal trough inserted in the small basement window, and the big black hunks of coal shoveled to slide down a twelve-foot metal trough. It made such a clatter that our whole end of town knew what was happening.

It was my job periodically to "fix" the furnace. This meant that every two or three hours I would descend to the basement and shake the ashes out by pumping a big cleat-wrench back and forth, then shoveling the ashes from under the grate into a three-foot high ash can. After that I would lay down several shovelsful of coal on top of the still glowing embers and adjust the dampers in the chimney pipes according to whether burning was to be fast or slow.

One evening we were dinner guests of Professor and Mrs. Leal Headley. The meal had barely begun when Mrs. Headley[1] said to their son, "Marston, will you fix the furnace, please?" I figured we wouldn't see him for a while. But all he did was walk to the nearby wall and "fix" the furnace by resetting the thermostat. That was it. They were the first in town to have oil heat. They also had a Franklin air-cooled automobile.

In the days before the New Deal and organized public welfare, men called hoboes used to come to the house and ask for something to eat. Sometimes they would inquire whether we had any work for them, but I can remember only once was such an offer accepted. Mother was hospitable and gave them a plate of food they could eat on the back steps. We heard that these people might put a mark on our house as a soft touch, but we never found one.

In those days, we had two mail deliveries a day. Groceries and ice were brought to the house by wagon. The horses made the

---

[1]Harriet Marston Headley was a daughter of the San Diego merchant/philanthropist George Marston.

streetwise English sparrows happy. When you picked up the phone, "Central" answered, and you gave her by voice the number you wanted. For food needs, Mother put in a morning telephone call to Federman's grocery store and read off her list. Later that day the Federman grocery wagon would arrive and deliver our order on our back steps.

The downtown meat market, its floor covered with sawdust, was separate from the grocery store and did not deliver. Before long, two national chain store outlets moved into town, the National Tea Company and the Atlantic and Pacific Tea Company (A&P). "Cash and carry" they were called. The prices were lower, and Federman's phased out. Milk, however, was still delivered to our back door by the Cantleys, who operated a dairy farm on the edge of town. This was before pasteurizing (we thought pasteurization ruined the taste), and a half-pint of cream would rise to the narrow top of the bottle.

Our ice was saved and harvested during the winter from the Cannon River and stored in a big icehouse on the east bank, tons of sawdust preserving it against the summer heat. Every day we put out a sign to say which multiple of twenty-five pounds we wanted. The ice man stopped his horse, moved to the back of his wagon, chipped out a cake, picked it up with his tongs, carried it to the back of our house, and put it through a small latched aperture into our ice box. We were discouraged from eating the refreshing chips as the towns along the river dumped their sewage into it. Red Grange, All-American football star at the University of Illinois in the twenties, fired up a generation of kids for the ice delivery business when news photos showed him hauling a chunk on his shoulders as part of his training the summer before his senior year.

We lived near the edge of town, and we could roam the hills, streams, and farmlands. My grade school friend, Howard Holden, invited me out to their family farm to explore the fields and play in a haymow. It was about a mile and a half walk from home, and one day I took my brother Stu. We pretended the haymow was a swimming pool, and dove from upper rafters. To this day, whenever I smell pungent hay, I think of that farm.

Our family occupied the Second Street house nearly a quarter of a century, and it saw all three of us children through Northfield High School. I was graduated in 1932, Stu in 1937, and Helen in 1944. It was in an upstairs room of that house where our mother died. And it was in the downstairs living room where she then lay in state, while loving friends came by to pay their respects.

The Grandmothers

We almost always had grandmothers living with us. Gertrude Stephens Hunter, widow of my paternal grandfather, Thomas K. Hunter, was small of stature and outlook. She would sit in her rocker and knit and philosophize. She often wore a shawl and a high choke collar. There was always something wrong with her, and my father said she "enjoyed poor health." She usually had a reason why she was not up to helping with the dishes or other household tasks. She was not much for the Revised Standard Version of the Bible; for her the King James Version was the only way to go. Also she did not take kindly to a preacher who read his prayers in the pulpit. If he didn't have it in his heart clear enough to pray without notes, he wasn't much account. Eloquent in favor of Prohibition, she was a one-issue voter, and said that repeal-advocating Franklin Roosevelt had "only one thing in his cranium—beer!"

My father's relationship with his mother was a zigzag road. He felt she treated him badly in childhood, thinking she favored his little sister who died at age three, and later the girl his folks adopted to take her place.

There was always some bitterness, and the association remained formal. Dad told me that when he would leave the house to go back to school or college after a vacation, she would be apt to say, "Well, Stuart, we were glad to see you come, and we are glad to see you go." Yet whatever the coolness, he was about as devoted a son as any one could wish for. He wrote her every week. I recall taking him ten miles northeast of Northfield to Randolph, a town earlier devastated by a tornado, to catch the Great Western train on its way from Saint Paul to Omaha. He had a free clergy pass, and about once a month he went down Friday night to visit his mother and returned Sunday night. She lived, along with our Grandmother Willard, at Omaha's Florence Home for the Aged. (When I addressed an envelope that way she wrote back that I could write just "Florence Home.")

Dad's mother's full name was Gertrude Evangeline Stephens Hunter, and she was married in 1882 to his father, Thomas K. Hunter. They are buried, with their little Helen, in Nebraska City where TK was serving the Presbyterian church when she died.

My mother's mother, Ideletta Lou Henry Willard, was of a different stripe. Both grandmothers were unswerving in their devotion to fundamental religion, but Grandma Willard was a workhorse and always gave out more than she probably should have, a latter-day "suffering servant." Her first husband, the grandfather we never knew, was Matthew Chambers Willard, a merchant in Galesburg, Illinois, who died in 1894 of pernicious anemia while in Providence, Rhode Island, on a business trip. His wife had been worried about whether his stock-market activity was, in effect, gambling. My mother was two years old when her father died.

Thirteen years later, Grandmother Willard married widower Joseph J. Lampe, mentioned earlier, a Presbyterian theologian who taught at Union Theological Seminary in New York and Omaha Theological Seminary in Nebraska. She survived both husbands and all three of her children. Her faith was a rock and she attacked life with great enthusiasm and dedication, punctuated by joy.

Music

It was a given that we children would have musical training, or at least some exposure. (Stu was to get into the French horn; Helen the clarinet.) As for me, from the fourth grade to the eighth, I dutifully took piano lessons, practicing seventy minutes a day, the extra ten (times six) making up for the hour not practiced on Sunday. My first teacher was Agnes Page, and I weekly trudged over to her house on Third Street. She was well along in years, or so it seemed to me. Her fingers were curled from arthritis, but they could still coax great tones from the piano. One day during a lesson we watched the Methodist church go by on rollers, pulled by a horse, on its way a few blocks to its new location. After four years of arduous effort, it was clear to all that Paderewski I was not. The lessons were dropped. What I learned, however, has been beneficial to me in music appreciation and amateur singing. Eight years later Agnes Page sent me a nice note from Glendale, California, congratulating me on graduation from college.

Town Characters

Every small town has its local personalities. One of ours we all suffered with was the man whose Saint Vitus Dance made it difficult for him to navigate down the street, but he still did not give up.

The police chief was W. D. Smith. A current gag was, "I know the whole Northfield police department—he's a great guy."

Frank Gibbs was not quite all there, but he had a wonderful spirit and hauled away everybody's garbage. We all respected and liked him. His first word to anyone he met on the street was an opinion about the weather. Frank stood straight and tall and dressed carefully for church every Sunday, taking a front pew seat on the Baptist side. Hearts were warmed when he found a nice, quiet, plump little woman who agreed to marry him. Their devotion was touching.

Campus Ventureland

The Carleton campus held magnetic enticements for a small boy. I rode around the curved walks with my wagon as though it were a Greyhound bus, and got good at reversing and coming alongside a curb. Major buildings under construction—a dormitory and a stadium, with their damp smell of fresh concrete—presented alluring labyrinths for exploration on evenings and weekends, each room and underground passage an avenue for adventure.

Gridley Hall, one of the early campus structures, was the dormitory for freshman women. Presiding over Gridley was Dean of Women Adella M. Catton, mother of Civil War historian Bruce Catton. Behind Gridley was a mounded-up potato cellar where vegetables for the dormitory kitchens were stored, also great for exploring. On the Gridley lawn were some huge horse-chestnut trees that produced hard, brown, shiny chestnuts that served as barter-coin among the younger set.

The college bookstore provided a perquisite for faculty types, such as wholesale prices on bigger-ticket items like typewriters. When the students went home for the summer and you could hear the squirrels crossing the sidewalk, the store would of course expect no customers for three months and had to clean out perishable goods. The price of candy bars was reduced. A friend and I bought up a goodly supply at three cents each and sold them for five. Not all. An undisclosed percentage of the inventory went down the vendors' hatch.

The college's Lyman Memorial Lakes were just right for community swimming in the summer and for ice hockey in the winter. For the former, there was a wooden platform in the middle, from which a lifeguard surveyed the scene. Swimsuits were one-piece, and both male and female chests were covered. Baggy Bermuda shorts had not yet arrived, and the male swim briefs of those days featured a sometimes proud codpiece decor.

By late November, the ice was sufficiently thick to make Thanksgiving morning the first day of a long ice hockey season. If the snow had already covered the ice, we drew a big circle, with pie-shaped paths out in the middle of the lake and played a catch game called "Fox and Geese." Big time skiing had not yet caught on, but we did a lot of small time cross-country snow traveling and tobogganing down the modest campus hills to the lake.

Small colleges generate a special camaraderie, families living near each other next to a tradition-enhanced school in a small town. Some of our professors cut their children's hair in their back yards. The kids called them "faculty haircuts."

In our early years at Carleton, there were two Hunters on the faculty—one was my father who taught English, and the other a professor of biology. They were soon called "Book Hunter" and "Bug Hunter."

Franz Frederick Exner, a chemistry professor with a thick German accent, who assisted many a Carleton graduate's passage into medical school, was a dedicated churchman who for some time was my Sunday School teacher. At times he was your classic absent-minded professor. He once turned up in mufti at a college function that called for black tie. His wife sent him home to switch. When he failed to return within a reasonable time, she went back to their house to check and found he had gone to bed.

Jess and Bess Robinson were good friends of our family. He was an economics professor and was the guru of generations of students headed for business careers. His Scottish proclivities were legendary. He bought his motor oil at Sears Roebuck and then, to the embarrassment of his passengers, asked the gas station attendant to put it in. For years the Hunters and the Robinsons alternated Thanksgiving dinners in their respective homes. I never figured out whether both families wanted to do this, or whether they were stuck and could think of no gracious way of breaking the pattern.

My friend Junior Sampson and I used to hike a couple miles south, to camp out on Wolf Creek, a small stream entering the Cannon River between Dundas and Northfield. We caught crabs and boiled them in water from the creek, over a fallen wood fire, in a pan from our Boy Scout cook kit. We were around twelve years old. As a backstop—as the crabs were meager fare—we brought along sandwiches and a hard boiled egg or two.

When we were younger, Sam and I, and all our friends, made a Big Deal of the Fourth of July. We were so worried we would oversleep and miss out on shooting off at dawn all our sophisticated firecrackers (later made illegal), that the night before we tied strings around our big toes, let them hang out our windows, so that the first one to awake would go and wake the other by yanking on the hanging string. Needless to say it was a useless gesture. We were both out on the street well before dawn until after dark.

When I was around twelve, I contracted scarlet fever, and for some reason the college infirmary had a room where I could stay during the infectious period. A Mrs. Allen was the head nurse, and the installation was called the Allen Infirmary, though I am not sure there was any connection. My Grandmother Hunter moved in with me, so we got pretty well acquainted during those weeks. She said the New Testament's Book of Acts was one of the most exciting adventure stories ever written, and I think we read parts of it every day.

There was a red-headed college student, Pat Wells, who was visiting a friend each day, and somehow we got into conversations as she sat on the porch outside my window. We were probably seven years apart in age, roughly twelve to nineteen. Maybe she liked "younger men." At any rate I quite fell in love with her. A classmate of hers, a handsome basketball player by the name of Behmler "Hippo" Carisch, was at the time unsuccessfully trying to make time with her but I was sure she was paying more attention to me that she was to him. She was graduated in 1929, and in due course was married to a Jack Sparks. Years later at an alumni gathering in California, I had a brief visit with Pat. When she died in 1997 in Midland, Texas, she was pushing ninety and could claim five grandchildren and a great grandson.

Across the lakes from the campus stood the college farm, whose herd of dairy cattle provided milk for dormitory dining rooms and employment for needy students. The farm had an imposing water tower, piercing the skyline to the northeast. One summer I dared myself to walk in tennis shoes, tightrope-style, around the four horizontal support girders, the topmost nearly a hundred feet in the air. Having done the top one first, the next twenty-five feet lower seemed less scary. I made it all the way around all four, in descending order, actually covering five girders at each level, as a kind of over-kill proof that I really did conquer the entire tower.

There was nobody around. There was nothing to hang onto. I looked at nothing but the girder beneath me. One slip and it would have been a while before my crumpled body would be found. Even today, I get chills in the night when I think of it. Charles Lindbergh, thirteen years older than I, had done the same thing on the look-alike landmark water tower in Little Falls, 140 miles to the north. His aim was to cure himself of fear of heights. My experience had the opposite effect.

Dad the Sportsman

My father was an outdoors man and a devotee of all kinds of games, unlike his oldest son. He was good at different kinds. As a graduate student at Princeton, he was a champion carom shooter in House tournaments. At Carleton he would repair most afternoons to the faculty quarters above the gymnasium for a mean game of pool or billiards. He loved the faculty volleyball games late every Monday afternoon. In cards, he excelled at something called "Pitch." He never got into golf, and quit tennis because, he said, he got too mad.

Fishing he liked just about the most. He used to take me out to favorite lakes, and I enjoyed being with him in the outdoors, but I never caught the fishing virus that absorbed him. He seemed to understand the psychology of the fish and predict what they would do. Sometimes we cast for bass, using live frogs as lures. Once dad noticed that his baited frog got up on a lily pad and tried with his forefeet to claw the hook out of his throat. It so moved him that from then on he would not use live bait. He quit hunting for a similar reason. He once hit a duck flying over, and noticed that one leg dropped down. He could not get over what he had probably inflicted on that duck and its family.

From his minimal hunting career he had retained a 22-caliber rifle and a shotgun. For Christmas he gave me an air rifle, a BB gun, and I planted quite a few tiny lead balls around the countryside. Before long he entrusted me with the 22. Mostly it was for perforating tin cans in gravel pits. When I arrived at the army, I had already been well trained by my father in how to clean a rifle with a cloth wad at the end of a long rod.

We never caught a rabbit or a squirrel. With a steel trap, though, I overcame quite a few gophers around the campus—after all we lived in the Gopher State—skinning the critters and saving their hides as souvenirs with loads of salt. This activity did not last long. Dad's theory was that the creative purpose of all these burrowing creatures like gophers and ants was to aerate the ground. Without them, he said, the earth's crust would become a solid rock.

One evening Osborne Cowles, a neighbor who was the Carleton basketball coach, came over to see us.[2] He was helping track coach John Millen run the Boy Scout Camp Pa-Huca on Fish Lake near New Prague fifteen miles west. He realized that at only ten I was not yet scouting age, but they had extra space at camp, and he thought I might make my way and benefit. My parents agreed, and I was off to a really highlight experience. Tuesday, August 3, 1926, I wrote in pencil on Camp stationery:

> Dear Mother:
>   I arrived here in Mr. Mader's car yesterday although we had a flat tire on the way out. The first day I swam a 100 yds. And I got a pin like this, [hand drawing of Red Cross Life Saving emblem]. I have passed my Tenderfoot Test and am working on my Second Class. I will write Friday. [Drawings of smacks and bear hugs.]

Symbolic "beaver skins" were awarded for motivational reinforcement, with a different colored skullcap for each advance we made. I received seventy-five "skins" for swimming across Fish Lake, and a couple hundred for memorizing all four verses

---

[2]Cowles was later to coach successful basketball teams at the universities of Michigan and Minnesota.

of the "Star Spangled Banner." I still prefer to sing the fourth verse at community events.

I made good friends with some kids from Faribault, particularly Nick Boosalis, son of a Greek-American restaurateur. One day a group of us took the fourteen-mile hike required for First Class through towns near the lake. On long walks later in life I have often recalled the leg chemistry, plus the feeling of achievement I experienced, on that hike near Fish Lake when I was ten years old.

The Facts of Life

About this time I began to be curious about the "F" word. It had not yet been elevated to its current acceptability on stage and screen. But the verb was no stranger to Northfield school grounds. I asked a friend what it meant. He rolled his eyes, snickered, and wouldn't say. So I said, "Then I'll ask my dad."

"No, don't do that," he anxiously responded, "it's about down here," and rolled his hands around in his pants pockets.

I had no embarrassment about talking about such things with my dad. I was sure he knew all about it and would level with me. So I asked him, and not long after we sat down together in our house and talked. He got out a sheet of paper. He was a fair artist and on the paper he drew graphic pictures of male and female genitalia, indicating what went where. He explained that God designed all this to produce children for the future, but that some people mistakenly did it just because it feels good. This was not the way to go; it was to be saved for marriage. I have always been grateful for this session between my dad and me, and that I found out this dimension of life not from the street but from the horse's mouth.

A generation later I gave the same message to our boys one night when we were holed up by a storm in Saint Ignace,

Michigan, waiting to get across to Mackinac Island. My drawings weren't up to my father's, but the thesis was his. Years later one of them recalled my words that night with scornful hoots. I once asked a pastoral counseling teacher why I bought my father's package and my kids did not accept mine. "You adopted the mores of your generation," he said, "and they adopted the mores of theirs."

2 Books rec'd Jan '03
from Willard Hunter.
525 W. 6th St
        Claremont CA 91711
New editor = Spirit of CAL
Bushman Never get Anywhere

-3-

NEVER ON SUNDAY

My parents were dedicated to developing a Christian atmosphere in our family. We had what in those days was called "family worship." After the breakfast dishes were cleared away, we gathered back at our seats at the table. Dad was in charge. He would start by reading a portion of scripture. There was no commentary or discussion. Then we got on our knees while he led us in prayer. I can still smell the leather seats on those chairs as I bowed my head into the upholstery.

In Northfield in the 1920s, our Sabbath mornings consisted of Sunday school at 9:30 and church at 11:00. The Northfield Congregational Church had a grand old building. In the basement was a gymnasium, and above that around the balcony were rooms for Sunday School and Scouts. Also a room and bath for two male Carleton students who planned to enter the Congregational ministry.

The pulpit was front and center, with the pews in circular configuration, reflecting the traditional Calvinist emphasis on preaching. There was no talk of anybody being "too young" to attend church. I began in infancy. As I got older, I sat there and absorbed whatever I could. Mother was pretty good at entertaining Stu and me during the sermon, sometimes rolling up "mice" in a twisted handkerchief hammock.

The ushers took up the morning offering, each carrying a long rod with a velvet pouch on the end. Once I noticed a man put in a five-dollar bill, and when we got home I said how impressed I was. Mother wasted no time straightening me out. With our tithing (giving ten percent to the Lord) she explained, we gave far more than five dollars.

The church was a merged Congregational-Baptist society. The minister, the Rev. Samuel Johnson, was devoted to his task. He made sense to me when I first heard him talk about George Washington Carver, "the wizard of the peanut," and when he spelled out J-O-Y as "Jesus first, Others next, and Yourself last."

The church organist was the brilliant James R. Gillette (1886-1963), professor of music at the college from 1923 to 1937. His unique Carleton Symphony Band toured throughout the country in the 1920s and 1930s. Gillette was the first American composer to write in the genre of symphony for wind band, transcribing and arranging works by Bach, Beethoven, and Debussy, and composing original works as well. At the U.S. Sesquicentennial in Philadelphia in 1926, Gillette was rated third among the nation's organists.

The Sabbath was made for man, not man for the Sabbath

We received monetary rewards for Bible memorization, a penny for each verse. I tried without success to collect more than once on "Jesus wept," the shortest verse of them all. Grandma Willard said if you read three chapters each weekday and five on Sunday, you could finish the whole Bible in a year. I got all the way through once, but it took me more than a year.

The Sabbath was rigorously observed. We never went to the movies or studied school lessons on Sunday. We did not swim at the community dock. The main idea was to treat Sunday differently from the other days and to concentrate on church and family life. When I asked why we could swim on Sunday at our northern Minnesota cabin but not at the local lake in southern Minnesota, the reply was that the latter was with "roughnecks." Up north it was with family. Dad figured six days with roughnecks were enough.

In my mind, this type of observance was a positive concept. True, there were prohibitions. But I always felt that in our family, Sunday was not a no-no day, but one where people kept themselves free to do happy and upbeat things together. Sunday observances were one of our benchmarks of Christian living, setting a tone for enterprises through the week.

Dad said our Sundays were lenient compared with the ones he knew as a child. He spent much of the day memorizing the Westminster Shorter Catechism, a question-answer statement of faith coming down through the tradition of Presbyterian Calvinism. Its classic opening:

Question: What is the chief end of man?
Answer: Man's chief end is to glorify God, and to enjoy him forever.

The Westminster Catechism, a copy of which was given to me by my two grandmothers as a twenty-fifth birthday present, was substantially operative with our generation also. The legality of Sunday activities was tested by the Catechism's category. If they were "works of necessity and mercy," they were OK.

Sunday afternoons were often devoted to walks, drives, and parlor games like Parcheesi and caroms. When our Model T Ford was a novelty, we used to go for a ride on the country roads around Northfield. Mother was particularly pleased with these trips. A favorite parlor amusement was to sit on a chair and spin a deck of cards, one by one, into a hat in the middle of the floor. Cards, which were forbidden in some families and groups, were allowed in our family for non-gambling competition. Games of chance and reward were out. I will never forget my mother's warning, "It is wrong to get something for nothing."

After Sunday evening popcorn we sang hymns around the piano, led by Grandmother Willard-Lampe, sometimes followed by prayers. One Sunday evening as I was climbing the stairs toward my room, my suspicious mother asked where I was going. I replied I was on my way to study for an exam the next day. She said, no I was not. I protested, "But if I don't study tonight, I'll flunk the exam tomorrow."

"All right, then you will flunk," she said, principle ahead of expediency.

I've heard people describe this kind of God-centered up-bringing as having religion "stuffed" down their throats, leading them never to have any part of it again. I did not have this reaction. I thought it was a good thing. I still do.

It was impressive to me as a youngster that a Philadelphia ordinance prohibited professional baseball on Sunday. During the World Series in the years 1929 through 1931, when Connie Mack's Philadelphia Athletics represented the American League, there was a day's delay whenever the rotation called for a Sunday game in Philadelphia. Such observance can make for an interesting witness. Sandy Koufax of the Los Angeles Dodgers alerted millions to the meaning of a High Holy Day when he declined to pitch the opening game of the 1965 World Series because it was to be played on Yom Kippur.

My father was against taking the Sunday newspapers, except during the fall when he "needed" to know the results of the Saturday football games.

When the Grand Theater in Northfield proposed a change in the local ordinance so that movies could be shown on Sunday, meetings were held in our church and I wrote against the change in the local newspaper. The measure passed narrowly, and Sunday movies have been shown there, and everywhere else, ever since.

When Christmas day fell on Sunday, we put off opening presents and other celebrations until Monday, as the Tournament of Roses in Pasadena does. The Vestling twins heard about this and came across the street. Louise asked, "How in the world can you possibly wait twenty-four whole hours?" My reply, which for years my father quoted, was: "Well, we've waited 365 days so far, I guess we can wait one more."

Our treatment of Sunday came down through a long family tradition. The Sabbath was central to the life style of our ancestors. My great grandfather Silas Willard, while helping to bring the Burlington railroad to Galesburg in the 1850s, also succeeded in preventing the trains from running through town on Sunday. After his death the trains began operating seven days, and the women in the family sold their stock in the company to avoid complicity. It was their version of what is now called socially responsible investment.

Fundamentalism versus Modernism

One of the great discussion topics of the 1920s was what was known as the Fundamentalist-Modernist controversy, a nationwide debate between those who held a literal interpretation of the Bible and those who picked up on latter-day intellectual criticism. The press focused on the Scopes trial in Dayton, Tennessee, July 1925, one of the first court cases to be called "the trial of the century." John T. Scopes, a high-school science teacher, went on trial for teaching Darwin's theory of evolution. William Jennings Bryan, celebrated orator and three-time Democratic nominee for president, led the prosecution, while the noted Chicago criminal lawyer, Clarence Darrow, directed the defense. Scopes was found guilty, but was fined a nominal hundred dollars. Five days later Bryan died of a cerebral hemorrhage. The Tennessee Supreme Court reversed the ruling on a technicality. In 1927 the U.S. Supreme Court denied a retrial.

Our family provided a micro ringside on the contest. Dad was a Fundamentalist and Mother was a Modernist, yet I never heard them argue about this. Each respected the other's views. Dad's position was that these smart alecks ("wise men from the east") relied as much on unproven theory as the Bible people did, and that nobody had been able to explain the so-called "missing link" in the alleged continuum between apes and human beings.

Dad's stance toward Bible revisionists came clear to me one evening when I returned from hearing the Rev. Richard Raines of Minneapolis' Hennepin Avenue Methodist Church, one of the most popular preachers of the day. I told Dad that in his sermon Raines referred to the story in Mark's gospel about the pigs into whom Jesus had introduced "unclean spirits," causing them to run down the hill and drown in Lake Galilee. Raines said he thought that what happened was that a swarm of bees came along, stung the pigs, and drove them bananas. Dad smiled and said, "It doesn't make any difference what he thinks."

I've since reflected that opinions of people today, one way or the other, do not affect whatever the facts were.

Mother, from a different perspective, told me more than once that she thought it was just as great a miracle, perhaps greater, for God to take millions of years to create the universe than if the whole matter happened within six twenty-four hour days. I have found this helpful, and have been puzzled by how many people try to polarize the matter around the wrong question. The real issue, in my view, is not how long it took, but whether there has been a creative intelligence behind it.

Celluloid and Cat Whiskers

The liveliest, and only, entertainment spot in Northfield, outside of the annual Rice County Fair, was the Grand Theater. Built as an opera house in 1899 by horse breeder and state legislator Alfred K. Ware, it was later converted for movies, although it was still used for community events, such as town pageants and Memorial Day celebrations.

Everett Dilley was owner and operator of the Grand in our time. There were two showings of the movie each evening, at 7:15 and 9:00. Before the main feature there was a newsreel from Pathé or Movietone, often with Lowell Thomas announcing. This was followed by a ten-minute comedy. I recall one in the silent days that featured Will Rogers measuring himself awkwardly from a Sears Roebuck catalog for a suit that came back badly distorted because of the inept measurements.

After the comedy came the main feature. We usually arrived early for the first show and waited impatiently, with or without popcorn. When it was time, Mr. Dilley would stride down the left aisle, to the cheers of the kids, disappear behind a curtained doorway leading to the appropriate switches, and the lights would dim. At the end of the feature, we were allowed to stay and watch the comedy the second time.

Sometimes we attended a motion picture at the imposing Minnesota Theater in Minneapolis, an ornate palace of the type most major cities boasted in those days. There would be not only a film, but also a vaudeville stage show. Big band music was provided by Lou Breese and his orchestra and by Eddie Dunstedter at the mighty Wurlitzer pipe organ. Starting below the stage and out of sight, Eddie and organ would be dramatically elevated into view by hydraulic lift.

I attended a show there once with my Grandmother Willard. The stage show segment featured a line of leggy chorus girls that made her uncomfortable. Afterwards she said to me, "I hope you were clapping just because everyone else was."

The RKO Theater on Hennepin Avenue in Minneapolis carried bookings from the vaudeville circuit. Ole Olson and Chic Johnson were especially popular. They stressed—at least in

Minnesota—Scandinavian-Jewish humor. Later they gathered the best gags from their vaudeville days and put together the popular Broadway show, *Hellzapoppin*, that had the forty-first longest running performance in New York history. I was pleased in the fifties to come to know Ole Olson at Mackinac Island.

Movie going in our family was rationed to once a month, and was confined to Fridays or Saturdays. "School nights" were off limits. My favorite star was Douglas Fairbanks. His bravado and athletic daring were so mesmerizing that when you came out of the theater, you could jump over a tall building. I remember asking, "Grandma, how in the world can you not go and see *The Thief of Baghdad?*"

"I think I will live just as long," she replied. I was not so sure.

When I came home from law school for a vacation, I discovered that sweet little sister Helen, eleven years my junior, the apple of her father's eye, and getting away with murder, was going to a movie every week. I asked Dad how come? His lame reply: "The movies are better now."

The radio came on strong in the 1920s. My father somehow obtained instructions on how to build a crystal set. This involved an antenna, made by winding a copper wire around a lacquered up cylindrical oatmeal box, with condensers, and a tiny square dish with a cat-whisker. The cat-whisker consisted of a small metal arm, with a tiny sharp wire at the end, with which he pointed to different places on a miniature crystal. Moving the cat whisker on the crystal brought in different broadcasting stations, which could be heard only by the person with earphones.

We heard not only Minneapolis / Saint Paul, forty miles away, but even some stations far, far away—Des Moines, Atlanta, Galveston, and the granddaddy of them all, KDKA Pittsburgh. The richer kids' families soon had tube sets that reached farther. A wintertime joke ran, "We opened the window and got Chile on the radio."

Sunday evenings we faithfully tuned in to the Seth Parker show, a down-home family program featuring Maine accents and mood hymns à la Garrison Keillor. My father was a great fan of Jack Benny and also Edgar Bergen's wooden dummy, Charlie McCarthy. Weekday evenings, everybody's favorite was the fifteen minutes with *Amos 'n' Andy*, the longest running program in the history of broadcasting—thirty-two years on radio and two on TV. Carleton College started up a small radio station, and my father was one of the announcers.

Dad also listened to Father Coughlin out of Royal Oak, Michigan, not because he agreed with all his positions, but because he thought the radio priest had a compelling style and was raising some populist points that should be heard. A great fight fan, Dad listened to most of the boxing matches, never missing a heavyweight championship. He was intrigued by the post-match comments of Joe Louis. He also listened to baseball, especially the World Series, and to the national political conventions.

Live and on Stage

Thanks to the town's colleges, we also had the chance to attend live performances. Tony Sarg's Marionettes, the world's greatest, were recurrent visitors. Their version of Robert Louis Stevenson's *Treasure Island* delighted all ages. Another performer who made a vivid impression was Wagnerian opera star Ernestine Schumann-Heink, who in her prime was considered the world's greatest contralto. She had sons who fought on both sides of World War I. For her concert, our family sat in the overflow choir loft behind the platform. Her voice had seen better days, but her stage charm was extraordinary.

Violinist Jascha Heifitz kept us spellbound. Another impressive personality was the Illinois bard, Vachel Lindsay. I remember him reading to us his moving "Abraham Lincoln Walks at Midnight." Carl Sandburg, appearing at Saint Olaf College, presented his trademark "American Songbag," with that shock of white hair, big guitar, and sonorous voice identifying in his organ tones with "the prairies of Illinois."

-4-

LINDBERGH, THE MODEL T, AND THE WEST

Minnesota's Lindbergh

In the twenties, barnstorming bush pilots worked the small towns with offers of airplane rides. One day a plane flew over our house. We always ran outside to see them. Suddenly there burst from this craft high in the sky a puff of leaflets that descended like confetti over the town. Eagerly we scooped up the first we could reach. Rides could be had at the Lashbrook farm, northwest of town. There were two pilots, and the rides cost five dollars. I wanted to go up, but my father was not about to risk his son's neck for five bucks.

I am sure that one of those pilots—tall, slim, good looking—was Charles Lindbergh. Who is to say it was not? He was in fact barnstorming in southern Minnesota in the late summer of 1923.

Four years later, on a Saturday evening, May 21, 1927, while we were walking down to the Carleton lakes for the May Fete, we heard from those who had radios that Lindbergh had landed in Paris. I was delivering Minneapolis papers in those days to Northfield customers. Because Lindbergh was a Minnesota boy (Little Falls), there was a special interest in the week's build-up before the take-off from New York.

The world exploded at the news of the flight. Nothing like it had ever happened, and will probably not again. The Sunday papers were full of it, but not everybody was pleased. Young fireball neighbor Malcolm Clark, probably eight and likely reflecting his father's reaction, was irate. Taking off his helmet he slapped it repeatedly into a puddle and shouted, "That man ought to be paddled, like this!"[1]

In August, my father packed us into our Model T Ford and drove us forty miles north to the Wold-Chamberlain Field in Minneapolis. There we joined ten thousand highly excited people to see the *Spirit of St. Louis* and its pilot. Lindbergh had embarked on a forty-eight state, welcome home tour. The word was going around the roped area where we stood that his plane had been sighted over Baraboo, Wisconsin, having taken off from Madison that morning on the four-hour flight to the Twin Cities. A stubble-faced man with an armload of banners paced up and down in front of us intoning, "Pennant, souvenir of Lindbergh—pennant, souvenir of Lindbergh—he done it!" The charming grammar, endearing to an English teacher's family, made the man's declaration a happy mantra for some time. "He done it."

The *Spirit of St. Louis* was expected at two o'clock. Lindbergh was making a point of the dependability of aircraft, and in the three months of the tour, he landed eighty-two times precisely at 2:00 P.M. Only once, in New England, did he miss on account of weather.

We could feel the excitement building. At five minutes to two, we saw the tiny craft approaching high up in the east. A shout went up. The silvery ship became larger and soon was coming in for a landing, piloted by someone who obviously knew what he was doing. The crowd could restrain itself no more, and surged through the ropes and the National Guard as though they weren't there. I wanted to go, but our "good-guy" code prevented us. Lindbergh managed to taxi his plane into a hangar, with the door clanging down just before the people hit, while he

---

[1] It was Malcolm who gave us another family gem. When asked if he was going to a certain event, he replied, "No, my cuckoo, cuckoo, cuckoo ma won't let me."

shouted angry remarks at the crowd, an up-close eyewitness told me, even threatening to call off the parade that was momentarily to take him downtown.

Later that day as we drove back to Northfield, we were no doubt like the folks returning from a Lincoln-Douglas debate. We all knew we had seen something momentous.

Air fever seized everybody. I started a Lindbergh scrapbook and packed it with clippings and photos. I wore a leather pilot's helmet with button-up chinstrap. *Youth's Companion* was urging kids to talk their elders into painting communities' names on the larger commercial roofs to help orient pilots. Neighborhood boys made model airplanes, and new expressions were in the air, like "monoplane" (the biplane was dominant before Lindbergh), "wingspan," "prop," "joy-stick," "three-point landing," "altimeter," "bank," "taxi," and "dope" (cellulose material to shrink or strengthen cloth surfaces, smelling like bananas). The world had changed, and so had we.

Religion and Automobiles

For twenty-five years of the thirty-three my father lived in Northfield, he supplied the pulpit of a rural Congregational church in Medford, twenty-five miles to the south. A number of Carleton professors in those days were, like Dad, ordained ministers, and the small churches around southern Minnesota, especially Congregational parishes, leaned on college people for help. Before Medford, Dad supplied various pulpits, one with the charming name of Blooming Prairie. Sometimes he and colleagues would go out Saturday and not return until Monday morning. For a time in the twenties he reached Medford by train, going down Sunday morning on the Milwaukee and coming home that afternoon on the Rock Island. Later he went on the Jefferson highway buses. And finally by his own car.

The church at Medford consisted of the families of farmers and artisans, requiring a simpler spiritual menu than the more intellectual fare relished by the academics in Northfield. It was in Medford that we first caught on to the gospel hymns like "The Old Rugged Cross" and "I Come to the Garden Alone." I laughed when I first heard the line that went, "And the voice I hear falling on my ear," because Dad sometimes talked about people being thrown out on their ear.

Sometimes after church we would drive another nine miles south to Owatonna and have Sunday dinner at the Owatonna Hotel. Once I accompanied Dad to Medford every Sunday for an entire year. He was a keen observer of advances in highway construction. We would notice improvements in the new stretches, like intermittent spillways for exiting rainwater from the surface. It was at this time that three-lane highways came into vogue—allowing for faster traffic to overtake slower. The problem was that too many vehicles moving in opposite directions were trying to use the center lane at the same time. So the experiment was abandoned.

Predictions of future lifestyles in the Minneapolis Sunday supplements piqued our imaginations, with their drawings of multilane, divided highways. They seemed a long way off. Other sketches showed huge passenger airplanes, some with sleeping accommodations even.

There was lots of excitement when Dad bought our first car in 1925, a Model T Ford. It was a two-door and coal black. Henry Ford, who built fifteen million "Tin Lizzies" between 1908 and 1927, said customers could have any pattern and color they wanted, so long as it was plain black.

Dad splurged a little on accessories, like a Boyce Moto-Meter on the radiator cap that was supposed to tell us when the engine was getting too hot. To measure the gasoline supply, we would pick up the driver's seat, unscrew the cap of the gas tank, lower a yardstick to the bottom, and determine the amount of fuel left by the soak line. We changed gears via foot pedals. To start, the left pedal got us going in "low." Shifting into "high" took place automatically when sufficient speed was reached that the driver could take his foot off "low." The middle pedal was "reverse" and the right one was the foot brake. Acceleration was by a hand lever protruding to the right from the steering column. On the left was another lever regulating the "spark."

Dad showed no resistance to my learning how to drive. I did so at age nine and did quite a lot of it. This was before drivers' licenses. Once when I pestered Dad to let me take the car around the block by myself, he let me, but I nosed into a gutter a couple of streets away, could not reverse out, and had to walk back to get him to rescue me.

I had to peer through the steering wheel to see the road. On our Sunday trips down to Medford, Dad let me drive. This not only made me happy, but it gave him a chance to go over notes for both his sermon and the adult Sunday School class he always taught after church. The first fifteen miles was to Faribault, a metropolis of 15,000 souls, and he thought it advisable, when we reached the outskirts, that he should take the wheel through the city. We managed to change over without stopping; I arched toward the ceiling while he slid under and over to the controls. South of Faribault we reversed the process, and I drove the remaining nine miles to Medford. On the return trip, north-bound from Faribault, we got a chuckle out of the sign across from a big cemetery, "Next Time Come to Stay!"

Family Reunion

One reason for our auto acquisition was a 1925 family reunion in Michigan, our first major auto camping trip. The relatives attending belonged to my mother's, the Willard, side of the family. The gathering was held at Charlevoix, Michigan, sixty miles south of the Straits of Mackinac on what was then called Pine Lake, later changed to Lake Charlevoix. The locale was a lakeside summer association called the Sequanota Club, founded early in the century by faculty members of Knox College.

One of Mother's first cousins, Henry Lampe, brother of William and Willard Lampe, was a Presbyterian missionary to Korea, and brought his big family back to the States on furlough every seven years. The idea was to get together at those intervals the descendants of Silas and Cordelia Willard, grandparents of my mother and the Lampes. Mother was delighted to discover that at Sequanota all three meals were served in the common dining room, and the women were relieved of cooking chores. Also it was the first time I had been introduced to a multiple choice of cold cereals.

We made the trip from Northfield to Charlevoix in our Model T Ford on terrible "washboard" gravel roads and camped along the way. This included pitching our tent every evening, and cooking morning and evening over our Coleman gas stove, the kind that took a lot of pumping to keep up the gas pressure. We made fifty miles each morning and a hundred miles in the afternoon. I was never very sharp on the mechanical side, and as assistant tent erector, I exasperated my father, who more than once called me "useless." It was a wound I carried for quite a while. Most of the time he was proud of me, but not when I was helping pitch the tent.

On the return trip, when we were driving west of Duluth, Minnesota, we had a flat tire that took a while to change. Another family, going the opposite direction, had some problem at the same place and time. Stu became instant friends with a couple of their children. After some thirty minutes, when both families were saying their good-byes, Stu burst into loud tears—his bawling could reach real volume. Dad asked, what's the problem? "They're keen kids," he cried, "and I'll never see them again."

Heading West

In 1930 we made one of those once-in-a-lifetime trips families used to make by auto to the West Coast. By this time, our Model T Ford had become a Model A, the company's response to competition from General Motors' Chevrolet. Henry Ford, after a year of secrecy and public speculation, had brought out his new creation in December 1927. In our new car, the old foot pedals were replaced by the new gearshift, and Dad had problems adjusting. So at age thirteen I drove most of that summer's 5,000 miles.

We visited relatives, plus Wind Cave, Yellowstone, Yosemite, and Glacier National Parks. Also the Black Hills, before the sculptures on Mount Rushmore. Helen was only four years old, and right at the outset she nearly died in the South Dakota heat. Her persistent carsickness brought a streak of color to the side of the car out of which she was always leaning.

Soon the rains came and turned the South Dakota dirt roads into gumbo. We had to wait a couple of days in Spearfish for them to dry out. On the left-side running board there was a rack into which we piled luggage and tent. Across the back of the car, a cabinet for food supplies had been custom-built by a carpenter friend. It had a hinged gate that dropped down to make a table. Up front, hanging over the radiator, was a canvas water bag that cooled itself through evaporation. I am sure the device helped our spirits, but it was never a very satisfactory thirst quencher.

Most of the roads were of gravel. The constant pounding of traffic tended to produce a cupping, or washboard, effect. Consequently, huge road-graders with angled blades regularly plied their divisions, smoothing the surface. We found better road maintenance in the west than we had in northern Michigan five years earlier. Cars would kick up a big cloud of dust, the faster the bigger, and if the wind was from our left we had to roll up our windows for each passing car. If the wind was coming from our right, then our dust rolled over the other car.

In the middle of Nevada one afternoon our way was blocked by one of the big road graders and a LaSalle coupe. The LaSalle driver had walked over to visit with the machine operator, and they had a lot to talk about. At length the former, a friendly, middle-aged man with an engaging smile, walked over to us, apologized for blocking the road, and gave each of us kids a handful of orange gumdrops. He said he was Death Valley Scotty, and before we said goodbye, he invited us all to visit him in his castle in Death Valley. Dad wrote this off as social badinage, but in later years he said more than once he wished we had accepted the invitation.

We learned later that the man's name was Walter E. Scott, born in 1872, meaning he was fifty-eight when we saw him. The colorful westerner had spent twelve years as a stunt-riding cowboy in Buffalo Bill's Wild West Show, then turned up in 1905 in Los Angeles with large sums of unexplained money. That year he chartered a three-car train and in under forty-five hours broke the Los Angeles to Chicago record. He liked to ride through Reno and toss gold coins to the bystanders. In the 1920s, with what he claimed was the yield of a secret gold mine, he built a two-million-dollar mansion at Stovepipe Wells in Death Valley, where he lived until he died in 1954. It turned out the secret gold mine was wealthy Chicago insurance man Albert Johnson, who was fascinated by Scotty's desert environmental concerns and his humor.

Our first objective in California that summer of 1930 was to visit Mother's brother, Silas Willard. Silas and his wife Martha lived in Palo Alto. He was a tall, strikingly handsome man with a booming laugh and lively to talk with. Martha worked at the University of California Press at Berkeley and took us to the publication offices where she showed us how she did proofreading.

Uncle Silas had visited us in Northfield in the twenties. We were impressed with his spanking new Reo Flying Cloud, which we helped him show off to the astonished neighbors. He also demonstrated how he called hogs down on his farm in Princeville, Illinois. After graduation from Knox College, Silas had gone into farming, but the farm was not a success. He always needed more money to keep it going, and I recall overhearing family conferences when his requests came in to his mother, our grandmother, whose resources he may have substantially drained.

Now Uncle Silas had bounced into insurance in California. Probably bipolar, he was in both farming and insurance always on the verge of a Big Deal. But none materialized, and five years after our visit with him, he brought his own life to a tragic end.

From California, we drove north to Oregon to visit my mother's older sister, Cordelia Willard Dodds, and her five children. Austin Dodds, Cordelia's husband, was an Omaha lumber dealer who moved to Oregon to enter the production side of the wood business. He took us through pungent pine-smelling sawmills, and showed us the long flumes whose rushing waters carried away the wood particles. Cordelia had a terrible case of asthma.

Austin and Cordelia told the story on themselves that although he preferred light meat, and she dark, they both for twenty years ate the opposite of what they liked, each thinking the other had the same preference as they did.

One of the Eugene movie houses was offering a free ticket to any one who would dive from the thirty-foot high board at the park's swimming pool. I had done this at scout camp in Minnesota, so had no problem in picking up the theater pass. The movie featured the Two Black Crows, forerunners of Amos 'n' Andy. Dad liked the line where one of them said his war-veteran brother got shell-shocked from eating peanuts in bed.

In Portland, we were impressed with the budding transportation center along the Columbia River, where rail, sea, air, and highway were developing near to each other. A new Pan-American World Airways' Clipper pontoon ship had just landed, promising more trans-Pacific service.

In that summer of 1930 the Great Depression was well under way. People were reaching for whatever they could. Two new ventures impressed us with their vigor. One was miniature golf, often called Tom Thumb golf. New courses were springing up on the edges of towns. The other was what my father was calling "cabin camps." We were pitching our tent every night, but with this new development, a family for a fee could skip that and sleep indoors. They were not yet called "motels."

The year before, Dad had bought a shore lot at "Pine Gables of the North," on Girl Lake near Longville, Minnesota, two hundred miles north of Minneapolis. At the close of our West Coast trip, he wanted to stop by Longville and see whether, after the excitement of the cross-country trip, we still wanted to settle down and spend future summers at one place. We decided that we did.

A Home on the Lake

So the next summer, 1931, we went to work building a cottage on our lot. We hired local carpenters, Ray Kinkel and his son, for the expert part. We ourselves did much of the other work, like installing the floorboards and nailing siding to the joists, also painting the exterior. To insure a water supply, the

Kinkels said they could "witch" a well for us. They whittled a fork out of a willow branch, and Ray held the top of the "Y" in two hands, the bottom of the "Y" pointing straight ahead. He crisscrossed the area where we would like to install a water pump. When something pulled the point of the fork downwards, a mark was made. The fork was then carried in a direction perpendicular to the first run. When the downward pull pointed to the same spot during repeated runs, it was determined that we would find water at the intersection. We did. Whether we could have without the interesting process, we do not know. There are those who scoff, but I became a believer.

As Stu and I grew up, we did not visit the cottage as much as younger sister Helen, who spent summers there with Dad and sometimes her friends. Not long ago, I stopped by the cottage at Girl Lake and visited with the family who bought it from us, decades ago. It looked pretty much the same. I was shown the penciled marks on the joist that I had made long ago chronicling my mile swim across the lake each year.

The Cities

In spite of the local papers urging us to "buy Northfield," my father went to Minneapolis for anything consequential like suits or shoes or Christmas presents. Besides, he liked the trip, and it seemed as though we went about every three months for a "fix," even in the dead of winter when our auto radiator sometimes froze.

Before my father bought our Model T Ford, we went on a gasoline-powered rail car called the "Dan Patch," named for Minnesota's famous racehorse. It picked up a lot of milk along the way, and the forty-mile trip took two hours, going by way of Lakeville, where the company had built an amusement park to attract rail riders. The Minneapolis terminal was ideal, on

Seventh Street at the heart of downtown.

I was probably six when I made my first trip on the Dan Patch, but I still remember some sensations, the most memorable when we crossed a high viaduct leaving Northfield. Looking down, unable to see any means of support, gave me the scary feeling I was again to experience on my first two-seater army plane trip twenty years later.

Like the San Francisco Peninsula people who talk about "The City", we spoke of "The Cities." In Minnesota one is careful to include Saint Paul along with Minneapolis. Garrison Keillor's radio base is located in Saint Paul at the F. Scott Fitzgerald Theater, named for another famous Minnesotan. In the old days there was a popular story alleging that the Minneapolis Chamber of Commerce had proposed a merger of the two cities, and suggested that the combination be named "Minnehaha"— "Minne" for Minneapolis and "Haha" for Saint Paul. Another tale reports that a Bible salesman was turned down flat by a prospect who said, "Nothing doing—you have all those stories in there about Saint Paul, and not one word about Minneapolis."

On our trips we sometimes stopped at Montgomery Ward's in Saint Paul, but mostly the focus was Dayton's department store in Minneapolis. Dayton's was to generate the Target discount chain, merge with Hudson's of Detroit, and together change their name to Chicago's Marshall Field's. In the Christmas season back then, Dayton's was especially interesting to kids. There were mechanically mobile figures and small train rides through dark tunnels. Once when we were lunching at a restaurant in the store, the waitress kept filling my water glass, and as a dutiful child, trained to consume whatever was before me, I kept drinking the water till I about blew up. Fortunately my father noticed what was happening and to my great relief rescued me from the obligation.

I remember also the police traffic regulators at the busy downtown intersections. A uniformed officer stood in the middle and turned the hand-operated semaphore "Stop" and "Go"—even in snow, slush or freezing weather.

All Minnesotans are shaped by the cultural and commercial influence of the Twin Cities, and we were no exception.

Political Glimpses

I recall an unfamiliar adult stranger invading our block one day in August 1923 and hawking big black headlines punching out news of the death of President Warren G. Harding. Vice President Coolidge had been sworn in the night before by kerosene lamp at his father's Vermont farm.

In 1924 Coolidge was elected president in his own right, and on inauguration day, March 4, 1925, all of us children at the Washington School were brought into the upstairs hall where a tube radio set had been installed. There we heard the scratchy broadcast of Calvin Coolidge's address delivered at the Capitol in his New England twang. It was the first national broadcast of a presidential inauguration.

The First Lady, Grace Coolidge, was the outgoing personality of the team. Their son Calvin Jr. died of blood poisoning, allegedly from a dye in his socks. Ten years later, when I was selling Real Silk Hosiery door-to-door in southern Minnesota, we made a point of our socks being made with poison-free dye.

In August 1927, from his summer White House in the Black Hills, Coolidge tersely announced, "I do not choose to run for president in 1928." My father said we need not worry; there was a fine man in the cabinet, Herbert Hoover, who could take Coolidge's place.

The only genuine whistle-stop experience I had came during the 1928 election campaign when we all went down to the

Northfield railroad depot to see and hear Joseph T. Robinson, Democratic candidate for vice president on the Alfred E. Smith ticket. His special train stopped briefly for the candidate, who was for years also the Democratic leader in the Senate, to say a few words. We were of course impressed and respectful, but as the train pulled out, one of my friends said, "Now where's my Hoover button?" Democrat Al Smith was the first Catholic to run for President, and part of the whispering campaign against him was that if he were elected, the Pope would come over and live in the White House. After the election, in which the Democrats were defeated, it was said that Smith cabled the Pope, "Unpack."

In junior high assembly, we had a mock political rally where kids representing both 1928 candidates spoke. I remember the speech of my friend Bill Watson, who was the son of a medical missionary to China and who was later killed in world War II flying "The Hump" in southeast Asia. Speaking for the Republicans and referring to popular advertising campaigns of the day, Bill said, "Remember, it takes two Smiths to make a cough drop, but only one Hoover to make a vacuum cleaner."

Everything was pretty Republican in our town. The rare Democrats were thought to have something not quite right with them, living, morally, on the other side of the tracks. We were startled when our friend Jesse Robinson, Carleton economics professor, said it didn't really make much difference whether the Republicans or the Democrats got in.

During the 1932 presidential campaign, Ruth Bryan Owen, daughter of William Jennings Bryan, spoke at Carleton on behalf of the Democratic candidate, Franklin Delano Roosevelt. I recall her making the point that FDR had been a good governor from the standpoint of the environment, having done well by the forests of New York state. She spoke in the college chapel, and its lobby was full of Roosevelt literature. Influential in bringing

Owen to Northfield was our acting postmistress, Anna Dickie Olesen, in the days when postal appointments went according to political patronage. We were proud that Olesen gave one of the seconding speeches for the vice presidential nomination at the national convention.

In the 1930s Minnesota became the preserve of the Farmer-Labor Party, an offshoot of the populist Nonpartisan League out of North Dakota. Progressive Republican Congressman C. A. Lindbergh, the famous pilot's father, who served in the U.S. House of Representatives 1907-17 from Minnesota, was allied with that movement. Hubert H. Humphrey was later to effect a merger between the Farmer-Labor and the Democratic parties in Minnesota.

The big Farmer-Labor star in the thirties was Floyd B. Olson, a silver-tongued orator who was elected Governor of Minnesota in 1930, 1932, and 1934, then was nominated for the U.S. Senate in 1936. He was favored to win that contest, but cancer ended his life in the middle of the campaign. He was a Depression counterpart in the North of Louisiana's Huey Long in the South, though less flamboyant, and he engendered much the same kind of broad-based populist expectations.

Olson was a popular platform orator with a rare talent for the spoken word. His statue at the capitol in Saint Paul is fashioned in the speaking mode. When he appeared for the centennial of Henry Schoolcraft's 1832 discovery of northern Minnesota's Lake Itasca as the source of the Mississippi River, we drove over from our northern Minnesota cabin to hear him speak. The big black limousines of the governor's party whooshing through the forest cathedral made an impressive sight. Another time, at a college convocation honoring two high-ranking army officers, we again experienced the Olson luster. My father was impressed with the deft way the governor used the military occasion to make a stirring peace plea.

Olson was reputed to carry on a profligate private life. A woman asked him after a meeting, "Governor, are these things we hear about you true?"

"My dear," he replied, "I'm afraid some of them are, and I hope you will pray for me."

Delivering the News

One of my happiest memories is of being a newsboy for Twin Cities newspapers. I started out with the *Minneapolis Journal*, an afternoon paper which arrived in Northfield by truck around four o'clock. Our distribution point was in a couple of vacant rooms in back of Manhart's coal office on the western side of the river. Sometimes when the truck was late, we would fill in time by smoking three-inch sections of the twine that had held previous paper bundles together. For cigarette paper, we wrapped the twine in dirty newsprint. It sure was bitter and hot, doubtless more lethal than tobacco. If we had inhaled, we'd have died. Cliff Hagen, our puffy, red-necked boss, provided my first introduction to the breathy aroma of alcohol. Cliff was also a beekeeper and had a honey business on the side.

The canvas paper sacks that we hoisted on both shoulders had carrying straps that were too long. The best solution was to fold a foot over and get someone with a sewing machine to "battle-stitch" the fold together. My route included the downtown merchants, mostly on the east side of the river, and I had to have three sacks—one over each shoulder for the residential sections of the route, and a third down the front, which I emptied through deliveries in the downtown stores. On Sundays, Dad let me use the Model T, a great help with the heavier papers and the envy of my peers.

Somehow, I got hooked on the funny papers. Two of the comic strips were especially gripping—one about a guy by the name of Webster and the other a college athlete called Ned Brant. There was also Gasoline Alley with Skeezix (the baby originally found on the doorstep and then grown to be a teenager before our eyes), chinless Andy Gump, Hairbreadth Harry, and Little Orphan Annie. I took to reading them all before launching forth on the deliveries, and the result was that I got fired. Cliff said the merchants could see the truck from the Twin Cities come through town, and wondered why their paper was coming so much later. My parents were terribly upset at this display of irresponsibility in their fair-haired boy who always did so well. After a few months, I applied again, and was re-hired. Cliff knew I had learned my lesson.

With the paper route came discretionary money. The *Minneapolis Journal* cost the customer ninety cents a month, seventy-five if they didn't take Sundays. We had to collect this every thirty days, and we were paid ten cents per customer. So with a hundred papers on the route, this meant ten dollars a month for the carrier. I wanted to buy a used Dodge coupe being offered by the local Ford dealer, who was willing to take my ten dollars each month. But the old maestro vetoed this plan, saying that all that kind of money should go to my education.

The paper routes in Northfield were great training. I began to learn something about business and how to deal with people. I learned how not to phrase questions. Once, while making the monthly collection rounds, I asked a barber, "Will you please pay for your paper?" He replied, "Will you please get your muddy boots off my carpet?" I recall a fierce sense of responsibility in that all those people were dependent on me for their news. Radio was barely a factor yet.

As I entered high school, I was able to acquire a route carrying the morning papers, the *Minneapolis Tribune* and the *St. Paul Pioneer Press*. I didn't have to collect from the customers, the evening guys did that. Heading out at 5:00 A.M. and getting the job out of the way before breakfast left me free for extra-curricular activities in the afternoon. It also gave me cover. Sophisticated students need not know that I was doing anything so uncool as peddling papers. I did this through my junior year. One winter it was five below zero Fahrenheit every day for a month. I was fortunate in that my route included the Carleton College dormitories. Just as I was getting good and frozen, I hit the heated dorms, peddling up to fifty papers at the students' doors, at the end of which I was thoroughly warmed up and ready to finish my route in the town's northeastern residences. I am so glad I knew nothing of the modern "chill factor." It was cold enough as it was.

I managed to finance quite a few candy bars and sweet rolls with my new wealth, leading to my father's comment, "When you get to be a newsboy, you spend your money like a drunken sailor." Somehow I got hold of a package of Thompson's Malted Milk, complete with an aluminum mixing can. No matter how much I shook the contents, I could not get my shakes thick like those at the soda fountain. It took me a while to realize that they used ice cream to make them thick. Junior Sampson and I rode our bicycles to Faribault, fifteen miles down and fifteen miles back, to slurp the thickest and best chocolate malted milk in the world, offered by the drug store in the Faribault Hotel. Price: fifteen cents.

Faribault, pronounced "Faribo," was and is the procreator of the world-famous blankets, many of which make their way onto airlines seats. Northfield and Faribault high schools were rivals in sports. One of our yells was: "There ain't no flies on us, there ain't no flies on us. There may be flies on the Faribault guys, but there ain't no flies on us."

Thumbing It

I saw my first big league baseball game in the summer of 1931. Junior Sampson wangled an invitation to visit his aunt and uncle in Chicago, and we hatched the idea of us two hitchhiking there together. We didn't think our parents would permit it. Sam's father had died years earlier, and his mother leaned on my father's judgment, quite confident, we think, that Dad would veto the idea. To everybody's surprise, he approved, so we got ready.

The first night we got as far as Waterloo, Iowa, where we slept out in a farmer's field in cinched up blankets. This was before sleeping bags. The next day we got rides all the way to Chicago. Junior's aunt, Mrs. Kimball, was particular about our behavior and asked us not to sit on the edge of the beds. I was swept away by the sights and sounds of the big city. Chicago made Minneapolis and Saint Paul look small time. Overpowering, animated billboards that simulated speeding trains dominated air space above Michigan Avenue. I had never seen so many African-Americans in my life. For many city blocks that ran for miles south of the Loop we saw not a single white face.

On day one, we figured we owed it to ourselves to attend our first burlesque show, picking one on State Street. Our attention was riveted, and I can still repeat some of the gags. I remember a hardened female veteran sashaying around the stage peeling off her gloves and then everything else, while singing "Please Don't Talk about Me when I'm Gone."

In the afternoon we saw a Chicago Cubs game at Wrigley Field. Luckily we were able to see Cub players Rogers Hornsby and Hack Wilson in action. Hornsby's 1924 batting average of .424 is still unsurpassed. Hack Wilson had hit 56 home runs the year before, setting a National League record that lasted 68 years until Mark McGwire hit 70 homers in 1998, again topped by

Barry Bonds' 73 in 2001. We never thought of trying for autographs.

On our return trip, we were lucky to flag down a man who was driving across Wisconsin to Saint Paul, thirty-five miles from home. Saint Paul, even with its streetcars, and their copy-cat destination signs, "The Loop," still looked like a small town in comparison to Chicago.

It was a happy boyhood. Compared with the fortune of so many of the earth's children, I feel I was blessed to have turned up in such a family, in such a town, at such a time.

"No lot is altogether happy," said Horace 2000 years ago. I have at times lashed out at my fate. But then I have remembered the Arab proverb, "I had no shoes and complained, until I met a man who had no feet."

THE KNOWLEDGE TRAIL

In school and college, I started as fair-haired boy and finished as Big Man on Campus. I can't remember being called "teacher's pet," but I was the conscientious type that teachers liked. In college I learned the importance of establishing a reputation in the first weeks of a class by being prompt, thorough, and well prepared. It was possible then to slip into a benefit-of-the-doubt overdrive for the rest of the year. My friend Fred Purdy used to quote his mother, "If you have the reputation of getting up early, you can stay in bed."

I never was "one of the boys," but I always made my way, and was welcomed for perceived skills of leadership. In athletics you would not call me a "jock," playing in the highly visible insider sports of football or basketball. Mine was rather the loneliness of the long distance runner.

Back in grade school (called "elementary" now) there were six of us first graders who it was thought would be under-challenged in the second grade, and so were passed directly from first to third. For the rest of my career I was a year younger than my peers. It made good conversation, but I always felt a year behind in things like athletic development.

My earliest public triumph, after kissing a cute fellow-first-grader on a street corner to the delight of a small crowd, was as a sixth grader being chosen to represent our school in the annual community Christmas pageant. I sometimes believed it was a portent of future success. I played one of the three kings, bringing the gift of myrrh to the Baby Jesus in the manger scene.

The other two kings, the ones with frankincense and gold, were selected from Longfellow (grade) School and from junior high.

The words I sang to accompany my gift were from the familiar carol:

Myrrh is mine; its bitter perfume
Breathes a life of gathering gloom:
Sorrowing, sighing, bleeding, dying,
Sealed in the stone-cold tomb.

In later years I wondered whether these lines were an omen of depression to come.

My first experience with formal education was at the Washington School, about a mile south of our home. Since we went home for the noon meal (all except for the farm kids with lunch-pails), this for us meant two round trips a day, or some four miles. We faculty kids from the north side of town liked to brag about those four miles. Our janitor was a tough looking character whose decaying teeth were brown with tobacco juice. Nevertheless, we all knew he was our friend. It was he who stood on the front steps at nine o'clock and rang a heavy handbell— the school's friendly persuasion to drop our games and hit the stairs indoors.

I was always intrigued to see at the corner of the blackboards the notice "Save," a word that later became so big in the computer world. I learned that teachers chalked the word as a message to the janitor that she wanted that material left on the board for the next day. We heard of a custodian, surely not one of ours, who, when he swept the floor with his oily sawdust compound, pulled the shades, thinking that if he could not see any dust rising, there in fact wasn't any.

Gum chewing in school was a no-no. Sometimes a teacher would stop it by saying to the offender, "Do you have enough for everybody?" Expecting the pattern to hold, a couple of us bought an ample supply of Wrigleys, and the next time Mrs. Wright asked whether I was chewing gum, I said, "Yes, but we have enough for the whole class," whereupon my accomplices started passing the goodies down the aisles. Mrs. Wright was adequate to the situation. "No," she said, "We'll all wait and stay after school for the treat." It's hard to fight city hall.

Mrs. Wright taught the sixth grade. She was of slight build, wore glasses, and had pure white hair. She was a strict disciplinarian, but had a smile and a warm, understanding manner to go with it. She was gentle with advice, as when she admonished us boys, when walking along the street, always to tip our hats when approaching ladies. One day she had every member of the class—individually, row after row, front to back—repeat the words: "A verb is a word that asserts." The sing-song rhythm helped us remember, and here I am three quarters of a century later repeating it.

I don't recall talk about church and state, but once in the middle of every week all of us kids adjourned to churches in town for an afternoon of what was called "Wednesday School." This was to satisfy the public's support for front-and-center religious training, while at the same time seeing that it not be at taxpayer expense. "Released time" was the official term. Most went off to the local Protestant and Catholic churches, with a few staying that afternoon in public school with their teachers. It seemed like a good idea, but the experience in the Congregational Church for me was an absolute mess. The volunteer teachers were not trained in how to keep discipline, and the kids took over in riotous fashion. I recall learning a few Bible truths, but mostly it was a waste of time.

We were drawn into the outside world each week with a four-page newsletter for schools called *Current Events*. It was done in an interesting way for kids. It seemed to me there was usually something about the Muscle Shoals power controversy (which resulted the next decade in the Tennessee Valley Authority).

Also we had news about President Herbert Hoover and his dealing with the 72nd Congress.

In late May every year, the school invited the town's "Old Soldiers" (Civil War veterans) to a Memorial Day ceremony. It was then called "Decoration Day" after the custom of decorating soldiers' graves with flowers. Four of these veterans of the Grand Army of the Republic (GAR) were still living in Northfield. One was not in good shape and died while we were kids, but J. W. Stebbens (1841-1932), a short, spry man, was still sharp and articulate. Each year he came dressed in his GAR uniform, sporting a trimmed, white beard and braid on his hat. Before he spoke, a schoolgirl intoned the long poem, "The Blue and the Gray," the North (blue)-South (gray) bridge-building poem by Judge Francis Miles Finch, with its chorus:

> Under the sod and the dew, waiting the Judgment Day;
> Love and tears for the Blue, tears and love for the Gray.

My biggest failure was the Palmer Method. This was an approach to handwriting introduced by Austin Norman Palmer, an Iowa business genius, who decided in the 1880s that the curlicued, stylized Spencerian style then in vogue was nice but too slow for modern needs. Palmer's method involved controlled strokes of basic arm muscles and endless practices of ups and downs and rounds and rounds. I never could get the hang of it. And while most of my classmates went forward and got their pins, I never did. I was relieved and happy when we moved on to junior high where they paid no attention to Palmer.

In junior high school we had an English teacher named Alberta Ackerman. A book enthusiast, she compiled a master list of around thirty books she wanted us to read, extracurricular, over the year. They were classics like Jack London's *Call of the Wild*, Ernest Thompson Seton's *Wild Animals I Have Known*, Richard Henry Dana, Jr.'s *Two Years Before the Mast*, and Hermann Hagedorn's *Boy's Life of Roosevelt*. I was and am a slow reader, and managed to get through the year without reading most of that list. In later years I have made up on some of them. I came to know Hagedorn personally, and was proud to report to him that at least I had read *his* book.

The Orange and Black

Our high-school principal, Anna Bernard, was a math teacher who presided over the assemblies with an iron hand. She was sometimes frustrated during the study hour with guys, steel tips on their heels, who walked to the water cooler in such a way as to enlist the entire study hall to beat time with their feet. After sixteen years of service, she retired at the close of our senior year.

The school colors were orange and black, like those of Princeton University. The fight song, "Northfield High School, Hats Off to Thee," was sung to the tune of the University of Minnesota's rouser.

At one rally Coach Vincent Hunt announced that from then on our athletic teams would be known as the Raiders, a salute to the town's famous bank robbery.

I played front-and-center roles in high school, like president of the junior class. The main responsibilities of that position were running the junior-senior prom and presiding at the banquet, held at the Carleton College tearoom. To jump-start the after-dinner action, I told a story I had picked up in O. O. McIntyre's column in the *Minneapolis Journal*:

> Clarence Budington Kelland, in toastmastering a recent dinner, said, "The role of a toastmaster is to be as dull as possible so as to make the speakers look good. As I look about the head table this evening, I see I shall have to rise to new heights of dullness."

One classmate predicted I would become an after-dinner speaker.

I caused quite a stir around town by the date I chose for the prom, Suzanne Cooke. My father wanted me to be altruistic and take the plain daughter of a faculty friend. But Suzanne and I had been thrown together that year as male and female leads in a high school play, a detective mystery called *The Tiger House*. She had a concert-quality soprano voice, had done well in state high school competitions, and sang in the choir of the Congregational Church, where we had first met in Sunday School as eight-year-olds. She was the adopted daughter of "Doc" Cooke, Director of Athletics of Saint Olaf College. Sundays he crossed the river, with Suzanne, to worship and take leadership in the Baptist branch of the Congregational-Baptist Church, being the only member of the Saint Olaf faculty not a Norwegian Lutheran.

Suzanne had a million-dollar personality, and we began to find time for each other. I had never danced before, so the week before the prom I got her to teach me the two-step and waltz one afternoon around a record player at her house. In the car she would sit close, and she knew how to make a guy feel terrific.

She made my parents feel something else. She had spent her sophomore year in California having a baby. Such was not unheard of among Northfield girls, but it was hardly normative in those days. Hushed conversations around town were her scarlet letter. Speculation as to the identity of the father was not conclusive.

My mother was anxious I not make any lasting gift that Suzanne could hold up and say, "See what he gave me." Candy or flowers were better, she advised. (As a certified El Cheapo, I didn't even do that.) My father had a long talk with me one afternoon. He said that one's reputation is a priceless asset, that mine so far was good, and hers was not. He hoped I would do the right thing. If it had been thirty years later, I might have told him to go fly a kite. But this was 1931. I had a lot of respect for the old man and I decided to make the move.

Suzanne and I planned to meet after the high-school commencement exercises, where she was singing in the chorus. From the auditorium we drove around town and ended up at her house. It took me a while, but I finally told her it was over. She cried. She understood. About her own experience she said, "It's a hell of a way to bring somebody into the world. That's the way I arrived." I kissed her—for the first time.

It was after midnight when I got home. My parents knew I was out with her, but they did not know it was the exit date. In a punishing mood, Dad locked me out. I made a little noise, but although Mother appealed to him for mercy, he had made up his mind. For the rest of the night I either sat in a rocker on the porch or walked around town. That day August Piccard had ascended to 52,000 feet at Augsburg, Germany, in a pressurized cabin he designed, the first used for manned balloon flight. With the dawn, and still dressed for commencement, I delivered my paper route, returned home, and reported.

Postscripts.

- Breaking up is hard to do, and I was less than sensitive. In effect I told her, "I'm OK, you're not OK."

- It was deflating to see, the very next night, Suzanne happily driving up to the movie theater with another guy, a Saint Olaf student named Marlin Sieg, to whom she would later be married. I wondered whether it had been my great personality that had attracted her or whether she was just programmed to charm the next guy who turned up. Her subsequent marriage, by the way, complete with kids, turned out to be permanent.

- How could she have made the switch so fast? I am guessing that Mr. Next had probably asked her for a date earlier, which she declined until our break-up, whereupon she might be free to communicate her availability.

A few days later, at the Grand Theater Memorial Day cere-monies, I delivered Lincoln's Gettysburg Address, a warm-up for the orator of the day, Roy L. Smith of Minneapolis.

I was fifteen years old.

Gamesmanship

Never quick or well coordinated, my performance in athletics was so-so. I made the high school football team my senior year and played substitute right end behind Sammy Anderson, who was tall, aggressive, and fast. Upon graduation, he received a basketball scholarship at Santa Clara University in California. He was one of the boys from the local Odd Fellows' home for orphans that each year contributed substantially to Northfield High School's athletic success. He was an outstanding end who played almost every minute of every game. Besides, much of the season I had a bad charley horse in my right thigh, which contributed to keeping me on the bench. We finished the 1931 season with a record of 10-0-0. One press account called it "probably the greatest football team Northfield High has ever had." Nine of the ten games were shutouts. Only one opponent scored at all, and that was with but one touchdown. The ten opponents scored only 6 points the entire season, while Northfield ran up 251.

Once when we were 53 points ahead of Farmington, and the game was about over, Coach Hunt didn't think I could do any damage and sent me in. Trying to give me a break, my friend Kenny Kelsey, the quarterback, called a play where I was to go out and catch a pass. But the opposing Farmington tackle dumped me on my rear end before I could make it past the scrimmage line.

In basketball, I was cut before the season began. Track I could manage. Few wanted to do the dull, painful training it takes to be a distance runner, so there was no competition. I ran the half-mile. I always said anybody is crazy to run farther than 220 yards. But I stuck with the crazies through high school and then college.

I bagged the usual summer jobs. One of them was picking potatoes at a peat bog five miles north of town in a community called Castle Rock, so named by the Milwaukee Railroad for a nearby vertical outcropping of sandstone that thrust like a castle into the air. Peat is a very black, soft substance that geologically is on its way to becoming soft coal. It is used in places like Ireland for fuel. When it sometimes catches fire in the field, it gives off a pungent smoke we sometimes caught when driving through the area to the Twin Cities. Apparently peat also provides great soil for growing potatoes. A factories-in-the-field type operator leased and planted the Castle Rock acreage and when the crop matured, hired high school kids to pick. A digging machine would bring the spuds to the surface, and then we went in and sacked them. There were scales in the field, and we could pick a hundred pounds a day. We were paid two cents a sack, two dollars a day, or twenty-four dollars for the two weeks we worked.

Through the "Periscope"

The Periscope was Northfield High's school newspaper, and it came out every two weeks. The English department each year chose the editor from the senior class, and for 1931-32 I was it. At an alumni reunion in the 1990s, I was able to purchase copies of every issue of the *Periscope* for that entire year.

We had class reporters that filed a few news items. But mostly I did the whole thing myself. I asked my friend Hughitt Hinderaker, who used to liven up conversations with funny angles, to write a humor column. "Hugh's Hitts" became a popular feature.

Fellow long distance runner Bob Larson, son of another Carleton professor, was a bright guy who knew a lot about everything. I asked him to be sports editor. One time I suggested to him a few changes in sentence structure. His response was, "What you want is for me to sound like you." From then on we ran his stuff his way. Later, when I experienced a positive personal reorientation through the Oxford Group program, Bob was impressed that I had lost my arrogance.

Besides writing and editing most of the copy, I was also responsible for headlines and the layout. There were two commercial weeklies downtown in those days, and the contract for *The Periscope* alternated between the two—the *Independent* and the *News*. My year it was the *Independent*, owned and operated by the Mohn brothers. In those days type was set by a hot-lead linotype operator, forming slugs out of molten lead. Every two weeks I spent hours around the flat marble tops, writing headlines, choosing type, making corrections, and fitting the puzzle together. Ralph Boone, an African-American pressroom foreman, was my instructor. What I learned under his tutelage about typefaces and layout helped me immeasurably in the many publications I produced in later years.

I became intrigued by the advertisements for Speedwriting and sent away for the set of instruction books. I worked pretty hard on the exercises, and although I did not finish the whole course, I learned simple abbreviations that have always been a help in making notes, both in college courses and in later lectures and meetings. Likewise with the typewriter. My Royal portable, a Christmas present from the folks, came with an instruction book—"How to Type (some impressive figure) Words a Minute." This I did complete, and my proficiency with the touch system has been of enormous help in school and college and my entire writing and speaking career, and of course on into the computer age.

When I graduated from high school, my father came up to me after the ceremony and congratulated me. I thought that was strange. Didn't every one graduate from high school? By the time I became a parent, I understood my father's appreciation that night, realizing what a lot of hard work and parental commitment it takes for a child to reach that milestone.

Then it was on to college, two blocks away.

"It is a small college, and yet there are those who love it."

So said Daniel Webster, describing Dartmouth College in a famous contract case he argued before the U.S. Supreme Court in 1818. It is true for Carleton and other colleges as well. I am sometimes asked why I did not attend Knox College in Galesburg, Illinois. My great-great grandfather, Matthew Chambers, was a founding trustee. The first board meeting was held in his log store in Knoxville in 1837, following chartering by the Illinois legislature, of which Abraham Lincoln was then a member. My great grandfather, Silas Willard, was also a trustee for a time. His son, my grandfather Matthew Chambers Willard, was a Knox alumnus and served on the board for twenty-two years. My mother and most of her numerous cousins were graduated from Knox. So I helped break the chain.

I don't believe the question ever came up. The main reason was economics. I graduated from high school in 1932, at the bottom of the Great Depression. My father was on the Carleton

College faculty. We lived a block from the campus. Faculty salaries were low, and tuition benefits for their children were one way to help compensate. So the choice was clear. Then too, my father was very high on the quality of a Carleton education.

I stood in line at the registrar's office in Leighton Hall in September 1932, a little bit proud I was only sixteen. As we were waiting, one student asked another, "How much do the extra fees come to?" The reply: "About a hundred dollars more than your folks figured."

The first year I lived at home off campus. Actually, it was like extending high school, as I did not participate much in college life. I attended class and went home.

A dramatic change in my life took place in my sophomore year. At a camp the previous summer, I had met a young man—Elbert—who was on the borderline of retardation. His father, a prominent Minneapolis banker, was concerned over his son's education. In those depression days, admissions policies were influenced as much by warm bodies with tuition money as by intellectual capacity. One never knew whether, if the father were treated right, he might become a donor. I was asked to be Elbert's roommate for a year, generally to keep an eye on him and be a buffer against possible mistreatment. His parents paid my board and room.

Elbert apparently made it through the year OK, but the experience for me was tremendous. I was particularly fortunate to draw an unusual threesome of table mates in the men's dormitory dining room: H. Meredith Sigmond, football scholar from Zumbrota, Minnesota; Randall S. (Pat) Herman, national track star from Oak Park, Illinois; and George Leonard, son of a prominent Farmer-Labor attorney in Minneapolis. All this brought me out of my shell and transformed my ability to meet and deal with people.

On the Stump

This freeing was abetted by another most liberating experience for me, debate and oratory. I majored in English, and minored in History and Speech. I was interested in a political career, and these subjects certainly strengthened communications skills. How to think on my feet was one of the best things I learned in college. One memorable experience was a debate held in the Old Capitol Building in Iowa City in 1935, where Vernon Fladager and I, Carleton's team on the affirmative, defeated Notre Dame.[1]

I was the college orator at Carleton in 1935 and 1936, representing the college both years in the Minnesota state oratorical championships. In 1935 I was defeated on a snowy winter's night by Bernard Levander of Gustavus Adolphus College, a Swedish Lutheran school on the Minnesota River at Saint Peter. I. M. Cochran, our forensic coach, continued to regard me as a winner and appointed me orator again for 1936. That year the state contest was held at Macalester College in Saint Paul. This time I was judged first, and went on to the interstate oratorical contest in Evanston, Illinois. There I won the western division, but in spite of our coach's confidence, I placed only fourth in the finals, beaten by a speaker I had bested in the preliminaries. Friends back at Carleton were shocked. One said, "I figured you must have fallen down or something." Cochran thought the outcome was due to the content of the speeches and the philosophy of the judges.

My oration was entitled "Disciplined Democracy" and stressed the importance of character and commitment. The winners were discussing government programs that were then

---

[1] The intercollegiate debate topic that year was: "Resolved. That the nations should agree to prevent the international shipment of arms and munitions."

being made popular by the New Deal. Cochran noted that when I was judged by small college people, I won, but when the judges were from the big universities, I lost.

Academics

One year I was busy with so many extracurricular activities that I reduced my class load to gain more time. It was a mistake. I found I was as busy as ever. This confirmed for me the wisdom of what later was known as Parkinson's Law: the volume of work expands to fill the time available for its completion. There is also the saying, "If you want something done, find a busy person."

In college I began a lifelong practice of taking a short nap after lunch. I picked this up from my dad, who came home from the college every day for lunch and a brief siesta. Around the dorm, guys talked of being in "the arms of Morpheus," or knitting "the ravell'd sleeve of care." This was all chalked up to "innocuous desuetude."

I was elected to the honorary academic society, Phi Beta Kappa, which in most schools recognizes the top ten percent of the class. The speaker at our installation ceremony was Harvard philosophy professor William Ernest Hocking. At commencement I was graduated *summa cum laude*. That year, when I saw I was corralling enough A's to come within striking distance of the *summa* range, I spoke with three of my professors to see what I could do to make sure. One of them was quite upset with me for what he regarded as less than honorable activity. Although he prided himself as a nonbeliever, he quoted scripture to underline his contention that I had things upside down. "Seek ye first the kingdom of God and his righteousness," he intoned, "and all these things shall be added unto you." I was chastened, but pleased that in the end I was able to go over the top. The college registrar confirmed that an office error left my name off the *summa cum laude* roster on the graduation ceremony's bulletin.

Long Distance Runner

In college I continued my long distance running efforts, cross-country in the fall and track in the spring. Freshmen were awarded cardigan sweaters bearing our class numerals. Upper classmen were issued pullover sweaters with "C" on the chest. I am a lifetime member of the Carleton "C Club."

In cross-country, I felt burned out and did not participate in my junior year. The last year, however, Joe Scammon, a classmate who was student coach, recruited me by saying that if I came out, I would probably be the only senior and would likely be chosen captain. Smart strategy, and I succumbed. In earlier years, Ray Conger had been our coach. He was an Olympic runner himself (Amsterdam 1928) and the only American to have defeated Paavo Nurmi, the great Finnish runner.

On a weekday run, I was puffing up one of the campus hills above the lakes (in cross-country you sprint up all hills). Afterwards Conger said, "Hunter, I think you have only one lung."

One of my fellow long distance runners was a good friend through high school and college, Bob Larson. Our dads were both Carleton professors—his in Psychology and mine in English. In high school, as mentioned earlier, he was my sports editor on *The Periscope*. We used to play squash together at the courts in Carleton's Laird stadium. During one game, on a wide-swinging backhand, I caught Bob in the eye, my racket shattering his glasses, splinters from which entered an eyeball. We took him at once to the Miller Hospital in Saint Paul, but his sight could not be saved. For the rest of his life he had the use of only one eye. Years later when I again told him how bad I had always felt, he said, "But it was only an accident." I said, "Yes, I know that's true, but I will always carry it with me." Bob, with his brilliant mathematical mind, subsequently enjoyed a distinguished career as an actuarial expert, and then retired to the Orange County coast of Southern California.

In my senior year we had a dual cross-country meet with Macalester College in Saint Paul. The Macalester campus stretches along historic tree-lined Summit Avenue, the home of some of the state's great lumber and railroad barons of the past, such as the Weyerhaeusers and James J. Hill, builder of the Northern Pacific. Part of the cross-country route went several blocks down Summit Avenue, using the grass-covered median. We had just arrived there when the midriff elastic in my waistband gave way. I held my pants up with my right hand for a block or so, but decided this was creating too much interference with my stride. So I stopped, dropped my pants on the grass and proceeded to the end. I came in either first or second as I recall. Of course, my jersey was long enough to cover the important areas, but I caught a ribbing in the sports column of *The Carletonian* the next week.

In the Midwest Conference Cross-Country championship meet that wound up the season, I was really lucky. This conference consisted of nine of the most prestigious colleges in Minnesota, Iowa, Illinois, and Wisconsin. The conference meet that fall was held at Carleton, but only one non-Carleton runner showed up. He was a star from Lawrence College in Appleton, Wisconsin, and he took first place. I came in second, ahead of the other Carleton runners, of whom I was captain. Being the only team in the race, we garnered enough points to win the meet. Since then I have been able honestly to include in my résumé that I was captain of the 1935 Midwest Championship Cross-Country team!

The Social Scene

Having grown up in Northfield, I recall the mandatory freshman-sophomore annual tug of war in the Lyman Lakes.

That had disappeared by the time I reached college. When I became a freshman, all the men in the class had to wear for the whole academic year a "beanie," a green skull cap with a yellow bill. Failure to conform resulted in discipline by the "senior court." This custom died with the arrival of veterans after the war. As did compulsory chapel and vespers.

There were no national-related fraternities or sororities at Carleton, but there were pale carbon copies (what's a carbon copy, grandpa?) called literary societies. In former days they had generated some debating activity, but by the time I got there they didn't have much social *or* literary function, either one. William Schacht of nearby Rochester, fellow runner and debater, summed up the situation. Those societies, he said, were like setting up door frames on the Bald Spot and asking people to step through them. When I was a sophomore and was "rushed", I decided not to join any. But my mother was terribly upset. She had experienced great joy and satisfaction in her sorority experience with the Pi Phis at Knox (which was a national); and she could not bear having me miss out. So I changed and accepted the invitation of the Corinthians. However in my senior year, Mother now gone, I led the dissolution of the Corinthians and was the spokesman for its demise.

The social life at Carleton centered mainly on the Saturday night dance at Sayles Hill Gymnasium. Dancing was not allowed at Norwegian Lutheran Saint Olaf College across the river. Nevertheless, my roommate Don Raish, campus social chairman our senior year, thought there should be some type of activity the two student bodies could engage in together in the interest of community fellowship between the two colleges. Mostly the only time students from the two colleges made contact was in a fight on the bridge over the Cannon River the night before the big game.

Accordingly, Don went to see Lars Boe, the president of Saint Olaf, and had a long talk. With zero results. Mingling did not fit with the cultural mission of Saint Olaf College. Don repeated to me several times Boe's question to him, "Are we going to allow civilization to make a mastic of us?"

Dancing on the Carleton gymnasium's hardwood floor did not make the basketball coaches happy, but everybody managed. Music was sometimes provided by campus combos, but when the budget allowed, the Social Committee secured outside professional bands.

Some of the dances were all-college, non-date, to make sure every girl had a chance. I think that at that time there were seven hundred students enrolled, four hundred men and three hundred women, a ratio which was believed to be best socially. But most of the dances were for couples, who traded segments on their dance cards. Everybody had a small folder, usually tied with a frilly tassel, providing ten blanks for names of dance partners—five before and five after the intermission. If you were pretty keen on your date, you tended not to share too many dances but to keep most for yourself.

The two most beautiful women on campus, Carolyn Haeberlin and Mary Shifflett, were believed to be out of the reach of any but the most dashing athletes. This was a challenge, and I decided to try. I was pretty nervous while Carolyn was coming to the phone. She said she had a conflict on the night I was suggesting, and her demeanor was so cool, I did not try again. Mary, however, was perhaps surprised but seemed happy to hear from me and accepted for a dance that fall. As soon as the word got out, I was inundated with requests to trade dances, and I think I gave up five. She was a classic beauty, with black hair and flashing eyes, the kind of coed the college publicity office took pictures of beside campus blossoms for use in the brochures. We went out together a few times that spring, but somehow we had trouble finding things to talk about. Finally, on a Sunday afternoon walk, I told her I didn't think it was working, and probably it was best we call it off. Her heart was not broken. I think she got over it. Others were waiting in line. She said that she appreciated me telling her what I thought. So often, she said, a guy quits without saying why, and a girl wonders what happened. So that worked out fine.

Mary later married Bud Wilkinson, football coach at the University of Oklahoma. They were ultimately divorced, but when he died, I wrote Mary a friendly letter. She responded with a nice reply and also told her round-robin class letter I had written. By then we were both over eighty.

Faculty Characters

At reunions an alum will sometimes ask whether there are still any colorful "characters" like the ones we used to know and love. A couple from our day come to mind. James Pyper Bird taught French with razzle dazzle. If he caught a coed touching up her complexion in class, he would throw a piece of chalk at her across the room. He sometimes tended to badger, as he did with me once regarding some contretemps about our family's dog. I objected out loud to his approach and asked him, in effect, to "get off my case." He did so at once, and he never treated me like that again. It was a lesson that helped me from then on—you can influence the way you are treated by your own firmness. To encourage a falterer Mr. Bird often paraphrased a line from Galatians, "And be not weary in well doing; for in due season you shall reap your reward if you faint not."

Keith Clark was another colorful personality. She came to Carleton with experience in journalism and government. A lively, quotable personality, she was pleased to be thought of as some one "outside the line," proud to be a "secret" smoker when such was forbidden to campus women. She taught history and was the energizer of the International Club, which brought knowledgeable speakers to the college. She and I ran into each other downtown one day, and we happened to speak of screen actress Jean Harlow, the sex siren of the day. Dr. Clark commented, "She has such a vapid face."

"Who looks at her face?" I asked.

Roy A. Waggener, popular lecturer in zoology both on and off campus, made some pronouncements I still remember. He said we live off one-third of what we eat, and the doctors live off the other two-thirds.

In another dimension, he asserted in class one day that the exhortations we were hearing in chapel and vespers could be a waste of time. The reason, he said, was that "Me being what I am and things being what they are, I cannot help what I do."

At the time I thought this was terribly subversive of the whole Christian ethos of free decision-making and character improvement. My brother, a psychology major, reassured me that this theory of behaviorism was receding in the scientific community. Later however, I myself came around to a view more on the Waggenerian side, leaning toward the determinism of Calvinist predestinarianism.

Students too added color. My dad liked to quote the undergraduate who after being expelled, boasted, "I've been kicked out of better colleges than this!"

Visiting authorities provided an important component of our education. I especially remember poet and critic Louis Untermeyer, who lectured one afternoon (it is possible he had an engagement in the Twin Cities that evening). He was particularly contemptuous of Edgar A. Guest, the folksy poet who was writing a sentimental column of verse every day from the *Detroit Free Press*, enormously popular and widely republished. ("It takes a heap o' livin' in a house t' make it home.") Untermeyer, on the other hand, leaned to the classical side. He told us with some glee of a woman who was a fan of Guest's and came up to Untermeyer after a lecture. She was incensed by his snide shots and asked him, "Mr. Untermeyer, what kind of car do you drive?"

"I drive a Chevrolet—why do you ask?"

"Well," she huffed, "Mr. Guest drives a Cadillac!"

Years later I had the privilege of visiting with Mr. Guest at a small luncheon at the *Free Press*. We talked about one of his recent poems, which I had found moving, where a little boy was playing sheriff.

"Art for Art's Sake"

One summer I "uncovered" on purpose, in the service of Art. At the Buckham Memorial Library in Faribault, there is a series of four murals on the interior walls of the library's upper level. They depict four aspects of ancient Greek life: intellectual, political, military, and athletic. Some people said the figures looked like me. They do. Here's why. At our home on Northfield's East Second Street, we did quite a lot of entertaining. Mother's problems with MS never slowed her down as a hostess. One of her specialties was blanched, salted almonds, with which I used to help her. Also she would usually bake Parker House rolls.[2] When we entertained dinner guests, she did the cooking, Dad did the carving and so on, and I did the table waiting. One

---

[2] I made a point later in life, when I was speaking at Faneuil Hall, to stay at Boston's Parker House, where the yeast-raised, buttery, soft dinner rolls were originally introduced in the 1870s.

evening, Professor and Mrs. Alfred Hyslop came to dinner. He was the chairman of the Carleton Art Department. I guess he liked the cut of my jib, and he asked my father whether he could invite me to be the model on some paintings he was commissioned to do. Dad agreed and so did I. The result was the Faribault murals.

Hyslop's studio was in drafty Williams Hall, one of the college's earliest structures. It was hard work, holding a pose for twenty minutes at a time with only a few minutes' break every hour. I was paid the student-work rate of thirty-five cents an hour. Standing there in the nude, sometimes chilly, was at first a little disconcerting, especially during the occasional incipient tumescence. But I got used to it, and the artist was thoroughly professional all the way. I was the only model who posed for all the figures, and there were at least four in each of the four murals. My diary shows we had posing sessions in April, July, and August 1933, lasting from two to five hours each.

Nearly fifty years later, in 1981, I went back to the Buckham Library in Faribault for the first time, took pictures of the murals, and sent the color photos to Alfred Hyslop, then well into his eighties and living in Tucson. He wrote back a warm letter of appreciation. I was glad for this exchange not long before he died.

Super Salesman

During college summers, I was a salesman for the Northrup King seed company of Minneapolis. Mr. Stanchfield, the general sales manager, asked me why, if I had not done all that well with selling Real Silk hosiery to housewives the year before, would this be different? I said that the door-to-door business, without supervised routes, was not the professional kind of selling his company stood for with established territories.[3]

Stanchfield assigned me to the counties of southeastern Iowa and northeastern Missouri. I learned what a "pot and pitcher hotel" was. The job was to visit the stores, mostly in small towns, where the company's seed rack was displayed, having been sent from Minneapolis on consignment. We counted up and collected for the seed packets that had been sold, and shipped the rest back to Minneapolis in the box they had come in. Many store owners believed they were the only ones who saved the boxes. But actually most did. I found one in the basement that was full of cockroaches, so I took it to the street to dump them out. The embarrassed merchant asked me not to do that, and I realized belatedly that he was not interested in having the public associate his place with cockroaches.

My territory then was just south of Iowa City, where my uncle M. Willard Lampe was the founding dean of the State University of Iowa's School of Religion. Some weekends I could spend with him and his family. One Fourth of July, I drove with him out to Washington, Iowa, where he was to be the Independence Day speaker. He made a good address, emphasizing that all people qualified for the rights in the Declaration of Independence regardless of the "pigment of their skin." It was the last time for forty years I ever heard anyone say anything on the Fourth of July, and it helped me start in the seventies an Independence

---

[3]During the summer of 1935, I sold Real Silk products door to door in Austin, Minnesota. Jay Hormel, the Austin meatpacker (Spam), had a French-speaking son, who was a fellow student at Carleton, and the latter invited me to the Hormel home. We had a lively visit with Mr. Hormel, who took delight in referring to me as a "super-salesman," although apparently not "super" enough to sell him any socks. He did explain to me his concept of a guaranteed annual wage, which his company was seriously considering. He was uncomfortable about hiring people away from established positions and then firing them after using them for a few months, when such people then found it difficult to return to previous employment.

Day Speakers Corner in Claremont where a broad cross section of citizens now say their piece.

Multiple Sclerosis

Meantime Mother was fighting the multiple sclerosis that had struck her years earlier. Its symptoms came and went, but she became increasingly weaker. Dad took us all down to Sumner's Studio for a family portrait, and she joked that he wanted to make an official record of the family before she died. Dad took on more and more of the family chores.

We were told that people do not die of MS, but of something else. Mother had suffered from the disease for eight years, but she was actually taken by pneumonia in the Depression winter of 1934. It was late January, at the end of the college semester, and I was in the middle of final exams. It was also a week of huge black clouds of dust ominously covering the sky, the kind that drove Oklahomans to California that year. The house was only a block from the campus, and I stopped to see Mother. As it turned out, it was for the last time. When I left her upstairs room I said, "Keep fighting." She responded weakly, "I'm too tired to fight." Two days later, February 1, 1934, she was gone.

That afternoon I had arrived at Goodsell Observatory to take a calculus exam. My math professor, Marion White, appeared shaken and said my mother was very ill, and thought I should go home rather than take the exam. I said I knew that the situation was serious but I could take the exam, and then go. She said, no you'd better go now. I think she had been told that Mother had already died but felt she should not be the one to inform me.

When I arrived home, Dad gave me the news. We cried and gave each other a big hug. The undertakers were there before me and soon were coming down the stairs with the body wrapped in a sheet. The next day they brought her back, and she lay in state for a day in our living room, while friends came by to pay their respects. I am told this is no longer the custom as it sets up problem memories among the family. But to me it seemed, and still seems, just right for her. The commercial mortuaries do a great job, and I am grateful for them. But for her friends to be able to come and say goodbye in her home, that meant a great deal to me.

I was eighteen and was not broken up over her departure the way Stu was, although at the time I did not see how everybody could go on running their businesses and making deliveries for example. Didn't the world have to stop, at least for a few minutes? It seemed to me a blessing that there would be no more suffering. Stu, fourteen, saw her as the bright spot in a sometimes difficult childhood. Mother was the one he believed really understood him. Helen was seven years old, and had not quite that depth of relationship. Dad told me that Stu had asked him, why did she have to go? He said, it may have been best on account of the multiple sclerosis. Then Stu asked, "But why did she have to have that?" With tears in his eyes, Dad said to me, "I could not answer."

For the funeral and burial in Northfield, a number of Medford people drove the twenty-five miles on a Saturday afternoon over wintry Minnesota roads to express their love. Dad had arranged with the undertaker to recover mother's Pi Beta Phi pin and her rings. He was especially touched by a tiny bird, possibly a wren or a cedar waxwing, that flew in over the grave just before the casket was lowered. It hovered a moment, and then flew off. Mother was forty-two, Dad fifty. We children were eighteen, fourteen, and seven.

Two years later, in 1936, Dad was married again—to Louise Curtis of Omaha. She was another unusually gifted woman— gracious, caring, and efficient. She was a church secretary, never before married, and she was not about to abandon her happy single life. But Dad was such a persistent suitor, she finally acceded. In the course of his strategy he sent me to call on her when she was attending a Glenn Clark Camp Farthest Out on a Minnesota lake, referring to me in his introductory note as his "ace." She had known my mother as a fellow student in Omaha's Central High School, and both were named Louise. My sister Helen was ten, and the new mother turned out to be for her the right person at the right time. Mother II was concerned over the wicked stepmother image of the fairy tales, but she was in fact the opposite. After sixteen years as a beloved member of the Carleton community, she and Dad retired to California, where she survived him by nine years.

-6-

"YOUR ARMS TOO SHORT TO BOX WITH GOD"

I was always up to my neck in college politics. Classmates seemed to regard me as a leader and put my name in for the key positions starting with sophomore class president. In our junior year, the spring of 1935, Chuck Duncan of Duluth made a fiery speech nominating me for student body president. He was designated by the Corinthian Society, of which he and I were both members, to undertake this assignment.

In the nature of things, I expected this and was fairly confident of the election's outcome. But a small challenge was thrown in the path of my game plan. I was nominated to be the student representative to spend the next two years at something called Carleton-in-China, probably modeled after Yale-in-China, teaching in a mission school at Fenchow in Shansi Province. The plan was for a student (male at that time) at the close of his junior year to proceed to this teaching assignment for two years, and come back for his senior year. The students on campus would then get the benefit of his China experience. The project, interestingly enough, was substantially financed by student contributions. This invitation intrigued me, not only because of the challenge of service in a whole new world, but more because the medical missionary in charge of the Fenchow hospital at that time was Dr. Walter H. Judd, who, as I will show later, had such a powerful influence on my life. Also some of those who had gone out there in the past had become foreign correspondents or state department types. I sought advice from wise and understanding faculty friends. Most advised me against it. The China ploy would be a dead end, they thought, and I was a cut above the kind of people that normally accepted that sort of thing. This was about all I needed. China before World War II was nowheresville, and so it became for me a "road not taken." I believed my career would be more likely to get somewhere if I remained with my class, got elected, and stayed on the ladder.

It was a decision I would always regret.

My political plan stayed on track. The opposing candidates were more on the intellectual side—Don Raish of Pierre (pronounced "peer"), South Dakota, who was my roommate our senior year, and George Zahner of Minneapolis, a fall Phi Beta Kappa, who later remained our class president for sixty years. All three of us had been nominated by the Carleton faculty as candidates for a Rhodes scholarship. Zahner was the only one who survived the Minnesota competition, but was then eliminated in the regional round in Des Moines. One faculty member commented that I was the only one of the three really to qualify, because of the Rhodes requirement that the candidate have a "fondness for and success in manly outdoor sports." I had lettered in two varsity sports, whereas the others were not into such activity.

Zahner was a brain, not much of a social bug, but Raish, a handsome, light-haired junior whom I nicknamed "Smooth," was going steady with Jean Todd, a senior who was student body president that year. I was going with Rosemary Ferguson, a smart freshman debater whose father was a Ford dealer in Eau Claire, Wisconsin. There were more freshman women like Rosemary than senior women like Jean. Consequently I knew that on the west (women's) side of the campus, I was in good shape. In the final vote I led the field with a plurality of about thirty-five votes, out of some three hundred cast for the three candidates. It came out about as I expected.

The first thing I did was to go to the college's president, Donald J. Cowling, and ask his advice as to how to conduct the office. He said he thought my predecessor had done it about right. I had the impression that he liked her establishment approach. She was not a boat-rocker.

My second step was to gather some of the articulate campus dissidents and write a questionnaire covering all controversial points we could think of, and some neutral ones as well, and send it to every student.

We had the survey printed and ready to distribute at year's end through the campus mail when the community was devastated by a college tragedy. We had to put off the survey for at least a week. It was spring, and for some time resentments had been simmering between students and the campus night watchman. Carleton's famed arboretum had become an attractive locale for "blanket parties" where couples wandered down in the evening by the moonlight to spend time in quiet contemplation of the wonders of each other's nature. President Cowling was of the old school and was disturbed by the activity which blankets in an arboretum would suggest. He ordered the night watchman to discourage same. The man carried a side arm for self-protection, and began showing up in the arboretum of an evening to spray beams from his flashlight around the lush flora. The result was explosive. Some of the young studs threatened to throw him in the river, and one night they menacingly encircled him. Frightened, the watchman fired his revolver, probably to scare or wound, but a bullet entered the stomach of Burt Krayenbuhl, a popular athlete and man about campus. He died three days later in the Northfield Hospital. The participants in the melee came through the college dining rooms that evening pleading for calm and for no recriminations. Sunday a solid bank of us attended Burt's funeral in South Saint Paul, his hometown. A court action resulted in clearing the watchman and the college of wrongdoing.

A week later our questionnaire went out, and Dr. Cowling was unhappy. He was long used to running everything himself and was doubtless concerned over what might be stirred up. But the results were surprisingly positive all around. There was even a solid majority in favor of continuing the compulsory chapel and vespers services. These were twenty-minute convocations Tuesday and Friday mornings, usually addressed by a faculty member, and sixty minutes Sunday evening with a visiting preacher, sometimes of national stature.

Apparently the students, at least that generation of students, thought the all-school gatherings provided a good community experience. The twice-weekly morning chapel services were addressed by faculty members, thus providing acquaintanceship with the ideas and life of able minds beyond one's own teachers.

Whatever unhappiness Dr. Cowling had with me did not last. We got along fine. We worked closely at the joint Student-Faculty Council monthly meetings, and he told an all-college convocation that my address in the chapel on Homecoming Day 1935 was "the finest student speech I've ever heard."

(One tends to remember things like that.)

In the political scene, in December 1935 I was one of two Carleton representatives (Ann Hartman was the other) to the convention of the National Student Federation of America in Kansas City. There I was elected chairman of the north central region of NSFA. Edward R. Murrow had been the national president 1930-32. The first evening of the convention I was having dinner with other student representatives. There was a particularly striking young lady with black hair and a great smile from Sophie Newcomb College in New Orleans, the women's division of Tulane University. She looked more like a prom queen than a student government representative. She authenticated her Southern credentials with her trademark comment, "I was fohteen years old before I knew that 'damn Yankee' was two words." After we had introduced ourselves around the table, she looked across at me and in a mellow drawl asked, "Wheah is Cahlton College, Mistuh Huntuh?" For the life of me I couldn't remember.

We were not always aware of it at the time, but were later increasingly conscious that in Dr. Cowling we were rubbing shoulders with a national leader. He came to Carleton at age 29 in 1909, the youngest American college president, and having earned more degrees from Yale than any other person. A philosophy major, he was also an ordained Congregational minister, and was active in the national church all his life. He remained at the helm of the college through World War II, retiring in 1945 at sixty-five. Like most college presidents, he stayed out of politics. But after the war he took on an objective with great seriousness. He told me he believed that the future of the country, indeed the world, depended on electing Harold E. Stassen president. Some time after that I had lunch with him in Saint Paul, and asked him why he did not accept any of the offers he must have received during his career to head up major institutions. He said, "It was a matter of fulfillment."

My father, who was not always on the best of terms with his boss, said that Cowling came out to Minnesota and took "this little one-horse, fresh-water college," and made it into a national institution. Laurence M. Gould, Cowling's colorful successor, referring to Emerson's famous dictum about institutions, said, "Carleton College will forever be the lengthened shadow of Donald J. Cowling."

When Cowling retired, there was a banquet in his honor at the University of Minnesota, sponsored by three entities that had benefitted from his leadership and fundraising skills— Carleton College, the state university, and the Congregational

Church. The *Minneapolis Star* carried a large photo of the honoree on the front page, and underneath were the words:

> Northfield Minnesota in its day has been noted for two great fundraisers, Jesse James and Donald J. Cowling. The difference between them was that Cowling never carried a gun.

Of course I enjoyed the kudos and attention of the student body presidency. I was sure this kind of success would continue steadily into the future. Following my speech at the Homecoming bonfire on the "bald spot," an area in the central quadrangle where grass did not grow because of the annual bonfire, Joe Markley, Carleton football hero of yesteryear and longtime Central High School coach in Minneapolis, came up to me and said, "I predict for you a great future." Back in high school, when I had driven safely home through a blizzard from a basketball game in Red Wing thirty miles away, my relieved mother looked lovingly at me and said, as only a mother could, "I think you are being saved for something great."

Maybe I was. But not quite in the way I had in mind. In the immortal words of Thomas à Kempis in *Imitation of Christ*, "Man proposes but God disposes."

My life at that stage showed some parallels with Richard Nixon's. We had both been brought up in the Depression era, with the solid values of small town American families, under the guidance of intensely Christian mothers. Both of us attended small colleges where we excelled in oratory, debate, and student government; both won substantial scholarships at prestigious eastern law schools; and we had similar aims. A squib in the college yearbook ran, "Next year sees Willie studying law at Harvard—he'd like to be Carleton's first White House occupant." Nixon, with frankly more ability, managed to stay the course. I did not. The Hound of Heaven never let me go. My arms were too short to box with God.[1]

I did not know it at the time, but many forces were already at work that would ultimately lead to a change of direction. One such, the person who perhaps had more influence on me than anyone except my parents, was Walter H. Judd (1898-1994), medical missionary to China in the twenties and thirties and United States congressman from Minnesota in the forties and fifties. I had first heard him speak when I was a high school senior at a young people's lakeside church camp west of Minneapolis. He was thirty-four years old, back from six years in China and studying under a surgery fellowship at the Mayo Clinic. His topic was "A Philosophy of Life that Works," a speech with which he had galvanized the quadrennial convention of the Student Volunteer Movement in Buffalo in January that year. A gifted, no-notes orator with a machine-gun, witty delivery, he was to make thousands of appearances before every conceivable kind of audience throughout his life. In that lakeside encounter, I was fascinated not only by his message but also by his oratorical style, his gestures, and inflections. They made his content exciting.[2]

---

[1]*Your Arms Too Short To Box With God* is the title of a landmark African-American musical dramatizing the Christian Passion story in a modern urban setting. It opened in New York in 1976 and has played summers in cities like Detroit and Los Angeles. The title is written without an apostrophe.

[2]I was included at a ninetieth birthday party for Dr. Judd at the Willard Hotel in Washington in September 1988. Senator Robert Dole of Kansas, who had served with Walter in the House of Representatives, came by and said, "In Washington everybody talks, but few listen. When Walter Judd talked, everybody listened." *The New York Times* called him "one of the most influential members of the House on foreign policy." It was said that at least 150 members followed his lead on international votes. Following his keynote speech at the Republican National Convention in 1960, he was almost named to the party's ticket as vice presidential nominee. Many think that if he had been, the GOP might have won that year. Mr. Nixon afterwards told Walter he believed that passing him over

He had a manner and a way with word pictures that fastened in my memory. He was surprised at how much of what he said on platforms I could play back to him, next only to his wife, he said.

When I was back at Carleton in the fifties, I heard him speak at Vespers. He said he knew of people who were trying to make Christians out of politicians. He may have been thinking of people like me, as he knew of my objectives in Washington.

"But" he said, "I would like to encourage young people to make politicians out of Christians. "O, but you say, 'You never get the people you want. You never get your first choice.' And I say, unless you work for your second choice, or your third choice, or your fourth choice, you are going to end up with your *last* choice."

Later, I heard him speak at The Claremont Colleges. I came home and said to Mary Louise, "That man makes the shivers run up and down my spine." She said, "Walter Judd could read the telephone book and make the shivers run up and down your spine." She was right. He could.

Back there in the early thirties I began to follow Dr. Judd around. I was impressed with the way he was able to hold large audiences of young people spellbound for two hours at a time—and even more with the impact he was having on me. His effectiveness arose from a combination of a brilliant analysis of problems around the globe, showing the relevance of the Christian way, and then a direct challenge—what are you going to do about its claims? My response proved to be basically the turning point of my life.

---

had been a mistake. A high moment for me was to be included as a speaker at Walter's memorial services in Maryland and Washington DC when he died in 1994 at ninety-five. His last words to me at the close of our final visit were: "The Chinese say that with clothes, the new are best—with friends, the old are best. You are one of the old."

Still, I hoped I would not have to go through with such a commitment. I was like Saint Augustine, who said, "Give me chastity and continence, but not just now."

One of Dr. Judd's penetrating quotations that continued to press me was one he had read in the Chinese classics:

If you are planning for a year, plant grain.
If you are planning for ten years, plant trees.
If you are planning for a hundred years, plant people.

Another of his proverbs I saw as relevant to my career decision was:

How prudently most men creep into nameless graves;
while now and then one forgets himself into immortality.

After one of his Vespers talks at Carleton, I went out to walk on the dark campus. It was a rainy night, and when I reached Observatory Hill, I looked up at the black clouds and said, "God, I will do anything you want me to do from here on."

Dr. Judd was focusing the issue for me. From childhood I had known that I had some kind of call to Christian service. This was the climate of our home. And it held me even as a student. Now, as college days were winding down, a personal struggle saddled me with an agonizing choice. The choice was between church and state.

I was aware that a "call" to Christian service did not necessarily entail strictly religious professions. One could also be "called" to enter politics or business or other vocations. Was it not important for positions of public trust to be filled with people of peerless integrity and, in case of a Christian, to carry those convictions into the public arena? This thought held much attraction.

I was intrigued by the blandishments of theological schools on "career days" in college. Albert Palmer, President of Chicago Theological Seminary, made an interesting comment, "Don't go into the ministry if you can do anything else." On the surface this looked appalling, a confirmation of one's worst fears that the ministry might be a catch-all for left-overs. What Palmer meant, of course, was that the ministry requires some one who is so motivated by his commission that anything else, for that person, is unthinkable. The Apostle Paul wrote, "Woe is unto me if I preach not the gospel!" It is something like the attitude of Helen Curran, the wife of Joe Curran, longtime National Maritime Union boss, who said of her husband, "I would rather be miserable with him than happy with any other person in the world."

"Do anything else?" I felt I *could* do something "else." I *wanted* to do something else. And that something else was to go into politics. Although I was dedicated to the church, I did not respond much to church people. Moreover, I did not see them doing much of anything that made a difference. The same old people were going through the same old motions.

My senior-year roommate Don Raish and I shared our agonies over end-of-student-days career choices. He thought it ironic that the two of us—he the campus social chairman, I the student body president—with people assuming we had it made, were moaning and groaning about the direction we would take after graduation.[3]

True, it was important for public-minded people to be dedicated to government service. But for myself, it was to be another way. Some time later this thought came to me:

It is important to have a good person in the White House.
It is more important to have a good person in every house.

---

[3]Don, after ten years in the airline business, became a lifelong Episcopal priest in Texas.

Two Men and a Message

In May 1936, just before commencement, two men visited Carleton at the invitation of President Cowling: Cleve Hicks, an Episcopal evangelist out of Massachusetts, and Randulf Haslund, a Norwegian dynamo who had recently found a new thrust in his life. They were representing something called the Oxford Group, and spoke at the college's Sunday evening vespers service. I was transfixed. At most of the services we received great advice, often from national figures. But never before had I heard practical stories of people *carrying out the advice.* Their talks gave graphic accounts of real people becoming different. I said to myself, "If half of what they say is true, I need to find out more."

Unlike our usual vespers speakers, the Oxford Group men did not leave town after their talk. They stayed on for a week in the college guest rooms, where they held interviews and conducted small-group meetings. At one of these, I was hooked. They talked about four absolute moral standards—honesty, purity, unselfishness, and love. They also talked about the guidance of God. And they talked about life-changing.

All of those impressed me right away. I knew that I had compromised on moral principles I had been taught by my family. I wanted to know God better, and was interested in the possibility that the Creative Force could transmit thoughts to me. And to help some one else find a faith and a new direction, I thought, would be the most wonderful experience in the world. Also, it was clear to me that human nature was at the heart of national and global difficulties. A change in human nature could be important in changing society.

Cleve and Randulf suggested we sit quietly with a pencil and a blank piece of paper, listen, and see what came. Whatever else entered my mind that night, one ribbon thought came that I never forgot. It went straight to the heart of my dilemma:

Men and not institutions will build the new world order.

I knew that all the laws, agreements, and treaties in the world, however necessary, were not going to touch the heart of what is wrong. People becoming different was the *radical* solution; it went to the *root*. I was not sure that reaching the hearts of people was something I would ever be good at. But I gradually concluded that that was where I would ultimately lay down my time, talent, treasure, commitment, and life.

At length I decided I would make the experiment. I could always go back "to the mess I was in," as they said. So I took four sheets of paper and wrote one of the absolutes at the top of each, asking God to help me make the check-up. I was surprised at how many things I wrote down. On the sheet labeled "Absolute Honesty" I jotted down a college expense account I had chiseled on. At that national student convention in Kansas City, I had been allotted an advance sum for expenses, with the understanding I would return what was not spent. However, while condemning political corruption on the floor of the convention, I had self-appropriated the difference, bought some clothes, and banked the rest. I was "honest" in the rationalization that it was payment for services. But "absolute" honesty was something else again. So I took it back.

Also I sent back some towels that belonged to hotels where I had stayed. I recalled a track teammate in a high-school locker room pulling out a towel that was marked "Hotel Albert." With tongue in cheek, he said, "That was my mother's name before she was married." There was a whole lot more to my cleanup than there is any point in covering here. I apologized to a professor for lying about class attendance. I developed a more unselfish approach to sex. I made amends to a guy I had resented.

What I noticed was that God became real to me for the first time in quite a while. It felt as though when the connections were brightened up, some Force out there started paying more attention. Psychologists may explain all this, but that is the way it looked to me. Things simply were different.

The experience seemed a practical follow-up to the Judd challenge.

"Incubator of Greatness"—the Harvard Law School

Suspicious that this meant Christian service I still pursued the political and went ahead with my application to the Harvard Law School for admission in the fall of 1936, and I was the recipient of one of the first two George Chase Christian fellowships for a Minnesota student to do graduate study at Harvard. I took it as a sign from the stars that I was on track.

Life magazine came out that year with an article on the Harvard Law School, featuring the numbers of graduates who made it big in government and industry—dubbing the school "an incubator of greatness." The phrase had a nice ring to it.

The experience in Cambridge, however, was not a happy one. For one thing, I could not shake the conviction I was in the wrong place. Secondly, from being somebody, I was now nobody, not nearly as smart as the new set of peers. Many of us had our noon meal at the refectory of nearby Episcopal Theological School. We of course discussed the morning's lectures. I was much better at repeating the professors' jokes than their legal points. Thirdly, the law presented itself to me as a giant game, like mathematics or a puzzle. I was never much good in that kind of territory. Finally, although in a civilized society the law is necessary, as one teacher said, to keep people from coming to blows, I could not shake the feeling that the system was not interested in solutions, but only in determining winners and losers.

Many judicial decisions, Professor Eddie Morgan frequently told us in his course in Evidence, could be explained by what he called the "adversary system." Developing the character of people involved interested me much more than making judgments between good guys and bad guys.

Law school was my first contact with the eastern United States. For one thing, first hour classes started at nine o'clock instead of eight. Noon turned out to be one o'clock. I thoroughly enjoyed becoming acquainted with the cultural opportunities of Boston, particularly the theater district. Many Broadway plays had try-out runs in Boston, and we saw some good shows. I recall especially George Kaufman's *You Can't Take It With You*, which came out in 1936.

Another cultural enrichment for us students was generated at Scollay Square (later renamed, with exciting bureaucratic flair, "Government Center"), which we held it our academic duty to visit on the occasional Saturday night. A landmark of the Square was the Old Howard burlesque theater where the girls were skilled at taking off their clothes. We had heard that Oliver Wendell Holmes, during his nineteen years as justice of the Supreme Court of Massachusetts, was a regular at the Old Howard, and we were sure that to associate ourselves with this aspect of the judge's experience would help advance our legal understanding.

In the fall of 1936, Time Inc. introduced an exciting pictorial magazine called *Life*, borrowing the name from a defunct humor periodical. It looked like a winner to me, and thinking it might become a collector's item, I became a charter subscriber. Apparently others had the same idea as those early copies turned out to be worthless and also a basement-space pain to my dad, who finally persuaded me to let him toss them out.

The year 1936 was also the first year I could cast a ballot. I voted for Franklin D. Roosevelt for his second term, mostly because of Cordell Hull, Secretary of State, and his free trade policy.

One afternoon during the 1936 campaign, I joined a large crowd on the Boston Common and heard FDR speak. He was introduced by the florid Boston Irish leader, former Mayor James Michael Curley. Roosevelt was running for his second term as president, and Curley was a candidate for U.S. Senator from

Massachusetts. As it turned out, Curley was unsuccessful in his bid against Republican Henry Cabot Lodge, Jr., who that year won his first of several elections to the Senate. On another occasion in the fall I attended a lively, mass rally for Curley in the Boston Garden, experiencing some of the man's storied eloquence. He was a graduate of the Emerson School of Oratory and was a stemwinder of the old style. With an eye to Boston's considerable Italian vote, it was announced that the candidate's favorite song was "The Isle of Capri." In his address to adoring backers he stoutly defended, in the name of safety, his boondoggle "public works" program, when he was governor, that had lined the highway with sidewalks clear out to western Massachusetts. Curley was one of the most colorful characters of Boston's history. His fictionalized story appeared in a Pulitzer Prize winning novel, *The Last Hurrah*, by Edwin O'Connor (Boston: Little, Brown & Co., 1956). Arthur M. Schlesinger, Jr., called it "The best American novel about urban politics." In the 1940s, when Curley had added "congressman" to his many portfolios, I had a visit with him in his Capitol Hill office.

Among the outstanding speakers who came to the law school in Cambridge was Speaker of the House Sam Rayburn. My main memory of his remarks was an exhortation to students from the northern states, long before talk of term limits, to keep their U.S. representatives in office longer, so that their seniority could give them the kind of influence in the Congress enjoyed by the long-serving southerners.

Gerald L. K. Smith, the spellbinding Huey Long lieutenant from Louisiana, recommended that Harvard establish a chair in Rabble Rousing. What the upper echelon students needed, he argued, was to learn how to communicate with the masses.

Harold Laski, the British socialist who was a great friend of Felix Frankfurter, frequently visited. He once described the *Harvard Law Review* as "pages of notes topped by a smattering of text."

Boston's historic sites and reenactments were also fascinating. I recall seeing a modern, red-wigged William Dawes reining his horse through Cambridge in support of Paul Revere's ride on Patriots Day, April 19. Since then the hooves and horseshoes of Dawes' mount have been imprinted in the sidewalk.

It was on the Boston piers that I acquired a taste for seafood. Oysters on the half shell were a new experience for a Midwestern palate. The Durgin Park restaurant became my all-time favorite. The place has not changed in a hundred years, and the red-checked cloths on the family-style tables are still a friendly delight. Whenever I have returned, as to deliver Fourth of July orations in nearby Faneuil Hall, or for whatever reason at all, I have dined at Durgin Park. The insulting ladies from south Dorchester in their dirty white muslin are still slinging the roast beef, oysters, and Indian corn pudding. On our last visit there, Mary Louise and I were waited on by a nice looking solid citizen with a solid personality. I said to her, "You're not big enough or old enough to be waiting tables at Durgin Park." She replied, "You want to bet?"

One of my happiest evenings in those law student days was a close-out bash at the end of our second year. How I was included in the party I do not recall. It could be that Parker Berg, a classmate from Pittsburgh who could not attend the party, asked me to escort his beautiful girl friend. She was a Wellesley College student also from Pittsburgh, and I wish I could remember her name. She was pretty terrific, and I toyed with the idea of betraying my friend's trust and stealing her. The party was a dinner dance at the Copley Plaza Hotel, and the entertainment was by Benny Goodman and his orchestra, including that night Lionel Hampton on the xylophone and Gene Krupa, the world's greatest drummer. Liltin' Martha Tilton was the female vocalist, and she sang, "This is my first affair, so please be kind." Since I was not long for the law school at that point, I have remembered this party as a kind of gala farewell.

In retrospect, I have always been glad for the law school experience. Many issues in public and commercial life I have better understood because of what I learned in the halls named Langdell, Austin, and Hastings. Brilliant professors, giants in their fields, made the place exciting. I sat in classes taught by Felix Frankfurter, later a Supreme Court justice; Erwin Griswold, former U.S. solicitor general and for twenty years dean of the school; Austin Wakeman Scott, who himself *was* the law of trusts; and Samuel Williston, almost ditto in the law of contracts. The school has always been in the news. At the turn of the century, five of the nine justices of the U.S. Supreme Court and at least fifteen Supreme Court justices of other countries had a Harvard Law education. I later returned for many of the five-year reunions.

Particularly vivid memories arise of Edward H. "Bull" Warren, professor of property law. To heap scorn on faulty logic he would cite the unwed mother's comment, "But it is such a *little* baby." To illustrate the importance of clarity, he often cited the "vicar's egg," referring to the cleric who when asked about his egg, replied, "Parts of it were good." Stories of the professor's alcoholic escapades in Boston went the rounds. He was the model for the character played by A. E. Housman in the motion picture *The Paper Chase*. When I flubbed an answer in class one day, he used with me the same words Housman said in the film to the baffled student, "Mr. Hunter, here is a nickel. I suggest you take it to the nearest telephone, call your mother, and tell her you will never make a lawyer."

Besides his own eccentricity, the Bull was expressing the tilt of the school in those days, which held that a good law education was one that toughened the student through a climate charged with brutality, failure, and fear. It was said that members of the first year class were told, "Look to the person on your left and the one on the right—one of you will not be back next year." Although Dean Erwin Griswold told alumni that this was a canard, it is true that, in our case, of the six hundred students in our entering class the fall of 1936, only four hundred of us returned for the second year. Following the war, the school concluded that such washouts were too expensive—for both the school and the student. The philosophy of admissions shifted toward the (shudder) Yale approach. More care is now used in the selection of entering classes, and today most Harvard Law students graduate.

I hung in there for two years. But then the Hound of Heaven caught up with me.

During my first year at law school, Cleve Hicks and an Oxford Group team were conducting meetings in the Cambridge area, coinciding with the tercentenary of Harvard College, founded in 1636. I attended a weekend Oxford Group house party in Hugh and Helen Scott's Wellesley home on the Charles River. It was not long before I knew that the jig was up. A number of solid citizens, some rather tough-minded types, the kind I did not think would be interested, convinced me that people can and do change and apply what they found in practical affairs. I was ready to jump in. Still, they counseled me to stay where I was, and I did so for two years.

In the fall of 1938, at the beginning of my third year at the Harvard Law School, an ad hoc committee from Oxford Group headquarters in New York came to Cambridge and waited on me in my digs. They invited me to join their team on a full-time basis. The moment of truth had arrived.

I took time off from studies, went to New York, and sweated over this decision for two weeks. My father was deeply distressed and offered to sell insurance policies if it would help keep me in law school. There was indeed a financial dimension: my grades were not good enough to retain my fellowship beyond the first two years. Charles H. (Chas) Haines, of the Lukens Steel family and an associate of Oxford Group initiator Frank Buchman since the early twenties, had made financial contributions to my third year. I was by now regarded as part of the family, for whom this kind of sharing was appropriate. But I think the team felt that if they were going to help underwrite me, they needed more of my services.

At Calvary Church in Manhattan, the rector, Samuel Moor Shoemaker, who knew my situation, decided to close his Sunday morning service with the hymn of James Russell Lowell, "Once to every man and nation comes the moment to decide." Trucking executive Fred Purdy asked me whether I was as willing to stay in law school as I was to leave. The Reverend Frederick Lawrence, Cambridge Episcopal priest, later bishop, thought it was terrible that I was being asked to terminate these studies, and Dr. Loring T. Swaim, national orthopedic authority, agreed. John Ray Snell, Harvard graduate student in engineering, thought it was a good idea to relinquish, because if I did not and obtained my law degree, it would be more difficult to abandon ambitions later on.

I did abandon them. It was a kind of death, the kind German theologian Dietrich Bonhoeffer wrote of in *The Cost of Discipleship*: "When Christ calls a man, he bids him come and die."

I pulled the plug. I cast in my lot. I burned my bridges.

7

SOUL SURGEON WITH A GLOBAL PRACTICE

It was in Sweden in 1938 that I was to have a foretaste of my first career. There I attended an all-Scandinavian assembly for Moral Re-Armament in the old Hanseatic League city of Visby on the island of Götland off Sweden's southeastern coast, and it was there that I first met Frank Buchman, initiator of the program. My first reaction was not all that positive. Was he cocky, or just sure of himself? It was soon evident that he had a magnetic effect on people, and an obvious power to motivate great numbers to achieve constructive ends. He also repelled many. Change agents do.

After my second year in law school, Cleve Hicks had invited me to an Oxford Group youth rally in Pennsylvania's Pocono Mountains, attended by several hundred young men from around the country. Cleve had Episcopal clergy training, and was especially good at motivating young people. He was a sort of Friar Tuck, with a round, happy face, who got a big bang out of life. Somebody said he looked like an unmade bed. "Why should I organize my papers?" he asked, "leaves don't fall from trees into files." Throughout his days, he kept in touch with people whom he had helped find a new life. Of all his possessions, he said, what he would most hate to lose were his six address books.

Cleve selected seven of us from the Poconos rally to attend the assembly in Sweden later that summer. (Such conclaves were still being called "houseparties".) I was lucky enough to be one of them. It meant cutting one more personal tie, as I had to resign from my summer job with the Northrup King seed company, where for the third year I was to be a summer salesman in southeastern Iowa and northeastern Missouri.

To finance the trip, Cleve raised funds from Howard Cheseborough Davison, one of our fellowship who lived in Dutchess County, New York. Howard was proud of his distant relationship to the John *Davison* Rockefeller family. He was later to marry the daughter of Abraham Vereide, initiator of the Washington breakfast groups and their Fellowship House.

Our transatlantic passage was via a Swedish ship, the S.S. *Drottningholm*, nine days New York to Göteborg. The weather was typically North Atlantic, and although as a boy I had been well experienced in carsickness, this was my first nausea at sea. I found that flat on my back in my small bunk was the place to be. I learned to like super-salty anchovies, and in later years generally chose anchovy pizzas. The waiter trained us in dining etiquette, asking that we place our utensils pointed to the center of the plate when we wanted it removed.

From Göteborg, we were driven at night across Sweden to Stockholm at breakneck speed in a rented car, a little hairy around blind curves, especially for us Americans, as Swedish autos were still driving on the left. A ferry took us to the island of Götland and its centerpiece, Visby, the "city of ruins and roses." It was lovely in August, and a large crowd from throughout northern Europe attended the assembly.

One reason for the intense Scandinavian interest that had developed over the previous months were books and articles about their involvement in the movement by popular writers, notably labor writer Harry Blomberg and novelist Sven Stolpe.

One of the stars of the meeting was a Norwegian newsman, Fredrik Ramm, who had flown over the North Pole in 1926 with explorer Roald Amundsen. Ramm was a breezy man with ruddy complexion and a great sense of humor who took some ribbing for his musical Norwegian accent. He urged us not to applaud the speakers. They were delivering a message, not presenting a performance, he contended.

Frank Buchman delivered the keynote speech at Visby, and it has been remembered as a turning point in the direction of his work. It was entitled "Revival, Revolution, Renaissance." In it he dealt with the tension between the personal and the global.

Buchman was sometimes called a "soul surgeon" because of a small 1932 booklet entitled *Soul Surgery*, written by his YMCA missionary friend H. A. Walter, who also authored the popular hymn "I Would Be True." Walter's surgery point was that in helping a person to remove what is wrong with one's spiritual body the caregiver needs to be as thorough as the professional who removes what is wrong with one's physical body. The guidebook highlighted Buchman's life-changing, or soul surgery, methods, using notes made by Buchman himself for a book he planned to author with Henry B. Wright, who died before it could happen.[1]

The soul surgeon term caused some amusement in the press, and Buchman let it drop. Life changing was always for him the key, but only as a necessary step toward world changing.[2]

---

[1]Wright was in charge of student Christian work at Yale when Buchman was working at Penn State, and they conducted intercollegiate student conferences together. Another leader of the conferences was my Uncle M. Willard Lampe, who at that time was the Bible Study Secretary of the Christian Association at the University of Pennsylvania, and who was later to found the School of Religion at the University of Iowa. Walter's *Soul Surgery* booklet pulled together the Wright-Buchman methods of winning people and popularized the "Five C's": Confidence, Confession, Conviction, Conversion, Continuance. These still appear sometimes in spiritual literature, including Twelve Steps material.

[2]Howard Clinebell, a world authority on pastoral counseling, told me he thought Buchman was the pioneer of person-to-person healing. Before his time people with a problem were apt to seek out an expert who had a certificate on the wall. Buchman, Clinebell says, led the way to a lay approach, one-on-one, mutual assistance, where like talked with like.

At Visby Buchman was acknowledging the personal core part of his work, but he was concerned that it not stop with the individual. He believed from the beginning that personal change must issue in social change. In 1934 he had said that the aim of the Oxford Group was a new social order under the spirit of God, "making for better human relationships, for unselfish cooperation, for cleaner business, cleaner politics, for the elimination of political, industrial, and racial antagonisms."[3]

In 1936 in the British House of Lords the Marquess of Salisbury had made a classic statement about what Buchman was up to.

The cause of the world's state is not economic, the cause is moral. It is there where the evil lies. It is the want of religion which we ought to possess. If I may use a phrase which is common in a great movement which is taking place in this country and elsewhere, what you want are God-guided personalities, which make God-guided nationalities, to make a new world. All other ideas of economic adjustment are too small really to touch the center of the evil.

Now at Visby, Buchman was trying to give traction to that idea. He put it this way:

Some of the people have come here hoping to be changed. That is very good, very necessary. Some of you have come here with the hope that you will learn to change others. That, too, is very necessary. But the danger is that some of you want to stop there. I am tremendously interested in a third point—how to save a crumbling civilization. That is the thing that interests me. But then I want a fourth thing. I want to reach the millions of the world.[4]

---

[3] *Remaking the World: The Speeches of Frank N. D. Buchman* (London: Blandford Press, 1961), 4.

[4] *Ibid.*, 4.

At this meeting I met some of the Swedish labor leaders and writers who were documenting what looked to them very much like a renaissance in the Northland. That was the kind of thing I wanted to help advance.

Pennsylvanian with a Program

Frank Buchman was a genial, intuitive, intelligent, compassionate man. He had eyes that both penetrated and twinkled. He had an intense caring for individuals and a bright vision for the world. His life (1878-1961) was intensely Christian and intensely pragmatic. His sure-footed sense of authority issued from his unquestioning confidence that God spoke to him directly and with clear accents of "thus says the Lord." He could thunder like the prophets of old. He could also be the gentle "uncle" at a child's birthday party. He had an extraordinary capacity to motivate brilliant men and women to dedicate all their time and money in fulfilling his global vision of world changing through life changing.

He said good food and good Christianity go together, that the way to the heart was often through the stomach. The tables he set became famous. At the same time food for him was always a health problem, leading to circulatory difficulties. He never had sufficient exercise, and he was always overweight.

In a way, Buchman was Mr. Human Potential ahead of his time. An airline pilot said he had produced "a wonder drug that makes human beings out of people." Yet he insisted that such change must always go on to play its part in transforming society. "Why not," he asked with his dying breath, "let God run the whole world?"

Born June 4, 1878, in Pennsburg into a Pennsylvania German family, where English was a second language, Frank Buchman was educated at Perkiomen School, Pennsburg; Muhlenberg

College, Allentown; and Mount Airy Seminary, Philadelphia. His mother was a devout German Lutheran hausfrau and his father a saloon keeper, store manager, and hotel operator. Young Frank picked up a good deal of faith from his mother and famous hospitality skills from his father. The latter had a background in the Evangelical and Reformed persuasion, and the son went to church in the morning with his Lutheran mother and in the afternoon with his E & R father. The two faiths shared the same building, across the street from the Buchman store, on the second floor of which Frank had been born.

After graduation from seminary he started the first hospice for poor boys in Philadelphia, but had a falling out with his board over a downsized food budget for the boys that he thought was mean. It was 1908, and he took a trip overseas to get away from the emotional turmoil the conflict had caused him. Stopping in England's Lake Country, Buchman came under the influence of an eloquent Salvation Army woman preacher, Jessie Penn-Lewis, and underwent a profound spiritual experience. It involved an apology to his board for his bitterness toward them and the release resulted in a new course for his life. He then served seven years as YMCA secretary at Pennsylvania State University and later as lecturer in evangelism at Hartford Theological Seminary, during which time he conducted renewal campaigns in Asia with Sherwood Eddy. In 1922 he launched out on his own and in subsequent years developed a force of full-time personnel around the world that at times numbered over a thousand.

Buchman was not only effective in one-on-one reorientation but added to this a capacity for developing small sharing groups. Paul Tournier, the Swiss psychologist and writer, gives him a good deal of credit for the rise of the modern phenomenon known as group therapy.[5] It was out of Buchman's weekly sharing meetings in New York and Akron that Alcoholics Anonymous arose.

Although he widely publicized Robert E. Speer's four absolute standards of honesty, purity, unselfishness, and love, which the YMCA leader early in the twentieth century held were a distillation of the Christian Sermon on the Mount, Buchman saw these "four absolutes" more as an introduction to the new personal and group life than as a set of principles for living. His own reliance was more on intuition than on rules, and it is probably fair to say that he himself was antinomian.

His Pennsylvania German[6] (Deutsch) background is one of the keys to understanding the man. German was his mother tongue. Buchman looked Pennsylvania German. His religion was Pennsylvania German. His frugality and sagacity were Pennsylvania German. His tastes were Pennsylvania German. His humor was Pennsylvania German. His outlook and lifestyle were Pennsylvania German.

Many of Frank's conversations and talks were peppered with tales reflecting the down to earth side of his Pennsylvania German background. One of his graphic stories I recall described the not quite bright boy who was selling apple butter and cottage cheese door to door in their Allentown neighborhood. The boy had two tubs, one with cottage cheese and the other apple

[5]Tournier is quoted by Garth Lean in *On the Tail of a Comet* (Colorado Springs: Helmers & Howard, 1988), 153.

[6]His people are sometimes called "Pennsylvania Dutch" although they have had no connection with the Netherlands. The explanation is they called themselves "Deutsch," which of course means "German," and the Anglos thought they were saying "Dutch." That language was dominant in the Allentown area for 200 years, and up until World War II, it was not possible to get a job there as a busdriver or waitress without knowing both languages.

butter. However, he had only one paddle with which he dispensed the two products. So by the time he reached the end of the block, you could not tell which was the cottage cheese and which the apple butter.

Frank Buchman was the cover story of *Time* magazine April 20, 1936, but the periodical was hostile from the beginning, and in its obituary kicked the man in his grave. There are those who claim there is no such thing as bad publicity. I can testify that *Time's* scurrilous attacks in the early thirties attracted me. I reasoned that their flip cynicism about everything might well mean that the Oxford Group had something going for it. My colleague Ray Purdy, a Princeton classmate of T. S. Matthews, longtime top editor of *Time*, identified Matthews as the source of the bias. (Matthews' autobiography, *Name and Address*, was a popular number—New York: Simon and Schuster, 1960).

In retirement Matthews had moved to England, so when I was there, I called and he graciously invited me to lunch at his quiet home an hour north of London, meeting me at the country railroad station. He confirmed that a convinced cousin of his, name of Cuyler, had informed him of the work, and that when Matthews was a student he had known Sam Shoemaker, early Buchman associate who then was in charge of the Philadelphia Society, Princeton's Christian campus center. I reported Ray Purdy's speculation that Shoemaker had presented a moral challenge to the undergraduate Matthews who, rejecting it, then had to find things wrong with the program. His answer to me was a scornful snort, and when I pressed him for an answer, he said that was his answer.

He told me with some amusement how a man in the Oxford Group once made a date to come to his office at *Time* to explain the movement. When he arrived, the man reported that he then was living with a woman not his wife, but that for a week now he had not seen her because he wanted to be "clean" when he came for the interview!

After lunch we shifted to other subjects and went out to a horse race on adjacent meadows. "You think he was a great man, do you?" he queried me about Buchman. I said I thought it was not a question of greatness or non-greatness but that honest journalism required an evaluation of the man's contribution to human welfare, whatever one's reservations might be as to style and methods. It was a cordial exchange all around, and he drove me to the railroad station for my train back to London.

Those related to "Frank" (first names were always encouraged) were initially known as the First Century Christian Fellowship. In the 1920s they were known as the Groups. Developing a following in American seaboard colleges, Buchman was asked to do a similar work in Oxford and Cambridge. In 1928, a team of Oxford students he had helped train were conducting a campaign in South Africa. There a railroad porter marked their car the "Oxford Group." They thought the words had a good ring. Buchman in those years was intrigued with things British and liked the association with the mother of great causes. For ten years, 1928-38, this program was known as the Oxford Group.[7]

Alcoholics Anonymous (AA) began in this period, in 1935, and was known for a time as "the alcohol squad of the Oxford Group." So it is natural they still use the Oxford name in referring to their progenitor movement.

In 1938 the name was changed to Moral Re-Armament. The shift came out of a walking meditation in the Black Forest when

---

[7]Buchman's work is not to be confused with the nineteenth-century Oxford Movement led by Cardinal John H. Newman, 1801-90 (known for his hymn "Lead Kindly Light") which aimed to revivify the Catholic church.

the thought came to Buchman that in the midst of the rush to war and the arms race, the basic world need was "moral and spiritual re-armament." He believed it would mean a better name. By dividing the syllables "Moral Re-Armament," he had a three-letter acronym, MRA, headline-friendly, of the kind made popular by the U.S. government in the 1930s. A problem with "Oxford" was that it sounded as though it might be a British debating society. "Moral Re-Armament" denoted an idea closer to the movement's aims. In 2001 the movement became known as Initiatives of Change.

It is hard to appreciate three quarters of a century later what a news personality Buchman was before World War II. Not only was he the subject of a cover story in *Time* in the spring of 1936, soon he was the subject of a big-time Broadway play (albeit negative about Buchman), staged by the top names in the business. On the night of July 19, 1939 he led the biggest meeting that had ever been held in the Hollywood Bowl. After the war he was nominated for the Nobel Peace Prize in 1951 and again in 1952.

As noted earlier, after the 1930s, the accent was more on the world stage, though still based on personal remotivation. There is sometimes a false debate where some argue that to change the system one must first change the person, as over against those who say that the system must change first. Buchman maintained it was ever both.

Jonathan Messerli, then president of Muhlenberg College, in dedicating a bust of Buchman on the school's Allentown campus October 19, 1991, noted that whereas many activists decide what is the moral thing for leaders to do and insist they do it, Buchman's strategy was to help leaders put into gear what *they* believed was moral.

His chief strategy headline was, New People—New Nations —a New World. His message was full of what he called "ribbon thoughts," ones that those who run might read—some he created and some he borrowed:

It's not who's right but what's right.

World changing through life changing.

You can plan a new world on paper, but you have to build it out of people.

You can't make a good omelet out of bad eggs.

Live to make the other person great.

Train ten other people to do it better than you can.

God gave us two ears and one mouth. Why don't we listen twice as much as we talk?

Some will come and others will think. (Send your invitations even to those you do not expect to attend.)

Seek out the key people. (Buchman agreed with international YMCA leader John R. Mott that to change the world you have to change those who run it. This led to the false charge that he was interested in only influential people.)

Human wisdom has failed, but God has a plan.

Man's extremity is God's opportunity.

Get movement into people rather than getting people into a movement.

Men's work for men and women's work for women. (This principle is still followed among the Twelve Step sponsors.)

Never speak beyond your experience.

Disagree without being disagreeable.

There's enough in the world for everybody's need, but not for everybody's greed.

If everybody cared enough, and everybody shared enough, wouldn't everybody have enough?

Later on, I will describe my own relationship to Frank Buchman.

Buchman and Hitler

Before any comment on Frank Buchman gets very far, the Hitler issue comes up. It has consistently been Buchman's most serious public relations problem. The difficulty arose from an interview published in the New York World Telegram, August 25, 1936, conducted after he had arrived from a trip to Europe. During the interview, while criticizing the Nazis' anti-Semitism, he expressed appreciation for Hitler's building a "front line of defense" against communism.[8]

The comment might have died with the next day's papers except that the sentiment was couched in a most unfortunate way, Buchman using the phrase, "I thank heaven for" the German leader because of his doing this. Most teachers, when trying to remotivate an obstreperous bully, will try to find *something* positive in the person's conduct to affirm. I think this is what Buchman was doing in this interview. Jimmy Carter was later to adopt a similar strategy, and he too was criticized for it.[9]

Buchman had requested a personal interview with Hitler in Berlin in 1934, waiting in vain for two weeks for a response in an

---

[8]Frank was probably aware of a statement the week before, on August 19, from the Catholic Church of Germany, which issued a letter of support for Hitler's public fight against Bolshevism.

[9]The reporter who interviewed Buchman and wrote the World-Telegram story was twenty-six year old William A. H. Birnie. In May 1974, twenty-eight years later, I interviewed him in his office at the Reader's Digest in Chappaqua, New York, where he had become a senior editor. Among other things, he said to me, "My memory of my talk with Buchman is that he wasn't endorsing or condemning Hitler. It was that with a totalitarian set-up, you were able to reach the key people easier than you were in a diffuse democracy."

across-the-street apartment. He failed to achieve the one-on-one meeting, but he did not give up. He believed that every human being, no matter how far gone, was a child of God and somehow could be reached. "The outstretched arms of Jesus Christ are also for the German leadership," he would say. During the 1930s, Quaker leaders also made personal overtures to speak with Hitler. On the other hand, Christian theologians Reinhold Niebuhr and Dietrich Bonhoeffer reacted strongly against this approach as unrealistic and advocated violence as a solution. Both wrote attacks on the Buchman life-changing approach.[10]

Some believed that since Buchman was "insufficiently critical" of Hitler, as one observer put it, he was soft on Nazism. On the contrary, (1) he believed that condemnation rarely produces change; (2) his philosophy and his record ran in the opposite direction—he worked postwar shoulder to shoulder with Nazi fighter Konrad Adenauer, who would have dropped him like a stone if he thought there was a shred of sympathy with the corrupt ideology; and (3) a Gestapo document discovered after the war roundly condemned the Oxford Group as antithetical to

---

[10]Reinhold Niebuhr, one of the most articulate Protestant theologians of the twentieth century, and Buchman were in agreement about the nature of the human being, that it was corrupted by original sin and needed restoration through divine intervention. Swiss theologian Emil Brunner, who took an active part in Buchman's religious renewal program in Switzerland in the 1930s, wrote a book, Man in Revolt, which Niebuhr told him claimed much of his attention during the preparation of Niebuhr's most famous book, The Nature and Destiny of Man (Gifford Lectures; New York: Scribner's, 1941). But when Buchman tried to bring redemption to a sinner named Adolf Hitler, Niebuhr labeled him "naive" and "dangerous" (Christian Century, October 7, 1936, p.1315).

In the same spirit German theologian Dietrich Bonhoeffer, Niebuhr's friend and colleague, abandoned the Christian commandment to love one's enemies and entered a bomb plot to murder the German dictator. Bonhoeffer wrote that Buchman's attempt in love to "try to convert Hitler" was "a ridiculous failure to understand what is going on." (Dietrich Bonhoeffer, Gesammelte Schriften , Vol. 1, Ökumene, 1958), 42-3. (Munich: Chr. Kaiser Verlag).

National Socialist aims.

Failing in the mid-thirties in a direct conversion attempt with the German leader, Buchman then switched to the public prints, the *World-Telegram* interview being a case in point. For three years, while the war clouds gathered, right up to the outbreak of World War II, the Pennsylvanian tried to reach the German leadership through the press—searching for words that might convince them that here was someone in the West who understood.

In September 1938, following the assembly in Sweden, Buchman held his first world assembly under the new name, Moral Re-Armament. The site was Interlaken, a mountain resort in Switzerland.[11] This was just before Neville Chamberlain and Hitler met at Munich. The banner headline of the Switzerland conference was:

INTERLAKEN—THE ANSWER TO VERSAILLES

Hitler was loudly complaining that the Treaty of Versailles that ended World War I had humiliated Germany, and that he was destined to lead his nation, by force if necessary, to restore his people's honor. Buchman's idea was that if he could communicate to Berlin through the press that there were forces on the Allied side that were willing to face the past honestly and change, it might give *der Führer* a new idea.

These German overtures were suspect in pockets of the

---

[11]From Sweden I drove with friends through Germany to the assembly in Switzerland. Staying overnight in Berlin, I was struck by the enormous energy of the German artisans and night laborers who were clearly giving their all to build the "Thousand Year Reich." At nine P.M. on downtown streets, the jackhammers were roaring to clear space for the sweeping new plazas. This was August 1938. World War II was one year away. I asked myself, "A thousand years?"

media. Yet the mind reels at the possibility of how the enormous loss of life, the expenditure of untold resources, and the devastation of environments wrought by the biggest war of history might have been avoided if the German dictator could have somehow been redirected.

Where will Frank Buchman stand in history? Historians tend to sideline people who operate in the spiritual dimension he chose. He fought no wars. He won no elections. Yet it is possible that his mark, above the battle, will be hailed some day.

It is not for me to make the definitive evaluation, but let me suggest three arenas.

Personal. In addition to the lives, families, and enterprises that were remade under his banner, it is safe to say that Alcoholics Anonymous never would have happened without Frank Buchman. He established the quality of life and the principles through which this derivative movement has brought recovery to millions.

Policy. A brilliant British career diplomat who occupied key world posts during and after World War II says Buchman represents one of five major forces that moved the U.S. away from isolationism to world responsibility. "There is no doubt in my mind," he writes, "that MRA's expanding work all across the United States, and the numerous visits paid by U.S. congressmen to MRA's European centers immediately after the war, contributed to the enlightened mood which prevailed in Washington at that time, leading to such historic postwar initiatives as the Marshall Plan. Indeed, Paul Hoffman, administrator of the Marshall Plan, described Buchman's work as 'the ideological equivalent of the Marshall Plan.'" Archie Mackenzie, *Faith in Diplomacy*, (London: Grosvenor Books, 2002), 42.

Mackenzie, who was in charge of press relations for the

British delegation to the organizing conference of the United Nations in San Francisco in 1945, reports, "When President Truman came to San Francisco for the signing of the Charter on 25th June, he met Dr. Buchman and thanked him for his work."

Global. Buchman's personal influence, one-on-one, on France's Robert Schumann and Germany's Konrad Adenauer, publicly acknowledged by both, plus his associates' influence on the thousands of industrial and political leaders of both nations who attended the MRA conferences in Switzerland after World War II, may have been the key factor in ending a hundred years of internecine strife between the two countries. The genius of French economist Jean Monnet in drawing up plans for postwar European integration was basic to the process. But he himself told Schumann in 1950 that they were "on the brink of making the same mistake as in 1919." History is strewn with brilliant plans that have been destroyed by the volatility of human nature. Buchman may have saved the plans—common market for steel and coal, leading on to the European Union—because he was able to bring to bear solutions in the human nature area.

It was this kind of international influence that resulted in the two nominations for the Nobel Peace Prize [12]

---

[12]Significant segments of this influence are documented in an impressive study by the Center for Strategic and International Studies (CSIS), Douglas Johnson and Cynthia Sampson, *Religion, the Missing Dimension of Statecraft* (New York: Oxford University Press, 1994). See chapters by Edward Luttwak, "Franco-German Reconciliation: The Overlooked Role of the Moral Re-Armament Movement" (37-57); and Ron Kraybill, "Transition from Rhodesia to Zimbabwe" (208-257).

Peter Steinfels wrote in the *New York Times* July 9, 1994: "One study describes the largely unreported success of the Moral Re-Armament movement in bringing together thousands of French and German citizens, including influential politicians, trade unionists, industrialists, educators, clergy, and journalists, for extended and intense meetings in Switzerland from 1946 to 1950. The gatherings laid the groundwork for the 1950 initiative of Robert Schumann and Konrad Adenauer to establish the European Coal and Steel Community, a major step toward the reconciliation of France and Germany and a united Europe."

An impressive evaluation of the man's world contribution was made by a veteran U.S. congressman on Buchman's hundredth anniversary. In June 1978, the communities of Pennsburg and Allentown held a commemorative dinner. Representative Charles E. Bennett of Jacksonville, Florida, was the keynote speaker.

Bennett, a World War II hero out of the Philippines theater, was elected to Congress in 1948 and held the seat for twenty-two terms, forty-four years, during which time among other things he authored the first arms control bill and the first ethics legislation. When he retired at 81, he was the second most senior member of the House of Representatives and Chairman of the Subcommittee on Naval Power of the Armed Services Committee. He was my best friend in Congress; I knew him for sixty years and I stayed with him and Jean in their home in Falls Church when I visited the Capitol. He never ceased to give public credit to Buchman's work for leading him to a profound personal change when he was a young Congressman new to Washington, dropping, for example a four-pack-a-day smoking habit and straightening out some relationships. His experience of the guidance of God with the group also, he felt, led him to a sense of inspiration for his arms control and ethics initiatives.

Here are his core words at the Buchman centennial:

> Everyone knows that the world cannot go on forever on this earth having wars. It is the most anachronistic thing that exists. That people kill each other by the millions to solve political, sociological, or economic problems, makes no sense to any one. Some time in history, hopefully not too far off, somebody is going to put the chemistry together to turn that around. And I think that a man who will have a lot to do with it will be Frank Buchman. For certainly for the first time I have been able to observe, a man really had a sort of brotherhood throughout the world that never really had been felt before, that could learn to love each other and learn in fact to end war in our time.

8

THE LOYAL LIEUTENANT

I gave all my time, and I mean all my time, sixteen hours a day without salary or title, to the Buchman program for eighteen years, 1938 to 1956, ages twenty-three to forty-one. This career took me for extended periods to Europe, Africa, Michigan, California, the District of Columbia, and points in between.

We were dollar-a-year people who never got the dollar. Expenses were it. It was like the young scientist who approached Thomas Edison for a job in his laboratories and asked about pay and hours. Mr. Edison replied, "We don't pay anything and we work all the time."

Buchman repeatedly said that our money came from "faith and prayer." We did a lot of praying, and somehow or other needs were always met. People in MRA who had resources were guided by God to share them. On a wintry Minnesota day I was getting dressed in my upper berth on a train approaching Saint Paul/Minneapolis from Chicago. The below-zero temperature made the steam hiss from the boilers, and frost was heavy where the wheels hit the rails.

In my quiet time as I rolled along, I had the thought to buy a hat. At the Minneapolis station my friend Ralph Beal, a businessman, met the train, and it was not long before he said, "I had guidance this morning to give you this ten dollars to buy a hat."

In the fall of 1938, my first assignment upon joining the full-time force of Moral Re-Armament started with a train trip from New York to Akron to attend a houseparty at "Stan Hywet," the fifty-room mansion of Mr. and Mrs. Frank A. Seiberling.

In those days our travel was mostly by rail, overnights by Pullman "sleeper." Upper berths were cheaper than lower berths. We estimated that a bus trip cost two cents a mile; train, three; and the rare plane ride, six. The railroads had a traditional respect for the church and provided ministers a ten percent discount. MRA workers were recognized as accredited evangelists, so we all carried clergy coupons, a considerable help in keeping expenses down. The discount did not apply to the sleeper portion.[1]

Alcoholics Anonymous

Frank A. Seiberling, founder of the Goodyear and Seiberling tire companies, and his wife and children were among those who had been drawn to the Oxford Group program by a series of Akron rallies in January 1933. A tire mold inventor, T. Henry Williams, and his wife Clarace opened their home for Group meetings every Wednesday evening, and it was out of those meetings that Alcoholics Anonymous began. Among those who attended the Williams meetings regularly were Dr. Bob Smith and his wife Anne. He was a prominent Akron surgeon, and an alcoholic.

Years later, I was visiting the Williams in their home and said, "T. Henry, you know something about Alcoholics Anonymous, don't you?"

"Sure do," he replied. "It started right there." He pointed to a spot on his living-room carpet where Dr. Bob Smith had finally, in the spring of 1935, acknowledged his drinking and knelt to surrender the problem. Two weeks later Bill Wilson, an

---

[1]It also did not apply northeast of New York. Episcopal Bishop William Lawrence, whose family had started a number of New England railways, persuaded them that the markdown was demeaning to the clergy.

alcoholic stockbroker who had found recovery in the New York Oxford Group and was on a business trip to Akron, made telephone contact with the Akron Group. First he reached Dr. Walter Tunks, the Firestone family minister, who referred him to Henrietta Seiberling, the Frank Seiberlings' daughter-in-law. Wilson told Henrietta he was a "rum hound" from the New York Oxford Group looking for another alcoholic whom he could try to help. "Manna from heaven," she said, her group having hoped for someone who could talk Smith's language as one alcoholic to another. She was able to bring Wilson and Smith together at her home for their famous encounter on Mother's Day, 1935. It was a meeting that M. Scott Peck calls "The greatest positive event of the twentieth century."[2]

At the weekend houseparty I attended in November of 1938, three years after that "positive event," Frank A. Seiberling, an impressive figure of a man, was in and out, while his wife, in addition to being a gracious hostess, was a steady participant in the proceedings.

Another in attendance was Dr. Paul Campbell, a young Canadian physician who was a rising star at Detroit's Henry Ford Hospital and was being groomed by Dr. Frank Sladen to take over as CEO. We were of similar age and, like me, Paul had

---

[2]M. Scott Peck, *Further Along the Road Less Traveled* (New York: Simon & Schuster, 1993), 150.

It is said that the success of Alcoholics Anonymous and its myriad addiction-solving emulators is owed, over and beyond the organizational genius of co-founder Bill Wilson, to the Twelve Steps he secured through his experience in the Oxford Group. These steps came out of the life-changing methods of Frank Buchman, and developed by his associate Sam Shoemaker, Wilson's spiritual mentor. In brief these steps involve: admitting the need for help; turning one's life over to the care of a Higher Power, who is then asked to remove one's listed shortcomings; admitting wrongs out loud to somebody; making restitution to those harmed; working at prayer and meditation; and passing the experience on to others.

been wrestling with career choices. Before long, he too decided to throw in his vocational lot with Frank Buchman and his Moral Re-Armament movement. For twenty years he traveled the world as Buchman's personal physician.

The Battle for Peace through Sport

Back in New York, I was put in charge of the sports celebrity program. Frank Buchman was to return from Europe in the spring of 1939. Moral Re-Armament had been launched in London in 1938, and was now to be introduced in the United States at three mass meetings—in New York, Washington, and Hollywood.

A key player in this sports effort was H. W. "Bunny" Austin, British tennis star, who had begun to enlist sports figures in what he was calling "The Battle for Peace" after a book he published by that name. He had decided to put his training for the next Wimbledon second to his urgent concern about the onrush of war. He was astounded to be fitting his baby daughter's carriage with a gas mask. Since athletes have wide acceptability, he reasoned, perhaps their influence could help avert catastrophe. Having signed up a number of British sportsmen, he crossed the Atlantic to make his appeal in North America, and I was assigned to be his man Friday.

A diminutive player with a superb voice, a warm smile, a British sense of humor, and a vivacious actress wife, Phyllis Konstam, Bunny had an entrée everywhere, even at the White House, where he was received for an interview with Franklin Roosevelt.

The dean of sportswriters of the time, Grantland Rice, was intrigued by Austin's ideas and provided access to just about everybody in the sports world, including Babe Ruth. We found on all sides that if Grantland Rice said it was OK, it was OK.

Then too, Bunny Austin's own credentials were impeccable. He had reached the tennis finals at Wimbledon in 1932 and 1938. No other male Briton has done that since. In the 1938 finals he lost to Don Budge, who soon turned professional, and Bunny was ranked number one in the world.[3] Now in 1939, he was about to make his last run at Wimbledon. His training was off because of his extensive work in his "Battle for Peace," but he told me later he believed he would have won if the modern rules for resting between sets had then been in force.

Bunny was also a Davis Cup star. He and Fred Perry, after a long British drought, won the Cup for the United Kingdom four years in a row, 1933-36. For twelve years starting in 1928, Bunny never failed to rank among the world's top ten players. A key to his success, he said, was his father's maxim: "The point of tennis is to hit the ball over the net and between the lines." He thought Australia's Rod Laver was the greatest player of all time, Budge second.

Before Bunny returned to London for the 1939 Wimbledon, the focus of our sports strategy was a manifesto signed by celebrity athletes calling for teamwork in home, nation, and world, "Moral Re-Armament through Sport." The aim was to build "a world team of sporting nations to win the race against chaos. Sportsmen morally re-armed can unite the world."

Among those we saw and signed up were Grantland Rice, Babe Ruth, Wilmer Allison, Henry Armstrong, Don Budge, Joe DiMaggio, Carl Hubbell, and Bobby Jones. Also Connie Mack, Mel Ott, Jesse Owens, Eddie Rickenbacker, Branch Rickey, Gene Tunney, and Ellsworth Vines. We had a rollicking visit

---

[3]In those days players leaving the amateur ranks became ineligible for the "grand slam" tournaments. Bunny Austin's last appearance at Wimbledon was in 2000. He was nearly ninety-three, just before he died, and he led the parade of champions around the park before the games began.

with former heavyweight champion Jack Dempsey at his Manhattan restaurant where he presided with such charm, but for some reason we did not ask for his signature, which we later regretted.

I was by myself when I caught Davey O'Brien on a campus slope at Texas Christian University in Fort Worth. He was the star quarterback on the nation's top-ranking football team, and had just won the Heisman Trophy for 1938. He wasn't very big, and I was struck by his modesty and friendliness.

One day at the Polo Grounds in New York, where the Giants were working out, we managed a happy visit with Carl Hubbell, Mel Ott, and Bill Terry—New York Giants baseball stars. They let Terry do most of the talking. Carl, a quiet man, showed more interest than the others. A friendly Oklahoman with floppy ears, he was known for a devastating screwball, delivered in a slow, cartwheel style. He won twenty games in each of five consecutive seasons, and in the All-Star game at the Polo Grounds in New York on July 10, 1934, struck out in order the biggest guns of the American League—Babe Ruth, Lou Gehrig, Jimmie Foxx, Al Simmons, and Joe Cronin—plus pitcher Lefty Gomez.

Our most memorable conversations were with legendary baseball figures Joe DiMaggio, Babe Ruth, and Branch Rickey. We reached DiMaggio at his quarters in the New Yorker Hotel, and he agreed to have breakfast with us in the coffee shop. It was May 1939. He was all the things you read about him—friendly, polite, quiet, soft-spoken, refined. He was the son of an Italian immigrant fisherman in San Francisco, and carried his 190 pounds gracefully on a six-foot-one frame. Already, at age twenty-four, he was a big star, some said the greatest center fielder ever. But you would never know it talking with him. That year his batting average was to hit its peak, .381. Of all the people we talked with, DiMaggio was one of the most interested. After signing the statement and about to depart for Yankee

Stadium, he said, "I really hope something will come of this."

Babe Ruth was very difficult to see. I suppose everybody wanted something. His playing days were over, and his cancer had reduced his activities a lot. Very few knew his telephone number, but Grantland Rice did. He urged the former slugger to see us, and set up a date at the Ruths' apartment in Manhattan.

Claire Ruth received us graciously at the door. It was a modest little flat, with many hangings from places they had visited. Her husband's face was florid, and we could see he was not well. But he was hospitable, listened attentively, leaving most of the talking to his wife, the attractive conversationalist of the family. We were not sure how much he was taking in, but before long he went into another room and came back with a huge trophy bowl the Japanese people had given him during a baseball exhibition tour of their country. Babe Ruth had clearly judged the theme of the visit to be international teamwork, and he wanted us to know that he in his own way was doing his part. He signed Bunny's "Battle for Peace" statement because Grantland Rice had signed it and said it was OK for him to. We had been there for half an hour.

Branch Rickey was one of the most interesting personalities of all. Here was a dedicated Methodist Sunday School teacher who chomped on long cigars—a hard-driving, big league baseball manager, who never stepped inside a ballpark on Sunday. Rickey is said to have been one of the three most influential figures in the history of American baseball—the others being Babe Ruth and Kenesaw Mountain Landis (who served as baseball's first commissioner 1921-1944). Not only was Mr. Rickey the father of the farm team system of player development, but he also personally integrated the national game, finding through a wide-ranging search just the right black athlete, Jackie Robinson, to do it, together with the supportive personal counseling that made it succeed. This had not yet happened when we knew him. I used to visit with him at the spring training ballpark in Sarasota. When Bunny read his sports manifesto to Rickey over the phone from New York to Saint Louis, and he came to the part referring to "what President Roosevelt calls 'the underlying strength of citizenship,'" there was a silent pause. "That name 'Roosevelt,'" he said, "I suppose I shouldn't feel this way about him, but I do." Bunny asked him what if it simply said, "the president"? That solution suited him, and Branch Rickey agreed to add his name to the statement.

National Launch

The big launching year for Moral Re-Armament in America was 1939. This thrust was pegged on huge rallies in three of the nation's most famous arenas—Madison Square Garden, New York, May 14; Constitution Hall, Washington, D.C., June 4; and Hollywood Bowl, Los Angeles, July 19. Although not heavily involved with the details of any of them, I was on hand for all three. Several features of the New York meeting stand out in memory. One was that Buchman was reaching out especially to the African-American community. He had heard a black leader say that many of his people were looking with hope to communism, and Frank wished to present an alternative.

Another was a pre-meeting audition that Frank held at the Garden for May 14th speakers. He had me try out, but for some reason I did not make the cut. For many of the years I knew him, Frank and I were good personal friends, and he was always interested in what I had to say—but not in public. There apparently was something about my style. He seemed to prefer the cultured British mode to the brash, Minnesota approach.

At the mass meeting at the Garden, there were many effective speakers, particularly a group of young Scots in their kilts. One of them barely got through giving his name, "Andrew

Campbell Mackay," before the house broke out in a roar. I was particularly impressed with the dignity of Dame Judith Anderson. The brilliant actress was forty-one and would live to ninety-three, with a lifetime of successes including *Mourning Becomes Electra, Hamlet,* and *Medea,* as well as television and nearly thirty movies. Anderson did not speak on her own, but movingly read lines entitled "The Golden Age," which set forth the aims of MRA as seen by British labor writer Harry Addison:

Three great tasks confront this generation.
To keep the peace and make it permanent.
To make the wealth and work of the world available to all and for the exploitation of none.
And with peace and prosperity as our servants and not our masters, to build a new world, create a new culture, and change the age of gold into the Golden Age.

I got into trouble with Buchman through over-zealous activity in preparing for the Madison Square Garden demonstration. Richards Vidmer, a sportswriter for the *New York Herald-Tribune,* had devoted a column to MRA the week before the meeting, where he waxed alliterative, saying, "Moral Re-Armament is magnificent and magnetic." He added that there could be problems if America adopted it and other nations did not, and closed with, "It must be universal and unanimous." In preparing the printed program for the Madison Square Garden event I used a telescoped version of Vidmer's column, leaving out all his qualifiers and making it read, without even any dots between the sentences, "Moral Re-Armament is magnificent and magnetic. It must be universal and unanimous."

After the meeting, *Time* magazine printed its expected scathing comment, focusing on my handiwork by saying, "This is what happens to 'absolute honesty' in the advertising age." Buchman discovered I was the perpetrator and called me on the carpet. I don't believe I've ever had a more thorough dressing down. To recover from this going-over, which Frank later said I had taken well, I was invited to Howard Davison's home in Millbrook, Dutchess County, to spend a quiet weekend of licking my wounds and healing my culpability.

I fell afoul of Buchman again when, at a small caucus in which I was included, I opined that we needed a plan for obsolete literature. The team had fallen into the habit of overprinting everything, and garages from coast to coast were filling with *Congressional Record* reprints, pamphlets, and books. The word "obsolete" was a hot button for Buchman. He asked what I meant. I said we had thousands of Bunny Austin's *The Battle for Peace* in the basement, and perhaps we could get rid of them to make space for the next publication. To Buchman, this was totally unacceptable. He said the work would explode across the country in the next two years, and there would be an enormous demand for Bunny's book and all else.

The other comment I recall Frank making during that period came during a discussion of the recovering alcoholics in the fellowship and their restiveness with the group discipline of MRA. They had their own ways, and, among other things, wanted to smoke. When they gathered separately, they were accused of meeting off on their own. Bill Wilson didn't like any one telling him what God's guidance was for him. There was talk of separation. Bill was quoted as wanting to deal only with the alcohol problem. Frank, who himself had an impressive record of helping alcoholics, said, "But we have drunken nations on our hands too." His aim was to make the regeneration ideas available to all—the statesman, the ordinary person, the addicted, the not addicted—a total program of remaking people and remaking nations. But Wilson said he did not want to save the world, he just wanted to save drunks. He took the New York alcoholics out of the Oxford Group in 1937. Dr. Bob Smith did the same in Akron in 1939.

Buchman's American headquarters was the parish house of Calvary Episcopal Church at 61 Gramercy Park, New York. Its dynamic rector, the Reverend Samuel Moor Shoemaker, had been a dedicated lieutenant of Frank Buchman ever since undergraduate days in the 1920s at Princeton. He had met Frank while a student teacher in China and the meeting had meant a transformation in Sam's life, a change he was able to pass along to a remarkable number of people. He became the nation's outstanding spokesman-practitioner of person-to-person evangelism, and as spiritual mentor to Bill Wilson he provided the ideas that became AA's Twelve Steps. I came to know Sam and his family and was included at events at their apartment on the sixth floor of Calvary House.

One of our fellow warriors arrived by an interesting route. In the late 1920s Henry Ford decided to give a major recognition event in honor of his hero, Thomas Edison. So in Dearborn, Michigan, in 1929 he staged a mammoth celebration of the fifty years of incandescent light, Mr. Edison having invented the bulb in 1879. One of the accompanying PR thrusts was a national contest to find a young scientist who might succeed Edison. There were competitions in all forty-eight states, and the finalists were judged by a blue ribbon panel, including twenty-seven year old Charles A. Lindbergh, two years back from Paris. The national winner, awarded a four-year scholarship at Massachusetts Institute of Technology, was Wilber Brotherton Huston, son of a Seattle bishop. (He was named for William Wilberforce, nineteenth century British anti-slave parliamentarian.) Of course the press soon dubbed Bill "America's Brightest Boy," and he was interviewed by Lowell Thomas and everybody else with a pencil or a microphone. He had already been drawn to MRA in Seattle and after graduating from MIT traveled as part of our full-time force. On occasion he and I roomed together in New York, and we became good friends. After the war he returned to science and was based at the Goddard Space Center in Maryland.

President Roosevelt

At the Washington meeting in Constitution Hall, I was impressed with the conviction of Harry Truman, who read the communication sent to the assemblage by President Franklin D. Roosevelt. Bunny Austin told me how the message was secured. He and his sidekick, British cricket player John Guise, had been invited to speak at Groton School in Massachusetts. The head-master was Endicott Peabody, Roosevelt's old teacher, who when asked whether the President would be interested in what they were talking about, went to his desk and wrote out and signed a note to FDR.

On the train to Washington, they ran into John Roosevelt, the President's youngest son, and asked his help. John said he was having breakfast with his father the next day, and would give him the Peabody letter. Following through that morning, Bunny rang the White House and reached Missy LeHand, FDR's secretary, who said, "Hang on a minute." After leaving the line briefly, she came back on and said, "Can you get here in twenty minutes?" They could and they did. Ushered into the Oval Office, Bunny said they were clearly in the presence of someone of "immense charm." The president said to his visitor, "Oh, I would recognize you anywhere from your photographs." Bunny suspected this was a ploy FDR frequently used. Roosevelt said that the Oxford Group "used to be laughed at somewhat, but now it commands great respect."

Austin replied, "We had a great meeting at Madison Square Garden, and people said the only thing that was missing was a message from the president. Would you like to send one?"

His reply, according to Bunny, was, "Sure I can do that."

After the meeting, Steven Early, FDR's press secretary, said to the visitors, "I don't think the president will sign this message for you."

Bunny replied, "I not only think he will sign it, he *said* he *would* sign it."

Early: "How many messages do you think the president is asked to sign?"

Austin: "I don't know how many messages, just as long as he signs this one. Excuse me, Mr. Early, are you the president of the United States or is Mr. Roosevelt?" "At the end of the talk," says Austin, "Early very graciously said, 'Come back tomorrow and I will have the message ready for you.'"

The Roosevelt statement, featured on the front page of the *New York Times* on 5 June 1939, the day after Truman read it to the Constitution Hall meeting, ran as follows:

> The underlying strength of the world must consist in the moral fiber of her citizens. A program of moral re-armament for the world cannot fail, therefore, to lessen the danger of armed conflict. Such moral re-armament, to be most highly effective, must receive support on a worldwide basis.
>
> *Franklin D. Roosevelt*

John Roots, a foreign correspondent who was a native of China and a longtime Buchman associate, had drafted the first two sentences. The president made some editorial changes in his own hand and added the last sentence himself; Bunny felt it strengthened the message by infusing a strong global tone.

To the West

From Washington, the move was westward to prepare for the Hollywood Bowl in July 1939. Among the overseas visitors were a number from Scandinavia, and it was decided that this contingent might spend fruitful time on the way west in Minnesota, an unofficial Scandinavian country in America's heartland. Since I came from there, I was included in the party.

It was on this occasion that I first met Minnesota Governor Harold E. Stassen, who had been elected the year before at age thirty-one, the youngest governor in the nation. He endorsed our meeting in the Minneapolis Lyceum Theatre, led by Buchman and featuring speakers from around the Midwest. One of them was the son of Northfield's W. F. Schilling, who had been a member of President Hoover's Farm Board.

During the evening Jessie Joy from Salem, Nebraska, told a fascinating story of how the spread of moral standards in her town had answered corruption in farm subsidy and welfare payments. It was such an appealing, down home, small-town account that Frank invited Jessie to travel west and speak at the Hollywood Bowl. Jessie had never addressed an audience larger than nine in her one-room schoolhouse.

The Hollywood Bowl meeting was a landmark event. A young *Los Angeles Times* reporter, James Bassett, who was later to become a top editor, wrote that 30,000 got in and 10,000 were turned away, making it the largest crowd in the famous amphitheater's history. I arrived just in time in a carload of labor union friends and my brother after a four-day drive from Minneapolis. One of the most impressive speakers was Louis B. Mayer, the second "M" in Metro-Goldwyn-Mayer. Others were a duo from the violence-torn Imperial Valley; one from the Teamsters and the other from the Associated Farmers.

I've always thought that Frank Capra, or one of his creative team, was in the Bowl that night. Two years later, he brought out a film rather obviously based on the Hollywood Bowl meeting—*Meet John Doe* It tells the story of a grass roots movement stressing honesty and teamwork among local folks, culminating in a national meeting. Capra later said this film was his favorite. The screen soda jerk that describes the team in his town might well have borrowed the speech of Jessie Joy. There is a strong Christian note at the end of the film where Barbara Stanwyck tells Gary Cooper he doesn't have to go through with his commitment to jump off the top of city hall to prove his integrity. "Somebody two thousand years ago did that for us," she says.

There was another film in those days that related to MRA, *Susan and God*. It went back to 1937 when Rachel Crothers, a dominant playwright for three decades, produced and directed her last Broadway play, *Susan and God*. The title role was given to the top stage personality of the day, Gertrude Lawrence. I saw it with some friends in 1938. The story was of a New York dowager who returned from England full of airy zeal for "Lady Wiggam's Movement," an obvious parody of Buchman's Oxford Group, widely publicized in the thirties. Susan flits around to meetings and protests enthusiastic love for humankind, while neglecting her alcoholic husband and lonely daughter. At the end, however, Ms. Crothers had the grace to have Susan unite her family through a moving genuine apology for her selfishness. The Buchman idea, after a ninety-minute beating, triumphs in the final ninety seconds.

By the time the movie rights to *Susan* had been purchased by Louis B. Mayer, the film titan had come to know Buchman and had hosted a motion picture luncheon for him and his entourage in July 1939, two days before the mammoth MRA meeting in the Hollywood Bowl. In fact, Mr. Mayer himself asked to speak at the Bowl meeting, where he declared, "The films can be ambassadors in celluloid for a new world."

Mr. Mayer mobilized his top talent for *Susan*, and one might say he, in his lights, was trying to do the best he could by Buchman. The latter had no illusions as to what a big time movie might do to his program, but his practice was always to co-operate, and he approved of the studio hiring some of his full-time personnel, including Cece Broadhurst, Canadian singing cowboy, and George Frazer, whose composition "Wise Old Horsey" became the repetitive theme song of the film for its entire 157 minutes.

Mayer's best director, George Cukor, one of Hollywood's all time tops, was tapped to guide the production. Anita Loos wrote the screen play. Front rank stars were called up from MGM's impressive stable—Joan Crawford, Rita Hayworth, Frederic March. Mr. Mayer was known for dominating the industry with his down-home, family-style movies, and one interpretation of his investing his best talent in the picture, and asking Buchman to supply some of his own personnel, was that he wanted to give Buchman's idea a boost. That the opposite effect resulted was probably more due to other factors.

Buchman aide Morris Martin tells in his *Always a Little Further* (Tucson: Elm Street Press, 2001) a dramatic story of how he personally stopped the cameras when it appeared that demeaning material was being filmed. Martin reports an exchange of cables with an MRA operative in India, who having heard of the team's participation, cabled a query, "Do we support *Susan and God?*" To which Buchman replied, "Certainly not Susan."

My guess is that basically the mogul was trying to help Frank get his message across. On his death bed Louis B. Mayer told Joel McCrea that Frank Buchman was one of four public men he admired most.

1939 was a big publicity year for MRA. The final dollop was another Hollywood item that also turned out negative for Buch-man, unless you believe there is no such thing as bad publicity. After the Hollywood Bowl meeting Mae West, or her agent, phoned Buchman and said she was interested in what he was doing and could they get together. Buchman was unclear as to who she was, and Morris Martin was able to fill him in that she was the leading sex symbol of the day and had recently been banned from the air for her overly suggestive Eve on a radio program. Buchman decided nevertheless to go ahead. There was something of the Woman at the Well about the scenario, and he had never allowed fear for his reputation to deter him from reaching out to people who reached out to him. In addition to Mae's carefully manipulated public sex persona, she was also known in Hollywood circles as someone who was making her own spiritual search.

I was there when Frank's party left for the appointment and saw their amused and perplexed faces when they returned. The meeting was of course a made-to-order publicity setup for Ms. West. Someone had thought to arrange for an Associated Press photographer to turn up in her Hollywood apartment. Buchman brought along a coterie of chaperones of mixed ages and sexes. But the photographer was equal to the challenge. Front pages around the world soon appeared showing the two principals—he in his gray business suit and she in her pink negligee—the evangelist and the showgirl. A publicist's dream for her. A bad news trap for him. Those who would trivialize his message got a nice break.[4]

After the Hollywood Bowl meeting, the traveling force from all the countries took a special train to the Monterey Peninsula for the "Second World Assembly for Moral Re-Armament." The Southern Pacific train left Glendale, the suburban station north of Los Angeles, and I never saw such a sea of baggage in my life. North of San Luis Obispo we oohed and aahed over the most striking horseshoe curve west of Altoona, and at Salinas, the lettuce capital, the train took a spur into Monterey. The VIP's

[4]See David Hanna, Come Up and See Me Some Time (New York: Belmont Tower Books, 1976), 158-60.

stayed at the Hotel Del Monte, the rest of us at Asilomar, a YMCA conference installation at Pacific Grove. Bunny Austin, just back from his final shot at Wimbledon, played a demonstration tennis match for the hotel guests.

In the dispersion following the ten-day assembly at Monterey, I was included with the contingent for follow-up work in southern California and landed in the home of a crusty but congenial attorney named Fred Barstow, who lived in Alhambra, the suburb immediately east of Los Angeles. One memorable Barstowism: "I don't believe anything I read in the papers. Whenever they have written anything about me, it has been wrong. The same must be true of the others."

During this period I met Paul Cornelius and family. He was a meatpacker, with a plant in a Los Angeles location later occupied by Farmer John. Paul's health was terrible, asthma was dogging him, and he was always pencil thin. Still he kept up a vigorous life. When he met MRA, he was locked in combat with a labor union and was keeping a revolver in his desk drawer. He solved the conflict, he said, through the guidance of God and was able to use his story in other conflict situations. Paul was the one who introduced to the team one of its most effective concepts, "It's not who's right but what's right." The saying became a central, and often successful, theme in a hundred labor disputes across the country. Paul and his "what's right" was a key factor in the reconciliation of the Dangberg Brothers , whom he had known through the meat business, resulting in saving their 30,000 acre cattle ranch near Minden, Nevada, from dissolution through fratricidal warfare.[5]

---

[5]We did quite a lot of work in the surrounding area, including Yerington, Nevada, whose newspaper carried the perky masthead:

Mason Valley News
The Only Paper in the World
That Gives a Damn About Yerington

Back in the Los Angeles area, we had been focusing on the San Gabriel Valley. The Mission San Gabriel had been founded in 1771, ten years before Los Angeles, but it still, east of Alhambra, had not been actively developed. There was a small, country, one-spittoon newspaper called the San Gabriel Eye Opener. Some called it a tri-weekly—they'd bring it out one week and try to bring it out the next. The alcoholic editor thought it would be a great idea to run a series on the faith of the American founders, and I was drafted to write it. For six weeks they carried my reflections on the beliefs and character of Washington, Adams, Jefferson, Henry, Franklin, and Lincoln. It was my first weekly column, and I have since been a regular correspondent for various journals for most of my life.

One of the architects of the strategy surrounding the southern California events, including the Hollywood Bowl, was Manny Straus of New York. His friend, Col. Arthur M. Wolfe, whom I knew, had introduced him to the program. Straus was a big-picture, Public Relations operator with a capital "P" and a capital "R." For example, he was the engine behind "I Am An American Day," a national interracial event in its time. His approach to public relations did not depend on press releases or importunity, but rather, he said, on doing "something the newspapers cannot ignore."

He was a friend of Louis B. Mayer and persuaded Hollywood's dominant figure to give a motion picture industry luncheon for Buchman and his international team two days before the Bowl meeting. Will Hays, called at the time the "czar" of the industry, served as master of ceremonies. Two hundred motion picture executives, actors, actresses, and civic leaders attended the luncheon at Victor Hugo's restaurant, including James Roosevelt, Walter Wanger, and Dr. Rufus von Kleinshmid, President of the University of Southern California. In the spirit of the visitors' message, actress Jeanette MacDonald and Mayer settled a long-standing feud at the luncheon.[6]

From Day One, Straus's aim was to reach as many of the world's billions as possible. He asked me to look up the population of Java, as he heard there were more people there than in any comparable area in the world. He persuaded Buchman to announce at the Hollywood Bowl on July 19 a program that would result in one hundred million people listening to God by December 1-3, 1939. This became the total preoccupation of the entire force for the next six months.

Straus was impressed with the focus our team was able to bring to big short-term projects, but said, "The Moral Re-Armament people can do more in three days and less in three months than any other outfit I know." Although Manny was greatly responsible for the national visibility of Buchman's MRA in the weeks before World War II, he became a little much for Frank, who may have felt the tail was beginning to wag the dog. I was at a meeting at which word arrived that Straus wished to come and help plan for the future. Buchman said he would not be interested in Manny planning for the work, but only in planning for Manny. It was the end of a most interesting and dynamic relationship.

The "One Hundred Million People Listening to God" program was a pretty tall order to deliver in four and one half months. Nevertheless, we all went at it. That fall we fanned out across the country, I back to Minnesota to beat the bushes in the precincts of my origins. Ralph Beal, president of a Minneapolis-based, industrial water-softening business, the Flox Company, and his family had been active in the program since the mid-thirties. He set me up in the Leamington Hotel, where I received

---

[6]Twenty-two years later, in August 1961, MacDonald's husband Gene Raymond would join Beulah Bondi, Joel McCrea and others of the Hollywood community to fly to Allentown, Pennsylvania for Buchman's funeral.

Silas and Cordelia Chambers Willard, maternal great grandparents, immigrated from Vermont and followed George Gale's vision of building an ideal community, church, and college on the prairie of western Illinois.

Silas and Cordelia Willard built this house at Chambers and Losey Streets, Galesburg, 1857-58, completing it the year Lincoln and Douglas debated at Knox College, a few blocks away. My mother was born in this house in 1892. It was at one time the headquarters of the Poland China Hog Association, later falling on hard times. In the 1990s Betty McNaught converted it to a bed and breakfast inn, "the Great House," and it is still a town landmark.

Silas and Cordelia's son, Matthew Chambers Willard, my grandfather, carried on their traditions in business and their landmark Galesburg home.

Galesburg Willard family mid-1890s. Mrs. Matthew Chambers Willard (Ideletta Henry) and her three children—Silas, Cordelia, and Louise (my mother). Their father (above) had died in 1894.

*Mother, Stella Louise Willard,
graduating from Knox College, 1914*

*My parents just after they were married, with my father's parents. Thomas K.
and Gertrude S. Hunter, Palmyra, Nebraska, where T.K. was serving at the time.*

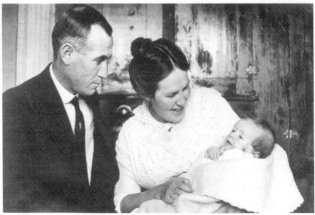

*The first born gets a
lot of attention.*

Payette River Valley and Emmett, Idaho, from "Freeze Out Mountain,"
north of Boise.

House in Emmett, Idaho, where I was born September 22, 1915. Located at 503
Washington, on the southwest corner facing east, it was the parsonage provided
by the Presbyterian church when my father was home missionary pastor 1915-
17. The dwelling has since been replaced by a bank parking lot, but not before
we visited there in the 1960s and saw the room where I joined the human race.

Farewell to Emmett. This is the scene as we pulled out for Omaha on the Union Pacific. It was 1917; I was two.

With my Mother, center, and Hunter grandparents in their Model T Ford, Kimball, Nebraska, 1917. In another eight years I would be driving my father's Model T in Northfield, Minnesota.

Northfield's proud boast for a hundred years.

*Jesse James (1847-1882) on his best behavior,
perhaps a shot from his press kit.*

Charles Lindbergh and his great flying friend Harlan "Bud" Gurney in the early twenties. Charles was barnstorming in southern Minnesota in 1923, and he may have been one of the pilots I watched take passengers up on short trips from a pasture on the edge of Northfield.

The return of the native to Washington School, Northfield, where my education was started, 1921-1926.

*Family potrait, Sumner Studios,
Northfield, 1926, Stu, mother,
older brother, Helen, dad.*

*Seventh birthday party in
Northfield. I'm on left.
Note three wore neckties.
Best friends were Carl
Vestling, tall in middle,
and Junior Sampson and
Kirk Roe, furthermost to
the right. Next to me is
Howard Holden, whose
family's farm east of town
was a favorite haunt.
Brother Stu in front.*

*Hunter home for decades at
407 E. Second Street,
Northfield. Mother died in the
front upstairs bedroom, 1934.*

Northfield High School football team 1931. My mother never raised me to be a football player. See top row, fourth from right. That year's team established the astounding record of 10-0, scoring 251 points to their opponents' 6. Except for eight and a half minutes as a substitute right end in the first and last games, I sat on the bench.

*Three Willards (children of Matthew Chambers Willard) and families meet in
Northfield 1922. My mother (Louise Willard Hunter) has the string tie. Her
brother, Silas Willard, is next to her, wearing the bow tie. Their sister, Cordelia
Willard Dodds stands second from the right, next to my dad, Stuart Hunter, at the
end. In between the Willard sisters are Martha Latimer (Mrs. Silas) Willard;
Matthew's widow, Ideletta Willard (Lampe); and Dad's mother Gertrude S. (Mrs.
Thomas K) Hunter. On the front row are Dodds and Hunter kids. My white head
dressing (for a ring worm condition) had to be changed by my mother every day
until solved by X-ray treatments.*

With brother Stu and sister Helen at Newport Beach, 1978.

TWH on right with British athletes, John Guise and Bunny Austin, and Carl Hubbell, New York Giants pitcher at the Polo Grounds, New York City.

Finale of "You Can Defend America", TWH center as King of the Rats being transformed from "Gimme" to "Give". The show originated in a birthday party in 1940 at Lake Tahoe, then was shown at the two national labor conventions, AFL and CIO. It was called a "pre-war public morale builder", was sponsored by city and state Defense Councils, and was seen 1940-41 by a quarter of a million people in twenty-one states.

Just before Mary Louise's and my wedding August 22, 1945, Petoskey, Michigan. Frank N. D. Buchman, initiator of the Oxford Group/Moral Re-Armament programs, is here flanked by the groom and the best man, John C. Wood. Three clergy persons participated, Buchman giving the closing blessing. This picture for years hung in the Buchman home in Allentown, Pennsylvania.

Pre-nuptial visit to Mackinac Island. (Steamship Algomah *in harbor.) We were married in Petoskey, thirty-five miles south August 22, 1945. I had just been commissioned in the Infantry at Fort Benning. Ralph Henry, Carleton English professor and news writer, thought this soldier-and-bride shot should go to* Life.

Bob, age three, with Frisky at Mackinac Island, winter of 1956.

With Tom, age three, at our home on Newark Street in Washington's Cleveland Park area, 1949.

Bob, 1970

Mackinac Island, 1951

*The family at Mackinac Island, 1955. Willard Merrell Hunter (1948), Mary Louise
Merrell Hunter (1916), Robert Stuart Hunter (1952-1971), Thomas Willard Hunter
(1915), Thomas Merrell Hunter (1946).*

We lived on Mackinac Island at various times from 1942-1956, the last five of those years were through the winters. The owner of "Little Bob's," Robert Hughey, was a warm friend, and a support to us in the loss of our "little Bob."

At Lindbergh's boyhood home at Little Falls, Minnesota, on the upper Mississippi. The first time I visited there was in 1927 just after the New York-to-Paris flight. The house, 140 miles north of Northfield, had been vacant, and that summer it had been almost destroyed by souvenir hunters. The family donated the 110 acre farm to the Minnesota Historical Society, and with Lindbegh's personal, on-the-premises cooperation it was restored to its original condition. A nearby museum that tells his family's story was remodeled and reopened to the public in 2002, in time for the celebrations of the 100th anniversary of the flyer's birth. From the above porch the year before he died, Lindbergh made a farewell address.

long telegrams from Sam Shoemaker and Ray Purdy in New York with material for placement with the media and Governor Stassen.

In the end we settled for a hundred million listening to words about the program on the radio. There is no question that millions did. One of the speakers was Senator Harry S. Truman. He also wrote President Roosevelt urging him to join with the others in the radio series in December:

> I sincerely hope that it will be possible for you to take part in this broadcast. I believe it would be advantageous if you could talk to Dr. Buchman on the subject. I think he has some information that will be most interesting to you.

Roosevelt responded that he believed the timing was not right for him to make an appeal for peace. War had broken out in Europe, and he was trying to persuade Congress to repeal the neutrality legislation so that he could help Britain resist the German threat. As to Truman's part that December, his daughter Margaret wrote:

> Dad topped this one [an address in Missouri] by giving a speech sponsored by Moral Re-Armament (MRA) calling on Americans to resist the amoral dictatorships of the left and right. The MRA people told him they were going to distribute three million printed copies of the address.[7]

General Erle Luce, owner of the Hampshire Arms Hotel, Minneapolis, was a key player in the MRA operation in Minnesota. Earlier that year, in February 1939, General Luce, the Rev. Charles Deems, rector of St. Mark's Episcopal Church, and Minneapolis Mayor George Leach had led the Minnesota delegation to the French Lick houseparty (the last of the assemblies to be called that) at French Lick Springs, Indiana. That was

---

[7]Margaret Truman, *Bess W. Truman* (New York: Macmillan, 1986), 213.

where Mark McKee of the Pere Marquette Railroad, and later the Pan American World Airways, came aboard. In May of that year Leach received Frank Buchman and his team at City Hall. As mayor he had accompanied Charles Lindbergh in the Minne-apolis welcome-home parade in August 1927. Now he had just been reelected Mayor, and a huge congratulatory horseshoe of flowers from the gambling industry graced his outer office. Frank told George his vision for Minneapolis was that it would be "a springboard for a new civilization."

"It might as well be," George responded, "it's been a spring-board for everything else."

We had conversations with Basil (Stuffy) Walters, who had been brought up from Des Moines by the Cowles family (*Des Moines Register Tribune, Look* magazine) when they bought the *Minneapolis Journal* and merged it into the *Star and Tribune.* Walters explained their flamboyant methods to build up mass circulation, in contrast to the *Journal's* traditional hue, and said "When I go to New York, I intend to read the *New York Times.* I actually read the *Daily News.*"

From Minnesota I was called back to New York for some matter on the sports front. It was the first time I had traveled by air, and I was pretty scared. This was 1939. Leaving Minneapolis in the evening, I changed in Chicago, where I was impressed with how few people were in the small terminal. There I boarded a sleeper plane, complete with a bunk and white sheets, stopping in Dayton briefly in the middle of the night. I was rather in awe of the flight attendants, risking their lives every night in this dangerous calling. In those days an attendant had to be under twenty-five, single, attractive, and a Registered Nurse. With the explosion of air travel, the airlines were soon happy to retain grandmothers.

There was a New Year's Eve vigil planned at Calvary House. And beforehand, Lillian Wood of Richmond, former Virginia state golf champion, invited a few of us to have dinner with Minneapolis-based golf star Patty Berg, one of the sports figures attracted to Bunny Austin's athletes-for-peace program. At the New Year's Eve midnight session, led by Buchman, people shared their convictions and plans for the coming year. Pete Hudgens, assistant secretary of agriculture in the Roosevelt Administration, came up with a memorable comment in his Georgia accent: "Ah'm grateful that what is going to happen in 1940 will not be limited to mah vision."

After that, Buchman's focus shifted to Florida.

-9-

REGROUP AT TAHOE

In January 1940 Irene Gates, a New York physician who pro bono looked after the health of the full-time team, including Frank Buchman, thought a few of us needed to get out of the winter weather. As often happened, a couple who owned a home turned it over to Frank for a couple of months, this time in Stuart, Florida. As I was shaking off a persistent flu bug, I was included in the party. While Buchman and the rest took the Orange Blossom Special, one of the popular streamliners that sped down the East Coast in those days, his chief of staff, Morris Martin, and I drove south in Howard Davison's LaSalle with a heavy load of the party's impedimenta.

On our way through Washington we had dinner at the Mayflower Hotel with our friend and colleague Philip Marshall Brown, a retired Princeton international relations professor. The date being January 30, Franklin Roosevelt's birthday, the major hotels were devoted to birthday balls raising funds for polio research. Ten days earlier FDR had been inaugurated for his third presidential term. Marshall thought these celebrations had not only a charitable, but also a political fall-out, as they inevitably garnered a wave of sympathy for the president.

At the house in Stuart, one of Frank Buchman's concerns was fresh vegetables. He personally went shopping for them and got us to join him in the kitchen shelling peas, or whatever. Drafting me to join around the colander, he said, "You do better with labor people if you work at things like this." He was also strong on serving meals buffet style, so people could eat what they wished, and not be subject to the amounts served up for them by some one else.

Ken Twitchell, a Buchman lieutenant since the twenties in Princeton and the thirties in Oxford, and a son-in-law of New Jersey's Senator H. Alexander Smith, was in the party. We went out for a walk one day and encountered an African American nurse with some children she was looking after. Frank, ever the evangelist, said, "Now Ken here has a boy at home, and he listens to God every morning. Ken's boy says, 'If you want to stop war in the world, stop war in the home.'"

I told Frank that I thought I would some day head up his work in the Middle West. He was quiet at the time, but at a meeting the next morning, he said, "One fellow talked to me about heading up the work in the Middle West. He isn't any more ready to do that than the man in the moon." Frank was still chewing on my carcass, with bad tastes left over from the Madison Square Garden days. He thought I was making Bunny Austin my god, instead of God, and generally thought I should shape up. This type of relationship would last for another six months, until I came through a spiritual experience that made everything different, including my relationship with Frank.

While our group's R & R in Florida in the winter of 1940 was winding down, activity was beginning to accelerate in California. The team had been invited again for the second year to participate in the San Francisco World's Fair, which ran for 1939 and 1940. Europe had been at war less than a year.

Two distinguished ladies from Holland had arrived in the United States—one, a senior, Madame Charlotte (Lottie) von Beuningen, and the other her junior companion, Annelou Teixeras de Mattos. They needed American assistance, and Jim Newton and I were assigned to accompany them across the country. After more time with Frank in Florida, we made our way across the continent by train from Jacksonville to Los

Angeles and San Francisco. Jim had good contacts in the major cities, and we met with mayors and reporters in Montgomery, Jackson, Shreveport, Dallas/Fort Worth, El Paso, and Tucson. At Pecos the train was scheduled to make an extended stop, allowing us, we thought, to take a sightseeing auto excursion. However, not arriving back in time, we had to keep our car and driver to help us overtake our train at the next station.

Jim Newton, who died in 1999 at the age of ninety-five, was a man who had to be experienced to be believed. He ought to have been in pictures, and in fact was the subject of a Walter Cronkite documentary near the end of his life. At age twenty he developed Edison Park in Fort Myers, Florida, and became intimate friends with Thomas and Mina Edison and Henry and Clara Ford, who had winter homes next door to each other across the street. Their friend Harvey Firestone was so impressed with the young man that he took him to Akron and at once began grooming him, at twenty-three, to be president of the Firestone Tire and Rubber Company.[1]

---

[1]Jim Newton became a key figure in carrying Firestone through the Depression—the only Akron rubber company that made money in the early thirties. At one stage he built four hundred Firestone service stations, opening two every week. In 1936, after eight years with the company, he felt it was too much rat race and left to devote his full time around the world to industrial teamwork and community development through the Oxford Group/Moral Re-Armament. For more on Newton's fascinating life and his friendships with the Edisons, Fords, Firestones, Carrels, and Lindberghs, see his book *Uncommon Friends* (New York: Harcourt, 1987). He included me on his writing team.

Newton is also credited with creating the conditions that made Akron the birthplace of Alcoholics Anonymous. Having met the Oxford Group as a teenage salesman, he was able, when he went to work in Akron, to bring a Firestone son, Russell, through to a spiritual experience that resulted in new-found sobriety. Harvey Firestone, the father, was so grateful for the miracle in his son's life that he invited Frank Buchman and an Oxford Group team to conduct a week-long saturation campaign throughout the city in January 1933. Among the Akron folks who responded was Dr. Bob Smith, who became a co-founder of AA.

Approaching San Francisco with the Dutch ladies on our transcontinental trip, Jim and I assumed we would complete the assignment and take them all the way to Seattle. However, Basil Entwistle and Bill Jaeger were in charge of the MRA operation in San Francisco, preparing for MRA Day at the World's Fair, and they claimed we were more needed there.

San Francisco's beautiful big bridges had just been completed—the Transbay in 1936 and the Golden Gate in 1937. Frank, in a Commonwealth Club address, spoke of "what bridge builders these San Franciscans are." Bridge building was a central theme of his work in the 1930s, and the theme song was "Bridge Builders," by MRA's Rodgers and Hammerstein—music by George M. Fraser, and words by John M. Morrison.

> On sure foundations build we God's new nations,
> Strong and clear, tells each year
> Of new bridged relations . . .

At the Fair, Art Linkletter, later to become a daytime television personality, was the producer of a show called "Cavalcade of the West." In it a lone cowboy sang a western song, which Cece Broadhurst, our in-house western singer, picked up and made into an MRA paean, sung on stages and at birthdays, "We're all rarin' to go."

We did our thing at the Fair. The youth marched with banners. Frank liked banners. European ideologies were using banners, and he wanted to compete. We got much attention. The newspapers devoted space. But something was missing, and Frank decided the force needed to regroup. San Francisco friends, the Crowells, invited him to spend a weekend at their cottage at Lake Tahoe. Captivated, he felt at once it was the place to pull the team together. Two older codgers, Frank Bannister with a tent-camp park, and Frank Globin with an inn on the lake, were responsive to the Buchman charm, and one by one beds were found, enough for all the full-time MRA force then in California, and a few from beyond.

Globin had been a bootlegger in the prohibition days, running loads of illegal juice from Reno to San Francisco. Now he was operating Globin's Al Tahoe, a rustic hotel on the south shore of the lake, where Nevada and California meet. He had an abandoned casino that projected out into the lake, enclosing unused kitchen and dining facilities, and he turned the whole pier over to us for the summer of 1940.

The Tahoe experience was a turning point in my life. Also in the lives of a number of the force. Buchman was clearly unhappy with my performance and style. At one point he said, "You are a stubborn Minnesotan. Unless you change, you'd better find something else to do." It didn't feel good, but it was a happy thought, to be able to get out of the misery. I had left law school nearly two years before. Here was a chance to get back in and finish my third and final year.

But then something happened. Like others, I had been rather duty-driven and going through the motions. The change can be summarized simplistically in the old concept—*let go and let God.* It meant a new surrender based on an acknowledgment of brokenness. The AA's have captured the idea in their First Step, which they got from the Oxford Group: "We admitted we were powerless." People who have not hit some kind of bottom don't take to such a thought naturally. But I realized at Tahoe that I could become different only if I abandoned pride and let God take over completely. I had had an experience of God earlier. This appeared to me to be an experience of Christ. Others found the same.

The team's new reorientation resulted in an extraordinary burst of creativity in writing and drama. Morris Martin, brilliant doctor of philosophy from Oxford, produced a pamphlet, *You*

Can Defend America, which was distributed by the millions in war plants, schools, and unions across the country. General John J. Pershing, World War I hero, broke a lifetime rule to write the foreword. The public relations office of the Defense Department called the pamphlet, "The finest statement of this nation's philosophy of national defense that has yet been written."

Out of Tahoe birthday skits, a musical stage play was created, also called *You Can Defend America*, for which Dick Hadden, composer of the Rutgers University fight song, wrote a rousing theme march. The use of the stage was to change forever the public presentations of the program, from speaking meetings to dramatic productions. A musical play could pull crowds better than talking heads. "All the truth you want to know about yourself with a kiss," Buchman said. "Sugar catches more flies than vinegar."

My own experience at Tahoe not only transformed my life, but had considerable impact on the group. This kind of spiritual occurrence is difficult to put into words. It was not quite a "Damascus Road" event, but something like it. It had a luminous quality that shook me down and made everything different. It was something like those recorded by William James in *Varieties of Religious Experience*.[2] In psychological terms, it was a manic-type boost. In theological language, it was my "second touch," as when Jesus healed a blind man enough so that he could see people "as trees walking," and then when he touched him again, he was "restored and saw every one clearly."

When in 1936 I had given my life to God and underwent a housecleaning through making amends for past wrongdoings, I experienced a divine presence in my life that ended a long period of doubt. The earlier experience did, however, leave me

---

[2]Gifford Lectures at Edinburgh 1901-02, frequently republished, (New York: Random House, 1999).

with a lot of self-effort. I had thought of myself as a good guy helping God and humankind. But I was confronted by the Apostle Paul, who in his letter to the Philippians first listed his proud résumé, and then added:

> But what things were gain to me, those I counted loss. . . for the excellency of the knowledge of Christ Jesus my Lord. . . and do count them but dung, that I may win Christ.
> (Philippians 3, 7-8)

One result of this experience was that I for the first time felt a part of nature, and no longer superior to other creatures. I believed that I had been made, just as a tree had been made, and by the same Creator, who had a distinctive plan for each created thing. It was my job to grow in conformity to that plan without a self-serving scheme, like the tree that did not wish to be anything but what it was created to be. I wrote a poem to describe this, which began:

> "I am just a pine needle . . . "

At the same time, arrogance crept in. I was so sure that all my thoughts were God talking to me, and that all my activities were being guided by God, that other people's ideas struck me as being inferior. Others needed to find what I found. I tended to dismiss resistance to me as the inevitable reaction to a pure spiritual challenge.

During this period, Jim Newton and Eleanor Forde, the first woman to work full-time with Buchman, had taken to going out to a pasture near the lake in the early mornings before breakfast for their early morning quiet times. It was so cold at the 6,000-foot level that we liked to get where the sun would strike as soon as it cleared the mountains rimming the lake. Jim and Ellie invited me to join them. It was clear something was developing between them—they were married three years later—so I was a third wheel. But we had a great time, and it established a bond between us that continued for sixty years. Even in his nineties, Jim would say to me on the telephone that whenever he came to the line in the Twenty-third Psalm, "He makes me to lie down in green pastures," he thought of our fellowship those mornings on the meadow. Another Tahoe memento he carried in his Bible the rest of his life was a copy of the poem I gave him at the time, "I Met the Master Face to Face."

During July and August 1940, I was able to transmit my new experience, or at least help others to find something like it. I lost all sense of fear, and confronted some icons that shook people up. One key person in the team had a big sense of self-importance, which I was able to puncture, and for six months he thanked me almost every time our paths crossed.

I was concerned about the relation between the team and Frank. Both they and he assumed he had a special pipeline to the Almighty, and it militated against people saying what they felt, "lest haply," in Gamaliel's words, they "be found even to fight against God." This attitude gave Buchman a lot of power and the team a lot of cohesive strength. When you have one person in authority who is always right, "groupthink" helps you to stick close together, without the problems of questioning or dissent. A few years later, at an MRA conference at Mackinac Island, nine-year-old Tony von Teuber, playing on the front porch of the Island House, said, "I notice that what Uncle Frank says goes around here."

I tackled this syndrome at Tahoe. Over fifty years later, a colleague and I were driving in Florida, and he recalled to me a statement I made in a team meeting in the Crowell lake cottage in 1940: "Frank, you say we are all sinners, but you never share any sins of your own." This of course shocked the group. It was total heresy, and the idea never got anywhere. Neither Frank nor any of his friends believed he had anything to confess.

Also I told Frank that he had created a hierarchy, where he was the Pope, a few of his cohorts, such as Ken Twitchell and Ray Purdy, were the bishops, and the rest of us were the peons. This made him angry, and that evening he walked down steaming from the cottage to the dock quarters where I was staying and took me for a walk to make clear how wrong I was. So that I wouldn't be getting ideas, he said he did not come down there just to see me.

At another team meeting in the cottage, following a group quiet time when all were encouraged to share any guiding thoughts that might have come, I stood and argued for a change of team strategy. We had produced a successful, million-copy-newsstand magazine, *Rising Tide*; we had staged mammoth meetings in the biggest amphitheaters from coast to coast; and we had made the message known far and wide. Was it not now time to concentrate on the core program of individual people becoming different and being encouraged to make their impact on their nations?

Lead balloon.

One of the first to respond was Ken Twitchell, about the most experienced and skillful of Frank's spokesmen. He started with appreciation: "I'm sure that Willard's new experience will be beneficial to us all." But, he added, with more experience I would see things more clearly. "When we were in South Africa [late 1920s] some of us were restive," he said, "and we got the idea that Frank needed to change. So we went to him and laid it out. But we soon found that *we* were the ones that needed changing."

After this, everybody felt better. Frank was restored as the king who could do no wrong, and the team was again secure in the consciousness that the pecking order was still in place. This was the pattern throughout. It was generally accepted in the fellowship that if you differed with Buchman, there was spiritual error somewhere that needed attention.

Sam Shoemaker too believed the work was slighting the personal development at which he was so skillful in favor of the bigger push. Some wrote Sam off with the judgment that his ambition was to become an Episcopal bishop, an objective that could be endangered by association with Frank Buchman. However that might be, he was about to quit Moral Re-Armament when Frank invited him and his wife Helen to Lake Tahoe. Frank's plan involved lavishing attention on the couple, and we all went down from Tahoe to Reno where the Shoemakers' train from New York was to arrive in the evening. There were floodlights and lots of western costumes. Ray Purdy was on a horse and carrying a flag.

The Shoemakers were pleased, had a great time, and confessed in the approved manner that the problems they'd been having with the fellowship were their own fault. But the reconciliation was temporary. The next year, 1941, Sam resigned and removed MRA from his parish house. It was a sad situation. I went with Frank on some of the calls he made on old friends who wondered how such a division could happen. He told them that although Sam may have resigned from him, "I didn't resign from Sam."

I tried to get Frank to consider whether there was something on *his* side that caused the break. Usually it takes two to tango. I even urged him to apologize to Sam. But it was early afternoon, and he rolled over to take his afternoon nap.

My own assessment is that Sam had the same problem that I did with the strategy that seemed more concerned with approval than with life changing. I thought that the stage-show tactic lent itself to this trend. From the time the drama strategy began, we seemed to measure success more by the numbers who crowded the auditoriums and the endorsements of public officials—

and less by the impact on communities because of changed lives.

That Buchman was at times at least intellectually aware of the danger is manifest in a comment he made the next year, 1942, to Ray Purdy in Saratoga Springs, New York, when he almost died of a stroke. "I was wrong," he told Ray, "I have been organizing a movement. But a movement should be the outcome of changed lives, not the means of changing them. From now on I am going to ask God to make me into a great life-changer." This, however, did not change the team's dynamics.

Although my inventive thrusts at Lake Tahoe had no visible influence on either the organizational structure or the overall strategy, there was an enormous change in my personal relationship with Frank Buchman. There was no more fear, and from then on, we were social equals. He still did not regard me as one of his planning insiders, but for years we remained good friends. Some of the old guard talked to me about it, even with a touch of envy.

I didn't lose all my challenges. On some of the lesser issues, he agreed with my judgment. For example, our overseas personnel had to register for the draft. It was 1940, and they were going to do so at Lake Tahoe where they were stationed at the moment. There was opposition to us abroad, and some of it focused on the draft issue. The team was saying that Tahoe was where the registration would be done because that's what Frank had decided. My thought was that it was dangerous to supply all those names and addresses to that small village. I told him I thought Sacramento would be safer. He agreed, and the whole plan shifted.

Once at Mackinac Island Frank was presiding at a meeting while seated in a high backed chair which some one doubtless thought was appropriate for his position. I told him that it looked like a throne, and he ought to occupy a modest chair to identify better with the troops. He immediately asked an aide to get him a different chair. (Interesting that David Gergen reports a similar furniture image problem with President Jerry Ford.) I must add here however, as minor as these incidents may seem, even such modest challenges were extremely rare in the fellowship. His mesmerizing charisma was so great that he was, by and large, regarded as infallible.

Buchman recognized that in me he had a political animal, and he encouraged me to meet people and attend hearings on Capitol Hill. This led to enlisting members of Congress to work for a new spirit of honesty and teamwork in the government. A number of times after that he commented on how I had "made my way" on Capitol Hill. I once wondered out loud whether I could have as much influence on politics by influencing the politicians as I would have if I had become one myself. That is probably not true, but it's an engaging notion.

In Michigan in the forties and fifties, we and our Mackinac Island conference center were often engaged with various state commissions, and in the later days Frank made me his legal representative, in charge of Lansing relations, adding the encouraging word that he had "a lot of confidence" in his appointee.

At times he would say, "Willard, you will bury me." I was not sure of the comment's significance, but I chose to regard it as a term of personal regard.

The morning of Frank's funeral, August 18, 1961, in Allentown, Pennsylvania, Morris Martin sought me out to say that I had been designated as one of the pallbearers. At the grave in Fairview Cemetery, standing next to Merrill Meigs of Chicago and ten others, I helped lower the casket into the Pennsylvania soil from which the man had come.

-10-

YOU CAN DEFEND AMERICA

Guests from Nevada communities came to Tahoe to see our musical review, *You Can Defend America*. One of them, who was known as Mr. Carson City, said, "You have to take this on the road . . . starting with us." Within a week it was showing in the capital of Nevada, and the following week in Reno, "The Biggest Little City in the World."

The response convinced Buchman that he had a marketable weapon for a national audience. And so it proved to be. Wherever we went, the message of "Sound Homes—Teamwork in Industry—a United Nation" seemed to hit the mark with an America gearing up to play its part in fighting the Axis powers. My part in the show was King of the Rats, the force of evil abroad in the land, manipulating people with my subjects, the "rats" of fear, greed, lust, and hate; undermining the integrity of freedom. My forces were ultimately overcome by the teamwork force symbolized on stage by the Statue of Liberty. The spirit of GIMME, as lettered on my chest, was in the finale replaced by GIVE. Corny—but folks responded.

Labor leaders who had visited Tahoe urged us to bring the show to the CIO convention, November 1940, in Atlantic City and after that to the AFL conclave in New Orleans.

John L. Lewis, president of the United Mine Workers, had boldly challenged the old American Federation of Labor (AFL), consisting of craft unions which, like the guilds of old, were run by the princes of labor organizing workers by *crafts*. Lewis believed that rank and file workers in the mass production industries were not receiving the benefits of unionization, and were being by-passed by the labor elite. He formed a Committee for Industrial Organization (CIO), advocating a new concept of "industrial" unions, as distinguished from "craft" unions. He was organizing workers by *industries* such as auto manufacturing, rubber, and steel, with every one in the same plant belonging to the same union.

It was exciting to be in that Atlantic City hall. Lewis, with his lion's mane and bushy eyebrows, his courtly manner and formal dress, had a pungent speaking style, often quoting scripture or Shakespeare. He had broken with President Roosevelt during the 1940 election campaign and had endorsed the Republican candidate, Wendell Willkie. Lewis had pledged that if Willkie lost, he would interpret the result to mean that labor did not accept his leadership and he would resign as president of the CIO. Lewis had allowed Communist support in his mass union drives, using their organizing skills, and planning to dismiss them after the drives were over. So the Communists believed their fortunes were better with Lewis than with others and at the convention made vociferous attempts to keep Lewis at the helm. They organized snake-dances through the hall, chanting, "NO RESIGNATION, NO RESIGNATION." Lewis's stone face was unmoved. When Roosevelt won his third term election that fall, Lewis kept his word and stepped down. Taking his place as head of the CIO was a Scottish-American coal miner, Philip Murray, whom Lewis had put in charge of organizing the steelworkers.

I met a cross-section of these upper-echelon labor leaders at the Atlantic City and New Orleans meetings. I was one of the "stars" of our show, and people liked to shake the hand of the bad guy. We staged the play in ballrooms near the assembly areas at times when the delegates could get away from their meetings.

From the CIO convention in Atlantic City we proceeded by

train to the AFL in New Orleans. Following that, some of the group returned to the West Coast. Basil Entwistle wanted me to return there and work with him. A few, however, were heading east, and when Ray Purdy, who was on his way to Washington, D.C., asked where I wished to go, the choice was clear. I had always believed that I was meant for government relations in some fashion. I was accepted, and for the ten years between 1940 and 1950, except for a hitch in the army, Washington was my brier patch.

Jack and Connie Ely were living on Kalorama Road at the time, but soon acquired the Mary Roberts Rinehart house at 2419 Massachusetts Avenue in Washington's diplomacy quarter. For nearly three decades their imposing residence was the embassy of the Moral Re-Armament program in the nation's capital. The Elys were a remarkable family, whose story has been told by Jarvis Harriman in *Matched Pair*.[1] The two had a combination of top-drawer family ties in New York and Washington circles, a commanding, statesmanlike physical presence, and financial resources to make possible their embassy-style contribution.

Albert H. (Jack) Ely, Jr., a New York attorney, Yale 1915, married Constance Jennings, a Standard Oil heiress, in 1927. The Ely embassy in Washington became a national and international crossroads point of exchange for people and ideas through many years. Colonel Truman Smith, General Marshall's ace intelligence officer in World War II, was a frequent visitor and was fond of asking, "How's everything at Hotel Ely?" I lived on the third floor in the early 1940s.

Having turned twenty-five, the constitutional age for membership in the U.S. House of Representatives, I again

---

[1]Jarvis Harriman, *Matched Pair: The Elys of Embassy Row* (Tucson: PoohStix Press, 1999).

dragged up the idea of making the big move toward elective office. I floated the idea to John Beck, one of my teammates. Rather impertinently he asked, "What do you have that you can bring to Congress?" My answer at the time, of course, was *me*. But the political situation was not favorable. I assumed I would be running in the Minnesota First District, which embraced Northfield, and the seat was occupied by a longtime veteran legislator, August H. Andresen, who was strong with the dairy industry and didn't lose elections. It was hard to imagine going up against him and his many friends. If I went, it would be for long-haul name recognition and building experience. The whole thing was hardly realistic, and having no base, and receiving no encouragement from the team, I dropped the idea.

Our objective as a force in Washington was two-fold:
1. to lobby for values and a new spirit in national politics and international affairs; and
2. to establish in the minds of national leaders the knowledge that here was a force of importance to the strength of the nation.

In retrospect, I think I settled too much for (2), which should have been a by-product of (1).

Nevertheless, there was solid accomplishment in lives re-oriented, resentments answered, apologies made, angry speeches torn up before delivery, families strengthened. One evening we had four senators and two congressmen listening to God in the Massachusetts Avenue living room. In a way we were in friendly competition with Abraham Vereide's breakfast groups, which tended to target the same members of Congress as we did, those that responded to the spiritual dimension in politics. One repre-sentative had a transforming experience that turned his life around as a result of decisions made with us. He so inspired the House breakfast group with his story that they wanted him to tell it at a weekend retreat—only they did not want him to mention that we were the ones who had helped him!

Perhaps the most exciting time in Washington for me came in 1944 when Senator Harry S. Truman and Congressman James W. Wadsworth conspired to bring the program to the heart of the nation's capital. Senator Truman's interest in MRA, according to biographer Richard Miller, who wrote negatively about it, was "intense."[2] In a letter dated October 30, 1940, the Senator's secretary, V. R. Messall, wrote that he was "very much impressed with the work they are doing and heartily approves this movement." In a personal letter to Frank Buchman January 1, 1942, Truman wrote, "I hope you have a successful year in spreading the desire for a reawakening of the moral code in this great country of ours." David McCullough's biography *Truman*[3] is silent on the relation of Harry to this activity, and so far he has not replied to my queries as to why. The fact is that during his last four years in the Senate, Truman was point man for MRA in Washington.

To opponents he stuck to what he had seen. George Seldes, editor of the magazine *in fact*, and a curmudgeon who for decades was a professional opponent of MRA without ever interviewing any one he wrote about, was a muckraker who created his own muck. He claimed in his autobiography, *Witness to a Century*, to have waved Truman off the MRA program. But the senator responded, "My interest in the organization was to get the work done. I don't know anything about the controversy

---

[2]Richard L. Miller, *Harry S. Truman: The Rise to Power* (New York: McGraw-Hill, 1986).

[3]McCullough lists Miller in his bibliography.

in connection with it, and care less."[4]

Truman made more than one national radio address on the subject and in December 1939, as mentioned earlier, urged President Roosevelt to join in.

He had been involved with the program ever since President Roosevelt asked him, as a Senate Democrat with a loyal New Deal voting record, to read his message from the White House on June 4, 1939, to a packed meeting in Constitution Hall. On June 8, 1939, the Senator inserted an extensive report of the event in the *Congressional Record*. After that, Truman became particularly impressed with the way these moral code ideas, which resonated with his own background convictions, were being applied in practice.

Twenty months after the Constitution Hall meeting and three months after he had been reelected for a second term as Senator from Missouri, Truman's Senate colleagues voted in favor of his proposal of a special Senate "watchdog" committee to monitor war industry contracts, making him chairman. They wanted to root out inefficiency, waste, and fraud, as well as to get a "bigger bang for the buck." The unit became known as the "Truman Committee," and the chairman began inspiring such widespread confidence that his name started being mentioned

---

[4]Around the 1990s, I had a number of friendly visits with Seldes in his rural home at Hartland-4-Corners, Vermont. He was reaching 100 years of age. Over the years he had stuck by his late wife Helen's insistence, in view of the temptations of the journalism world, that they have but one martini each day, which he was happily offering visitors to his Vermont hillside home. He was clear-headed enough at this age, but it was a little late for him to shift attitudes, although he did say that if he was wrong on Buchman, he should think about doing something. I had conferred with executives of his publisher, Ballantine Books, in their New York office, including the chief attorney, and in good lawyerly fashion she declined to apologize for the libels (claiming fascist endorsements, for example) they had published about Buchman in *Witness to a Century*.

for higher office. During his investigations he found that MRA was producing interesting results. In one inspection report he said:

They have rendered great assistance to the all-out war program by creating the spirit of co-operation between management and labor, reducing absenteeism, heightening all-around efficiency, and increasing production.
Press release November, 1943

Besides Truman, another approximately one hundred members of Congress were attracted to the program. One of them was James W. Wadsworth from Genessee in upstate New York. He had been a Member of the Senate, and although he was now serving in the House, he was still addressed as "Senator." He was said to be one of the few Congressmen who could change votes with a speech.

Truman and Wadsworth agreed to address a city-wide event in Philadelphia where the industrial teamwork play *The Forgotten Factor* was sponsored by leaders of labor and management in Philadelphia's shipbuilding industry. The headliners from Washington made an impressive team—a Democrat from the Senate and a Republican from the House.

The Forgotten Factor, by Alan Thornhill, was an industrial play, giving a true-to-life look into the families on both sides of a bitter labor-management dispute, a breakdown that had crippled their company. The play's dramatic denouement, where the two sides are reconciled by the discovery of their common humanity and newfound understanding of each other's aspirations, stirred audiences from coast to coast. Sometimes by its own catalytic power the drama pulled opposing factions together. At the presentation at Philadelphia's historic Academy of Music, Jack Kelly, former Olympic oarsman, the city's leading brick contractor, Pennsylvania Democratic leader, and father of Princess Grace of Monaco, called it a "two-handkerchief play."

Both Truman and Wadsworth spoke from the stage after the play. Truman said:

I wish I were thirty years younger to see this thing work out. I know it is going to. . . . America today needs fundamental moral truth. We have seen it brilliantly and entertainingly presented tonight.

Academy of Music, Philadelphia, November 19, 1943

Since the play was proving to be a morale builder across every kind of barrier, it was natural that people should call for a front and center presentation in Washington, D.C. Truman and Wadsworth agreed to do a repeat.

The National Theatre was engaged for May 14, 1944, and the capital's military and political leadership received personal invitations from Messrs. Truman and Wadsworth, each of whom signed a thousand letters. I was looking down from the Senate gallery one day, and saw Truman seated at his Senate floor desk, piled high with those invitations, signing away as the speeches droned on.

I met Harry Truman only once. It was April 1944, and the National Theatre event was only weeks away. John Roots, who was at the heart of the planning and particularly persuasive with Washington leaders, took me to the Senate Office Building late one afternoon, along with Canadian cowboy singer Cece Broadhurst. Truman and Broadhurst both had birthdays on May 8, and Cece said, "Since the Senator doesn't have time to sing a song for me, I'll sing one for him."

Oh Senator Truman, he gathered a few men
To form a big Committee,
To investigate production rate
In every industrial city.
Can't help but admire the Senator's fire . . .

Harry was pleased. "That fellow's got it," he said. We stood around the outer office, his staff having gone home. I was struck with how quickly he made decisions. I didn't hear, "I'll think about it," or, "Call me tomorrow." It was "yes" or "no"—right now. And with great good cheer. Later in the White House he became known for this style of decision-making.

Invitees to the National Theatre were to write or phone their RSVPs to the Willard Hotel, the prestigious landmark where Lincoln stayed in 1861 the week before he moved into the White House. A number of us organized ourselves to staff temporary quarters there, and we answered the telephone, "Truman-Wadsworth Committee."

Before long there were ominous whispers in the wind. One day Matt Connelly dropped by. He was Truman's legislative man, very friendly and political. He wondered whether it would be all right with us if we did not say "Truman-Wadsworth Committee," as it was so close to "Truman Committee," a name he was obviously trying to preserve. We said yes, of course, and from then on we answered with merely, "National Committee."

Out in Detroit, some of our people were conversing with Daniel Tobin, the pre-Hoffa president of the International Teamsters Union, explaining who was sponsoring the show at the National Theatre and planning to come. Tobin said, "Truman won't be there."

"What do you mean, Truman won't be there? He's committed."

"I know, but I'm telling you he won't be there."

Tobin turned out to be right. Robert Hannegan, Democratic National Chairman, had begun to promote the idea of Truman for vice president in the election that year. Everyone knew Roosevelt was a sick man and if he were reelected, the party's choice for vice president would likely become president soon. Harry was reluctant, as the record of vice presidents succeeding to the White House had often been unhappy. Nevertheless, a loyal party man, he bowed to the advice of the pros who then doubtless told him he had best sever ties with all groups, however worthy and however explainable. And that was the end of Truman's direct association with MRA.

The Democratic National Convention of August 1944 was one of the most dramatic that I covered in those days. For one thing, I was able to spend some time with Hubert Humphrey, who was still little known, but who was already beginning to pull the Farmer-Labor and Democratic parties of Minnesota together.

Mr. Roosevelt's frail health put the big focus on the vice presidential nomination. A number of candidates had their backers, including the incumbent Henry Wallace, Roosevelt's vice president since 1941, and Supreme Court Justice William O. Douglas. At Mackinac Island before going to Chicago, I was predicting Harry Truman, largely because of the integrity he projected from his Senate watchdog committee. When he got the nod, I was credited with prescient political savvy.

In Chicago the night before the convention finally acted, I got into a taxicab, and by some kind of fortune found I was sharing it with Colonel Harry Vaughan, Truman's World War I buddy who had been a political crony ever since. In a happy and talkative mood, Harry confided in me that the top brass of the party had just concluded a meeting in a room under the convention platform and had agreed that it would be Truman the next day. And that's the way it turned out.

That night following the nomination I was in the hall on the twenty-seventh floor of the Conrad Hilton Hotel, thinking there was bound to be some action in the environs, when Jack Kelly came out of a room, recognized me (I was surprised, as we had not had all that much contact) and congratulated me on putting our "man over." That's how much the party leader of a major state connected Truman and us. The next day on the street, the last day of the convention, Jack saw me and repeated the congratulations in similar words.

War Clouds

The major part of the MRA force gathered in June 1941 for a strategy conference at Plymouth, Massachusetts. The progress of the war was not all that good for the Allies. On May 10, 1941, Rudolf Hess, the number three Nazi, parachuted on to the 157,000-acre Scottish estate of the Duke of Hamilton. The European editor of *Collier's* magazine, William Hillman, "announced with confidence" that Hess was a follower of Buchman and that his motive was to make contact with the Oxford Group for the purpose of negotiating a peace. Hillman was known to have links in the State Department, so the speculation was taken seriously in other publications, such as the *Christian Century*.

Buchman was of course intrigued with the implication and took time with the team to get reactions as to what this meant. None of the theories satisfied him. When all had finished, he gave his response with a down-home Pennsylvania story about a persistent rumor that a well-known single lady was getting married. Friends called on her and asked point blank, was it true? "No," she sighed, "but thank God for the rumor." There was some satisfaction, he implied, that responsible persons in the press might think he had that kind of clout.

The big news of the month came from Detroit where Henry Ford signed a contract with the United Auto Workers (CIO). It was June 20, 1941. Ford had been the last holdout of the Big Three auto-makers, saying he would close down the entire company before he would agree to the union's demands. Yet overnight he switched and gave them everything they asked for, including dues paid directly to the union via payroll check-off.

Why? Ford later said to his production wizard of forty years, Charles Sorenson, that when he went home that night and told his wife that he would not sign the contract and was closing the plant, she was horrified.

> She said if that were done, there would be riots and bloodshed, and she had seen enough of that. If I did that, she would leave me. She insisted that I sign what she termed a peace agreement. I felt her vision and judgment were better than mine. I'm glad I did see it her way. Don't ever discredit the power of a woman.[5]

One of the influences at work with the Fords may have been the conversations Clara Ford had been having in her home, Fairlane, with my friends Jim and Ellie Newton, who kept her apprised of their labor-management teamwork advances in Michigan industry.

In our gathering at Plymouth, with some encouragement from Frank who told me to "keep prophesying," as at Tahoe in 1940, I launched forth to right some of the wrongs and shake up some of the deadness I saw around me. My efforts met with hostility, and thinking at one point I was going to be fired, and rather hoping I would, I filled out applications with the U.S. Army Air Corps for pilot training, complete with endorsement from my father, just in case. The team kept me on, the air corps application died in my briefcase, and I dropped back into my shell.

From Massachusetts, we responded to invitations from people in the state of Maine to conduct what in 1941 became the first School for Home Defense. At Tallwood on Lake Maranacook west of Augusta, as at Tahoe, we were offered an abandoned camp and put it in shape. This Home Defense program was supported and visited by Brigadier Francis Wilby, commanding

---

[5]Charles E. Sorenson, My Forty Years With Ford (New York: Norton, 1956).

officer of the First Corps Area, United States Army.

In August 1941, Winston Churchill met Franklin D. Roosevelt at sea off the coast of Maine, where they produced the eight-point Atlantic Charter. Frank thought he might be able to see their ship, and asked his driver, John Wood, to take him up to the top of Mount Desert, above Bar Harbor, but the conferees were anchored beyond the horizon.

Glenn Clark, spiritual writer and group leader, also visited us at Maranacook. He had just completed one of his Camps Farthest Out at the Isle of Shoals and thought he had a commitment from Buchman for the two to pray together for the world situation. But Frank backed off. He was not keen on identifying with "spiritual leaders"; he was more interested in relating his work to statesmanship. In childhood I had known Clark when he was track coach and professor at Macalester College. He came from Saint Paul to our home in Northfield to pray with my father for our friend John Millen, the Carleton track coach, who was dying of cancer. At Maranacook he took me to one side, in confidence, and said he was praying I would become president. Obviously his success rate as a prayer authority was not improved.

We had reports that professional critic Tom Driberg from Great Britain was in the area. It turned out he spent six months in 1941 in the U.S. digging up negatives on MRA for his book, *The Mystery of Moral Re-Armament* (see page 211). Driberg was a Member of the House of Commons and posthumously revealed to be a double British-Russian agent in World War II.[6] All our people were ordered to clear out of the Maranacook quarters, the policy then being not to talk to journalists when negative

---

[6]Garth Lean, *On the Tail of a Comet* (Colorado Springs: Helmers & Howard, 1988), 302N.

publicity was in the air. I thought this was a mistake, but it was the paranoia of the time. This stance was only changed with the arrival on the scene of British journalist Peter Howard, who was eager to take on all comers.

During the summer, we went out from Maranacook with *You Can Defend America*, all the way from potato-land on the Canadian border (we had a special song, "Up in Aroostook County where the best potatoes grow") to the sand and cottages of Cape Cod.

I valiantly played my role as the chief rat, the essence of evil subversion, and was complimented, but I was pretty depressed the whole time. Part of the problem was that I wanted to join the armed forces. Actually, I was opposed to militarism and was not all that keen about the war, but it looked like a patriotic way to be released from the frustrations of the program I was in. Those I talked to felt my thinking was inadequate and that I could do much more for the country where I was. Frank called me in and read a letter he was proposing to the Selective Service System, asking that I be one of the full-time workers eligible for deferment as necessary to the war effort. When he finished, he said, "Now, Willard, is this what you want?"

At that point, I lied. I said, "Yes, Frank, that's fine." The psychological pressure to stay was greater than my courage to buck it. It was at that time, in the fall of 1941, that Sam Shoemaker broke with Buchman and the team, and withdrew his Calvary Parish House in New York from participation in the work. I was in sympathy with Sam's position, as mentioned earlier, but did not have his resources to make such a move. Nor did I believe that breaking off was the answer. I decided to stay with Buchman. Three years later I was drafted into the army.

-11-

THIS IS THE ARMY

I had been called up for the draft in 1942, but was rejected for what they said was an inguinal hernia. On a repeat in 1944, no evidence of such could be found. It is possible that by then they needed more warm bodies. Inducted at Fort Snelling in Minnesota, I proceeded with several hundred others by slow cattle train through the Middle West, arriving finally at Camp Fannin, a big installation carved out of sweeping pastureland just out of the rose capital, Tyler, Texas.

It was August, and the temperature in East Texas was 120 degrees. When we arrived, we noticed that although our newly arrived bodies were soaking our uniforms, the officers who were acclimated through months of service were crisp and dry. Some of the GIs wanted to give Texas "back to the Indians." They were the ones who sang with great gusto, to the tune of "John Brown's Body,"

> When the war is over, we will all enlist again.
> We will, like hell, we will!

Others settled down with a little more positive outlook. There were even those of whom it was said that they had "found a home in the army." I leaned more to that camp. I enjoyed every minute of it, almost, especially the humanity of it all.

For one thing, *everybody* was in the army, and I got such a kick out of rubbing shoulders with people of all walks of life, many of limited education, even some who could not read. Also the spontaneous barracks humor was exhilarating. It was a new world. My father was impressed with how much happier I was in the army than in my civilian calling.

Another profound impression was the army's philosophy of education. Outside of a schoolroom blackboard, I had never seen a visual aid. In the army the charts on easels were a great help. What most struck me was the statement by the teachers, enlisted men and officers alike: "If you don't get this material, it's not *your* fault—it's *our* fault." I had never heard a teacher say that. I had always understood it was *my* fault. I said to myself, this is going to revolutionize all of education.

Our company's chief sergeant at Camp Fannin was Bernard Norton of Ludington, Michigan. The first hot afternoon he met with us and gave us a stream of violent profanity, which we took to mean that he was to be obeyed, and that dire consequences awaited any one dumb enough not to catch on. He was a smart hombre with a high-school education and proud of being demonstrably tough. He did not like his army duty, got drunk every weekend, and served with flair. At the morning fall-out in front of our barracks, he bellowed out his instructions for the day. Sergeant Norton took a liking to me, and I did not get chewed out too much. I could carry a tune and he called on me to carry a few, along with the company guidon, on marches. We would trudge along, sometimes miles to the outer ranges for our training exercises, while I led the gang in old faithfuls like "Roll Out the Barrel" and "It's a Long Way to Tipperary."

We would hear from a sergeant something like this: "When that whistle blows, I don't want to see nothin' but a cloud of dust. And when that dust blows away, I don't want to see nothin' but sixty statues." To emphasize his seniority, he would say, "Soldier, I've stood at attention longer than you've been in the army" or "I've used more ink signing the payroll than you've drunk GI coffee." One of our sergeants, when the company might be standing around uncertainly, was apt to call out, "Let's do *something*, even if it's wrong!" Another would approach a GI who was wearing a little stubble and say, "Soldier, next time you shave, stand a little closer to the razor."

We had to clean our rifles every evening in the barracks and pass inspection by one of the sergeants. I discovered that if I cleaned mine right after supper, I would be there all evening, as the sergeant would always find some defect in my work and make me keep at it. But if I left it until close to lights-out, I could complete the chore in fifteen or twenty minutes and it would pass. The sergeant always passed a rifle before bedtime.

A number of us on an occasional weekend would rent a car with driver to take us the hundred miles west from our camp in the tree-covered hills of East Texas to the plains country around Dallas. We didn't ask how the drivers handled the gas-rationing situation. We sometimes spent Saturday night in the Adolphus Hotel. Clean sheets were a refreshing treat. After a Sunday morning breakfast in the coffee shop, we asked for our check and were told the gentleman at the next table, who had left, had taken care of it. He probably felt good about having done a small deed for "men in uniform," and we appreciated the kindness he showed to a few homesick soldiers.

Years later, I took my family back to Tyler, and at dusk drove around the old haunts. Camp Fannin had reverted to farmland, and landmarks were hard to come by. I was able to find the still-standing post theater, where we used to fall asleep after lunch watching Frank Capra training films. The rest of the area had receded into the arms of time.

Officer Candidate School

At the end of the four months of basic infantry training at Camp Fannin, I was accepted for Officer Candidate School at the Infantry School, Fort Benning, Georgia. However, I had no more than landed there than I developed a hydrocele, an accumulation of fluid in the testes, requiring surgical repair in the base hospital. The operation and recovery took four months, from January to April 1945, after which I rejoined another officer candidate class.

During this interim period I became a daily army newscaster for the hospital occupants. This opportunity came about as a result of a course I gave on Military Organization at an afternoon assembly. This is a subject the army required everybody to deal with, and I had taken my turn. Instead of grinding through the usual boring routine, I started with the President of the United States as Commander-in-Chief, went on to the civilian control of the military, described the Department of Defense, and took it on down to the enlisted man. The presentation was loaded with material they could recognize from the news. The officer in charge said he had never heard it explained so well to an assembly of GIs, and as a result he asked me to take on the daily newscast.

Being in a hospital, many of the listeners came in bathrobes or crutches. A hundred to a hundred and fifty men turned up every day. My news sources were the Columbus, Georgia, morning paper and a sprightly daytime radio talk program featuring Kate Smith and Ted Collins. The outstanding event I covered during this brief newscasting career was the battle of Iwo Jima, February-March 1945, which I followed for the audience every day on a huge map.

Between my stint in the military hospital and plunging back into "shavetail" training, I was given a brief leave, and I used it to visit family and friends, culminating in getting engaged to be married on a transcontinental phone call. All that excitement I have recorded in the next chapter.

Returning to Fort Benning from the leave of absence, I plunged into training to be an army officer. The motto at Fort

Benning was "Follow Me," a quotation from the New Testament which bespoke the school's heavy curricular emphasis on leadership. The need for such training was expressed in a frequently cited gag, "I wouldn't follow him across the street to the PX for a free beer."

The classes ahead of us were always calling out, "Go Back!" when we intersected with them at areas like Harmony Church in the outer reaches of Fort Benning's 189,000 acres. (A narrow gauge, coal-smoke-belching railroad took us from one training ground to another.) Their mantra was good-natured advice to quit while we were ahead. Things were a lot tougher in their cycle, they claimed. But we didn't believe their claim: "They sure are babying you guys." So we took in stride their advice to "Go Back."

My fellow candidates elected me their class president, so I represented them with the upper brass, although opportunities for democratic dialog in the army are, in the nature of things, limited. In the contest to be named speaker for the class at graduation, I prepared a leadership talk on "Follow Me? or Go Back?" but lost out to a son of the superintendent of Atlanta schools. It probably would have made no difference in the outcome, but I started preparation too late, and by the time I got around to the writing I was exhausted from a sleepless, thirty-six-hour bivouac in the woods.

On occasion the candidates would sing with some gusto an unofficial Infantry School ballad to the tune of the Cornell University anthem (the first line referring to the rivers of Columbus, Georgia):

> High above the Chattahoochee and the Upatoi
> Stands our noble alma mater, Benning's School for Boys.
> Forward ever, backward never, "Follow Me" and die!
> To the port of embarkation. Next of kin, Goodbye!

Back at Officer Candidate School, one of my classmates was George "Scotty" MacFarlane, whom I had known since 1938 when we met at a youth renewal camp in the Poconos of Pennsylvania. His specialty was the exuberant singing of Scottish songs made famous by Sir Harry Lauder. Born in the old country, he had an authentic accent to go with it. He was good at personalizing new words for the old tunes as called for by whatever celebratory occasion was up.

Scotty and I managed to enlist a half dozen classmates to get up each morning a half hour before the camp stirred and gather in the telephone lounge across the street for fellowship, sharing, and prayer. For some of them it turned out to be a sort of lifeline.

My experience with a "port of embarkation" and good-byes to "next of kin" came months later, in December 1945, when I almost, but did not, sail for Europe. I was within a gangplank of joining occupation forces in Germany when I was cleared to return to the industrial reconciliation home front.

My orders called for my army exit to be processed at Fort George Meade, between Washington and Baltimore. It was December 1945. I drove from Washington up and back in the Elys' dark green Buick convertible, the same car in which I had chauffeured Charles Lindbergh two years earlier. Friends won't believe this, but as I drove back home from Fort Meade, a civilian for the first time in eighteen months, I actually cried at the wheel. The army had been one of the happiest experiences of my life.

-12-

MARY LOUISE

For our fiftieth wedding anniversary in August 1995, our sons treated Mary Louise and me to a lively banquet for friends in Claremont, California. People reminisced and sang original songs. Fifty years is a long time—a half century, come to think of it. During that time, we lived on both coasts and in the middle. We had our ups and downs. It was by no means endless bliss. But somehow we managed and we hung in there. We're glad we did.

I knew Laurence J. Peter, and spent quite a bit of time with him in his last days at his home in Palos Verdes Estates. One of his favorites, of the many "Peter Principles" with which he made his reputation, was this:

> "All marriages are happy. It's the living together afterwards that causes the problems."

At that fiftieth party, Mary Louise and I were allowed time to share thoughts near the end of the festivities. This is what I said:

> If there is one word about this partner of mine, it is—Terrific! She's been the glue and the motor and the inspiration for so much of it. Especially with the children. She's been the one with the ideas—and the follow-through —on what to do about the extras in their education, health, music, paper routes, and on and on. The head deacon in our church in Lee, New Hampshire, called her the "balance wheel" in our family. She has put up with the moods, the highs, the lows, the medical vicissitudes. In riding herd on our income tax returns, she has kept us out of jail. In short, this operation would not

have gone much of anywhere without Mary Louise. And she has been putting up with this for over fifty years!

There are at least two protagonists in any love story, which makes our romance a story I cannot tell alone. Mary Louise will chip in from time to time with her own perspective.

It all began after the 1936 Harvard-Yale football game in Cambridge, Massachusetts. A mutual friend of ours who lived in a Boston Brahmin brownstone on Commonwealth Avenue had put on a post-game party that weekend, to which she had invited a dozen students from New England colleges and universities. I was in my first year at the Harvard Law School, and Mary Louise Merrell of Indianapolis was a junior at Vassar. We did not make much of an impression on each other at the time. The purpose of the gathering was to consider how to make a difference in our lives, in our schools, and in the world, so opposite-sex checking was not necessarily high on the agenda. Although it was hardly love at first sight, I never forgot Mary Louise as an interesting and friendly person whom I would like to get to know.

Which I did. But it took a while.

I have to tell you a little more about Mary Louise, in addition to my tribute to her on our fiftieth anniversary. She has been a kind of Girl Scout all her life (having reached Eagle rank in her youth). She takes most things very seriously and is super conscientious. Her first reaction to many suggestions is no. This gives her room for maneuver and time to sort out which **no** should become **yes.** She likes to think all around the picture, and to ask the question that one of her professors taught generations of Vassar students to ask, "What else is also true?"

She was always a standout student, e.g. Phi Beta Kappa at Vassar. At Shortridge High School in Indianapolis, which alumnus Kurt Vonnegut has referred to as a high school that provided a college level education, she was a Greek student and was the editor of the school's daily newspaper one day each week. A lifelong quality tennis player, even in her eighties she has impressed her peers.

In 1940, four years after we met, she was in Philadelphia and called on her summer neighbor and Hoosier friend, Mrs. Wendell Willkie, whose husband was about to be nominated as the Republican candidate for President. Mrs. Willkie immediately drafted her to be an assistant during the campaign, much to the apprehension of Mary Louise's Democrat father. She almost made the transcontinental whistle-stop campaign train.

In 1938 there was a big change in both our lives. She graduated from Vassar, and I left the Harvard Law School. Both of us (within six months of each other) were invited to become part of the national staff of the Oxford Group.

> *Mary Louise: In all honesty, I can't recall a clear impression of Willard on the weekend we met. But after Willard left the law school, our paths began to cross. I remember other women praising his abilities and commitment. He had quite a coterie of female admirers, and seemed to stand out in any group.*

We found ourselves thrown together on various projects, particularly on what we called the "government team," a hardworking cadre who concentrated on trying to bring a new spirit to municipal, state, and national government. Like me, Mary Louise had a natural interest in government. She had been an economics major at Vassar, influenced by the excitement of the New Deal and the professors from Poughkeepsie constantly interacting with Washington.[1]

---

[1]An interesting coincidence emerged. At Vassar Mary Louise was a classmate of Katharine Meyer, publisher of the *Washington Post* 1969-79, while concurrently I was a member of the same Harvard Law School class as her future husband, Philip Graham.

In the spring of 1941, Howard Blake, Warner Clark, and I were commissioned to tour the Midwest. Our announced mission was to promote Daphne DuMaurier's *Come Wind, Come Weather* (New York: Doubleday, 1941) a group of home front, mostly MRA-instigated, war stories from Great Britain and pulled together by the famous novelist. We saw most of the governors and quite a few mayors in the heartland, of special note being Harold Burton, mayor of Cleveland, whom we would see much more of in Washington when he became a U.S. senator and then justice of the Supreme Court. He was particularly enthusiastic about our war morale handbook *You Can Defend America*. This Midwest trip climaxed in negotiating sessions in Lansing with the Michigan Governor's office leading to the establishment of the MRA conference center on Mackinac Island.

Of the many interesting people we met on that journey was Rowland Allen, personnel director (1925-52) of the L. S. Ayres department store, for years the major emporium of Indianapolis. The city and state has long been known for its conservatism, and in contrast Allen was an avowed Socialist and an American Civil Liberties Union activist known for his crusades against right wing initiatives. That he should occupy a key position in Indiana's business establishment was a tribute to his apparent skills in caring for the store's employees.

Mary Louise was on assignment in Indiana at that time, living with her parents in north Indianapolis, and I was billeted in their guestroom for two weeks. I think that did it. It was hardly a Hollywood romance. We were drawn together not only because of mutual interest in all ramifications of the political world, but also by a common bond of loyalty as Midwesterners to the American heartland from which we both sprang.

Mary Louise: My father was a lawyer, had been president of the Indiana Bar Association and later, in 1947, became a judge in the Nurnberg trial of the I.G. Farben Company (chemical cartel). Mother joined the League of Women Voters as soon as her youngest child was in school, and became state president. So there was plenty of conversation on current and political issues around the dinner table, and Willard fit in well. Dad was a staunch, lifelong Democrat, Willard from a Republican background. But this didn't seem to interfere with dialogue. My father, for the life of him, could not understand how Willard could leave law school after more than two years, and his commitment to MRA—and mine—was totally beyond his comprehension. I remember Father asking Willard more than once, "But where will you be five years from now?"

I think she "fell" first. I discovered she arranged little things so that I would move in the proper direction. When a group would go to some destination by a cavalcade of cars, somehow or other I would find myself in the same car as she. The same thing would happen in an elevator. I felt her devotion was impressive and my own feelings were responding. By the time I was drafted into the infantry in 1944, we were definitely friendly, and regarded as a couple by some, although dating was not within the mores of the fellowship.

When I was stationed at Fort Benning early in 1945, the thought came into my mind that I should ask her to marry me. Next question: how to ask? I shared the thought with George "Scotty" MacFarlane, my army buddy. In those days one did not make a major move like getting married without checking with Frank Buchman, our mentor and CEO. Frank was in Los Angeles, but when my leave materialized, I wanted to go to Washington. Although I would not yet have "clearance" for popping The Question, I could talk with Mary Louise and check out whether it looked like a good idea to go ahead.

An eerie thought came up on the screen. The name also

looked important. There might be something special about being given "Mary," the Mother of Jesus, and "Louise," the Mother of me. This is one reason why I have not followed her friends of younger days who call her "Mary Lou."

The military was good about giving GIs transportation breaks, and I was able to bum a ride with Lt. Col. Harry Conley, who happened when I turned up at the Fort Benning air strip to be flying a two-seater AT-6 training plane to Washington.

Mary Louise and I did have several happy visits over the next two days, but of course, always in the company of others. One occasion was a picnic on a hillside below the Robert E. Lee Mansion at the Arlington National Cemetery.

On the side, I shared my plans with two of my colleagues who were old friends and who had really happy reactions. Later Mary Louise shared with me how angry she was when she learned I had talked to others before speaking with her. Soon there were good-byes, and I flew commercial transport to Minnesota to see my parents. Above the Pennsylvania mountains, I struck up a conversation with an attractive young flight attendant from Williamsport. I was surprised, and felt guilty that on a trip where I was planning to be engaged, I could allow myself to be semi-smitten, even for a few minutes, by another woman.

Settling in for a couple days with my folks in Northfield, my father particularly was amazed at the developments. I was nearly thirty, and he had about resigned himself to my being a bachelor for life. My stepmother was pleased when I described my intentions, but concerned by what she considered my rather clinical approach to romance.

The next afternoon, I enlisted a Minneapolis friend, Theone Beal, to go with me to call on Esther Glewwe Stassen, wife of the Minnesota Governor, at their home in South Saint Paul. Harold's parents joined us for a few minutes. I shared my hopes with Mrs. Stassen, and she wrote me a nice note wishing me well with my lady.

Time was running out. It was now Tuesday, and I had to be back at Fort Benning in a week. I flew from Minneapolis to Los Angeles, landing at the Burbank airport, LAX being still in the future. Paul Hogue met me, and as we drove away he looked north to the San Gabriel Mountains, which at the time were bright and clear, and said, "That's the Warner Brothers lot. Looks like the real thing, doesn't it?" My purpose was to seek Frank Buchman's approval for going ahead with my plans to propose to Mary Louise. He was staying at Ronald Colman's San Ysidro Ranch in Montecito, near Santa Barbara, and I arrived by car from Los Angeles Wednesday afternoon, marveling, as on many trips since, at the scenic beauty of the rail and highway corridor between the mountains and the sea.

That evening there was a public presentation of *You Can Defend America* at Santa Barbara's famed Lobero Theater. Frank wanted me to speak at the performance. It was sometimes intimated that he was pacifist, as he was articulate about world peace, and he wanted people to know that his boys were serving in the armed forces. I was in uniform and I did my thing. Frank liked what I said from the stage, particularly as I had reported on the Stassen family. He sensed that the audience leaned Republican, and the Minnesota governor was a contender in the forties for the Republican presidential nomination.

The next day, April 12, everybody was talking about President Roosevelt's death. He had been stricken with a cerebral hemorrhage at his winter home in Warm Springs, Georgia. Harry Truman had been sworn in as president. That evening *You Can Defend America* was staged at the U.S. Marine base in Goleta, the future campus site of the University of California at Santa Barbara. We ate in the mess hall beforehand and when I set my tray down next to Frank's, I asked him what he thought of the news. "Oh, I expected it," he said. Many people did.

I spent the night at Frank's quarters in Montecito, and when

I pressed him for an answer about Mary Louise, he said, "I don't have any specific guidance about that, but I think it's all right." That, of course, was all I needed. The problem then was to get to a phone. My intended was a continent away.

My air reservation back to Georgia fell through, but the folks on the phone who manage military transport priorities said the chances were much better from San Francisco. So on Friday afternoon, Paul Campbell, Frank's physician and aide, drove me to the small mission-style air terminal in Santa Barbara, and I boarded a United Airlines DC-3, complete with two typical California blonde stewardesses, and headed for America's most beautiful city.

That evening Mrs. Frances Bird, a Boston dowager who had rented an apartment overlooking the Bay for the duration of the United Nations organizational meetings, invited me to a dinner party and to spend the night. Among the dozen or more dinner guests I remember were Eugene von Teuber from Czechoslovakia and Francis Bradley from Boston. I told them all what I was planning to do, and they were excited to be on the inside of this happy expectation. "All the world loves a lover." At length I asked the hostess if I could use the telephone, as by now it was about ten P.M. in Washington. She showed me a little booth.

When Mary Louise, working at the Ely home on Embassy Row in Washington, learned the incoming call was from San Francisco, her secretarial notebook snapped to attention. There was a good deal of liaison between our team at the United Nations action centers and Washington, and she was a coordinator on the eastern end. So she was surprised when I came on and started talking about what a wonderful sunset we were experiencing over the Golden Gate. (Later she visited that apartment and determined I could not possibly have seen the sunset from that little booth!) I then got down to business:

"Mary Louise, I love you very much, and I am asking you, would you marry me?"

"O, Willard, you know I would."

She did not say, "It's so sudden," or "I need to think about it." It was "Yes," right now. Apparently she had thought it over all she needed to.

It was Friday the thirteenth.

Mary Louise: My memory of that phone call and the following day is quite blurry. What had happened seemed almost unreal—agreeing to a life commitment on a phone call? I do remember feeling the need to see each other and talk to each other, and promoted a trip to Georgia. I think I was in a daze, perhaps partly in surprise at my so very quick response to Willard's proposal. A phone conversation with my parents introduced a note of reality, because Mother immediately wanted to know about wedding plans, which had not crossed my mind.

Transportation out of San Francisco to the East was becoming impossible, so on Saturday I flew back to Los Angeles. On Sunday morning Frank Buchman, who had earlier returned from Santa Barbara, drove with me to the Burbank airport. I recall that when I took my seat on the DC-3 and looked out at the farewell party on the ground, I made the sign of the cross to Frank, and he returned it. I appreciated his coming to see me off. He was not too well. He had suffered a stroke two years earlier, affecting his right hand and leg.

All went fine until Phoenix, where I was "bumped" from my plane by an army officer with a higher priority, leaving me a little panicky around the edges. I had to report for duty at Fort Benning; time was running out, and I was on the ground without a propeller. Those transportation priority women had heard a million sob stories, but I got hold of one on the phone who was a sweetheart. She made me feel special, and before long she got me on another plane to Atlanta.

By this time Mary Louise had made her way by train from Washington to Atlanta, and in the small hours I phoned her from Dallas, and wherever else we stopped. I remember complaining how slowly the plane lumbered through the night. She was staying on Atlanta's Ponce de Leon Avenue at the home of our friends, the Guy Woolfords, hospitable folks who entertained many a soldier from the surrounding bases on weekends.

As you can imagine, we had a great reunion at the Atlanta airport—our first encounter since we were engaged. We didn't have time for much more than a sit-down breakfast before we had to leave for Fort Benning. Not far off the main route to Columbus is Warm Springs, so we decided to stop and pay our respects at the site where the president had died three days earlier. We signed our names in the book and added the words "72 hours."

Soon I was immersed in becoming an officer in the U.S. Infantry, and Mary Louise returned to Washington.

Mary Louise: Long-distance engagements were not unusual during wartime. He wrote lots of letters; I went to San Francisco and spent a few weeks serving as a kind of apprentice to the Swiss woman who was cooking for Frank Buchman, mostly very special meals for his guests. This was considered vital training for a bride-to-be.

On my way home to Indianapolis by train, I stopped for a few hours in Omaha to be looked over by Willard's two grandmothers, who both lived in a "home for the aged," as it was called then. Then there were a couple of pleasant days in Northfield with his parents and sister Helen, before meeting my mother for some shopping in Chicago. I squeezed in a luncheon with Willard's sister-in-law Betty, who let me know that it was a very good idea to become part of the Hunter family.

Mary Louise paid me a visit halfway through the four-month training to go over wedding details. Army assignments, of course, determined most of our timing, but out of the small window of opportunity, she picked out August 22, just one month before my birthday, September 22. She hoped it might help me remember the date. Some of the years it worked.

Mary Louise: All through these weeks wedding preparations had priority. Where would we be married? My family pulled hard for Bay View, Michigan, where the family cottage had been central in our lives every summer as long as I could remember. Willard and other teammates pulled for Mackinac Island, where an MRA assembly, including many friends, would be in progress. There were strong words, and even tears, but in the end a ceremony at a Petoskey church and reception at the Bay View cottage won out.

This wedding was a challenge and stretch for my parents, both because of their serious qualms about the life on which their daughter was embarking and because of the hurdles imposed by wartime rationing. Mother made a round trip on the train, sitting up all night, from Bay View to Indianapolis in order to get some of the food, clothes, and flowers that seemed essential to her. She also engaged to play the organ at the ceremony her Bay View friend Dudleigh Vernor, composer of "The Sweetheart of Sigma Chi." She went all out, dealing successfully with every obstacle, and I was more than grateful then, and continue to be.

After four months' effort in Officers Candidate School, I received my commission. It was awarded on August 18, 1945, four days after V-J Day, which brought an end to the war all over the world. I became a second lieutenant in the U.S. Infantry, with orders to report in ten days back to Fort Benning as a Tactical Officer in the Officer Candidate School.

I had piled up a lot of memories, the chief of which was, near the end, arriving at the dining hall for breakfast the morning of August 7, 1945, and reading in the Columbus paper that an atomic bomb had been dropped on Hiroshima the day before. It was a new word for us—and a new world for everyone.

Since there were only a couple of planes out of Columbus each day, I had taken precautions months in advance of booking reservations so as to make the wedding on August 22.

Mary Louise: Willard, now a second lieutenant, arrived on August 19. He and two army buddies flew in a small plane to the nearby town of Charlevoix, and Dad and I went to meet them. Almost predictably, and to my father's lasting chagrin, we had a flat tire on the way back to Bay View, easily fixed by the army friends. Then a gala Sunday dinner with cousins, aunts, grandparents and all, and off to more festivities at Mackinac.

August 22 was sunny, with a brisk breeze blowing off Lake Michigan. By three o'clock all was ready. Three ministers waited at the front of the church: Willard's father; his uncle, William B. Lampe, who that year was moderator of the Presbyterian Church USA; and Frank Buchman. I recall getting awfully apprehensive at the last minute—such a big step into a lengthy uncertainty. But my father said later that I raced down the aisle, pulling him along.

We had to hurry away from the reception so we could catch the last ferry across the Straits of Mackinac to our thirty-six hour honeymoon at Cedarville, in Michigan's Upper Peninsula. I remember saying as we drove north, "After all this, I really don't feel as if I know you very well." But now I wonder, do we ever know another person "very well"? There are so many mysteries in human relationships.

-13-

THE CAPITOL CONNECTION

Soon after I was demobilized in December 1945, and Mary Louise and I changed pursuits from war to peace, we rejoined the MRA force that was engaged in California. We should have spent our first post-army Christmas in Indianapolis with the Merrells, but we had to be up and doing. We spent the first six peacetime months of our marriage in the Golden West.

MRA supporters in the Los Angeles area had purchased the former Women's Athletic Club, designed by the famous woman architect Julia Morgan, for use as a West Coast center. Those of us in the so-called full-time team lived in the homes of MRA adherents and worked with them to make MRA a household name in the West.

Harry Damerel of Covina, head of the Damerel-Allison Company, was a power in the California citrus industry, one of the pioneers in preserving orange juice so it did not have to be drunk right after squeezing. He was also taking leadership in the MRA thrust to bring a new spirit to the area. Although he was Republican, he was a longtime backer of Democratic Congressman H. Jerry Voorhis. To show how close the relationship was, Jerry asked Damerel to look after his San Dimas home while he was away in Washington. And he, with Jerry's parents approval, invited Mary Louise and me to live in the Voorhis home for the first six month of 1946.

Before going to Washington in 1936 Jerry had developed the Voorhis School for poor boys in San Dimas. It was financed by his parents, Ella Ward and Charles B. Voorhis, a Chicago automobile sales executive and Vice President of Nash Motor Company. I had known Jerry since 1939 when he and I shared the speakers' platform at Armistice Day ceremonies in Alhambra. He reminded his listeners on that occasion, now known as Veterans' Day, of Lincoln's call "to care for him who shall have borne the battle and for his widow and his orphan." I had also conferred with Voorhis a number of times on Capitol Hill. A reporter told me off the House floor, "There goes the hardest working member of Congress [the House had voted to name him just that]. The trouble is he brings up so many issues that hardly any of them go anywhere."

When Jerry left the Voorhis School to go to Congress, successor leadership was wanting and the place eventually closed down. The family gave the buildings and grounds to the State of California, and after World War II the campus became a staging area for building California State Polytechnic University (Cal Poly Pomona). Jerry and his wife Louise, however, retained the headmaster's house as their domicile in California, and this was the dwelling that Mary Louise and I were privileged to occupy in 1946. The wall gas heaters made me realize for the first time that even sunny California homes needed heat in the wintertime. We lived there through the spring until the Voorhis returned to conduct Jerry's last campaign—against the young Republican Richard Nixon.

Years later the Voorhis and the Hunters moved to retirement communities across the street from each other in Claremont, California. He was a deeply spiritual man, dedicated to the Episcopal persuasion, and he readily consented, with some conviction, to my interviewing him about his personal pilgrimage on a weekly radio program I hosted on behalf of the Claremont School of Theology.

Jerry and I visited from time to time at the University Club of Claremont. One of the programs I gave at the Club was on Will

Rogers. As usual I asked whether any one in the audience had met Rogers. Jerry came forward and said that when the family had the school in San Dimas, their baseball team was playing Webb School at the San Dimas Campus. There was a small crowd, and shortly a middle aged man wearing a hat came and sat by himself in the bleachers. Jerry suggested to his sister she go over and invite the gentleman to join them in the family area. So she went, engaged him in conversation, and soon said, "May I ask your name?"

"Will Rogers," he replied. The humorist's son Jimmy was playing on the Webb team that day, and Dad came out to watch.

The Voorhis-Nixon controversy, of course, made the two of them highly visible principals. I saw quite a lot of both of them in Washington—Voorhis during the war and Nixon after. Both were supportive of our work. So when in 1978 I was helping eastern Pennsylvania leaders put together events recognizing the hundredth anniversary of Frank Buchman, I thought the appearance of these two antagonists on a national unity platform might be a demonstration of reconciliation. Perhaps if they got together, they might work out some accord or healing.

Consequently, I invited both to come and speak. Nixon did not say yes or no, saying only that in spite of differences, he admired Voorhis. Jerry, however, I talked to in his downtown Claremont quarters, which looked like a congressman's office, the walls lined with autographed photos, in thin, black frames, reminders of the great and near great he had known in Washington. Jerry was thoughtful, but after a moment he said he had better decline. He did not wish to help in the slightest way a project that would help give Nixon a platform for any kind of comeback.

I asked Jerry, would he be willing to pray for him? He was

startled, but in a moment he said, "Well, I suppose a person should be willing to pray for anybody."

When Jerry's wife was dying, I went over to his apartment, and we said prayers together. I closed mine with the "Evening Prayer,"

> O Lord, support us all day long of this troublous life
> till the shadows lengthen and the evening comes,
> and the busy world is hushed, and the fever of life is over,
> and our work is done.
> Then by thy mercy grant us a safe lodging, a holy rest,
> and peace at the last,
> Through Jesus Christ, our Lord. Amen

At the end he said that was his mother's favorite prayer. He had heard her say it many times.

A Night at Ciro's

People used to think that if you lived in southern California, you'd see movie stars all the time. The fact is, you hardly ever do, that is unless you eat at places like Ciro's. I remembered that name from childhood movie-magazines. And it seemed like a good place for a party to celebrate a snaggle of birthdays coming up in May 1946. It was expensive, but you only live once. Situated at 8433 Sunset Boulevard, a spot later to be occupied by the Comedy Store, Ciro's was from the 1940s to the 1960s the glamorous watering hole of the stars. The powerful, make-or-break movie columnists Louella Parsons (Hearst) and Hedda Hopper (Chandler's *Times*) made the place their headquarters, complete with tableside private telephones wired direct to their news rooms.

The birthdays involved Mary Louise, plus her Vassar class-mate Eleanor Morris and Vera Louise Irwin, a friend and colleague from Indianapolis. The party broadened out and took in a happy group. Mary Louise and I drove in from San Dimas, where we were housesitting the Voorhis home. The birth of our first son, Tom, was four months away.

We invited my cousin Betty Lampe Erickson, who, while waiting for her husband Sheldon to come back from the wars, was in the movie business as secretary to a producer. Then there was Vera Louise's boyfriend, Alex Drysdale, a P-38 pilot from the Pacific Theater. Other members of the party were Don Birdsall, good friend, member of our wedding, and veteran of the Adak front; Ellen Lee Blackwell, a friend from Vassar days; and Francis Bradley, co-conspirator on the government front.

The menu, as you might expect, was exotic. Years later Ellen Lee told me she never forgot my admonition, "Folks, remember you have had breast of guinea hen. I don't want any one leaving here saying they had chicken." The hard-boiled, albeit efficient, waiters looked like Mafiosi hit men.

By good fortune, we were seated at the table next to that of Jack Benny and Mary Livingston and their friend Gary Cooper. Merle Oberon and her escort were seated at a table on a mezzanine level, and the Bennys invited them to come over and join them. They all seemed to be having a good time in happy conversation. They were also enjoying the blue humor of Joe Brown, a stand-up comic who had endless bawdy verses up his sleeve. At one of his lines, Benny doubled up and pointed his chin toward the floor. Jack was known for his professional courtesy in laughing hard at other comedians' material.

Peggy Noonan, presidential speechwriter, quotes Ronald Reagan as saying that in his Hollywood days, "he wanted to save the world, and joined every group that said it knew how."[1] This is an interesting comment, as during that period he participated in the MRA meetings in Los Angeles, had strategy lunches with

---

[1]Peggy Noonan, *When Character Was King* (New York: Viking, 2001), 54.

friends of mine, and endorsed the public messages.

In California I saw a good deal of Frank Buchman, who was still recovering his strength after a stroke and preparing for the challenging years ahead. He was not in the best of health. Sometimes, when I would come into the Clark residence where he was staying, in Los Angeles's Saint James Park, I could almost touch the gloom. People were accustomed to waiting for Frank to set the pace in all things, even the mood around the house. If he was happy, the rest were. If he was downcast, they took the cue. I regarded this as unhelpful and tried to wade in with a joke or a dash of gossip from downtown. Often he would smile, and soon everybody looked a little brighter. I made it my business, if I was unable to come up with big thoughts for the next ten months, at least to provide some human warmth for the next ten minutes.

Behind the Biltmore Hotel in downtown Los Angeles those days, there stood the Biltmore theater, since torn down. One of the plays we saw was *Harvey*, the whimsical tale of a lovable alcoholic who has a large imaginary rabbit for best friend. The play was later made famous by James Stewart in the movie. At the Biltmore, the lead was played by Joe E. Brown, the friendly comedian with the oversized smiling mouth. I mention the play because all my life I have quoted one of its lines.

Psychiatrist Chumley is lying on a couch talking about himself, in a reversal of roles. He says to Harvey's friend, Elwood Dowd, that what he would like would be to go to a place outside Akron with a beautiful woman. He does not want to know her name, and he wants to tell her everything about himself. Dowd responds, "But don't you want her to say anything at all?"

Chumley replies, "I would want her to put her hand on my brow and say, 'Poor thing—you poor, poor thing.'"

I think that would be real cool.

Washington Assignment

Following the first six months of our marriage in California, we were based for most of the next six years in Washington D.C. When senior officials like Ken Twitchell and John Roots were away, I was in charge of the Moral Re-Armament office in the commodious home of Albert H. (Jack) and Connie Ely at 2419 Massachusetts Avenue on Embassy Row.

Buchman, as I have said, got me started on our program on Capitol Hill, enlisting members of Congress to work for a new spirit of honesty and teamwork. It was he who urged me to attend the Congressional hearings and get to know the people.

One of our duties was to recruit American delegates for international conferences. In September of 1948, we gathered together a delegation of industrialists and political leaders to attend the MRA conference at Caux-sur-Montreux, Switzerland. The group included Senator Harry Cain of Washington, Congressman George Smathers of Florida (who was to defeat Claude Pepper for the Senate in 1950), and former Senator Rush D. Holt of West Virginia, the youngest person ever to be elected to the upper house. Also the mayor of Richmond, Virginia, a former governor of Virginia, the Rev. J. Blanton Belk of Richmond, Larry Alldritt, a Miami electrical engineer, and Jim Newton, former Firestone executive.

I was impressed with the power of the staff people on Capitol Hill. Senator Cain's administrative assistant, Art Burgess, committed his boss to the trip before the latter heard about it. He knew the senator's upbeat interests and his schedule and thought the trip would be good for his image. It was interesting to learn how these types think. He said it was all right for the senator to be high minded, but Art's job was to get him reelected. "In order for him to be a great senator," he said, "he has to *be* a senator."

Our plane was a Pan American charter. Pan Am vice president Sam Pryor and another Pan Am executive, Mark McKee, hosted a dinner for our party at New York's Roosevelt Hotel the night before we took off. In those propeller days trans-Atlantic air passengers had to stop at Gander (Newfoundland) and Shamrock (Ireland) for refueling. After we left Gander that night and were out over the Atlantic, our engines began to go out one by one. Returning to Gander for repair, mechanics said they found iron filings in the engines. It was too melodramatic to talk about sabotage, but Larry Alldritt recalled that a man who had visited his machine shop in Miami, and who turned out to be a Communist, had shown unusual interest in the timing of the charter.

We were twelve hours late arriving in London, in the evening instead of morning. A hotel reception for us was laid on, attended by a half dozen British members of Parliament who livened up the meeting, when they agreed with a sentiment, by saying, "Hyuh Hyuh" (British for "Hear Hear"). Senator Cain, one of the best orators in Congress, was chosen to speak for the Americans. He timed himself by lighting a cigarette at the outset of his remarks, and closing when it had burned down.

This is reminiscent of Bishop Fulton J. Sheen, the witty Catholic orator with the flashing eyes, whose mid-century television show at one point topped that of Milton Berle, "Mr. Television" himself. Sheen was asked how he could finish his program so accurately without a moment to spare either way. He replied, "I have a memorized wind-up, often including a quotation, that takes forty-five seconds. When the red hand on the clock sweeps to the forty-five second mark, I drop whatever I am saying and go directly into my conclusion, which is completed when the hand is straight up."

After the conference at Caux, Jim Newton, Larry Alldritt and I took most of the party on a short tour in Europe. We conferred one evening with the Prime Minister Alcide de Gasperi of Italy, who came out from a session of the Parliament to chat with us. Congressman Smathers carried a tape recorder with him, which he used to interview statesmen for his radio program in Miami. Back in London, Smathers linked up with his old friend Jack Kennedy—they had both been elected to Congress in 1946—to take a three week tour through England and Ireland.

The next year's delegation to Caux, in June 1949, was an official one, created by a United States House of Representatives resolution authorizing Speaker Sam Rayburn to appoint and finance five representatives, three Democrats and two Republicans, to attend the conference in Switzerland. Prince Preston of Georgia was named chair of the delegation. They flew in a U.S. Air Force plane.

James Wadsworth of New York and some of the most powerful men in the House hatched this trip, originally proposed by my colleague DuBois S. Morris, Jr. They included Charles A. Eaton of New Jersey, James P. Richards of South Carolina, E. E. Cox of Georgia, Wadsworth, and Preston. Unfortunately, of these leaders, all of whom were well informed and supportive of MRA, only Preston decided to go and the selection of others fell to lower-tier members who had little concept of the mission. The newspapers caught up to that, and the overall image was not the best. Somebody suggested that the trip was a breach in the barrier between church and state, whereupon John McCormack, Democratic leader in the House, commented, "Separation of church and state was never meant to separate a person from his God!" The delegation brought back a beautiful Swiss clock from Switzerland as a gift to the Speaker, probably paid for by the taxpayers.

One consistently critical British journalist wrote that the project was put over in the House when few members were present. On the contrary, the seats on the floor that morning were almost all full, an unusual situation. The House was convening at eleven instead of the normal twelve o'clock because of an important matter coming up after the Caux vote. I was in the gallery.

Our government team determined that I should go to Switzerland also to help the delegates. The five were mostly very attentive and took in the conference events. We punctuated the earnestness with some sightseeing. One day, we took them to Gruyère, home of the famous cheese. Frank Buchman, who was pretty good himself at showing sights to visitors, mildly reprimanded me for not having the Americans in their assembly seats during an afternoon meeting that featured a key French industrialist who was pivotal to the Franco-German rapprochement that was to lead to the Schumann Plan and European Union.

When the delegation returned home, Preston made a thorough report to the House of Representatives at the microphone in the well of the House. He showed me his text in advance, and I think I took too many liberties. Later I told him I should have let him say it just the way he saw it.

Not long after that, I called on Representative Albert Gore of Tennessee, father of Al Gore, Jr. Gore the elder was upset over the House's action and said he would never vote for another such project. He was disturbed also about some elderly lady in Sweden who he heard had given money to MRA. I wondered whether he would have been so agitated had an intelligent lady given resources to a cause he liked. But there was no point in arguing with someone as steamed up as he was. I never saw him again.

While I was attempting to hold things down in Washington, I received a letter from my friend John Vandewater, an attorney in Whittier, California. He was to join the law faculty at the University of California at Los Angeles, specializing in labor law, and was later appointed U.S. Labor Commissioner. In 1947 John wrote me there was a new congressman elected from Whittier by the name of Richard Nixon. He thought I should try to make his acquaintance. I did, and it lasted a long time.[2]

Not long after that I was in California, and Rowland Harker, a missionary back from Japan, took me, and my sister Helen, out to Whittier to meet the Nixon family. Rowland had been a debate partner of Nixon's at Whittier High School. The visit resulted in many more and led to warm friendships with the family, particularly Hannah, the mother, whom Richard properly called a "saint" (I have never seen a person live her faith so completely). Helen helped Hannah baby-sit for Tricia and Julie at times and was her escort when she attended a Moral Re-Armament assembly in South America, where students apologized to her for stoning her son on a trip the year before. The last time Helen and I saw Hannah was in a rest home in southern California. She was rather far gone with Alzheimer's disease, and before long we attended her funeral in the Friends Church in E. Whittier.

---

[2]At the Republican National Convention in Philadelphia in 1948, I was cruising in the unlighted areas back of the speakers' platform after midnight when I ran into Dick Nixon. He was a first year Congressman, and he and I had spent some time together in Washington. I did a piece on him in the *New World News*, a monthly newsmagazine, featuring a picture of him and Pat on a bicycle amid the Tidal Basin's cherry blossoms. The photo is displayed in the Nixon Library in Yorba Linda. Although we were now approaching the wee hours in the convention hall and many had left and gone to bed, Walter Judd was delivering a fiery address, vintage Judd, placing fellow Minnesotan Harold Stassen's name before the convention for the GOP nomination for president. Behind the platform Nixon greeted me by name with smiles, as political people do. I said, "Dick, I think Walter is going to stampede this convention for Stassen." Judd had a mesmerizing effect on me; he might, I speculated, on every one else. I thought the power of his oratory at a convention just might be like that of William Jennings Bryan, who stampeded himself into the Democratic nomination in 1896. "You might be right," Nixon said, "unless the Dewey people have it already bought and paid for, with ambassadorships and everything." (The next day New York Governor Thomas E. Dewey was nominated for the second time. Stassen would run for president every four years for the rest of his life.)

Only once did I see Richard Nixon's father, Frank, when he was sick in bed behind the family grocery store/restaurant in Whittier. He was twinkly, yet lived up to his feisty reputation. When Richard reached the Senate he had his father come to visit him in Washington and tried to interest him, without much success, in attending congressional hearings to occupy his mind.

It was during this time that Richard brought to the attention of the Senate the World Assembly for the Reconstruction of Pacific Relations in Los Angeles, sponsored by Moral Re-Armament. I wrote a speech for him on the subject, and it appeared in the Congressional Record July 5, 1951. In it he spoke of attending with other senators the MRA assembly in January of that year at the Shoreham Hotel in Washington. He said he had been particularly impressed by the men he met who were formerly Communist Party leaders in their countries and who had found a superior ideology.

The family members we came to know best and have kept up with over the years are Ed and Gay Nixon. I first met Ed in a hospital near Whittier when he was recovering from an oil drilling accident. He looks like his mother and his brother, and is a dozen years younger than Richard, whom he regarded as a father figure. In 1966 Ed was a laboratory technician with the Bell Company in Washington, and he took our Bob and me into his home for a week while we were finding a house for the duration of my sabbatical at the Brookings Institution. Ed later went into international business with his other brother, the late Donald Nixon, and he and Gay have based in the Seattle area, where she has been an elementary school teacher. Ed said Don's wife Clara was the glue that kept the tribe together, remembering all birthdays. Ed got us tickets for the dedication ceremonies in November 1990 of the Richard Nixon Library and Birthplace in Yorba Linda, California.

I used to go with Jack Ely, a friend of hers, to call on Mary

McLeod Bethune in Washington. She was a grand lady with unusual acceptance among the major races in the nation's capital. Jack was a beloved presence in the city's black community. When he spoke at one of their churches, the chairman said, "He may look like a white man, but he has a real black heart."

Mrs. Bethune had founded Bethune-Cookman College in Daytona Beach and then had become an advisor to Presidents Roosevelt and Truman, having been made a divisional director in the National Youth Administration (NYA). She helped us get better African-American representation into our publications, and she endorsed our wartime booklet *You Can Defend America*, saying "it breathes the spirit of the Emancipation Proclamation." In later years she said that the human fellowship she had found there described—resulting among other things in a dramatic reconciliation with a prominent white dowager of Richmond, Virginia—was "the crowning experience of my life." A big-screen color film, with that title, was made of her career.

The two greatest Congressional friends we developed during my time in Washington, men who throughout their lifetimes backed the cause and worked out the new spirit with their families and political careers, were representatives Charles B. Deane of Rockingham, North Carolina, and Charles E. Bennett of Jacksonville, Florida. Later, when Charlie Deane was dying of cancer, I was able to get President Nixon to write him a note to the hospital from the White House, which pleased him. The two had arrived together in the House of Representatives in 1946.

During one of my visits to Charley in the hospital, he told me his guidance was that I would write his biography. At once I treated the idea as a significant assignment and started to pull together some notes. I talked to a North Carolina foundation that backed historical projects, but we ran out of time, and the family was not all that keen on including an outsider on the project.

During the war and early postwar years we saw something of Senator Truman and his family, especially the women. In our scrapbook we have invitations from Bess Truman to two White House teas in the 1940s. My wife, Mary Louise, and our friend Frances Roots (later Hadden), a gifted, professional pianist, who could play anything Margaret could sing, spent afternoons at the Truman home, often joined by Margaret's college friend, Jane Lingo. They were both students at George Washington University. Bess's brownies earned rave reviews.

On the opening day of the baseball season in 1948, the Hunter family was given box seats that happened to be located a few feet from the president's, where all three Trumans were ensconced with friends. The president, first in war, peace, and baseball, threw out the opening pitch, and when it was time for the seventh inning stretch, led the crowd to their feet. In between, I got the impression Margaret was trying to catch my eye, and when she did, she put out a friendly little wave along with her million dollar smile.

The month before, March 1948, three years into her father's presidency, Margaret accepted Mary Louise's invitation to join us for tea at our house in Washington's Cleveland Park sector. We were surprised she could be reached by a direct call to the White House. She arrived right on time, being delivered by a long, black White House limousine, accompanied by a driver and a Secret Service agent. Already her father was having problems with General MacArthur, but of course she gave us nothing more than a discreet glimpse.[3]

Margaret was on a soprano solo concert tour that spring and volunteered the opinion that critics are often frustrated performers. Two years later her father scorched one unfavorable critic, Paul Hume of the *Washington Post*, with an irate letter that achieved instant fame.

I was first introduced to Hubert H. Humphrey in 1939 by some of his labor friends in Minneapolis, and we had breakfast together at the Minneapolis Club. He was still a political science instructor at Macalester College and was yet to become Mayor of Minneapolis. While he was mayor in 1945, Hubert and his wife Muriel attended a summer MRA conference at Mackinac Island accompanied by a team of Minnesota labor leaders. I was just back from military service, still in uniform, and had the privilege of introducing him when he addressed the assembly.

In his senate years we saw him and Muriel in Washington from time to time, and during his 1968 candidacy for President, while war protesters were storming outside, I was included with Hubert at a small lunch at Pepperdine College, Los Angeles, at the invitation of President Norvel Young. Rajmohan Gandhi, a senator in India and grandson of the Mahatma, said that of all the American statesmen he met, Humphrey breathed the ideas of Moral Re-Armament better than any of them. Hubert accepted my invitation to participate in the Frank Buchman centennial in 1978, but in the end he became too ill to address the convocation at Muhlenberg College they hoped for, and he

---

[3]Margaret was unusually gracious, for someone in her position, about answering letters. She and I had kept up quite a few exchanges when I was in the army, and I wondered whether she might have felt she was making a small morale-building contribution by responding to people in uniform. At any rate Margaret Truman (Mrs. Clifton) Daniel, who reflected the genuineness of her parents, is one of the most charming people I have ever met.

died as the centennial year began. Muriel succeeded him in his senate seat and sent a message to the occasion.

Another warm friend who backed the cause with considerable enthusiasm was Sid Carnahan, a Congressman from Missouri. He at one point joined a special train delegation from Washington to New York for the Broadway premiere of the musical *Jotham Valley*. A number of people whose opinions we respected urged us to take it to the Great White Way. The most enthusiastic was Senator Blair Moody of Michigan, formerly Washington correspondent for the *Detroit News*, who had succeeded Arthur Vandenberg in the Senate. The play had been well received across the country but the hard nosed New York critics kept their enthusiasm under control. One headline ran, "Cast Enjoys Jotham Valley."

Sid Carnahan was also a delegate to the international Moral Re-Armament Assembly at Mackinac Island in 1951. Years later his son, Mel Carnahan, became Governor of Missouri and then ran for the Senate in 2000 against John Ashcroft. Mel and his son were killed in a plane crash, and Sid's daughter-in-law, Jean Carnahan, was named to take the Senate seat Mel had won posthumously.

One spring, probably in 1949, on returning from the west coast to Washington, I unexplainably contracted the mumps. I had no idea where I could have picked this up. But between planes at O'Hare Airport, not wishing to take home whatever I had to the kids, I decided to stop in Chicago, booking myself into the Conrad Hilton Hotel. Not knowing what the trouble was, I checked with the hotel doctor, who diagnosed it at once and wanted me out of there pronto. Without delay I landed in Chicago's Cook County Hospital, a huge operation—much of it charity related. I was pretty sick, and my brother Stu, who lived near Evanston at the time, came to see me every day. Mumps being a children's disease, the walls in my area were adorned with huge painted animals. Cook County is also a training hospital, and teaching doctors were constantly bringing groups of medical students to check me out. I was up against rates charged to non-Cook County residents, and I had no money. Fortunately Mary Louise had become friends the summer before at the Democratic National Convention with Elizabeth Conkey, a member of the Democratic National Committee and a power in the Cook County government. In a few minutes my bill was wiped out.

Back home in Washington, knowing the reputation of mumps, I was concerned about fecundity. Not a problem in this instance apparently, for after that we were able to conceive our third son, Bob.

Immigration

Part of my government relations portfolio was to look after immigration matters. We had personnel from various countries coming and going, and their status needed to be clean and sharp. Because of misinformation, apparently planted somewhere in the Immigration and Naturalization Service (INS), thirty of our full time people in early 1949 were hung up on various U.S. borders, some of them for weeks.

On this issue I may have made my most valuable contribution to the practical work of MRA. Senator Alexander Wiley of Wisconsin, ranking Republican on the Senate Immigration Committee, arranged for me a personal conversation with Tom Clark, Attorney General, who in turn sent me to my friend INS Commissioner Watson Miller. Clark and Miller were favorable to our work and had taken some part in it. Miller at once asked me to draft a memorandum, which he then sent to all INS field representatives, declaring in part:

Moral Re-Armament is a world force having as its principal objective adequate ideological preparedness of free nations for the ideological conflicts in which the world is now engaged. . . . Its objectives are recognized by the [Justice] Department as worthy and helpful in the strengthening of democratic forces throughout the world.

The document was dated April 1st, and I was worried that when it landed on some desks, it might be regarded it as a joke. Apparently it was not, and all personnel in question were at once released to cross the borders.

Charles Lindbergh heard about this outcome and asked our mutual friend, Jim Newton, if he could talk to me about it. Lindbergh had been stymied in bringing into the country a number of Romanians whom he was trying to help. We met one Sunday afternoon in Jim's room at the Shoreham Hotel in Washington, and I told him what I had done. Lindbergh seemed to be encouraged by the possibilities and thanked me. His modesty came out, I thought, when he expressed the hope that nothing he did would in any way interfere with MRA's relationship with the INS.

A few weeks after the border hang-up was solved, in the summer of 1949, I was in Chicago drumming up attendance at the international conference at Mackinac Island. As a fellow Midwesterner in and out of Chicago, I had met Mrs. John Alden Carpenter, the North Shore socialite who was the wife of the famous composer and the grandmother of Adlai Stevenson III. She had long been a warm friend of our work and on this occasion she came to a downtown luncheon where I was a speaker. After the luncheon she approached me and asked me whether I could come to the Carpenters' apartment that evening to meet some Chicagoans she thought might be interested. Of course I accepted.

The next week Peter Howard came through Chicago. He was

the British journalist who had become number two in the work and was to succeed to the world leadership of MRA when Buchman died. I always thought Peter saw in me the qualities that the English find objectionable in Americans. At any rate he decided out loud that I had ambitiously elbowed my way into the Carpenter circle and made clear his view that this was not acceptable behavior. Not long after, the question came up again with Buchman at Mackinac. He allowed that ambition was a bad thing, that in Chicago it was OK for me to work with travel agent types, but that people like Mrs. Carpenter were the equivalent of cabinet-level, and that it would be best to leave such to others.

I was outraged. I doubt whether either of these superiors knew that just three months earlier I had single-handedly made my way with a member of the U.S. President's cabinet and saved the bacon of a considerable segment of Buchman's full-time force, releasing them for service in advancing his cause. But in that climate, defending oneself was ascribed to the sin of pride, particularly defending oneself against a hierarchy that was always right. I was being a terribly Loyal Lieutenant. I saluted and kept my mouth shut. I should have spoken up, though, and I wish I had. It would have been good for them to hear what I had to say. And it would have been good for me to say it. One of my professors who later read my account of this asked, "What happened to absolute honesty?" An excellent question. I replied that at that point absolute unselfishness would take precedence. At any rate, in the words of the old spiritual, I "never said a mumblin' word."

Although my work with the Immigration Service may not have been all that much appreciated by my friends, it was prominently noticed by a professional enemy. Tom Driberg for months left his seat in the British Parliament and international spy work to write a scurrilous book.[4] In it he quoted from the INS memo I had drafted which pronounced that MRA's objectives were "recognized by the [Justice] Department as worthy and helpful in the strengthening of democratic forces throughout the world." Driberg was at a loss to explain such an evaluation coming from official sources, but opined that it was "a result, no doubt, of long-sustained pressure and intrigue."[5] I had been in Washington ten years and had learned how the city operates, but I would prefer to substitute "persuasion" for "pressure," and "strategy" for "intrigue." I never met Mr. Driberg, but I like to think he paid me a compliment.

---

[4]Tom Driberg, *The Mystery of Moral Re-Armament: A Study of Frank Buchman and his Movement* (New York: Knopf, 1965), 149.

-14-

MACKINAC ISLAND

After 1950, the Hunter family base shifted to the Midwest. We lived for a time with Mary Louise's parents in Indianapolis, where all three of our sons were born, and in 1952 moved to Mackinac Island, Michigan. We were a family of five, including Tom, Bill, and Bob—at that time aged six, four, and almost 3 months.

Mackinac Island, the historic crossroads of the Great Lakes, had been the scene of international Moral Re-Armament conferences every summer since 1942. We made our home there five years, 1952-57. Tom and Bill both learned how to read in the Thomas Ferry School, housed in the old Indian headquarters, over which Indian agent Henry Schoolcraft presided the previous century. It was from Schoolcraft, incidentally, that Henry Wadsworth Longfellow obtained north-country Indian stories for his epic poem *Hiawatha*.

The Straits of Mackinac (pronounced "Mackinaw") connect Lake Michigan with Lake Huron, and they separate Michigan's upper and lower peninsulas. Mackinac Island, nine miles around, lies to the east in Lake Huron. In the seventeenth and eighteenth centuries, it was the military and commercial key to the control of the Northwest. Waterways were the only route to the west, and the Straits of Mackinac were the funnel through which, in the North, everybody and everything had to go. Whoever commanded Mackinac Island controlled the Northwest. Three nations' flags have flown from the old fort on the bluff—French, British, and American.

The first explorers were French missionaries, among them the Jesuit Père Marquette (1637-75), who is buried at a mission he founded across the straits at Saint Ignace, named for the founder of his order, Ignatius Loyola. At the close of the French-Indian wars, Mackinac Island was ceded to the British, who then lost it at the end of the American Revolution. During the War of 1812, the British recaptured the fort in a surprise overnight attack (you can still see "British Landing" there), but lost it again to the Americans in the Treaty of Ghent in 1814. The island fort continued, and after the Civil War it became America's first national park. In 1895 the U.S. government turned the area over to the State of Michigan, which for over a hundred years has maintained most of the island as a state park.

Through the centuries, Native Americans have made Mackinac Island a focus of activity, with some traditions of peacemaking between tribes. That is one reason why the place became a central location for John Jacob Astor's fur trade, following the War of 1812. The warehouse barns are still a stop on the horse-drawn tours.

A young army physician, Dr. William Beaumont, made medical history after a French Canadian trapper named Jacques Saint Martin was shot in an 1822 island fight. Beaumont helped restore him to health but was unable to close the man's stomach wound. Since the doctor could see inside directly, he was able to make important discoveries about digestive processes. He sometimes had to bribe Saint Martin to come back so he could observe at first-hand what happened to food as it worked itself through a live intestinal tract. The *Reader's Digest* story (October 1951) was entitled "The Window in Saint Martin's Stomach."

The first Protestant missionary was the Rev. William Ferry, who built a church and a mission school for Indian children. The latter subsequently became a hotel, and it was at Mission House during the Civil War where Edward Everett Hale, who was holed up in a three-day storm, wrote his most famous story, "The Man Without a Country."

A park commissioner in the centennial year, 1995, said, "The essence of the island is history, horses, and fudge." No automobiles are permitted on the island. Eleven fudge shops emit their seductive aroma on the village's short main street, and the crowds that come on the ferries and leave the same day are called "fudgies."

My relationship to Mackinac Island had begun in 1941. It was wartime, and Howard Blake and I were commissioned to negotiate with state officials in Lansing for conference space. The wartime showings of *You Can Defend America* in the Detroit area had brought key labor and management personnel into the Masonic Auditorium, including people like automaker Henry Ford and autoworker Victor Reuther. Morale was a vital factor in the Detroit industries supplying war materiel. Some viewers said they thought they knew what they were fighting *against*, but this helped them see what to be fighting *for*. People felt the need for a place where different groups, particularly labor and management, could have time to work out together what a new quality of life would mean in practical terms.

Among the people we worked with there was a growing interest in developing a conference center in the Upper Midwest. State officials said they had an abandoned hotel on Mackinac Island that might be revived—the Island House—a relic of bygone days when the Vanderbilt interests constructed the Grand Hotel, and the Cudahys, the Swifts, and the Armours had huge mansions on the bluff.

The Moral Re-Armament teams had the seasoning of two successful summer conferences—1940 at Lake Tahoe in California and 1941 at Maranacook in Maine—and they had developed enough experience to take on a major conference program at Mackinac. Henry Ford, with the help of Charles A.

Lindbergh and others, was building bombers at his Willow Run plant, near Dearborn. Buchman was talking to Ford about establishing a "Willow Run in the War of Ideas," a center, he said, "to produce the ideas that will answer the 'isms.'" He likened the re-tooling of industry to the re-tooling of "our thinking and living to meet a changing world."

The Fords had Buchman and a number of the team as their guests at the Dearborn Inn. The couple attended several of the showings of *You Can Defend America* and enjoyed a huge birthday party at the Inn. After one of the showings, Henry asked to talk to me, the "bad guy" in the show. Mostly, it turned out, he wanted to give me a brief talk on the simple virtues. I recall he especially mentioned the Ten Commandments.

We gave one performance for cadets for whom Ford was responsible, who were being trained at a naval training station in his plant. That evening, Charles Lindbergh was Buchman's chauffeur, calling on him beforehand at the Dearborn Inn, and delivering him back afterwards. Unfortunately, according to Lindbergh's diary, on the rides to and fro Frank chose to tell Charles about the congratulations he had received for his sixty-fourth birthday. Charles knew all about congratulations and might have responded to more personal spiritual fare. But who knows? Lindbergh also wrote that Ford grumbled about Buchman overstaying his welcome at Dearborn. A year later though, when Buchman lay at death's door with a massive stroke, Ford telephoned him with his personal greetings.

Mrs. Ford suggested to Frank that Mackinac Island might be a place where he could get away for some rest. Buchman visited the island and thought something could be made of the Island House. Governor Murray van Waggoner had seen *You Can Defend America* in Detroit, picked up on the conference center idea, and turned the negotiations about Mackinac Island over to his administrative assistant, C. W. Lucas. In the spring of 1941,

Blake, Warner Clark, and I conferred on the subject with a number of state officials in Lansing.

The key figure was Wilfird F. (Bill) Doyle, chairman of the Mackinac Island State Park Commission. Doyle wielded state-wide influence for half a century and was a perpetual member of the Park Commission. In his day job he was Lansing's leading lobbyist, whose clients included Michigan chain stores, theaters, and beverage industry. Bill was enthusiastic about our coming to Mackinac. It was wartime, and there was a general depression in the tourist industry, exacerbated by the islanders' low morale. To Bill Doyle, we looked like a ray of economic hope. He invited forefront MRA operatives Howard Blake and his wife Peggy, and Charles S. "Sciff" and Helen Wishard, to come to the island, where he put them up for the summer of 1941.

Because of depressed times, the Island House had gone back to the state for inability to pay taxes. The oldest hotel on the island, and one of the largest, it was becoming an eyesore, and the state was anxious to get it moving again. MRA held out promise. It was ours for a dollar a year. The old dowager inn on the lakefront, with its four stately porch pillars, was in terrible shape, "being slowly carried away by the rats," as one official said. Our team tore into the grease and grime, propped up the ancient stove, and got the place ready in time for the arrival of the first delegates in July 1942.

Its north-of-the-border counterpart, *Pull Together Canada*, joined the American cast of *You Can Defend America*. The two shows were invited to present a joint performance at the Grand Hotel, and much of the top echelon of Michigan leadership was there. Afterwards, Bill Doyle mounted the stage and said, "You've brought a new spirit to the north country. We hope you will make Mackinac Island your permanent national head-quarters." It was the last kind word Bill Doyle said about our work. For the next twenty years he single-mindedly threw rocks in the road. We never knew why. My own theory was that the man was a big-time promoter for special interests, and although I never heard him accused of corruption, if a wave of honesty should sweep Michigan, it might cramp his style.

Out in Los Angeles I had a chance to talk with a prominent newspaperwoman about how to approach the press in Michigan. She was Adela Rogers St. John (1894-1988), one of the century's foremost Hollywood chroniclers. As William Randolph Hearst's premier woman feature writer, she was front and center at national events as well as movie happenings, and covered the Lindbergh kidnaping case in 1935, which she named "the trial of the century." She was a great help to us for a spell in the 1940s. She spoke at meetings and at the MRA center, formerly the LA Women's Athletic Club on Flower Street, conducted classes for our younger people in how to write for and deal with the press. During a lull, I had a conference with her on our public relations problems at Mackinac Island arising from lobbyist opposition. Her strategy, like Manny Strauss's, was not to importune editors, but to create action that they had to cover.

Before we went up there, Bruce Anderson, manager of the Olds Hotel in Lansing, and nephew of R. E. Olds, the automaker, told Howard Blake and me there were two people on the island whom we should not fail to see—W. Stewart Woodfill, owner of the Grand Hotel, and Otto Lang, manager of the Arnold Transit Company. Although there now are several ferry companies competing for the lucrative passenger traffic, Arnold, owned by Senator Prentiss Brown, was the only one at that time serving the island, and it still carries most of the freight. Both Woodfill and Lang were helpful and cooperative throughout the tenure of MRA on Mackinac Island.

The Grand Hotel, whose bright gleaming front is the big visual landmark from the lake, had been established in 1887 by the Vanderbilt railroad interests. Young W. Stewart Woodfill signed on as desk clerk in 1919, at age twenty-three. Working up to manager, he bought a third interest in the enterprise, sold it to his partners just before the stock market crash, and bought the hotel back in 1933 for "peanuts." Over the fifty years of his association, Woodfill made the 262-room hotel an international showplace, advertising its 682-foot-long veranda as "the longest porch in the world." So many walk-through tourists turn up every day that the hotel has had to charge admission just to look-see. The "Esther Williams Pool" on the front lawn is named for the swimming celebrity who starred in a movie filmed on the island. (*This Time for Keeps*, 1947, featuring also Jimmy Durante and Lauritz Melchior.)

Woodfill was the driving public relations force that persuaded the people of Michigan to undertake the Straits of Mackinac Bridge linking the upper and lower peninsulas of Michigan. Designed by David Stein, the bridge has the world's third longest span. The Steins were regular visitors to plays and other events on the island while the bridge was going up. It was completed in 1957, and every Labor Day, led by the Governor of Michigan, thousands walk across the bridge in an annual rite. W. Stewart Woodfill died in 1984 at eighty-eight.

Each summer, over a thousand people from all over the country and some foreign nations came to the MRA teamwork conferences at Mackinac Island. During the war, armed forces personnel spent their leaves there. Behind the Island House was a barn theater, a rustic wooden structure that lent itself to plays and meetings.

When I was drafted into the U.S. Infantry in 1944, I said farewell to Frank on the Island House walk. George Welsh, mayor of Grand Rapids, known in Lansing as "the Silver Fox" because of his white mane and political acumen, was there and spoke to me afterwards, more than once, of being moved by our father-son style of off-to-war farewell that day.

After the war, I reported back for civilian duty at Mackinac. My first highlight assignment was being chosen at a 1946 meeting to introduce Hubert Humphrey, who as mayor of Minneapolis addressed the conference.

As the operation expanded, the Island House was soon outgrown; homes and small hotels were rented, and some purchased. Among the heaviest contributors to land investment for new campus areas were our friends, T. Henry and Clarace Williams of Akron, Ohio.

New construction in the island complex was needed, and in the 1950s a bigger theater was built. Other conference facilities and residence buildings began to rise on Mission Point. When our family moved to Mackinac, I was among several dozen volunteers from around the world who committed their energies to the construction. During the summers Mary Louise and the boys did considerable shuttling between the island and her family's summer place in Bay View/Petoskey, thirty-five miles to the south.

The design of the new theater (1954-55) called for roof-support beams made of peeled pine logs. To secure these, we obtained permission from the forest service to harvest ripe trees on Bois Blanc, the largest of the three islands in the Straits of Mackinac. Reginald Sheppard, a sourdough handy man from the Canadian woods (he could recite in toto Robert W. Service's "The Cremation of Sam McGee") undertook to procure the logs. He figured it would be a fine educational experience for two greenhorns to assist him, and he selected Eric Peterson, an accountant, and me. Reggie was a good teacher, and we felled the big timbers, trimmed them, and moved the logs toward the beach with our cant hooks in a couple of days. The test then was to transport them across four miles of water to Mackinac Island. Reggie also had enlisted Bob Amen, a superb mechanic who had helped keep in shape the tanks on General Patton's Red Ball Highway in France. He brought an outboard motorboat over from Mackinac. We tied the twenty-five logs into a three-tier boom, secured them behind the boat, and set off.

What we did not count on was a strong headwind, which within an hour completely neutralized our forward motion. The outboard motor was singing a sweet song at what might have been some six miles an hour, but the opposing wind was above that, and we sat still in one spot. It became clear that we would run out of gasoline, with no progress at all. And night was coming on. A command decision was called for. We agreed with Reggie's judgment—the logs had to be cut loose. The consoling thought was that the wind would probably blow the logs back to Bois Blanc's northwest shore, from whence they came. With any luck we could go back and get them another day. So the logs were set loose to drift back and the boat went on.

To calm our shattered nerves on our return to Mackinac, we put in for a brief stop in an eastern cove on Round Island. By this time it was really dark. We still had enough gas to jump across to Mackinac, first waiting for a huge ore boat to pass. When you are underneath one, it is huge. Arriving on Mackinac Island, our relieved families were glad to see us. Friends had been watching for us with spyglasses, but we did not believe those who told us that the church bells that were ringing when we arrived were for us.

Three days later, we retained Bud Welch and his Buddy-L launch, went across, found the logs fairly close together on the Bois Blanc shore as we had hoped, chained them up and towed them back.

Superb Swedish woodsman Sven Lindstrom peeled the logs, notched and fitted them with bolts. Today you can see those logs towering toward the roof at the Mission Point Theater. This construction was so satisfactory that a similar style was adopted for the Great Hall, a few yards to the east. The latter has a circular design, and when one of the Indian workers first saw it, he with some wonder quietly said, "Tepee." It has informally been called that ever since. For the Great Hall logs, we went to a commercial firm which felled the trees near the famed Tahquamenon Falls, trucked them to the harbor at Saint Ignace, and floated them to the island.

The story of these buildings, which Jim Doherty, editor of the Petoskey News Review, said was the first major wintertime construction in the area, is recorded in a documentary film, for which I had the honor to be both a cameraman and the narrator: Mackinac—Island of Renaissance. The movie can be viewed at the Fort Mackinac Museum.

All of this activity required domestic and logistical support, and a number of families in MRA's full-time force, including ours, became year-round residents. In addition, I was made legal representative of Moral Re-Armament, in charge of Lansing relations. Except for the isolation, Mackinac is an attractive place to live. The style of life is rural; sleigh bells jingle on real horses and real sleighs (no cars summer or winter). In those days you would go into the woods before Christmas and cut your own tree. The straits freeze over, and enough of the rest of the Great Lakes also to shut down shipping. An exciting experience is afforded when the harbor freezes over on a quiet night. This provides a glassy surface on which people can skate unrestricted throughout the harbor. Not so when the water is riled during the freeze; then it is too rough, and a confined rink has to be shoveled out.

One Saturday, I decided to accompany some island folks on a walk to Saint Ignace, six miles across the ice. The straits currents sometimes eat the ice from underneath, creating thin spots that keep things interesting. Walkers often place pine bows around a danger area. Knowledgeable teamsters drove horses across. More recently, propeller-powered aerosleds have become popular. On that Saturday, the dozen of us went over and back on foot. Some were shopping to dodge island grocery prices; others were picking up welfare checks.

When we lived on the island, the American iron and steel business was more prosperous than it later became. A steady procession of huge ore boats plied their way past Mackinac Island on their way from the northern Minnesota mines to the steel mills of the Chicago area. (Those destined for Ohio and Pennsylvania passed several miles to the east of us.) Sometimes these ore boats would salute and sometimes not. Perhaps they were greeting only fellow lake craft.

One imposing, classy craft stood out from the rest and charmed every one's imagination. It was the *Wilfred Sykes,* flagship of the fleet owned and operated by the Inland Steel Company. It measured 678 feet long by 70 feet wide, and its graceful lines gripped all whom it passed. It was brand new when we first saw it, having been commissioned in 1950, and at the end of the century it was still carrying ore from Duluth to East Chicago.

One Sunday as the family was having dinner at Bennett Hall, by the waters of the straits, we talked about the *Sykes* and how great it would be if the captain of that magnificent ship would greet us when going by Mackinac Island. So we took a paper place mat from the table and the boys wrote on it a letter to the captain of the *Wilfred Sykes,* in care of the Inland Steel Company, Chicago. We had heard that the Great Lakes greeting signal was three long blasts on the horn and two short ones, so that is what they asked of the captain. Within a month it started. As far as I know, it has been going ever since, and whenever the boat plows the narrows between Round and Mackinac Islands, the people know the captain remembered. Maybe there is a sticky, refrigerator-door type of reminder, fixed near the pilot's wheel. All because three little boys fifty years ago wrote a letter to a sea captain on a table place mat.

Ralph "Speed" Couls, local haberdasher and dry-cleaner, was the town's genial mayor. He was a good friend and a lovable alcoholic. We were concerned that the Doyle forces might exploit his weakness in the interest of municipal decisions damaging to our position on the island. Through one winter a few of us tried to give Speed some fellowship and had a kind of modified AA meeting with him night after night. We sang a lot of songs, told stories, ate ice cream sundaes, and played records like "Cool Water."

Because of his life style, Speed was always having business problems, like being behind with his creditors. One day the Red Ball Overshoe Company from Mishawaka, Indiana, telephoned and diplomatically asked about the chances of his paying what he owed.

"You're not worried about that bill, are you?" Speed asked, "because if you are, I'll stop. There's no use both of us doing that."

Speed was well liked on the island, and when he died, the local Protestant church was packed out. The eulogy was given by the Rt. Rev. George West, formerly Anglican bishop of Rangoon. Every one wondered whether there would be the customary unreal statements about the departed, and what the distinguished visiting cleric would have to say about somebody like Couls. The Bishop was up to it. He had had an operation for throat cancer, and couldn't talk very loudly. In his firm stage whisper he declared, "They say that . . Speed . . .had his problems. . .(*pause*) . But then . . . so have I."

Our oldest son Tom was six when we moved to Mackinac. He had a stuttering problem, and is still grateful, four decades later, to Pat Squires, his one-room teacher, who had the same difficulty and took special pains to draw him out. Also she put her foot down when anybody tried to make fun of his distress. For years, every time any of the family returned, we visited with her. Tom was good friends with Dorman Kumsi, of an island Finnish family, a daredevil who knew not the meaning of fear, especially when tobogganing down the island bluff around blind corners onto Main Street.

Second son Bill remembers chasing frogs for fish bait, in a pond-swamp on the far side of the island. He says that whenever he is on a ferry approaching the harbor, it feels to him like coming home. In recent years the family has returned, complete with grandchildren, for a ritual nine-mile bike ride around the island.

Bob was two months old when we moved to Mackinac. When he was four years, he struck up a friendship with Frank Buchman, who told Bob he wished he had a hundred like him. "Holy Mackerel," Bob responded, "that's a lot of people." Bob rode a little tractor around the horse paths, and when Frank commented on his "truck," Bob asked Frank's secretary to inform her boss that it was not a "truck" but a "tractor."

Near the close of our Mackinac Island years we acquired a friendly beagle, which Bill dubbed "Frisky," an accurate assessment of the pooch's personality. It was a gift to us from Donald and Margaret Jamieson of Indianapolis.[1] Frisky was a durable dog, very patient with the boys. He lived a long life for a dog, fifteen years, thoughtfully expiring in the spring of 1970, just before our youngest was graduated from high school.

---

[1] Donald was a nephew of Booth Tarkington, and, along with his brothers, was a model for the Hoosier novelist's characters, Penrod and Sam.

-15-

AFRICAN ASSIGNMENT

The Mackinac Island chapter of my life was punctuated by a year in Africa, 1953-54. Frank Buchman in 1952-53 had taken a force of 200 people and three plays to India, Ceylon, and Pakistan. There was talk of a sequel mission to the continent of Africa, and I hoped I could get in on that. I applied and was accepted. The family was safely ensconced at Mackinac Island along with other families running the winter operation there, and I do not exactly possess the handy-man skills that the construction and maintenance at Mackinac needed. The Africa opportunity, with its speaking, writing, and public relations assignments, was something I could do.

I was away for a year, and whether this deprived the boys of anything I could have given by living with them and their mother that year I do not know. We regarded the mission to Africa as a major engagement in the world war of ideas. And war separates families. It looked like an opportunity to make a difference in constructive race relations on a key continent and to help leaders of both sides to effect peaceful and corruption-free transfer of control from the European colonialism of the past to the indigenous leadership of the emerging African nations. I signed on. As it turned out, Buchman withdrew from the mission on account of health.

The first stop was Caux, Switzerland, the international conference center that was opened in 1946, immediately after the war. In 1945, two Swiss professional men, Philippe Mottu, a diplomat, and Robert Hahnloser, an engineer, had visited

Mackinac Island. They were convinced that a Mackinac-type center in Europe was needed immediately to provide moral and spiritual direction for postwar reconstruction. They returned to their country, found an abandoned resort hotel at Caux-sur-Montreux, 3,000 feet above the eastern section of Lake Geneva with a beautiful view of the Dents du Midi. Caux Palace was 200 yards long and eight stories high, and they were able to save it from demolition. Scores of fellow Swiss were enlisted to make the financial sacrifices necessary to acquire and restore the beautiful old architectural treasure. They changed the hotel's name from "Caux Palace" to "Mountain House," recognizing its spiritual roots in Mackinac's "Island House."

Now in 1953 I was lucky to be at Caux during the visit of Robert Schumann, former foreign minister and prime minister of France. Schumann told the press of the background help MRA had been to him and Germany's Konrad Adenauer in reaching the postwar agreements between France and Germany that led to European union.

As we prepared at Caux for the expedition to Africa, we made side trips to Berne, the Swiss capital, and to Salzburg in Upper Austria, where we conferred with the regional Prime Minister, Josef Klaus. The coffee shops, we were told, were much as they were in Mozart's day and more business was being done there than in offices.

In Frank Buchman's absence, the leadership of the Africa safari was delegated to Bremer Hofmeyr of Johannesburg and Roland Wilson of London, two longtime international activists in the program. Hofmeyr, a Rhodes Scholar, came from a distinguished South Africa family, his cousin, Jan H. Hofmeyr, having been deputy premier. In the tradition of the team, those delegated for top responsibility in any project or area appropriated the Buchman style of leadership. The assumptions were that God spoke with special clarity to those in charge, that wisdom emanated from the top, and that every one else was to follow along. At first, Hofmeyr and Wilson made the decisions, and we loyally backed them. After a couple of months this changed, and decision-making became more collegial.

Our task force consisted of eighty-four people from nineteen nations. One was Mme. Lottie von Beuningen, whom Jim Newton and I had accompanied across the United States in 1940. She had returned home to Holland, and had done outstanding work in the Dutch resistance to the Nazis. Another grand dame was Lady Hardinge of Penshurst, whose father-in-law had been Viceroy of India. Also in the group was Seumas, the Marquis of Graham, and his mother and sister. Later, upon the death of his father, Seumas became the Duke of Montrose and a member of the House of Lords. Others in the party were British stage personalities Ivan and Elsie Menzies. Ivan was known around the British Commonwealth countries as a Gilbert and Sullivan star. He performed some numbers on our trip.

In addition there were ordinary folks—young people, business types, homemakers, and me. At Caux, we buckled down for intense rehearsal before departure. The stage was to be our entry into the nations we were to visit in Northern and Southern Rhodesia (now Zambia and Zimbabwe respectively), South Africa, Nigeria, and Ghana. It was decided to present Peter Howard's play The Real News, dramatizing a new spirit in the world of journalism. Later, on the road, we added The Boss, also written by Howard, portraying an approach to industrial teamwork. In The Real News, I drew the role of St. John (British pronunciation: "Sinjun") Fish, the hard-bitten editor.

Loudon Hamilton played major characters in both plays, the publisher in the first and the title role in the second. Loudon was one of Frank Buchman's original associates, and was sometimes introduced in jest as "In Whose Rooms" Hamilton, for it was in his rooms at Christ Church, Oxford, that the Oxford Group began in 1921. In the old days, Frank used Loudon as his warm-up man for meetings large and small, as he was good at telling funny Scottish stories. His timing was perfect. When he was through, the audience was mellow. He is long gone, but I can still remember a half dozen of his best ones.

Before we left on the African trip, Ray Purdy, American MRA executive, had an interview with John H. Johnson, from 1942 the creative publishing genius behind *Ebony* magazine, long-running chronicler of African American personalities and events. Johnson was interested in our expedition and asked that I file stories with him on what we found. Also, a Chicago radio station requested tape-recorded reports. I began doing both the writing and the recording, but soon stopped; I was unable to get the material past Bremer Hofmeyr. He felt my style did not fit with what he thought was called for.

Preparations all in order, our party left the Geneva airport early in December 1953 for our trip south. The first stop was Athens, then Cairo, Nairobi, and finally Lusaka. At Cairo I bought a string of miniature wooden camels, which we still use as supporting cast in our family's crèche at Christmas time. Stepping off the plane at Lusaka, the soft tropical air reminded me of Florida's. The vegetation was tropical, and red clay was everywhere. We were met by local friends and billeted in homes. Having spent time in London, I was struck by the fact that the English in Central Africa were more "English" than were their countrymen in England. Customs in the old country had changed, but in Africa the British accent, the British tea, and trappings of "empire" remained the same, only more so.

Many times we ran across the trail of empire builder Cecil John Rhodes (1853-1902) who began enterprises there at age seventeen, developed the Kimberley diamond mines, formed the De Beers Mining Company, and virtually built a nation of his own. Rhodes, who became prime minister and virtual dictator of the Cape Colony, dreamt of British rule "from Cape to Cairo." He restricted voting among illiterates, saying the franchise was for "all civilized" persons; developed the area to the north, naming it "Rhodesia" in his honor; and left his fortune to public service. His bequests included an endowment for the Rhodes Scholarships, providing for 170 students each year from former British colonies, the U.S., and Germany to study at Oxford University.

Our play, *The Real News*, was well received. For one thing, it was live stage entertainment, rare in Central Africa. Some of the revolutionaries I talked to were afraid MRA was a cooling chamber to reduce their passions for freedom and justice. Others, like Godwin Lewaneke, an activist with the African National Congress (ANC), reacted more positively. He had attended the conference at Caux the year before and said that as a result of his experience there, he believed he had become a more effective revolutionary, as he was now "fighting with clean hands." Many in the independence movements were also concerned over the crippling effect of corruption.

The original inhabitants were Bushmen and Hottentot, with Bantu (Zulu, Swazi, and others) coming down from the north in the seventeenth century. Before that the Dutch, needing a food and water-supply station for their explorations of the Far East, settled the Cape of Good Hope and always claimed they had occupied the region before the black people did. The British captured the Cape in 1806, and the two European powers struggled for a hundred years, culminating in the Anglo-Boer War of 1899-1902, won by the British.

Henry Macnicol from Scotland, who had arrived in South Africa before us, confirmed that the race issue was paramount. People could talk about little else. There was great apprehension. It was a wrench to see the signs on railway carriages, "Slegs blanks" ["Whites only"]. One knowledgeable businessman said, "We figure we have ten more years before one of the bloodiest revolutions of history." That was 1954. It took forty years for the revolution to be realized, and miraculously, with universal gratitude, it came in relative peace.

Alan Paton (1903-88), former national president of the South African Liberal Party, had achieved a world reputation for his book, *Cry, the Beloved Country,* a heart-rending novel about apartheid. He had just brought out another we were reading as trip preparation, *Too Late the Phalarope.* Bremer Hofmeyr had known Alan Paton earlier and went to visit him and asked whether he needed to have quite so much sex in the book. Paton's reply was noncommittal.

Albert J. Luthuli, who had been the chief of South African Zulus and had been a teacher in the mission school where he had been educated in his youth, was now since 1952 the president general of the ANC of South Africa, a post he held until his death in 1967. When we saw him in 1954, because of his anti-apartheid activities, he was under house arrest, and could go no more than a few yards beyond his tiny farmhouse in Groutville on the Indian Ocean coast. So a group of us drove out there and put on a condensed version of our show for him in his living room. He was a tall, handsome, friendly man, active in the Congregational Church, and appreciative of our fellowship. Six years later, in 1960, he was allowed to leave the country to accept the Nobel Peace Prize, awarded in recognition of his non-violent struggle against racial discrimination, the first African to receive this prize.

One of the most spectacular sights was Victoria Falls on the Zambezi River at the western end of the border between Zambia and Zimbabwe. Beside the falls stands a heroic striding statue of David Livingstone (1813-73), the Scots missionary-explorer who in 1855 was the first white man to come upon the falls. We spent Christmas there. The falls are one mile wide and plunge

420 feet into a narrow gorge. They are five times as wide as Niagara and two-and-a-half times as high. The plumes of mist and the roar of the cascade are perceptible from twenty-five miles away, and the Africans have long called the falls the "Smoke That Thunders."

Other memorable sights included the trip on the famous Blue Train from Johannesburg to Cape Town, reminiscent of transcontinental American rail journeys in former days. Cross-country auto travel reminded us of early times of the automobile in America, except that on long stretches there was one paved lane down the middle, requiring cars approaching each other to move their right set of wheels onto the dirt shoulder. Cars had to be rugged to stand the conditions, and at that time Chevrolets were regarded as the most durable.

We had a chance to see how the government of South Africa worked. The legislative headquarters were in British Cape Town, the administrative in Afrikaner Pretoria, and the judiciary in between in Bloemfontein. When the parliament sat from January to June, the government offices in Pretoria packed up files and moved to Cape Town. I had a chance to sit in the legislative hall and watch Parliament. The English Liberal Party was the minority and expressed opposition to the Afrikaner majority, but it was said that on the racial question, their views were much the same.

Cape Town is a spectacularly beautiful city. One of its charms is the thin cloud that rolls over the edge of flat Table Mountain at four o'clock every afternoon. It is called the "Table Cloth on Table Mountain."

One evening in the Cape Town City Hall, a Moral Re-Armament meeting packed out the Hall's public auditorium. Both black and white speakers were on the program—the first time a Cape Town public platform had been integrated. The speakers included Dr. William Nkomo, founding president of the African National Congress Youth League, and George Daneel, Spring-bok rugby football great who became a "dominie" (preacher) in the Dutch Reformed Church, the religious bastion of the Afrikaner rulers. Before the meeting, I was standing on the steps of the City Hall and fell into conversation with Albion Ross, who was covering the evening's event for the *New York Times*. I told him I had long been impressed with his coverage of the crushing of Czechoslovakia by the Soviets in 1948, especially remembering his comment that the Czechs were amateurs overcome by professionals. He said that's the way it was. He made an observation about South Africa: "These people [the Afrikaners] are not fascist rednecks out to oppress everybody. They are caught in a trap, and they act as creatures do in a trap."

Just then, the *Cape Times* reporter who was assigned to City Hall that evening came by and said he had to do something else that evening, and would I cover the event for him? So I did. Afterwards, I got a few together to check the story I had written. The only correction I recall was to change "bloody revolution" to "blood revolution," because, I was told, the word "bloody" in British circles is profanity. I took the copy to the news building, and the next morning the story appeared on the front page of the *Cape Times* under the headline, "White, Black on MRA Platform." Months later, in June 1954, Frank Buchman, in his annual birthday world message, devoted several paragraphs to quotations from that article. He never knew I wrote it.

From South Africa, our party flew to West Africa, where we presented the plays and held conferences in Nigeria and Ghana. We took our message not only to Lagos, the capital of Nigeria, but reached all sections of the country, including the far north on the edge of the Sahara.

West Africa, which is near sea level, received low attention from European colonists, who preferred the higher altitudes of eastern Africa with its more hospitable environment. Somewhere in Nigeria there is a monument to the mosquito, which kept the white man out. Also there are no natural harbors on the west coast. We were there before an artificial one was built at Lagos, and we were intrigued by the ancient methods they were still using. Ships had to stand out from shore while their cargo was unloaded by hand into dinghies that were then rowed to harborside.

Nigeria is the most populous nation in Africa, thirty-three million when we were there in the 1950s, nearly a hundred million today. Its territory is more than twice the size of California, and is rich in resources, especially oil. We found that there were three main tribes and languages—Hausa in the north, Yoruba in the west, and Ibo in the east. The latter two regions showed the Christian influence of a century of Protestant evangelism; the north was solidly Muslim.

A few years earlier in Washington I had come to know the strong man of the east, Nnamdi Azikiwe, affectionately known as "Zik." He was an American-educated Ibo who was in control of eastern Nigeria, the leader of his own, the dominant political party, the National Council of Nigeria and the Cameroons (NCNC), and publisher of sixteen newspapers. Tall, handsome, powerfully built, eloquent, he could adapt his remarks to any kind of audience, whether well-educated elite or illiterate peasants. He had attended both Lincoln University in Pennsylvania and Howard University in Washington D.C., and when he returned in 1950 to deliver a commencement address at Howard, he accepted our invitation to come to tea. He made a hit with us by surmising that our four-year-old Tom had "a high IQ."

Azikiwe, one of those working for independence from the British, had become so frustrated with the foot-dragging in

London that he had decided to go east of the Iron Curtain for help. En route to Prague, he accepted a friend's invitation to visit the Caux assembly center. The experience had changed his perspective.

Azikiwe began to see that his problem might be more with his fellow Africans than with the British. He picked up on the idea of taking responsibility for his own part in the breakdowns instead of blaming others. He heard a song he started to quote, "When I point my finger at my neighbor, there are three more pointing back at me." The idea that "it's not who's right but what's right" became a basic policy with him. He canceled his trip to Eastern Europe and returned to Nigeria, where he apologized to opposition leaders for his conduct in past dealings. The result was that he and his fellow negotiators developed a unity in their approach to London officials, who then felt a new confidence in the African leadership. Nigeria was the first African nation to achieve independence without bloodshed.

Now in 1954, Randulf Haslund and I drove over to the Azikiwe home in Onitsha on the Niger River, forty miles west of Enugu, the Ibo capital. We had a friendly visit with Mrs. Azikiwe and Zik's mother, who were looking after the four children while their father was busy in Lagos. After independence, Zik became the first governor general of Nigeria. He encouraged the election of the Hausa leader in the north as premier, since that area had the larger population. Over the years, we exchanged Christmas cards, and on the last one he hand-wrote. "We are still working things out on 'not who's right but what's right.'"

Our 2,000-mile rail journey included a week in Kano, capital city of the Hausa region at the base of the Sahara desert. We were there during Ramadan, the holy month of fasting for the Muslims. Our host was the Emir of Kano, who turned out to be completely in the pocket of the British authorities. He would make no decision without checking with them. The British police, having had severe riots during Ramadan the year before, were concerned that we did not fully comprehend the volatility of the situation. They asked us for an orientation conference at their headquarters, and of course we accepted. We did have very good showings of the plays to very big audiences, with no disturbances.

One officer spoke a memorable line: "It is important that justice be done, but it is also important that justice appear to be done."

Paul Hogue had ongoing responsibility for coordinating the MRA action in Nigeria. He and his wife Maia and team had settled in a home for headquarters on the other side of the river from Lagos, a nice house, but plain and with the non-plumbing outdoors. Bremer Hofmeyr believed such an important regional outpost should be in a more prestigious location and might be more influential if located in the vicinity of the parliamentary buildings in downtown Lagos. Paul believed he was in the right place, identifying with surroundings where labor people felt comfortable. I think Paul won, as he was staying on there, and Bremer was moving along to our next and last stop, Ghana.

Ghana was formerly known as the Gold Coast, and the British had ruled the territory under that name for over a hundred years. Official independence was to arrive two years after we were there, but in 1954 Kwame Nkrumah was the president, and in charge of the government in Accra. As a young man, he had been a pupil at Aggrey School in Ghana under the tutelage of Norman Young, a Canadian whose widow, Grace, and daughter, Eleanor, were in our party. Norman was killed at Dieppe in the costly Canadian commando attack on the north French coast in 1942. Grace and Eleanor had a happy reunion hour with Nkrumah in his office. Dr. James Kweggis Aggrey, "Aggrey of Africa," for whom the school was named, had been one of the luminaries of African advancement in former days, and was the originator of the figure that likened black and white people to black and white keys on the piano. "You need both for harmony," he said. The piano keyboard symbol graced the front gate at Aggrey School.

Whether it was the climate, the hard work, the diet, or genetics, or all of the above, I fell apart on the west coast of Africa. I had hit a manic streak and apparently spoke inappropriately from the platform and played fast and loose with my part on stage. I was relieved of my roles in the play and in public relations and was put up in an apartment with medical doctor Andrew McKay to cool off. This separation lasted for a couple of weeks, when it was decided it would be best if I would return to the United States.

The team arranged for me to fly to London with John Main, who was on his way back to Canada. This took three days, as the small plane flew only in daylight hours. We stopped overnight at Dakar and at Tangier.

Frank Buchman thought I should return to my father in Minnesota, which surprised me, as I wondered whether he remembered I was married. My father was annoyed. He figured that since I was Buchman's "employee," my health and welfare problems were no longer his but Frank's. Of course, Buchman did not operate like a corporation, but rather like a family, and his philosophy for health and welfare was to farm it out wherever he could.

At any rate, I rejoined Mary Louise, the three boys, and my sister Helen for the month of August on Woman Lake in northern Minnesota. After that I visited my parents, who had retired to California, and I then returned to Mackinac Island to participate in the 1954-55 winter's construction program.

-16-

HIGHS AND LOWS

The Roller Coaster Complication

Two to three million Americans experience manic depression. The problem is also called the bipolar disorder. One tends to shrug off the statistics. "That means somebody else." But it has happened to our family. It has happened to me.

The National Institute of Mental Health defines the affliction as involving episodes of serious mania and depression. Medical reporter Gloria Hochman's description: "The person's mood usually swings from overly 'high' and irritable to sad and hopeless and then back again, with periods of normal mood in between."

It is a condition that makes its victims feel as though they could conquer the world, and then later convinces them that life is not worth living. It has many forms and its timing is not predictable. One writer notes that it is sometimes accompanied "by dazzling creativity." Dr. Kay Redfield Jamison calls it "the only psychiatric illness with a good side."

I first became aware of the condition in myself in 1954 when I was on my assignment in Lagos, Nigeria, on the west coast of Africa. It did not strike me as an illness, rather a liberation. But others called it "some kind of break." I had to drop out, return home to America, and regroup.

After that, I found myself in memory flashing back to earlier incidents of depression and elation to which I had ascribed various other causes. My first year in Harvard Law School was a real drag. Family photos back home at Christmas time in 1936 show me as unusually sad. That depression may have been a reason why I did not do well on my Rhodes Scholarship candidate interview with the Minnesota committee that December. Conflict at the time over choice of career is discussed in another chapter, but chemical bases were doubtless present. Later depressions I have since identified, as in Los Angeles in 1946, shortly after I was mustered out of the army, when everything was gloomy for a month or two. Friend Scotty MacFarlane said he was impressed by my determination—no matter how low I felt—to pick up my guts and carry on.

What may have been the first real manic came at Lake Tahoe in 1940, and it presented itself as a spiritual experience that was enthusiastically affirmed by colleagues. It may well have been the kind authenticated by pioneer psychologist William James in his *Varieties of Religious Experience*. It came as a release from inhibitions, improved relationships with people, brightened perception, and increased sure-footedness. It played a role in the renewal that bubbled up in the MRA task force at Lake Tahoe.

My acceleration lasted several months before it dried up, and was triggered again the following year at an extended meeting in June of 1941 at Plymouth, Massachusetts. My release came about, I thought, as a result of my taking up certain corrective matters with the leadership of the group, things I had locked up. These two bursts of emancipation, in 1940 and 1941, appeared to result from things I said or did. After that the eruptions emerged without identifiable antecedents. When they came, they appeared to be super-creative, putting me in touch with the wisdom of the ages and the inspiration of the prophets and statesmen. I had been impressed with the claim of William James:

Most people live, whether physically, intellectually, or morally in a very restricted circle of their potential being. They *make use* of a very small portion of their possible consciousness, and of their soul's resources in general, much like a man who out of his whole bodily organism, should get into a habit of using and moving only his little finger.

Boston: *Familiar Letters of William James*
Atlantic Monthly, 1920

This has often been translated into the idea that we use only a tenth of our brains; the other nine-tenths goes unused. I was convinced that I had found the secret of tapping into the total resources of body, mind, and soul.

I likened myself to the Old Testament character of Joseph in Egypt. When depressed I languished as he did in prison. When released, my obviously superior judgment would surely be recognized by Pharaoh and drafted for national leadership.

Twice I declined professional help and had to be committed to a hospital, in each case for three months. The first time was in 1956 when I was working on a construction job at Mackinac Island, and started throwing my weight around in a big way, making it clear to those in charge how each job should be done. Accompanied by a doctor friend, I was sent for a break to Minnesota.

Escaping at one point from what I regarded as unwarranted domination, I headed for the railroad station in Saint Paul. Missing the Soo Line train back to northern Michigan, I conscripted a taxi to beat the train to the first stop in Wisconsin, thirty miles up the line. It was the fall of 1956, and Richard Nixon was campaigning for reelection as vice president. I had known him as a congressman when we lived in Washington, and I thought I would catch him at his campaign stop in Manistique.

Arriving too late, I took the bus down to Saint Ignace. I made the mistake of phoning my arrival time, and at the bus station I found a carload party waiting for me. One of them was Irene Gates, a medical doctor, and their message was that they all, including Frank Buchman, believed I should return to Minnesota, and were prepared to drive through the night to deliver me. The size of the party and their idea of timing surprised me, but there was nothing for it but to go along.

At a gas station stop at four in the morning I thought of running away through the woods, making my way to an airport, and flying to the Menninger Clinic in Kansas. If I was going to get psychiatric treatment, I was going to go first class.[1] I decided to forego the hassle though, and before dawn we arrived at the Miller Hospital in Saint Paul, later razed to make way for the Minnesota Historical Society Museum. There, Ralph Beal on one end of the steps and Ken Twitchell on the other were standing guard to avert my escape.

I accepted the family blandishments to enter the hospital for check-up and tests, which I assumed would take a couple of days. But when the doctors wanted to keep me there longer I said I would not submit to that kind of control. At that point my father and wife decided to blow the whistle and obtain a court order. Earlier, when I was talking with Dad in the living room of a friend's home in Minneapolis, all of a sudden he broke down and cried. My situation was that devastating to him, breaking his

---

[1] A dozen years later I would be invited to head up the development department at the Menninger Clinic. I had been earlier contacted in Washington by the clinic's treasurer, and did some public relations consulting for them, including an annual meeting at Topeka. Some time after that, Dr. Roy Menninger, president 1967-93, encouraged by his brother Walter, came to call on me in 1968 at the Independent Colleges office in Los Angeles. He gave me cogent reasons why I should stop what I was doing and join up with them. However, it did not look to me like the next step for either of us, and I was able to get them someone better qualified than I, Claremont friend William Cassell, who later became president of Heidelberg College in Ohio.

heart. I of course thought that he just did not understand the situation.

As time went on, Dr. David Norman, the psychiatrist on my case, told me that this stay would be a matter not of days but of weeks. The stay eventually stretched out to three months. Near the end, he said, "When you realize you are sick, then you are getting well." Norman told me that there was no rational basis for the three months; it was purely a matter of experience. The record showed that patients completing three months were less likely to return than those released sooner. He also said that psychiatric practices of twenty years earlier looked to his fellow professionals as barbaric, and he was quite certain that what they were doing in 1956 would look barbaric twenty years hence.

The manic side of the business is delicious. Sophie Tucker, the last of the red-hot mamas, is credited with the line, "I've been poor and I've been rich, and believe me, rich is better." Manic is rich. If you are not Superman, you are at least Douglas Fairbanks, or Walter Mitty. Nothing is impossible—physical, social, or political. Same with treasures. When Mary Louise and I were engaged, I was an officer candidate at Fort Benning. Walking into a fine jewelry store in Columbus, Georgia, I ordered a beautiful $2,200 diamond ring. I figured the money would turn up from somewhere. Friend Jack Ely said, "I've often thought about backing you for public office, but you show no fiscal responsibility." I was persuaded to return the ring. A generous friend provided a family heirloom I could give my beloved.

When I hit that big high in Africa in 1954, I was sure I could run a four-minute mile. On a tennis court with a friend who was a fine player, I was confident I would beat his socks off. By some fluke he beat me. Playing the lead in a stage drama throughout Africa, the crusty editor of a big daily, "St. John (Sinjun) Fish," I completely changed the interpretation without warning to the other players. I made a speech to a crowd of Nigerians in the Onitsha town square, on the Niger River, and became the incarnation of William Jennings Bryan.

Aging? I had the feeling that my molecules would not be affected by the normal processes of time, and that somehow I would substantially retain a youthful physique, as in Shangri-la. A camera without film would somehow take pictures anyway. Nudity was an urge. I kept wanting to take my clothes off, when no one was looking of course, and I went skinny-dipping at night whenever I could. I thought that everybody who became concerned over my comportment would understand if only they had the proper insights. I had special revelation to which others were not privy. And besides, I was going to be elected to high office in 1960. In fact I *was* elected to office in 1960, not all that high, receiving a unanimous vote to become Secretary of the Far West District of the American College Public Relations Association. That wasn't what I had in mind. Like I say, a funny thing happened on my way to the White House. The prophetic signals got switched.

In England I was telling people that I was the obvious actor to play the role of Lindbergh in the forthcoming movie *The Spirit of St. Louis.* Somehow, I was passed over in favor of James Stewart. I also announced I would soon be writing a syndicated daily column in the American newspapers, with the impact once exerted by Will Rogers. I did write a newspaper column for sixteen years, although it was weekly, not daily, and carried in two, not four hundred, newspapers.

With the manic, fluency improves, memory brightens, uncertainty flees, fear fades, and self-confidence zooms. Between Plymouth, Massachusetts, and Boston, I once was driving a carload of passengers and believed I could pass a car going up hill and could trust my personal radar to inform me about oncoming traffic.

Depression, on the other hand, is literally the pits. You don't want to do anything. All is a slow drag. You can't think of things. You don't remember what you should. You feel bad. Food tastes terrible. It does not help at all for people to try cheering you up. If they tell you things are not as bad as they seem, they simply don't understand that things actually are worse than they seem. Happy material is irrelevant. I found relief listening to Johnny Cash sing, "I'm So Lonesome I Could Cry," and Tracy Nelson giving out with "It's a Sad Situation." Those songs understood the state of affairs. Tennessee Ernie Ford's gospel songs also helped.

My family felt a threat in the highs more than the lows. When I start talking too fast and become more active, it tends to alarm them. This is the mood that has caused so much trouble in the past. But depression? Well, he's depressed and will get over it.

When depression settles in, a person feels totally abandoned. Here is how our youngest son Bob expressed his in a last journal entry,

GOD, WHERE DID YOU GO? Daddy - what happened to you? Why did you leave me? Mother - where are you now? I'm still here - right here - I didn't go anywhere - I need you now more than ever - I have nothing to stand on - Why did you go?

Echoes of the Psalmist come to mind, "I will say unto God my rock, why have you forgotten me?" (42:9)

When the depression is really bad, you know that *anything*, maybe even eternal damnation, would be better than what you are going through right then. You are simply not going to put up with this superimposed torment one more day. You are going to take charge.

I was not really suicidal, at least not suicidal enough, except for a day in 1969. I had a weekend leave to go home to Claremont from the Glendale Adventist Hospital. Sunday morning while Mary Louise was listening to the broadcast of our church service, I got out a big butcher knife from the kitchen, and was going to do it while she was trying to find some comfort amidst the distress her husband was causing her. But I chickened out. As she drove me back to the hospital, I contemplated opening the car door and throwing myself into the traffic. But in both instances, I could not bring myself to inflict such a trauma on her. Back at the hospital, I was going to walk away and jump off a nearby highway bridge being constructed. But a friend saw me and waved, and I knew I would soon be targeted by the staff. That particular depression was ended by electroshock therapy at the hospital.

But I became clear that one suicide per family is enough and I never again seriously considered it as a way out. I would stay and take it. "You decided that in the name of love," my counseling training supervisor, William Zeckhausen, observed at Laconia, New Hampshire, in 1972, when I was taking training to be a counselor.

The idea of a political career, abandoned years earlier, was now totally unrealistic, confirmed two years later when disclosure of a similar history caused Senator Thomas F. Eagleton of Missouri to be booted off the national Democratic ticket in 1972.

One Sunday afternoon, our youngest son Bob (the two older boys were away at college) and Mary Louise's mother and I had been out to dinner at the Pomona Valley Mining Company restaurant. I had been made chairman of a blue ribbon, self-study commission at the church, and the depression was making me deeply dread the meeting that afternoon. It was clear to everybody in the family, particularly myself, that I was mired in the Slough of Despond. Back at the house, I was brushing my teeth, and Bob, seventeen, came to me. With tears welling in his eyes he said, "I don't like to see you so sad, Daddy. I love you." As I write this, tears are welling in *my* eyes.

Just as things are not as terrific as the manic persuades you they are, they are not as bad as the depression wants you to believe. One of the doctors helped me to treat the depression like a third person. When exaggerating the bad, I could say, "That's not me, that's the depression talking." I found that speaking and preaching while in depression were agonizing. Yet if I stuck to it, the presentations did not come out too badly, and the ones delivered under each condition—whether high or low—were in the end of much the same quality.

In the spring of 1970, I took on the task of reorganizing the public relations of the Claremont School of Theology in six months. I was pretty depressed at the time, and recall having a bad time forcing myself to return to the campus each afternoon after having lunch and a nap at home a few blocks away. Sometimes when my superior asked me a question, I couldn't think of anything to say. Yet during that time I was able completely to revamp the corporate image of the institution through a new look in the publications and to bring an aggregation of the nation's top religion writers to the campus, resulting in major features in *Time* magazine and the *New York Times*. Although those months were agony, I still was able to produce.

Abraham Lincoln, who spent much of his life under what was once called "melancholia," has once again supplied a pertinent story. Speaking in Milwaukee in 1859, he produced this treasure:

> It is said an Eastern monarch once charged his wise men to invent him a sentence, to be ever in view, and which should be true and appropriate in all times and situations. They presented him the words:
> "And this, too, shall pass away."

How much it expresses! How chastening in the hour of pride! How consoling in the depths of affliction!

Although I was never very keen on a manic period "passing away," the depressive found much hope in the idea. Many a time I have been carried along by gritting my teeth and hanging on, knowing the condition, some day, would pass away. There is a relevant line repeated three times in the gospels:

"The one that endures to the end shall be saved." (Matthew 10:22)

A sign in a homeless shelter counsels:
When you come to the end of your rope,
tie a knot in it and hang on.

My French professor at Carleton, James Pyper Bird, was fond of encouraging his students with a paraphrase of this verse:

"And let us not be weary in well doing; for in due season we shall reap, if we faint not." (Galatians 6:9)

Right away I was faced with the issue of honesty, what to reveal to others. Could I get a job coming out of a mental hospital? Does a college want someone with such a record on the staff? I decided to face it head on. I thought I needed to bare my soul to only one officer at Macalester College, and decided to tell President Charles J. Turck. Before we came to an agreement, I told him I had recently come from three months in the hospital and told him why. Unscientifically he looked across the desk, smiled, and said, "You look all right to me." I never told any one else at the college, even though my immediate superior was curious as to why I should have changed careers after eighteen years.

Three years later in 1959, when President Robert J. Bernard of the Claremont Graduate University interviewed me with an eye to my joining his staff to set up a development program, I told him, still with some trepidation. He also smiled and said, "Those things happen." After that, I never felt I needed to bring the matter up again. I have never ducked the issue, or lied about it, but I have not advertised it.

The mental health stigma is painful. After one of the hospitalizations, a doctor said not to worry, my treatment was similar to a gall bladder operation, and people should so regard it. Nice words, but people do not so regard it. They do not equate mental health and gall bladder health. I have found over the years that I do much better, am more acceptable, am more readily considered for leadership, among those who do not know my background.

Those who do know are polite. But they put me in a box. This is true, I believe, even of members of my family. When our youngest son Bob, a freshman at Harvard, made his first suicide attempt by swallowing sleeping pills, the family kept the news from me for twenty-four hours while Mary Louise and a minister friend made Bob's hospital arrangements. Unsure of my reaction, they, perhaps unconsciously, assumed the role of parents to me as well as parents to Bob. They assigned me the role of a son that needed caring for. It feels something like bearing the mark of Cain.

When our boys were of high-school age, our family was considered as possible hosts for a year to a visiting international student sponsored by the American Field Service (AFS). As soon as the medical history came out, that opportunity ended.

The stigma is becoming less acute in society at large. Rosalynn Carter, wife of the thirty-ninth president, has made mental health a special concern. In 1996 she wrote to constituents of the "important news" of "historic legislation" requiring insurers to cover mental health disorders on a basis equal to physical illnesses.

The use of language has become more constructive. I spent time in a Concord facility that used to be called the "insane asylum," a term one of our parishioners was still using in the 1970s. When I stayed there for months in that period, the official designation was simply the "New Hampshire State Hospital." It has a better ring to it.

It has been helpful for prominent people to come forward with explanations. Actress Patty Duke did so in *A Brilliant Madness* (New York: Bantam, 1992). Johns Hopkins psychiatry professor Kay Redfield Jamison, a world authority on manic-depression, candidly records the story of her own encounters in a most perceptive book, *An Unquiet Mind* (New York: Knopf, 1995). Author William Styron (*Sophie's Choice, The Confessions of Nat Turner*) graphically describes his rendezvous with the monster in *Darkness Visible* (New York: Random House, 1990). Styron says that "depression" is a "wimp of a word" for an illness that is a "howling tempest in the brain." Without putting down various therapies, he says, "For me the real healers were seclusion and time."

It has also helped to read of others visited with the syndrome, like Abraham Lincoln, Oliver Cromwell, psychologist William James, TV newsman Mike Wallace, Broadway producer Josh Logan, who wrote of his illness experiences in *My Up-and-Down, In-and-Out Life* (1976) and *Movie Stars, Real People and Me (1978)*, telecommunicator Ted Turner, entertainers Rosemary Clooney and Charley Pride, and actors Vivien Leigh and Burgess Meredith. It has been suggested that Winston Churchill was of the same fraternity and that it was an advantage to his wartime role—a more placid personality might not have had the plunging leadership necessary to win the war. Of course Churchill's mood variations apparently were well within bounds.

The stigma is hardly reduced by knowing that Josef Stalin and Adolf Hitler were sufferers. Julian Lieb, psychiatrist in Wood-

Ellie and Jim Newton, at their home in Fort Myers Beach, Florida, where we spent many happy hours as their guests. Jim included me on his writing team for Uncommon Friends, *the story of his personal friendships with Edison, Ford, Firestone, Carrel, and Lindbergh.*

Frank N. D. Buchman (1878-1961) initiator of the Oxford Group/ Moral Re-Armament programs (later called Initiatives of Change), which spawned Alcoholics Anonymous. He was nominated twice in the 1950s for the Nobel Peace Prize. An airline pilot said Buchman had produced "A wonder drug that makes human beings out of people."

With Sir Gilbert Rennie, then British High Commissioner for Central Africa, Lusaka, Zambia, December 11, 1953, at the African premiere of the newspaper drama The Real News *by Peter Howard—I played the editor, St. John Fish.*

British tennis star Bunny Austin going over with baseball legend Connie Mack his pre-war "Battle for Peace" and "Moral Re-Armament Through Sport." To the left is John Guise, British Cricketer. I was with Bunny on this occasion and on dozens of interviews 1939-1940, including a memorable New York Hotel coffee shop breakfast with Joe DiMaggio and tea with Mr. and Mrs. George Herman (Babe) Ruth in their Manhattan Apartment.

With Minnesota Congressman August H. Andresen and Cecil "Happy Baker" Morrison, Canadian wartime bread czar; Minnesota businessman Ralph B. Beal; and Massachusetts state house correspondent Loring T. Swaim in 1943.

Mary Louise (right) at work with Mary Jane Merrill (no relation), formerly state president of League of Women Voters. Mary Louise has been a regular observer for the League at the Claremont City Council.

At the Willard family church in Galesburg 1994. The memorial window is inscribed to great grandmother H. Cordelia Willard.

Claremont School of Theology commencement 1977, with President Gordon E. Michalson and Vice President Buford A. Dickinson.

Addressing an all-college convocation at Heidelberg College, Tiffin, Ohio, 1983. The school president, William Cassell, was a friend from Claremont days.

Fourth of July oration, Independence Hall, 1982 Spoke for a record 34 hours, 8 minutes, and was pictured in the Guinness Book of World Records 1984 and 1985.

With the governor of California, who spoke at the annual luncheon on May 23, 1969 of the Independent Colleges of Southern California in Los Angeles. I was executive vice president 1967-70.

Walter H. Judd with President Dwight D. Eisenhower. Judd was Congressman from Minnesota 1943-63, much of that time serving on the House Foreign Affairs Committee and named by the New York Times as one of the most influencial Representatives on foreign policy. He came within a whisker of being vice-presidential nominee in the 1960 election campaign. In his missionary-to-China days (1925-38), I met him in Minnesota, and he became a profound motivational influence in my life. When he died in 1994 at age 95, I was privileged to speak twice at memorial services for him in Washington.

With Hubert H. Humphrey, presidential campaign, Los Angeles, 1968.

The Palapala Ho'omau (Eternal Word) Congregational Church, Kipahulu, Maui. Charles A. Lindbergh asked to be buried in the churchyard. I was a frequent speaker at the traditional community Thankgiving service held here each year.

With retired Pan-American executive Sam Pryor at the Palapala Ho'mau church, 1980, which he restored and where he and Lindbergh are buried.

With the Pahukoa family, Keanae, Maui, midway between Kahalui and Hana. Harry, right, a highway construction worker, helped dig Lindbergh's grave. Pearl (Lei) is a teacher and lay minister ('kahu'- shepherd). Son Tewa is in back.

Speaking at Petoskey, Michigan, 1993. "The Spirit of Charles Lindbergh" *was published that summer.*

Lee, New Hampshire. We served the yoked churches there and in Madbury 1970-76 while I was at the same time a student at the Andover Newton Theological School in Boston. The Lee church education/fellowship building in back was completed during that time.

Fourth of July oration, 1981, Petoskey, Michigan waterfront lasting five hours, fifty minutes.
News-review photo

Speaking at Mission San Juan Capistrano, August 1981, in salute to Los Angeles Bicentennial. For years I visited the mission on Saint Joseph's Day, March 19, to welcome the swallows back from Goya, Argentina just before the vernal equinox.

With Karl Fritjof (Fritz) Rolvaag in June 1981 at the historic Northfield bank where I spoke on "The Fascination of Jesse James." Fritz and I were fellow runners on the high-school track team. His father, O.E. Rolvaag, was a Norwegian novelist (Giants in the Earth) on the faculty of Saint Olaf College. Fritz became Governor of Minnesota and Ambassador to Iceland.

Philadephia soapbox, May 25, 1987, the 200th anniversary of the opening of the Constitutional Convention.

Old State House, Springfield, Illinois, 1981, speaking in the room where Lincoln delivered his "House Divided" address, accepting U.S. Senate nomination in 1858, prior to the debates with Stephen A. Douglas. The George Washington portrait is the room's only surviving item that was present in Lincoln's day.

State Journal Register Photo

Grand Marshal of the Fourth of July Parade, Claremont's Centennial Year, 1987.

*Moderator of Town Meeting,
1997, at Pilgrim Place
retirement community,
Claremont.*

Little Traverse Bay, Lake Michigan, with Mary Louise's brothers and spouses. Her family have summered nearby for over a hundred years.

Speaker at Carleton Alumni Reunion Baccalaureate Service, 1991.

Bill and Tom Hunter on a northern Michigan lake cruise.

Bill and Sharon and children in Michigan, 2000. Clayton and Laurel (his) and Casey (hers).

Gwen and Tom show happy pride in their offsprings' graduations the same weekend in 2000 at Bellingham, Washington—Aeden from Western Washington University and Irene from Squalicum High School.

At Speakers' Corner, London's Hyde Park, on Fourth of July, 1984. Spoke for six hours. Four self-appointed hecklers turned-up; I developed friendly relations with three.

50th wedding anniversary, Claremont, August 22, 1995.

bridge, Connecticut, writes that Hitler, on one side, "was despairing, indecisive, isolated, unable to care for himself . . . impaired concentration and memory . . . afraid of water, horses, and the moon . . . survived six suicide attempts before succeeding with the seventh." On the other hand, he was "egotistical, arrogant, grandiose, loquacious, aggressive and irritable . . . delusions of omnipotence, invincibility, and infallibility, violent mood swings, rages, racing thoughts, and pressured speech."

Lieb continues, "Hitler committed suicide in 1945." Four years later, Australian psychiatrist John Cade established the therapeutic value of lithium in treating the manic-depressive disorder. Lieb asks what humanity might have been spared if lithium had been available earlier.

Philip Graham, who ranked tenth in my 300-member Harvard Law School class of 1939, and who became Washington's premier publisher, was chewed up by the demon. He married Katharine Meyer, a Vassar classmate of Mary Louise's and a daughter of Mr. and Mrs. Eugene Meyer, owners of the *Washington Post*. Soon after he joined the Meyer family, Phil was put in charge of the paper and rapidly became the Washington news industry's rising star. James Reston of the *New York Times,* wrote in his autobiography, *Deadline* (New York: Random House, 1991):

> Graham was an attractive, intelligent, almost recklessly witty man. He was not deterred by lack of newspaper experience, or modesty, and before long was not only running the *Post* but also telling me how we should be running the *Times*.

That was the manic side. The depression drove him, on a visit to their Virginia farm in 1963, to kill himself with a 28-gauge shotgun. He was forty-eight.

There is some literature on the role of parapsychological

influences in the prophets. At seminary I wrote a paper on these traits in shamans around the world, noting that "shaman" is a name coming from Asia to describe medicine men who look after the spiritual side of the people and usually possess magico-religious powers.

The eminent Hebrew philosopher Abraham J. Heschel, of the Jewish Theological Seminary of America in New York, contended in a landmark book, *The Prophets* (1962), that leaders like Moses and Elijah were made possible by unbalanced thought processes. He devotes an entire chapter to "Prophecy and Psychosis," and states,

> Rejection or false recognition, together with the mental stresses and strains, the acts of self-denial necessitated by complete dedication, the effort and agony experienced in trying to bring intuition to expression, are too severe not to affect the sensitive balance of a human being. It is a miracle that a creative person manages to survive . . . . Neurosis should be regarded as that which challenges an artist rather than as that which makes him an artist. It was not Isaiah who produced prophecy; it was prophecy which produced Isaiah.

William James in *Varieties of Religious Experience* wrote,

> If there were such a thing as inspiration from a higher realm, it might well be that the neurotic temperament would furnish the chief condition of the requisite receptivity.

Scholars believe the prophet Ezekiel was cured of some nervous affliction. In the New Testament accounts, it is the people we would say were "off their rocker" who were the first to recognize in Jesus the messiah qualities that later emerged. "He suffered not the devils to speak because they knew him," wrote Mark. Perhaps the reason the story of Christ has struck such a vital nerve throughout the ages is that it has appealed not just to the heart and mind but also to the deeper psyche.

Mircea Eliade, in *Birth and Rebirth* (New York: Harper, 1958), notes that the shamans almost all exhibit some kind of psycho-pathic tendencies. He attributes the strange behavior to "the agonizing news that one has been chosen by the gods or the spirits." The "call" which God has laid on the heart of a future spiritual leader can be very unsettling:

> On the one hand, it is not true that shamans always are or always have to be neuropathics; on the other hand, those among them who had been ill became shamans precisely because they had succeeded in becoming cured.

Harry Emerson Fosdick, first minister of the Riverside Church in New York and national radio pulpiteer earlier in the last century, wrote of an early mental breakdown, hospitalizing him for three months. He believed it strengthened him for his later ministry.

I was helped by a speaker at a Macalester College convoca-tion in the 1950s who talked about the Old Testament story of Jacob wrestling all night at Peniel with an angel. During the struggle, the mystical figure "touched the hollow of his thigh. . . the sinew that shrank." At the breaking of the day "the hollow of Jacob's thigh was out of joint." He was a better man, but he *had a limp*. The speaker added that encounters with God often leave one with a limp.

From then on, I had a different perspective on my limp.

The Apostle Paul suffered from something he described as a "thorn in the flesh," which he suspected was sent as an antidote to hubris. Three times he prayed "that it might depart from me." It was probably more like thirty times three, but the message he received was that God's grace was sufficient and that God's "strength is made perfect in weakness."

Most gladly therefore will I rather glory in my infirmities . . .
in reproaches, in necessities, in persecutions, in distresses for
Christ's sake; for when I am weak, then am I strong.
(2 Corinthians 12:9-10)

I have decided to accept this posture for myself and have
come to believe that in some strange way, in spite of the pain
and the humiliation, the manic-depressive syndrome is a part of
creation. It would be preferable, in my opinion, if it did not
happen, or at least if it did not happen to me. But apparently the
owl called my name.

The shame of this affliction is severe. Yet in the nature of
things people seem to find some fascination and even hope in
defeat and failure. Every Fourth of July, and sometimes in
between, I present "Casey at the Bat." It is said to be the greatest
sports poem ever. One thing that fascinates us about this
remarkable story is that Casey struck out. If he had stepped up
to the plate and, as he was expected to, knocked a home run out
of the park and won the game for the Mudville Nine, we never
would have heard of the story. What makes it so universally
appealing (William de Wolf Hopper said he gave the piece
10,000 times from stages coast to coast) is that the Mighty Casey
struck out— and lost the game. I heard Charles Schulz (the
Peanuts Gang) tell a group of us wannabe writers that Charlie
Brown would never be permitted to win anything.

The mistake at the mint makes the coin a collector's item.
The irritating grain of sand in the oyster produces the pearl.

I hope it is not sacrilegious to suggest that Christ on the Cross
has a similar appeal. Robert Hamerton-Kelly says that if Jesus
had not experienced that failure, he would have dropped out of
sight, known, if at all, as an itinerant preacher handing out pithy
sayings in the nature of "a stitch in time saves nine."

It is not fair. But who said life is fair? Our political system
enjoins us to be just. So does God. But He or She operates under

a different set of morals from what we do. When I was in the New Hampshire Hospital in Concord, a lady from our Madbury church came to call on me. Her prominent businessman husband, noted for civic-mindedness and good works, was dying of cancer, and I, her minister, who had sacrificed a career for the Cause, was in a psychiatric ward. "Where's God?" she asked, "what's the use?"

You have to come to terms with your life as best you can, and realize that unexplainable mysteries abound.

One thought I like is that the genes in question are spread around over many people over long periods of time. In the evolutionary process, we are all somehow connected. If it takes what I had to help produce a Lincoln or a Moses, then I can be thankful that what I have has contributed to something big and useful, even though I myself was not one chosen to produce something big and useful.

There is also the troubling implication of heredity. The evidence indicates that the distressing genes are a family matter. My mother's brother Silas Willard was manic-depressive and took his life in a Palo Alto park. Our youngest son Bob ended his by jumping from a Boston hotel. When I was first hospitalized, my sister Helen and husband Frank McGee had not yet started their family, and wondered whether they should, in view of the potential danger. (They subsequently had two children, who have turned out fine.)

And then there is lithium. Patty Duke's co-author, medical reporter Gloria Hochman, writes in A Brilliant Madness:

> Until the early 1960s, mental illness was considered to be rooted in psychological trauma (faulty parents, unhappy childhood) . . . long-term psychotherapy was the way to exorcise the ghosts of the past . . . . While the nature-versus-nurture debate is not yet settled, there is little doubt among mental health practitioners that certain forms of depression and manic depression are surely biochemical illnesses.

I was in on the ground floor with lithium. Approved by the government in 1970, it was prescribed for me that fall by Dr. Kenneth Tilletson, a psychiatrist in Belmont, Massachusetts. He said to take it six days a week, "never on Sunday." Apparently I was too far along, or there was something wrong with the dosage. When the glory hit at the end of 1970, lithium failed to keep me out of the New Hampshire Hospital. But over the long haul since, it has been apparently very helpful.

At that time I started smoking Salem cigarettes, really to see whether I could get hooked and unhooked. Also I started collecting *Playboy* magazines. I installed a telephone in my dormitory room at the seminary and called a midnight Boston talk show, telling the host about my trip to Israel. The family started to become concerned, and I sensed they would be making moves.

One evening I was cruising downtown Boston, saw a fortune-teller sign and decided to see what the lady had to say about my future. She was an attractive, forty-something, Asian-Indian with children eating supper in the next room. She obviously wanted to deal with me quickly and return to the family. She looked at my palm. She had a good-looking, unsupported front, and took my comment on it in stride. The majority of her observations and predictions seemed standard stuff, but one item later stuck in my mind because of events the next day. She said I should look out for a big man who might not have my interests at heart. I paid her fee of ten dollars, and she bustled off through the curtained doorway to rejoin her family.

The next day Bill Gregory, a towering figure of a man, turned up at Andover Newton. Tall, broad-shouldered, and athletic, he was the minister of the United Church of Christ in Lincoln, Massachusetts. A good deal bigger than I, he had been commissioned by his friend Ed Meury of Durham, New Hampshire, to make sure I would not run away. His assignment was to deliver me to the New Hampshire Hospital in Concord. He, and my family, of course had my "best interests at heart" according to professional lights at the time, but because I knew he was an instrument of a long-forthcoming incarceration, his interest and mine did not look similar to me.

Our oldest son Tom, who was then himself a seminary student in New York, turned up for the family crisis. I managed to escape to the local commuter rail station to get myself lost in Boston. But the train did not arrive until Tom turned up, and the family took me into custody. When I saw what was happening, I decided to be realistic, stop fighting the problem, and submit. That evening I was checked into the Concord facility. Gregory was surprised that I put up no resistance and asked why. I said, "Bill, they told me in the army, 'If rape is inevitable, lie back and enjoy it.'"

How did that fortune-teller know?

Another shot of mania came along in 1973, just over two years later. I was falsely suspected of discontinuing medication. The psychiatrist I had been seeing in Dover, New Hampshire, had prescribed something extra, in addition to the lithium, and later said I could discontinue that extra medication. This was interpreted by some as my refusing to continue.

In the quarter century since 1973, the swings have smoothed out. Moods have come and gone, but nothing like before. I like lithium because it is a natural clay out of the ground. Some manufactured mood-control chemicals I found to dry up both mouth and intestines. So even in the hospital, I would spit them out whenever I could. I figured that if they were having a bad effect on the physical processes I could observe, there must be adverse results with other bodily functions that I could not. Lithium comes up clean and natural, an original element you find on a high-school chemistry chart.

Lithium is a metallic chemical element, the symbol being Li, soft, silver-white, and the least dense metal. It is a base for some lubricating oils in the automobile industry, and in metal alloys. Lithium is widely distributed in nature, being found in the soil, in plants, animals, the human body, and the sun. It was discovered in 1917 by J. A. Arfvedson, and, as mentioned earlier, its therapeutic value in treating manic-depressive disorders was established in 1949 by Australian psychiatrist John Cade. Twenty-one years later, in 1970, it was approved for distribution by the U.S. Food and Drug Administration.

In the sixties I was under the care of two Jungian psychiatrists, Dr. Frantz and Malcolm Dana. Frantz was a busy doctor from Sherman Oaks who was consulting with me during my stay at the Glendale Adventist Hospital in 1969. The sessions were usually brief. He was strong on the therapy of free-flow drawing and working with clay. He did not care whether I drew or shaped any particular objects. He wanted me to fantasize. I was terrible at all this, but I was a little better at *writing* fantasies in essay form. I came up with some interesting stuff, which our Bob said was among my best productions. Frantz wanted me to get into a group in Claremont where I could doodle in clay or plasticene. I found a group but it was so unsatisfactory that I soon quit.

Malcolm Dana, more Jungian, was a retired college president and a part time counselor. He was strong on dreams, and got me to write mine down and report them at each session. Then without hesitation he would tell exactly what each element of each dream meant for me. He called dreams "personal scripture" and believed they came from God.

The 1973 manic episode coincided with my graduation from Andover Newton Theological School with a Master of Divinity degree. At the graduation ceremonies in the big Baptist church in Newton Centre, I received the annual Carroll Whittemore

Award for Excellence in Preaching. I thought the recipient ought to say a word of acceptance and appreciation. When there was appropriate movement on the platform, I approached President Roy Pearson. Apprehensive, Dean George Peck advised him in a firm whisper against it, but the president gave in to my insistence. My words of appreciation to the donor, a large office supply distributor nearby, for encouraging the art of preaching in a day when it was in a relatively low condition, were well received. Afterwards Psychology Professor John Bellinsky said my request obviously came from the manic, but what I said was good and needed saying.

Two weeks later, I was considerably higher. I had invited former China missionary and U.S. Congressman Walter H. Judd to deliver the address for my ordination in the little Congregational church in Lee, New Hampshire. It was Sunday, May 27, and I decided that in the afternoon, I would seek inspiration from the sea. Driving in my Volkswagen Bug to the New Hampshire shore, I picked up a group of hitchhiking University of New Hampshire coeds. I had brought along a bottle of olive oil, and when they spread out their picnic gear, I told them I was being ordained that day, and would they assist in the process through anointing me with oil and adding any sea incantations they might care to render. Which they did.

After this, I couldn't find my car in the confusing beach parking area, so hitch-hiked back to Lee too late for the supper for honored guests in the parsonage, but in time for the service itself. The Judd discourse was brilliant, as usual, a little too political for the occasion, but helpful. At the end, when the ordinand is usually called on to give only a benediction, I launched into a twenty-five minute address. It made the evening too long, and people were concerned I had gone overboard. The school district had lent us their video recorder for the evening. After several viewings, in embarrassment I threw the tape away.

There followed another three months in the New Hampshire Hospital. It was the summer of 1973, and the Senate Watergate investigations were on, so I spent a lot of time in front of the tube. The hospital supplied free tobacco and cigarette papers, probably to ameliorate boredom, so I learned how to roll my own, like the movie cowboys. It was great-tasting tobacco, and even after I got out, it took me a year or so before I got off the stuff.

The best thing that happened that summer was a sharing group I developed of six to eight men who met every morning after breakfast for scripture, sharing, and prayer. Our guide was *How to Read the Bible* by Edgar J. Goodspeed. One of the group, who seemed to benefit from the sessions, was a recovering alcoholic. In gratitude he gave me his own beat-up copy of *Twenty-four Hours a Day*, the popular AA daily devotional guide that came out of AA's parent, the Oxford Group.

Bill Zeckhausen, who the summer before had been my mentor in Clinical Pastoral training at the New Hampshire institution for the retarded in Laconia, said he knew I was there but decided not to bring his colleagues in to see me, as I might be embarrassed. He was right, and I was grateful for his sensitivity.

All this time, the parishioners at the two New Hampshire churches I was serving, Lee and Madbury, were patient and generous and continued to allow me a paid leave of absence.

In the fall, I returned to both pulpits, and to classes at Andover Newton, where in three more years I received a second Master's degree.

From then on, there have been no hospitalizations or disruptions of work. I am deeply grateful that the path has been smoothed out.

-17-

UNDERWRITING AMERICA'S FUTURE

College Public Relations and Fundraising

My career in college administration, 1956-70, came about as something of a fluke. The determination was made because of something else, and it lacked the conviction of my other vocational choices. Of all the flawed decisions I have made in my life, this one ranks near the top.

The choice arose out of the health situation described in the last chapter. After eighteen years of devoting full time to the Moral Re-Armament program, my nervous system apparently was asking for a reduced tension lifestyle. In 1955 it was generally agreed I needed a different vocation.

As I was getting ready to leave the Miller Hospital in Saint Paul, and being advised to change careers, I thought that now might be the time to complete my third year of law studies and collect my Harvard degree. However, I was denied re-admission. They said their experience with returning students who had "abandoned" law studies for twenty years, as I had, was not good.

I pursued the normal paths, preparing a résumé and talking with friends. I had marketable skills, particularly in writing, editing, and public relations, burnished by years of government relations and communications work in Washington, Michigan, and Africa. The avenues that most interested me were politics and journalism.

Mary Louise and I got in our borrowed car and visited editors

in southern Minnesota, particularly Northfield and the attractive Mississippi River town of Winona. I wondered whether I
could, from a newspaper base, work myself into running for
public office, a long-held wish. It was an unrealistic will o'the
wisp in view of my medical history. So that soon dropped out of
sight.

Al Clague, whom I had known through MRA, helped greatly
in my job search. He was a skilled advertising artist at Batten,
Barton, Durstine, and Osborne (BBD&O), Bruce Barton's New
York advertising firm, which maintained major offices in Minneapolis because of heavy-hitter accounts with the grain milling
companies and other big Minnesota firms. Their resident partner
in Minneapolis was Jack Cornelius, Clague's boss. Al arranged
for me to see him.

Macalester College

Cornelius at once told me that Macalester College in Saint
Paul was looking for a public relations person. DeWitt Wallace,
founder of the *Reader's Digest*, was now backing an expanded
fundraising agenda for the school. They were beefing up staff.
Wallace's father, James Wallace, had been the Presbyterian
president of church-related Macalester at the turn of the century
and had kept the struggling institution alive during dark years
through sheer will power. His son, impressed with his father's
self-sacrifice for the cause, had in the past taken tentative steps
to help, but this time he was serious about doing something to
fulfill his father's dream. He had found a consultant in whom he
had confidence, Paul H. Davis, former top fundraiser for
Stanford and Columbia, and the two of them began to make big
plans. Cornelius was helping strategize the appeals, and in a true
advertiser's spirit counseled, "Don't sell the steak—sell the
sizzle."

DeWitt Wallace had been born on the campus in 1889. He had been a student there two years (1907-09) before splitting for Berkeley to become, he said, a "playboy of the western world." Macalester College had been established in 1885 by Edward Duffield Neill, who had served President Lincoln as a White House secretary. The Presbyterians took responsibility from the beginning. The campus lies midway between Minneapolis and Saint Paul, not far from the Mississippi River.

I was drawn to the idea of serving a small liberal arts college, a cause to which my father had given his life. I had pleasant memories of Macalester from my student days at Carleton, thirty-five miles to the south. I had run track and cross-country meets at Macalester, and it was there that I had won the Minnesota oratorical championship in 1936. Then too, all my days I had labored in the vineyards of the nonprofit world.

Cornelius arranged for me to meet the college's president, Charles J. Turck, in his office near Saint Paul's stately Summit Avenue. We struck up a rapport immediately. He offered me a job as Associate General Secretary of the college, explaining they believed in unimportant-sounding titles for fundraisers. The college scene did not grab me as an employment opportunity, however, so I looked around further. Cornelius also sent me to the editor of the *Minneapolis Tribune*. There I was offered the position of night wire-service editor, pulling together every night stories from the news agencies. Salary: $6,000 a year. Whenever prospective employers asked what compensation I needed, I thought of my father's annual salary of $2,800 in the 1930s, and, I'm sure inadequately, doubled it for inflation. I liked the newspaper idea a lot. It looked exciting, and I thought I could do well. Also, the *Tribune* owned the big CBS station, WCCO-TV, and maybe someday I might slip over into television news.

But the family and the doctor were against it. They thought it would be too harrowing, poring through pressures at midnight.

A college campus looked just the ticket to them, ivy-covered walls and quiet contemplation. Of course that was not the side of education that was involved. But in view of the situation I threw the switch for the campus position. It was not as interesting to me, but I have to say here that my Calvinist streak generally tilted me in favor of the less desirable. James Reston of the *New York Times* used to say that the Calvinist was never so happy as when he was miserable.

My mother often quoted the lines, "Of all sad words of tongue or pen, the saddest are these, 'It might have been.'" I still think the news job was more my cup of tea. But instead I spent fourteen years in college development. It turned out to be my "lost decade." There I reached my level of incompetence.[1] (I later became friends through Will Rogers events with Laurence J. Peter, who actually gave me one of his Certificates of Competence.) Son Bill asks, if it was a lost decade, why did I not get out of it earlier? Good point. Partly it was due to my feeling that God had put me there for the security of my family. If that were true, my personal satisfaction was irrelevant. If I had listened to motivational tapes, popular at the time, like Earl Nightingale's, I might well have switched to something else. But I had long tried to keep personal ambition behind me, and my challenge was to care for the family and do my duty.

Having said all that, there is no question that the fourteen years in college development turned up many lively and rewarding experiences. One was the friendship of DeWitt Wallace and the chance to work with him and a number of his top colleagues. Among these were senior editor Stanley High and *Digest* business manager Al Cole, who was also national president of the

---

[1] See the Peter Principle, the theory that employees within an organization will advance to their highest level of competence and then be promoted to and remain at a level at which they are incompetent.

Boys Clubs of America. For two weeks in 1957 I was a guest of the Wallaces at their Chappaqua Guest House while I worked with some of the top *Digest* personnel in producing for Macalester a fundraising booklet, *Underwriting America's Future by Giving to Education.* The title was suggested by Stanley High. The design was by the *Digest's* art director, C. O. Woodbury, who repeatedly declared his aim in graphics was "immaculate conception."

In 1921, after service in World War I, DeWitt Wallace moved to New York and married Lila Bell Acheson. The two of them started their little magazine in an apartment over a garage in Pleasantville, developing the most successful publishing venture ever.[2]

As a support instrument in fundraising, Messrs. Wallace and Davis wanted a publication like the one put out periodically by Pomona College. The so-called Pomona Plan of life-income gifts was beginning to be taken up by other institutions. This is a plan whereby a donor gives a capital sum or real estate to the college, which invests it, paying back to the donor income from the principal for life, after which the capital sum goes absolutely to the college. Our people wanted to get going on it. And they wanted a booklet as attractive as Pomona's. I was tabbed to produce it. I counseled against making the publication look like Pomona's, saying it ought to look distinctively our own. I was overruled on this and paid for it later when the daddy of Pomona's planned income program, Allen Hawley, gave me a dressing down for the copycat approach and said he was "ashamed" of me.

---

[2]To them the name "Pleasantville" expressed the upbeat philosophy of their magazine and they kept it as the company's post office address even after they moved upriver to Chappaqua. Wallace was to contribute approximately fifty million dollars to Macalester during his lifetime, and more continued to flow from his estate.

During this time the Wallaces included me at their home in Mount Kisco for a back patio luncheon. It was late fall, and "Wally" explained that they enjoyed outdoor dining so much they extended the season to where they "practically had to wear ear muffs." He showed me a heavy iron bed in the corner, an antique he had picked up, which he said had been hauled through the Napoleonic wars by a French general to accommodate his mistress.

The Wallaces had an extraordinary humanity about them. Lila said they had just come back from visiting *Digest* bureaus around the world; she was impressed by the special feeling of warmth at each bureau. I thought to myself that this might well come from the kind of people this remarkable couple attracted and the influence of their missionary parents.

A minor incident focused for me Wallace's attention to individuals. In the summer of 1976, I was driving near New York on my way west and stopped to pay a call at High Winds, the Wallaces' Mt. Kisco residence. No one was home, so I slipped a short note under the front door. Six months later I received a Christmas card signed "Wally" and above it this handwritten line, "Sorry to miss you last summer." I wondered how many thousands he thought of in such a way.

Among the other Macalester pluses were my opportunity to revamp the other publications and start up a lively newsletter, *Macalester Report*, for the masthead of which I dug up the Clan Macalester's official Scottish tartan. Along the way I learned that I was better at public relations than at fundraising.

The first time I met DeWitt Wallace, he and his wife Lila and I were seated together in the bleachers at a college function in the Macalester gymnasium. School officials were still interviewing me, and that night they were running me by the donor who was financing the program. We hit it off well, and apparently he gave the appropriate nod. He asked me right away about television experience, and I said I had taken part in a number of TV interviews. He was keen on the new TV program being proposed in which the college was to have a part in the new Minnesota Public Television, just getting started. The consultant retained by the college thought I had the right personality and voice for hosting Macalester TV programs.

Two problems arose. First, the TV woman ran into flack from old-guard professors who thought the host should be an established "Macite" rather than a Johnny-come-lately staffer. Second, our fundraising consultant, Paul H. Davis, and our communications chairman, Minneapolis advertising executive Erle Savage, both were opposed to putting any development office energy into television. They believed staff should not be diverted away from the nitty-gritty of fundraising off to the dubious side eddy of propagating general good will.

The incident brings up what some might consider an offbeat spiritual issue. At the close of my hospitalization in 1955, the psychiatrist advised that I change careers and get into something where I would receive more recognition. The MRA emphasis was on "God-filled nobodies." The doctor thought this was too selfless for me.

The only thing was, when I got into college work, selflessness was still the key. I had been told that Davis had a three-point program for fundraising:

(1) volunteers, (2) volunteers, and (3) volunteers.

In the first conference I had with him, he emphasized vigorously how we were to remain behind the scenes and make the volunteers look good. He said that he and his wife were Quakers, and they tried to follow the modest style. He cited the criterion for administrative aides at the FDR White House, "a passion for anonymity." I think John the Baptist's comment about Jesus came up, "He must increase, but I must decrease."

And so I concluded, through "circumstantial guidance," that despite the psychiatrist's professional judgment, the Big Guru in the Sky would continue to prescribe for me the denial of self.

In retrospect, I fudged. I began attending college public relations conventions. I wrote articles on aspects of the business I knew, and my byline began to appear in professional magazines. A naturally political animal, I was chosen to fill "ladder" positions in the profession and in 1962 was moved up to CEO of the Far West District of the American College Public Relations Association (ACPRA).

Incidentally, that year Richard Nixon was running for Governor of California. He was meeting with another group in the San Francisco airport hotel where our district conference was being held, and we persuaded him to address our college promoters. He made a good politician's eloquent remarks about the importance of supporting higher education. Then as he left the platform he caught my eye, put his arm around my shoulder, and told the delegates, "If this man does as good a job for you as he has for the causes he and I have been associated with, you will go places." The reference to "causes" was to the Moral Re-Armament program, of which he had been supportive when he was in the House and the Senate. As mentioned earlier, I wrote a speech for him when he was in the Senate.

In the old days church-related colleges used to conduct an annual event called Religious Emphasis Week. When I was at Presbyterian Macalester, one of these was conducted by Dr. James H. Robinson, pastor of the Morningside Presbyterian Church in Harlem. Jim Robinson was developing a student exchange program called Operation Crossroads Africa, and President Kennedy was to consult with him on ideas for the Peace Corps. We got to be pretty good friends, and when I next visited New York, I was his guest at the church's huge community center in Harlem. He asked me not to call him "Jim" while I was there, as he thought it important that his young people see my kind of people treating him with respect. He said he grew up in Cleveland and played with Jesse Owens all the time, beating him in every track event, the 100, the 220, the long jump— everything. When I asked why we had not heard of him, he said, "Jesse was twelve and I was sixteen."

During my fundraising career I became a member of the national board and then the executive committee of ACPRA, and for a time was on the medium "short list" of prospective candidates for national president. ACPRA later merged with the American Alumni Council to form the Council for the Advancement and Support of Education (CASE). ACPRA published and distributed my book *The Tax Climate for Philanthropy*, 1968, which was on the shelf of many a fund-raising officer across the country for years.

We enjoyed Minnesota life, especially I who grew up there. When I was a kid in the twenties, our Dad drove us from North-field to Minneapolis to see the Ringling Brothers-Barnum & Bailey Circus. It was one of the most exciting experiences of my young life. So thirty years later, when the circus was scheduled to show in the Saint Paul Auditorium (they had long since abandoned pitching the Big Tent every day), I said to our boys, this we have to see. I was more gripped than they were, and near the end I said, "Look, Bob, in a minute a man will get shot out of that cannon way up into the air and will land on the big net on the other side."

"Yeah, I've seen it on TV," he said.

Another memorable event was the centennial of the state of Minnesota, recognizing its entry into the Union May 11, 1858. The main celebration was a 1958 mass meeting in the University of Minnesota football stadium where John Foster Dulles, Secretary of State, was the featured speaker. Judy Garland, who grew up in Grand Rapids, Minnesota, was on the platform, ready to do her part. She asked for a glass of water, and Minneapolis Congressman Walter Judd drew the gallantry assignment, which took him across the stage from where the water was to where she was. When he arrived with the liquid, she asked him what was in it, making the crowd laugh and Walter exaggeratedly shrug his shoulders. Judy sang several numbers, closing ("Is it that time already?" she asked) with "Over the Rainbow."

The Claremont Colleges

When I was working at the *Reader's Digest* offices on the Macalester book, I received a telephoned invitation from Henry Mudd to meet him in his New York office. Henry was the Los Angeles-based CEO of the Cyprus Mines Corporation and Chairman of the Board of the newly founded Harvey Mudd College in Claremont, named for his father, who was a mining associate of Herbert Hoover. They were looking for some development help for the new college, and Paul Davis, who was consultant to both Macalester and Harvey Mudd, had told Henry that he believed I was the only one in the country that could handle the job they had in mind. It was an involved portfolio, half time with Harvey Mudd College and half time at the Claremont Colleges' coordinating institution, to become known as the Claremont University Center and Graduate School. After a visit to Claremont, it struck me as an unworkable arrangement, and I turned it down.

A year later, however, the Claremont people came back with a different proposal. Paul Davis was persistent, and persuaded the central unit's president, Robert J. Bernard, that I was the one who could set up a development program for the central institution by itself. I telephoned DeWitt Wallace for his advice, secretly hoping he would say that if I were leaving Macalester he would like to have me on his staff at the *Digest*. He did not, only giving out a standard sentiment that I should decide in favor of whatever I felt was best for me.[3]

Claremont's reputation was and is world class, and everybody told me this was something that should not be missed. My friend Laurence M. Gould, president of Carleton College, told me that if I did not take it, he would not speak to me. In the end, after Mary Louise and I had agonized, we finally decided to go for it. It loomed as a great opportunity and the next uncertain step in our revised career avenue. We included the boys in the decision. I still have Bill's words in his writing: "If Daddy wants to go, we'll go."

The Claremont Colleges have become one of the leading educational centers of the world. The oldest, largest, and richest of the cluster, Pomona College, was founded in 1887 by the Congregational Churches of Southern California. The college's shield still bears the motto, "Our Tribute to Christian Civilization." Begun in a house in the city of Pomona, it moved in 1889 to Claremont, three miles to the north near the Santa Fe railroad tracks, to accept the gift of a boom hotel gone bust. It was thought that after a year and a half the name "Pomona" was so well established that it should not be changed. That is why one finds Pomona College not in Pomona but in Claremont.

Following World War I, under pressure of rising student applications, Pomona faced the question of whether to enlarge indefinitely to become another big California university, or to say no to all but a few applicants and maintain its small-college values. It was decided to do both—grow bigger by small units.

---

[3]"Wally"—only intimates were supposed to call him that, but he did sign letters to me that way—once told me that his practice, when asked advice, was to find out what the person wanted to do, and then advise him or her to do that.

James A. Blaisdell, Pomona College president 1910-25 and
founder of the Claremont Group Plan, wrote in a landmark
letter to Ellen Browning Scripps on October 3, 1923:

> My own very deep hope is that instead of one great,
> undifferentiated university, we might have a group of
> institutions divided into small colleges somewhat on the
> Oxford type—around a library and other utilities which they
> would use in common. In this way I should hope to preserve
> the inestimable *personal* values of the small college while
> securing the *facilities* of the great university. Such a
> development would be a new and wonderful contribution to
> American education.

The man's genius lay not only in dreaming the great dreams
but also in inspiring those with resources to make the dreams
come true. He said that enlisting financial support from someone
was like saving his or her soul. It helped release a person from
self through dedication to a cause beyond self.

Ms. Scripps was one of those who responded to the Blaisdell
vision. She was a member of the famous newspaper family and
was now living in San Diego. Born in London, one of thirteen
children of an English bookbinder, she had been brought to the
United States as a small child. She was the first woman graduate
of Knox College and as a student attended the Lincoln-Douglas
debate in Galesburg, Illinois, October 7, 1858. With her brothers
she founded the *Detroit News* and later the first newspaper
chain. She was instrumental in establishing Scripps College for
women in 1926. To help make practical the wider Blaisdell
dream, she provided funds to nail down 250 acres of land to the
north of the existing campuses, space still being held for future
colleges.

I too responded to the opportunity of making a contribution
to education in Claremont. The challenge was definitely an
important reason that I said yes to Dr. Bernard's invitation to
"throw in your lot with us."

I was good at special events and received high marks for managing a packed ballroom banquet event in Los Angeles at the Beverly Hilton Hotel launching an all-Claremont Colleges joint fundraising drive to meet the challenge of a matching grant of eighty-five million dollars from the Ford Foundation. The speaker of the evening was Robert F. Goheen, President of Princeton University, accompanied by his board chairman.

Also I was in charge of the black-tie ceremony dedicating the Garrison Theater, a performing arts center for the colleges. It took place in December of 1963 and was a real coup. We enlisted Scripps professor and humorous author Richard Armour to be master of ceremonies. The Pomona College people invited actor Richard Chamberlain, an alumnus. I managed to persuade western star Joel McCrea, also a Pomona graduate, to join us for the occasion. Chamberlain at twenty-eight and McCrea at fifty-eight, both local products and representing different genres of the entertainment industry, presented a dramatic contrast.[4]

It was during this period that I became friends with Henry Kissinger. Part of my Claremont portfolio was to staff something called the Friends of The Claremont Colleges, which twice a year gathered the entire constituency of the Claremont group for a prestigious focus event. Often the occasion resulted in a book comprising the lectures by the visitor—delivered at a black tie California Club dinner downtown Los Angeles and at an all-college convocation in Claremont.

At a Harvard event in Los Angeles I heard Kissinger, then a Harvard professor, speak on the global situation. I thought he

---

[4]Joel McCrea, western veteran of over eighty films, and his wife Frances Dee, were Frank Buchman's best Hollywood friends. I accompanied the couple at the Will Rogers Centennial in Claremore, Oklahoma, in 1979, and wrote a memoir "I Remember Will Rogers" for Joel for *Modern Maturity* magazine on his friendship with the cowboy philosopher, with whom he had lunch twice a month for five years.

had an unusual grasp of events and an out of the ordinary vision for the future. I set my cap to enlist him, and he accepted. Since it was my responsibility to see he had everything he needed during his two days with us, including various student and professor seminars, he and I operated in pretty close quarters. I took him to a tailor in the city of Pomona for a rental tuxedo. He flattered me by asking advice as to the order of his presentations. At the opening of his address in Claremont's Bridges Auditorium, he said he was glad there were no formal public speaking courses there because, "at Harvard mumbling is a sign of profundity."

Our conversations covered an interesting spectrum. He was still doing position papers for Nelson Rockefeller, and was strong for his patron nosing out Barry Goldwater for the Republican presidential nomination in 1964. Henry was fed up with the Kennedy White House and had stopped accepting consulting assignments with them. I urged him, in light of what he was saying about the Kennedys, to think of how he could help bring a new spirit to the White House. The next week Kennedy was assassinated, and Henry wrote me recalling the pertinence of our conversation.

He was gracious to reciprocate with generous hospitality the next year when he was faculty chairman of the Harvard summer school. I was attending a college officials' convention in Boston, and he included me at the head table for the opening lunch at the university along with his mentor, Professor William Yandell Elliott. "He was the first person I ever met," Henry told me "who took an interest in me and convinced me I could do something." Afterwards he took me on a walking tour of the Harvard Yard and environs. We talked about the assassinations of South Vietnam President Ngo Dinh Diem and of the American President Kennedy, both in the month of November 1963. Kissinger was convinced the destruction of Diem had been ordered at the highest level in Washington, and the sequence of the two murders "almost makes you believe in God." (Before his death, JFK acknowledged his policy regarding Diem was wrong.)

Kissinger met with our Harvard student son Bill to advise him about his curriculum, but Bill soon switched his major to economics. Over the years Henry and I exchanged correspondence.

Another outstanding event was a trip by trustees and friends of The Claremont Colleges to Oxford University in the spring of 1966. Since our college cluster had been roughly modeled on the Oxford plan of smaller units around common facilities, it was a natural. Filling a chartered plane, we made a three-week trip. We arrived in Oxford in an April snowstorm ("Oh, to be in England now that April's there," crowed the media) and stayed for a week. There was a choice of accommodations—an eighteenth-century dormitory room or a modern one. I chose the former, as it seemed more authentic, albeit chilly.

From top professors we heard lectures on the philosophy of an Oxford education, including heartfelt expositions of the tutorial system, pros and cons. Our group then had two weeks to tour in Europe wherever they wished before gathering back in London for the return. I took to Oxford recording equipment, transcribed all proceedings, obtained mailed corrections and clearances from the participants, and with Jo Hartley produced a book on the Oxford story, *Dialogue on Higher Education: Claremont, Oxford, Great Britain* (Claremont: Claremont Colleges, 1996). Sir John Maud, Senior Don of University College, the oldest of the Oxford cluster, said it was about the finest description of what happens at Oxford he had seen. A clever speaker in the English tradition, Sir John made a hit with audiences, British and American, by tucking in Shakespeare's line about Cleopatra, "Age cannot wither her, nor custom stale her infinite variety."

That autumn, 1966, I worked up a sabbatical year for myself, rare for administrators. I had to raise money for it, and was granted by my boss, President Louis T. Benezet, a year's leave of absence. My good friend Joseph B. Platt, president of Harvey Mudd College, arranged with his friend Kermit Gordon, the director of the prestigious think tank, the Brookings Institution in Washington, to appoint me Guest Scholar there for a year. The story of that year is laid out in a succeeding chapter, "Taxes and Patriotism."

Independent Colleges of Southern California

When I came back from the sabbatical in the spring of 1967, I was approached by Harold Fasnacht, president of La Verne University, and Norvel Young, president of Pepperdine College, on behalf of the Independent Colleges of Southern California (ICSC). They were looking for an executive vice president.

During the year I was gone, a director had been hired to re-place me at Claremont University Center and Graduate School as top gun in development. I was asked to take a subsidiary position in planned giving, reporting to the new director. I understood the president's desire to give everything a new look, but I did not think I could be put in this position. So the Fasnacht-Young proposal seemed a good way out.

ICSC is a United Way type of program whereby small colleges make their common appeal to corporations for their support. It reduces the duplication of fifteen college presidents calling on the same businesses. In short they put "all their begs in one ask-it." ICSC is one of over thirty statewide organizations doing the same thing, a movement that was started by Frank Sparks when president of Wabash College in Indiana.

Members of the Southern California association are Califor-nia Lutheran, Chapman, Claremont Graduate, Claremont

McKenna, Harvey Mudd, Loyola Marymount, Mount Saint Mary's, Occidental, Pepperdine, Pitzer, Pomona, Scripps, La Verne, Redlands, San Diego, Westmont, and Whittier.

This too was a difficult assignment. For one thing, it meant an hour's commute each way every day to Los Angeles, somewhat helped by a carpool with some friendly bankers. At the downtown office during my three-year term, I was able to revamp the publications, put on some great annual lunches (California Governor Ronald Reagan was the speaker in 1969), and boost the annual take to over a million dollars for the first time. One wrinkle I initiated, that they had not thought of before, was to enhance our income by investing donated funds during the period between the time the gifts were made and the time they were distributed to the colleges. Also we moved the office out of a dingy, run-down area of the city into one of Los Angeles's new skyscrapers, considerably improving our image. However, the quarters foisted on us by an over-enthusiastic trustee were too lavish. My successor took my advice and moved to more middle ground.

One Sunday we were attending an event in the First Methodist Church of Pasadena, and on a bulletin board I saw a notice that the next Sunday Martin Luther King was to speak in the Los Angeles Coliseum. I said to the boys, "We have to go to that. That man will emerge as a great historical personage, and you will want to have seen and heard him." So when the day came, a hot Sunday afternoon, we drove to LA and took our place in the bleachers. Two things he said I remember. He agreed that "you can't pass a law that will make you like me, but you can make a law that will keep you from lynching me. And that could be very important to me." The other affirmation that stood out was that the Black people had taken the biblical question, "Is there no balm in Gilead?" and turned it entirely around into a mighty affirmation, "There is a balm in Gilead—to make the wounded whole."

In those days the public relations program for the Independent Colleges of Southern California consisted largely in a television program, "On Campus," which appeared on KNBC every Sunday afternoon. Each college was featured in turn for a full half hour. Dave Bell had been brought from Ohio to produce the feature, and he reported to me. Dave was to go on to bigger time motion picture production. The on-camera host of the show was George Fenneman, formerly Groucho Marx's straight man on TV's "You Bet Your Life."

One of the member colleges was Loyola University, and when their week came around, we were able to get Bob Hope to participate. He had a son studying at Loyola's law school. So when we printed up our annual report, it was a natural to picture Hope in the television section of the brochure. It was my privilege to present him a copy and have a brief visit in his dressing room at the NBC studios in Burbank. The occasion was his periodic visit to the studios to do pro bono public service messages for agencies he backed. He did one for us that night, just after one for the Little League. While the latter was being set up, Hope was standing on the stage with two little leaguers, their baseball caps straight and their fists in their mitts. Filling in time, the comedian tried to engage them in conversation—what was their name, what did they call their club, their hometown? They froze, speechless. At length Bob said, "Hey, you kids aren't any good without your writers either, are you?"[5]

One of the highlights of this period, which ran from 1967 to 1970, was working with Si Fluor, chairman of the ICSC board and chairman of the petrochemical giant, the Fluor Corporation, founded by his uncle. Si was a thoroughly *human* human being. In addition to his business responsibilities, he was into all kinds

---

[5]Hope's chief writer, Gene Perret, was a reader of the newsletter *Words*. See Appendix H.

of public service endeavors, particularly health and education agencies in Orange County, where he worked and lived. He was also a fundraising power in the Republican Party. One day he heard me on KCBS radio making a one-minute response to a station editorial. I was objecting to the radio spokesman bad-mouthing generalizations about politicians. I advocated the encouragement of politics as an honorable profession. At the California Club that day he was enthusiastic about my talk and said, "We ought to run you for governor." Hearing this from a sure-enough kingmaker was quite a thrill, even though made in passing. It was about as close as I ever got to high public office.

Another amusing side pocket of this "might-have-been" alley was the number of people who should have known better but seemed interested, without any encouragement from me, in my becoming a college president.

- My uncle, M. Willard Lampe, founding dean of the School of Religion, State University of Iowa, wrote the Carleton College selection committee highly recommending me as their next president.
- Paul Smith, president of Whittier College and Whittier trustee John Stauffer earnestly asked me to consider succeeding Smith at Whittier. Stauffer laid on a special lunch at the California Club to press the case, and Smith included me and Mary Louise at an insiders' commencement lunch with astronaut Frank Borman.
- William Davis, Emerson Electric Company CEO in Saint Louis, courted me intensively in 1964 to consider the presidency of Iowa Wesleyan College, of which he was a trustee. The school even sent a faculty representative to call on me in Claremont, but I don't believe my answers about education policy were satisfactory. Also they wanted a candidate who had a Ph.D degree.

- A leader in the Colton, California, United Methodist Church more than once urged me to put my name in for the presidency of Crafton Hills College near San Bernardino. I declined.
- One fan was even talking me up for Sarah Lawrence College in Bronxville.
- Carleton's Laurence M. Gould told me he had written Coe College in Cedar Rapids, Iowa, suggesting they consider me.

All of this was indeed gratifying, but I never had a serious offer and am glad I never became involved with any of it. Administration, financing, and personnel are not my thing. I never had much luck even hiring a secretary. It is probably an issue of outer personality rather than inner ability. A clergyman whose ministry involved years of campus work across the country said he always thought of me as the college president type Also the public speaking probably gave people ideas.

I am not a college president, but I could play one on TV.

I thoroughly enjoyed dealing with the dozen presidents of the Independent Colleges of Southern California for the three years I served their group as executive vice president. Bur even that, I concluded, was not really my cup of tea. One day Mary Louise asked, "Do you want to do this for the rest of your life?" A good wifely question, and one I took very seriously. At length the clear answer was No. Next question: then what *do* you want to do? That one took a while.

At length I decided to switch again. I realized that from childhood, I had recognized some sort of call to full-time Christian service. I felt I had responded to that call in earlier years by devoting eighteen years to the Oxford Group/Moral Re-Armament program. Perhaps now was the time to get back to basics. I matriculated in the Andover Newton Theological School. I became a preacher at two rural parishes in southeast New Hampshire. The year was 1970. I was fifty-five years old.

-18-

PAPERBOYS

Our boys are named Tom, Bill, and Bob. Somehow Dick and Harry got left out. Thomas Merrell Hunter was born in 1946 (our baby boomer), Willard Merrell Hunter 1948, and Robert Stuart Hunter 1952.

Growing up in Claremont, California, they delivered daily newspapers. When I was that age, this activity was one of the best things I ever did, and we were pleased our boys had the opportunity. The three set something of a record. For a total of six years they served the identical route in Claremont for the *Pomona Progress Bulletin*. When Tom completed two years, he passed the route along to Bill for two, then Bob for another two. The route was not far from our house. Needless to say, these carriers were splendid in every way and were loved by all their clients. We were known as "the parents of the paperboys."

The 1960s were for everybody intense years, heavily influenced by deep bitterness over the Vietnam War and the ongoing struggle for civil rights. Our boys were strongly opposed to the war. The draft was not an issue for Tom (clergy) or Bill (medicine), but it always hung over Bob, who wrestled with conscientious objection. His case for this classification was rejected because he was not opposed to *all* wars, just this one.

In the public schools of Claremont, the three boys followed similar pursuits. All were given leadership positions and were top students. (I'm not making this up.) All ran cross-country, played varsity basketball, and led their tennis teams.

Thomas Merrell (Tom) Hunter

Indianapolis, the home of their two loving maternal grand-parents, was the birthplace of all three boys—each delivered in the Methodist Hospital. Those were the days when fathers were not welcome. A retired navy officer friend on Mackinac Island, Edward Tellefson, referred to an old navy tradition where a commanding officer would say to an ensign applying for what is now called paternity leave, "Son, for the laying of the keel you were essential; but for the launching of the ship you are irrelevant."

Before Tom's birth on September 14, 1946, Mary Louise had a forty-hour labor. So when I was notified in northern Michigan, I had time to fly to Indianapolis. On the plane I was able to share the happy anticipations with seatmate Tom Hickey of the Hickey Freeman clothing family.

Arriving at the Indianapolis hospital at dusk on the thirteenth, I tried every way I could to get in, without success. To the hard-nosed receptionist who was typing away on file cards (by now it was midnight) I said, "Can't I even go in and hold her hand?"

Without looking up she said, "You can't even hold mine— I'm too busy."

In later life Tom was a conscientious boy and charged at life with enthusiasm. He was graduated from Claremont High School in 1964, Amherst College in 1968, and Union Theological Seminary in 1972.

He carried the weight of being the oldest, consciously or unconsciously, worked hard, avoided fights with his brothers, and aimed to please us all.

When we moved to Mackinac Island in 1952, it was not clear how long we'd be there and whether the boys should be enrolled in school for a temporary period. Tom, aged six, was determined, so we signed him up at the local Thomas Ferry School. It was not a one-room schoolhouse, but it was close. Tom had begun to develop a stuttering problem, and we were fortunate that one of his teachers, Pat Squires, had been through it also. She was a great help too. Throughout her life, as mentioned earlier, Tom made it a point whenever he returned to Michigan to seek her out and express his appreciation for her help with this issue.

All three boys earned good grades, but Tom had to work a little harder for his than Bill did. He was on the cross-country and tennis teams, and named to the Honor Society.

In his early teens, Tom developed a long-range relationship with a New Mexico travel camp called the Prairie Trek. It was sponsored by the Cottonwood Gulch Foundation, founded by a teacher and outdoorsman out of Indianapolis, Hillis Howie, who developed an experience for young people by means of a combination travel camp and base operation south east of Gallup, New Mexico. Tom fit in as a camper immediately and soon was asked to be a counselor and wilderness trip manager, which he did for eight years.

When the time came, we took Tom to inspect colleges starting in the West, then the Midwest, but with a nudge from an Amherst-grad uncle, he finally went all the way east to Amherst. He does not look back on the experience as the dear, happy college days of song and story, but rather as a lot of hard work, both in studies and campus jobs. He sang in the glee club, became, as an undergraduate, its manager for a national tour, and as a graduate student came back to manage the glee club's world tour in 1970. He also lettered in cross-country, as he had done in high school, and ran the 1967 Boston Marathon in under four hours.

Tom majored in religion in college and then did neighborhood social work for a year in Manhattan under the auspices of the General Theological Seminary (during which time he was mugged twice, once with a knife at his throat), followed by three years uptown as a student at Union Theological Seminary.

After we moved to California in 1959, we sought out people who might help Tom with his stuttering, and found Dr. Joseph G. Sheehan, Professor of Psychology at UCLA, who with his wife Vivian made a helpful therapy team. The Sheehans referred Tom to their mentor in Kalamazoo, Michigan, where he was later to take work with perhaps the nation's best, Charles Van Riper. The results were remarkably successful. The condition still surfaces occasionally, but he has the art of getting through it. Ironically his entire career has involved public speaking. For five years on KGO radio (ABC) San Francisco he hosted a three-hour Sunday morning talk show, with consistently high ratings.

Billing himself a "minstrel" to kids and their teachers, Tom conducts workshops in schools, churches, and conventions designed to enhance children's learning skills through the use of music. He is co-producer of an annual teacher's camp in the Pacific Northwest. He writes his own songs and markets CDs and cassettes. A sixth grader after a concert asked him, "Are those real songs, or do you just make them up?"

Tom is ordained in the United Church of Christ, Congregational, and in his earlier career was Assistant Pastor at Ladeira Church south of San Francisco, and for five years was pastor of the Lummi Island church in Puget Sound. Since then his ministry has been in music, dedicated to making a difference among children and their teachers.

Tom married Gwen Alley, and with their two children, Aeden and Irene, make their home on Twin Ponds Farm near Bellingham, Washington, the community where Gwen grew up. She has Native American genes and works with high school students of that background as well as at an alternate school for "at risk" youth. Their new spread east of town allows space for animals, which Gwen is certified to use for therapy with children.

Willard Merrell (Bill) Hunter

When Bill was born in 1948, I was traveling in Europe and made the mistake of asking to be told when Mary Louise went to the hospital, as well as when the baby actually arrived. I received the first message, but not the second so there was an anxious week with no information. In Paris, where I was covering a United Nations meeting, I still had not heard. That week I was a guest in the home of M. and Mme. Jean Terray. He was a business executive related to Ferdinand de Lesseps, builder of the Suez Canal. Sympathizing with my distress, he asked why did I not call my wife on the telephone?

"You don't understand," I said, "she is all the way across the Atlantic Ocean, and then some."

"Call her up," he insisted, asked me where she was, went to the hall, spit a few sentences in French into the phone, and returned saying, "The call will go through at ten o'clock."

You can imagine, this being 1948, that there was fluttering in the dovecotes at the Methodist Hospital in Indianapolis. They had to roll Mary Louise out into the hall for the phone. The connection was fine, it was all good news, and we settled on the name right there on the trans-Atlantic phone, Willard Merrell Hunter. As in Tom's case, we were drawing from both sides of the family.

Whether or not Bill was ever really happy with his first name, he has been able to escape it with the nickname we gave him as a baby, "Bill." He is "Dr. Bill" in his medical practice in California's Humboldt County, and the word "beloved" is often used in public references to him.

Bill graduated from Claremont High School in 1966, Harvard College in 1970, and the Medical School of the University of California at Los Angeles (UCLA) in 1974.

He was between the ages of four and eight when we lived on

Mackinac Island, and particularly responded to the charms of living on the island. Those were the years when the Straits of Mackinac Bridge was being built, opening in 1957. It was exciting for the boys to watch it rise across the water six miles to the west.

He was an excellent student, a born leader, and an independent thinker. Fitting in was not a high priority for him. Starting off in the car for church, we sometimes had to wait for Bill to come out of the house. One time his mother asked, "Bill, why are you always last?"

"*Somebody's* got to be last," he said.

We never learned how he was able to assert mind over matter. Each fall during baseball's World Series championships, he managed to fall sick for that week. In those days the games were played in the daytime. Each day he managed to stay home. If it wasn't the flu, it was something equally debilitating. His suspicious mother would be determined to pack him off to school, but she went by the objective thermometer, and somehow or other, come October, Bill produced a fever that lasted just long enough.

Bill showed a political ambition in junior and senior high school that never returned. When he was in junior high, he and I had a talk about the office seeking the man and not the man the office. Lousy idea, he thought. He did not see any national political leader who had waited to be sought. At Claremont High School, without tipping his hand as to what he was doing, he laid out a three-year plan for becoming student body president, and was elected on schedule for the year 1965-66.

In athletics, Bill was an all-out type. One hot, smoggy afternoon, at the end of a cross-country run, Bill passed out, having given it his all. At a tense basketball game in Chino, when the other team was ahead by one point, Bill, surrounded by the pressure of silence, coolly sank two free throws. They put Claremont ahead, and the fans went wild.

From the time he was a little guy, Bill was susceptible to advertisements hawking moneymaking schemes. He was going to make a mint through selling Kalart greeting cards and so sent off for the proffered supply. Somehow the units did not move, and his parents for years "ate" Kalart cards. Same with a super-sensational vacuum cleaner that was going to put him in fat city. To show what a climate his managers created, a fellow recruit asked Bill why would he want to go to medical school and pass up an opportunity like this? His director said he simply had to find a home for *at least one* of those machines. Guess whose that turned out to be. It was an excellent product, and we used it for a long time.

As a paperboy Bill entered a contest where three new sub-scriptions would win him a turkey. It was November, and Bill really wanted to give his mother one for Thanksgiving. He was so appealing in this urge that I simply had to help him by driving him around the prospect area one evening. He was persistent and winsome, made a lot of calls, but no sale. He took the disap-pointment better than his father. I started to cry.

On his paper route, Bill was not so much interested in the business as in enjoying his customers. Unlike Tom, he was always losing money from under-collecting. When returning from picking up payments, it would turn out that he spent more time talking with folks than in collecting their money.

Bill was valedictorian of his high school class, 1966, and at the awards ceremony at the end of his senior year, it seemed as though he was called up to receive just about every one. A handsome devil, the girls were ever alert. One mother reported to us that her daughter said she thought Bill was getting interested in her: because "he tripped me today."

Bill matriculated at Harvard College, where after his first year in a Civil War era dormitory in the Yard he lived in Dunster House on the Charles River, and sang in a group called "Dunster's Dunces." Although he already was thinking about becoming a doctor, he continued the broader studies and was graduated as an economics major in 1970.

Those final four years of the sixties were times of intense protest, and Bill was one of those who felt strongly that his generation, the nation, and civilization itself were at an important crossroads. They were prepared to put life and career on the line. Harvard students were outraged at what they felt was the complicity of the university in the war. President Nathan Pusey called in the police to resist the student onslaughts.[1] Bill threw himself into a struggle in the Harvard Yard, tossed a rock at a cop car, and landed in the corner of a *Life* magazine photograph. At the commencement exercises, Bill was one of a substantial minority who did not wear the cap and gown. There was a rental fee of five dollars for the regalia, and he chose to contribute the saving to the Black Panthers Defense Fund.

During his senior year Bill drove to New York, picked up his brother Tom and proceeded to Washington where they demonstrated in a huge war protest march from the Capitol to the White House. He signed up as a marshal, joining the group that locked hands outside the buses parked around the ellipse to protect the White House from untoward invasion. Some demonstrators criticized the marshals for selling out. They heard jokes about how congressional leaders and the president were probably looking out at the demonstration and as a result saying, "This is it. We're shutting down the war today."

Applying to a number of medical schools, Bill was accepted at UCLA. He wanted a small town and a family practice, and he

---

[1]Pusey said later he had not handled that situation well, particularly in the use of the police.

spent his residency years at UC Davis, in Sacramento. He married Nonae Sears of Belmont, California, and they moved to Garberville, population 1,200, two hundred miles north of San Francisco in the redwood forests, built their own home on a high hillside in nearby Benbow, much of it with their own hands, and reared two children, Laurel and Clayton. Nonae has a degree in public health, has served on the local school board, and directed the summer waterfront activities south of town. Daughter Laurel, born 1980, hopes for an international-oriented career, studies languages, and before finishing college at California State University at Monterey Bay, had already lived and studied in South America, Italy, and Washington, D.C. Son Clayton is a wiry, quick athlete, all sports.

Bill and Nonae came to an amicable parting of the ways, and Bill's second marriage was to Sharon O'Day, a Registered Nurse in charge of post hospital care in Fortuna, California. She has a son, Casey, about the same age as Clayton.

Family Activities

Our boys all played their stint in Little League baseball. We were lucky not to get sucked into the high-pressure echelons where the boys act like men and the men act like boys. Tom and Bill were both pitchers. Once when Tom hit a batter, he was pretty shaken up over how serious it might have been.

We were blessed by excellent Boy Scout programs. In Minneapolis we belonged to the Westminster Presbyterian Church, not only because I was working for Presbyterian Macalester College, but because of the strong Scout leadership, headed by Kyle Cudworth, a Pillsbury flour executive, who was a genius at the development of young men. This carried over to fine experiences at the church-owned Camp Ajawah on a lake northeast of town.

When we moved from Minnesota to California, we were fortunate again to fall into a strong program under Scoutmaster Jesse Shaner, who emphasized a successful camp-out program. Each month the boys and dads spent a night at one of the state or national park facilities. A favorite was Joshua Tree National Monument near the U.S. Marine base at Twenty-Nine Palms. Indian Cove, at the north entrance of Joshua Tree, was marked by huge boulders, strewn by some prehistoric upheaval, over which the boys delightedly crawled till exhausted—and famished. All three of our boys became Eagle Scouts in Claremont.

By 1959, when we moved our family to California, Claremont was still surrounded by orange and lemon trees. They were soon to be bulldozed to make room for rapid housing expansion and schools—but not before we got a taste of the old agriculture. Claremont in fact had been made by colleges and citrus, and an issue in town at the turn of the century was whether preservation or demolition would be the fate of the big packing house on the tracks that had put millions of oranges on the Sante Fe railway cars to be rolled to the East.

The dramatic part came on the nights of frost, possibly a half dozen times each winter. A person could be wiped out in a single night. A grower and his brother-in-law, Fred Dundas and Leonard "Agee" Shelton, who lived across the street, religiously listened to the radio weather reports on LA's KFI every night at eight o'clock. When frost was expected, they went into action. Several times our boys were drafted to man the smudge pots as were many others around town. It was an all night job, and the kids participating were excused from school the next day. The smudging was accomplished by use of oil heaters in the groves. The clouds of smoke they belched out kept the frost away from the fruit.

Smudging caused a severe housekeeping problem. The gunk would seep through all cracks. We discovered that in the house we bought on Eleventh Street a previous owner had installed a fan blower that when turned on blew into the house and kept the air pressure inside the house slightly higher than outside, thus preventing the smudge from blackening the curtains.

A hallmark of our family time together was music—lots of it—with more enthusiasm than expertise, although Tom made a professional career of it. All three of the boys took piano lessons and performed in the standard recitals. From there they branched out, Tom to clarinet and bassoon, Bill to oboe, and Bob to cello. All took part in high school orchestras and at commencement exercises played "Pomp and Circumstance" forever. All three learned the guitar as an aid to socializing, and this instrument became an essential part of Tom's professional life. Along the way Bill picked up the violin and has become an accomplished fiddler, joining local groups and regional rallies whenever his medical practice has allowed. It seemed as though Bill could play any stringed instrument placed in his hands. At one stage he had also mastered the mandolin.

Many times we all made music together, with Mary Louise at the piano and me carrying the vocal part. Sunday evenings there were hymns, and on trips in the car—spirituals, folk songs, and Stephen Foster.

The boys and I had many happy times hiking in the hills north of Claremont. I guess Mary Louise figured this was a "guy" thing, and she used these interludes for a little peace and quiet back at home. Just above where we lived, on the slopes of Mount San Antonio ("Old Baldy"), we could immediately enter wilderness areas protected by the Angeles National Forest. One would never know there were more than ten million people living below us in Los Angeles County alone. We went most weekends and always took our beagle, Frisky. Since on weekdays we had to keep him inside our back yard or on a leash, the let-'er-rip weekends in the hills were his Promised Land. His brains were all in his nose, so we kept him off city streets. But through the canyons he could take off after coyotes or whatever appealed. Sometimes we would lose him, but returning in an hour or so we could always count on his circling back to the area where we had separated.

On a hike up Ontario Peak we saw a herd of Big Horn Mountain Sheep. Fred Dundas, our lemon-growing Claremont neighbor, was with us and said that in thirty years he had never seen such a sight. One of our first California summers all five of us trekked over the Kearsarge Pass and camped near the famous John Muir Trail that goes from Yosemite to Los Angeles.

One time we took a week to hike from west to east across the Sierra. We started at Sequoia National Park and hiked into the Kern River valley, then up over the top of Mount Whitney (highest outside Alaska, 14,494 feet), and down to Bishop in the Owens Valley. Every night we camped out on the ground. Fred's brother-in-law, Leonard "Agee" Shelton, whose son Robert ("Rabbit") went with us, donated the rental of horses to take us up the long incline that got us started and said, "Willard, this is the smartest thing you've ever done."

He was right, it was.

While we were climbing Mount Whitney, we came across an elderly lady, seventy something, leaning up against a rock in the shade. "How's it going?" we asked.

"Fine," she said, "I'm waiting for my mother."

Farther up the trail, we found a man and a bucket of golf balls. With a long driver he was whacking them thousands of feet down the vast canyon below.

Robert Stuart (Bob) Hunter (1952-1971)

Our memories of Bob may be a little sharper, because after his brothers had gone off to college we had him all by himself for his four high school years. There were many activities the youngest of the three had with us that others did not. For example, Bob and I hiked to the bottom of the Grand Canyon and slept by the river overnight—going down on a footpath and back the next day up the Bright Angel Trail, the one the mules use.

Bob lived with us without the others in Washington, D.C. 1966-67 during my sabbatical year at the Brookings Institution, sharing capital city experiences like the RFK Stadium and sportscaster Warner Wolf.

Then too, Bob was a compulsory journal keeper, and his diaries have, post-mortem, revealed interesting reaches of his life.

In-house traumas also play their part in drawing family members together. Bob was still at home when I was hospitalized for manic-depressive syndrome, a searing experience for everybody.

Finally, Bob's early death created a special link. Death has a way of enhancing its own, as for example, the special feeling we have for presidents who die in office.

From the very first, Bob was a charmer. In second grade, the teacher told us the other children wanted to be in his group. Even when he developed his stuttering problem (we thought it unusual to have two in the same family), he seemed to incorporate it into his innate charm. He also showed an unusual sensitivity to what was going on in people around him. When we lived in Washington 1966-67, he attended the District's leading junior high school, Alice Deal. Classmates called him in the evening with math problems, and he would spend half an hour on the phone talking them through.

While we were there, one of Bob's friends back in California wrote that it was important that he let her nominate him for class president the coming year, when he would have returned to Claremont. He declined. Two years later, however, he accepted their pleas and agreed to run for student body president. He was elected and served 1969-70. The office sought the man. A hyperbolic faculty adviser said that Bob had ushered in "a new kind of high school leader, not just in Claremont but in the nation as well."

At Harvard he had a similar effect. A classmate wrote about Bob a few weeks into their freshman year:

> I consider him the best friend I had at Harvard. I was able to talk to him when nobody else would listen. His friendship was actually the real stabilizing factor in my rather painful and difficult adjustment to this college.

In high school Bob developed the normal religious doubts. Earlier he had whole-heartedly adopted the traditional package. When he was a youngster, someone gave him a subscription to Norman Vincent Peale's *Guideposts* magazine, which he devoured each month as soon as it came. Every year he asked for a renewal as a present, unaffected by the cynicism of peers or brothers. At a Billy Graham meeting in the LA Coliseum, he decided to go forward to reconfirm the commitment he felt he had already made.

Active in his church youth group, even after he had begun to entertain doubts, he proposed at a congregational meeting a self-study for the church, and his recommendation became known as the "Hunter Amendment." There is a tree in the Claremont Congregational (UCC) courtyard dedicated to his memory.

Bob often came up with an interesting angle. The day after the Dallas assassination in 1963 he said, "Daddy, I've decided not to mow the lawn today, out of respect for John F. Kennedy."

His appeal often pulled at my heartstrings. For example, like his father his do-it-yourself skills were not all that great. In a national test, his verbal expertise was rated tops; his mechanical aptitude, zero. One time when he was struggling with what looked like a simple manual problem, I said, "Bob, they train chimpanzees to do that kind of thing." His eyes filled with tears while he murmured, "But I'm not a chimpanzee." It was one of those things I wish I had never said. He gave a similar response once when he was being especially inquisitive. I said, "Bob, curiosity killed a cat." Same misty-eyed reaction, "But I'm not a cat."

Like his brothers before him, Bob excelled in cross-country and tennis. Early in his senior cross-country season he broke a bone in his foot and had to train for six weeks on his bicycle. At the regional meet he overtook the favored runner and won the race in the closing yards. He was captain of an undefeated tennis team where he could be counted on to go for the "winner." This tendency to be decisive, almost compulsively so, usually made him "go for it." The high school yearbook, *El Espiritu*, called him the "sparkplug and playmaker" for the basketball team. He was known for the bold pass or daring shot, sometimes at the final gun.

He had lots of friends. He had blond good looks, and carried the stuttering nuisance with considerable grace. He was something of a heartthrob, and one mother wrote us, "I think Bob was my favorite one of all the boys who stopped by to see our girls."

Bob was a compulsive student as well as a compulsive athlete. Coming home from school in the afternoon, he could not bring himself to do anything else until he had completed his next day's assignments. At Alice Deal he was smaller than the other basketball players, but he fought his way onto the team by sheer guts. At the National Airport early one morning, I pointed out Bobby Kennedy coming through the terminal and suggested he might like to speak with him. Bob charged up, acquired the senator's autograph, and then threw it away. He said he obtained it only to prove he could.

Bob, like Bill, was accepted at Harvard and several other schools, saying it was pretty hard to turn down Harvard. He chose their option to delay entrance for a year. In hindsight this looked to us like a mistake. It seemed to add to his confusion. He toured the nation as a freight-riding day laborer, gathering general experiences and struggling with heavy thoughts. But his life did not move ahead. And always hovering over him was the Selective Service.

In the fall of 1970 in Eureka, California, he picked potatoes and wrote these comments in his journal:

> October 4—I'm beginning to learn how to live economically and still eat well. One technique is small- time shoplifting. So far I've acquired peanuts and cheese that way.
>
> October 20—I'm sure many just go along with their philosophy for their own personal ends, like me stealing from the grocery store. I had no reason to do that, except I somehow thought it was OK because I was liberated. I've now decided it's a bad thing because it reduces trust. And in a society where there is no trust there is fear, suspicion, and hate in its place, such as is demonstrated by my working partners. That is one necessity, I believe, to have in a society—trust of each other. If you don't have that, the society can really no longer function. . . . and that appears to be where we're headed.

Apparently depression was beginning to get to Bob, and by the end of the year he was not in good shape. He started smoking marijuana as a sophomore in high school, and it is said that continuous use over time tends to depress. He said that the mountains, which had so many times revived him, were no longer able to work their magic. As a culmination of his year off, he planned to make a trip to Europe, obtaining his passport pictures in the process. But soon he canceled his plans and, homesick for his friends in California, split once more for the West Coast.

Here again he was dashed. His friends had moved on with their lives, and he did not find the reunion he had hoped. Having been at the pinnacle of high school success, he was like the Dustin Hoffman character in *The Graduate*. Life was empty and nothing appealed. College, he decided, was a chance for one more try, and he poured himself into being a Harvard freshman.

But his depression advanced, and not three months into his first year, on December 11, 1971, he compulsively ended his quest with a decisive jump.

We were at home in New Hampshire when we heard the news. Our friend Roy Kent, Newmarket undertaker, went down to Boston at once. I asked him on the phone not to move the body until we got there. We arrived at the Boston morgue around five o'clock, six hours after he fell. They wheeled his battered body out on the gurney, and I had a few moments to say goodbye. Mary Louise preferred to stay in the car.

There was a glint in one of Bob's eyes that sparked for half a second the ridiculous hope that he could come back. I put my hand under his shirt and felt his chest. I was surprised to feel that his body was still warm after that much time had elapsed. I knelt beside the cart and kissed his cold forehead. Then they wheeled the cart away. Next time I saw Michelangelo's *Pieta* I felt a strangely warm bond, a parent holding a lifeless son.

Tom flew in from his speech semester in Michigan and Bill from his medical studies in Los Angeles. My sister and brother came, as did one of Mary Louise's brothers. Messages arrived from Claremont, poignant ones from Bob's high school friends expressing their loss. Nine years later at their tenth class reunion they were telling the newspapers that his memory was central to their preparations. Two years after his brother's death Bill at his wedding would tearfully wish Bob were present. Mary Louise noted that whereas we as parents would miss Bob for thirty years or so, Tom and Bill will for much longer. Tom phones us almost every year on Bob's birthday and deathday.

At the service in the Lee church we placed Bob's backpack and miniature camp stove in the front area, where the casket might have rested, representing his quest and the "magic" of the mountains. My brother Stu spoke of drawing future strength from this experience. I closed my remarks with Shakespeare's lines, "Now cracks a noble heart. Good night, sweet prince, and flights of angels sing thee to thy rest."

He was, indeed, a sweet prince.

Three days later we scattered his ashes in the December snows below the Kancamagus Pass in the White Mountains of New Hampshire.

We were moved by Harvard President Derek Bok thoughtfully inviting Mary Louise and me to his office to talk about Bob. Harvard averages one suicide a year.

I put up a plaque on the north wall of the Madison Hotel to mark the spot where Bob fell. On the marker I had inscribed the words of the father of one of Bob's Claremont classmates, a boy whom Bob had helped through some tough times:

> I am certain that the world is much better for having had
> Robert Stuart Hunter
> as a member of its congregation for even nineteen short years

The sympathetic hotel owner, Paul Manus, said he appreciated a father being so devoted to a departed son, and he wanted to do what he could. His secretary, Pat Hall, was warm-hearted in her hospitality each time I visited Boston. She arranged the details for the dedication of the plaque and gave a hotel-sponsored reception afterwards.

Others in the family had different views about the Madison

Hotel. Tom says, "Bill and I wanted to blow the place up."[2]

At the Boston police department and the city morgue, I tried to discover every detail I could about Bob's death. The police were not anxious to show me much. Doubtless they had had experience with distraught fathers and may have suspected I was going to sue somebody for something. A year after Bob's death I made an anniversary visit to all the stops—the hospital, the psychiatrists, the morgue, the Madison Hotel, and the police headquarters. Captain Joseph McCormack of the Identification Division finally and reluctantly brought the pictures out. The photos were grim. Bob's legs were shattered, something I had not been aware of in the morgue the year before. His head was pointed toward the *east* and the Boston Harbor, over which the sun rises on the city each day. Whenever we sing the communion hymn, "Let us break bread together on our knees," I think of Bob.

> When I fall on my knees,
> With my face to the rising sun,
> O Lord, have mercy on me.

He fell on his knees with his face to the rising sun. O Lord, have mercy—on me, and on him.

Alan Hunter, no relation, for years the pastor of the Mount Hollywood Congregational Church in Los Angeles, told us he and Bob happened to be in a small sharing group one Sunday morning when Bob was asked to identify some symbol that would represent what his life was like. He answered, years before *Forrest Gump*, that it was like a feather that started in the sky and floated in the air, swinging back and forth to the ground.

Bob kept an extensive diary and obliged himself to record his

---

[2]In fact Manus sold the Madison to the Federal government, which then imploded it and replaced it with the Thomas P. "Tip" O'Neill, Jr. office building.

thoughts on almost every subject. He was especially good at appreciating those around him. Here's what he wrote when the family was worried about me:

> This shook us up pretty bad. I took a moonlight hike in the mountains that was fantastic. Everything was so great. The full moon shining on the mountains, the smell of everything. I saw a deer, the beautiful sunrise . . . I did a lot of thinking and I think I came out on a really good level. As I told Bill, every incident like this really makes you think things through.
>
> It forces you out of your normal thought patterns, and you really have to grapple with things on a deep level. Especially since it has to do with someone we really love. . . . Any of us can fall off the tightrope of reality, and that's what happened to Dad. Because reality is only a tightrope that we walk to get through life. There is so much around us that we can't possibly conceive of.
>
> But I think I came to the conclusion that this, too, is part of life. And because of that, we have to accept it, accept it unconditionally and gratefully and know that it is valuable and valid. It makes us realize that life never works the way we want it to. We can never control it or mold it, because we are only one small part of something much bigger than us. . . . and life is good. It really is. . . . It is awe-inspiring, magnificent—just like the mountains, the sun, the moon, and the earth. We can only understand it and experience it in our soul. And Dad's experience is as much of this universality as anything else, so it too contains that goodness.

In our Claremont church one Sunday morning the youth group presented a lively arrangement of an old Negro spiritual. Bob had the solo part and he belted out several times the refrain, "I ain't got time to die."

Yet somehow or other, as will we all, he found the time.

Mary Louise and I have been very, very lucky. We hope we did something right. We sure tried. But our family—far beyond anything we could possibly have made happen ourselves—has been a gift of grace.

-19-

PREACHING IN COUNTRY CHURCHES

In 1970, at fifty-five years, I left California to begin a new career with study at Andover Newton Theological School in Boston.

I had been restless for some time in the college promotion work, and wondered whether the church, as I had contemplated in youth, might still have possibilities for service. Through Tom Trotter, dean of the Claremont School of Theology, I learned that President Gordon E. Michalson was looking for help in the school's development department. Trotter suggested that Michalson might welcome my assistance half time, while I at the same time could take some theological courses to see whether I wanted to pursue that field. I did this, and on the professional side I was able in six months to revamp the corporate image of the school and generate national press coverage. The former was accomplished by revising all campus publications, and starting up a plan for campus signs. The latter I was able to do by peddling an environmental conference at the seminary as a meeting on "The Theology of Ecology" and enlisting coverage by the religion writers of the *New York Times*, *the Washington Post*, *the Los Angeles Times*, plus a stringer from *Time*. All resulted in impressive features. At the same time the trial classroom work I undertook helped solidify the shift in careers. At the end of the six months I was invited to stay on in Claremont, but we felt it was time to make a clean break, and besides Mary Louise had always wanted to live in New England. So we were off to the East Coast—for six years.

Economic realities made it important that I secure a church job while at the seminary. This I was able to do through the headquarters of the United Church of Christ in Boston. I was made student pastor of two small Congregational parishes in nearby New Hampshire, Lee and Madbury, a few miles inland from the Atlantic Ocean. The two were called "yoked," as they had a common pastor and an Interchurch Council. Thus I was able to jump right into the ministry without waiting for three more years of education. The seminary faculty wanted their students to spend more time on campus each week than I did, but they never objected to my schedule.

Although the greatest tragedy to befall our family took place during this period, the loss of our youngest son, the satisfaction of living in rural New England was for us a first-rate experience. For myself it was great to be two people—Monday through Wednesday, a student in suburban Boston—Thursday through Sunday, a shepherd of two flocks in southeast New Hampshire. I was thirty years older than the other seminary students, but they accepted me as one of their own, even electing me to the student council. Also the seminary let me leave campus clothes and study materials in my dormitory room throughout the school year, even though they only charged me for the nights I actually occupied the quarters.

I made pretty good friends with some of the professors. Maybe the best was James Luther Adams, a well-known Unitarian theologian who taught for years at the Harvard Divinity School. When he retired there, he joined the faculty temporarily at Andover Newton, where I came to know him. He is named among the top three theologians in the history of Unitarianism, was translator and biographer of the German-American theologian Paul Tillich, amateur cinematographer of Nazi activities in prewar Germany, and author of many essays and books including *On Being Human Religiously* (Boston: Unitarian Universalist Association, 1976). He was an extraordinary individual in every way, with a gift of making each student feel he was very special. His classroom sessions were not always the best organized, yet he insisted that some of the most productive class experiences he had were the result of diversions into wide-ranging tangents.

Adams's name has been closely associated with voluntary associations and their importance in a democratic society. He was interested in my book on the role of tax deductibility in promoting voluntarism and assigned portions of it for advanced reading in his Andover Newton class. He was criticized, being such a creative, cutting-edge thinker, for not publishing as much as he should. But I believe the problem was not procrastination, but rather that he was constantly absorbed in helping his students publish *their* creations.

He provided one of the best blurbs that boosted my book *The Spirit of Charles Lindbergh: Another Dimension* with the quote, "Helps to explain why, for the time, Lindbergh changed the reputation of human nature."

Another good friend at Andover Newton was Professor John Billinsky, head of the seminary's pastoral care department. He "owned" the second floor of the administration building, and often dominated faculty meetings with his brilliant mastery of *Robert's Rules of Order*. He stopped attending the daily chapel services because one morning students served tomato juice and crackers for communion. He was always clear as to what should be done and how, and at the same time had a great heart. When our son Bob made his first suicide attempt, I met with John in his office, and I never have heard any one pray more fervently that some one would be healed.[1]

---

[1]Billinsky was an eminent Jungian, dedicated to spiritual solutions, and for years carried on an active controversy with Massachusetts Mental Hospital and its Freud-oriented Harvard influence. Mass Mental was where Bob stayed between attempts, and we noticed they had a mechanistic approach, not allowing him, for example, to exercise by playing basketball, so as to keep his repressions bottled up for sharing in interviews.

A third faculty friend was my preaching teacher, Eddie O'Neal, a powerful black football star who later occupied the Bartlet Chair of Sacred Rhetoric at Andover Newton. He had a rhythmic, charismatic preaching style and at the end of every sermon he issued an altar call. He was encouraging about my preaching, and I think he had a good deal to do with my selection as the winner of the Carroll Whittemore Excellence in Preaching Award.

Mary Louise landed an excellent job in Durham as Administrative Assistant to Harry Day, the Director of the New England Center for Continuing Education, a project of the six New England state universities and located on the campus of the University of New Hampshire (UNH). She so fell in love with New England that six years later she did not want to go back to California.

The New England Center for Continuing Education, on the University campus, was the creature of the six state universities in New England, and its logo was a hexagon, not unlike Chrysler's. The building has attracted visitors just to see the structure, which was designed by Los Angeles architect William Pereira, whose credits included the Transamerica pyramid building in San Francisco and the University of California campus at Irvine. The structure was built so that its upper reaches blend into the trees and the lower stories into the native geological outcroppings. The Continuing Education Center has been discontinued, and the building taken on for UNH purposes.

One of the highlights of Mary Louise's experience at the center was providing support for launching the Elderhostel movement, described in another chapter.

The churches were seventy miles northeast of the seminary, and it took ninety minutes for me to drive each way. Often I used this time in the car to memorize material like opening sentences and benedictions for worship services; also scripture passages, poetry, and even some Shakespeare. This memory backlog has been helpful to me ever since.

We lived in the Lee parsonage, which long ago had been erected in the old style, immediately next door to the church, standing on highway 155 in southeast New Hampshire, fifteen miles west of Portsmouth. The Lee and Madbury churches are five miles apart. On Sunday I preached at the 9:30 service at one and at the 11:00 service at the other. Each year they switched starting hours.

We had not lived in New England before, and it took some getting used to. The conventional wisdom is that you must live there for decades before you are really accepted. But every one was gracious to us right away. One incident struck us as having a rather New England hue.

George Webb was the head deacon in the Lee Church. Each weekday he commuted twelve miles to Rochester, New Hampshire, where he taught science in the high school. He was a veteran of many tours as deacon, and knew how everything worked.

We had a rather small attendance when we came, a dozen or so. Feeling the need to do something, I talked to him about it, "George, how about getting a group together to make some calls to interest new people?"

Said George, "We always counted on 'Mahshall' (Marshall) Stevenson to do that." (Stevenson was my predecessor.)

"I know, George, but now you have a new minister."

"Yes, but you have the same congregation."

Another rejoinder that sounded like New England came from our down-the-road neighbor Mary Booth, the widow of a Boston businessman. One of her friends, whose husband was not long for this world, moaned to Mary, "I don't know whatever I will do if anything should happen to my David."

"Well," Mary said, "you'll find out."

The Holy Land

During our first year of the new profession, I seized an opportunity to visit the Holy Land. I had always been impressed by reports from visitors of the meaningfulness of walking the dusty roads trod by the Biblical personalities. Now that I was constantly dealing with Biblical material, it seemed a good idea to acquire on-the-ground experience. I signed on for a tour to take place the last two weeks of August 1971. I paid the low rates of the tour group, but since their intra-Israel reservations were full, once I landed at Tel Aviv I was on my own. It turned out to be a perfect arrangement. I was free, for example, to *walk* the six miles south from Jerusalem to Bethlehem and the twelve miles north from Jerusalem to Bethel—and beyond that, part way to Shechem. Where it was too far to walk, as to Galilee, Jericho, and the Dead Sea, I could buy my own individual bus tours, sometimes for only part of a day.

I identified with original accounts as much as possible. Approaching Bethlehem in the evening, with a bright star overhead, I threw my sleeping bag on the ground and spent the night in Shepherds' Fields. Then walked into Bethlehem in the morning. From the Christmas card scenes, I thought of Bethlehem as being in a valley, and the shepherds coming "with haste" down from the hills. On the contrary, Bethlehem is built on the top of a hill (doubtless for security at the time) and the shepherds would have had to trudge *up*.

Near where they think is the nativity area it is a little disturbing to see, hear, and smell the belching buses lined up for people to visit Manger Square. At first I was irritated by the seemingly tasteless way some of the shrines looked, loaded with smoking censers, swinging lamps, and garish superstructures. Later I became more charitable, and felt appreciation for those people's devotion, who had chosen *their* way of expressing it.

I walked five miles northward from Jerusalem to the spring where the Holy Family spent the night after participating in the Passover. The year of the story, Jesus was twelve, and this spot is where his parents missed him, he having stayed behind to philosophize with the temple elders. How do they know this is the spot? It is the only watering place that would have been a day's journey north.

Above that is Bethel. I arrived there also at dark and rolled out my sleeping bag in the place where in the sixteenth century B.C. Jacob spent a night while running away from his brother Esau. Like Jacob I found a friendly rock on which to lay my head. For some reason I thought of Ruth St. Denis, whom I met in 1939 at a press conference she held in Los Angeles. "Jacob's Pillow" was the name of the dance center she and her husband Ted Shawn founded in the Massachusetts Berkshires.

Looking to the east, I did not see Jacob's ladder, but there was an eerie night cloud formation that looked like a tall man stretched out on his back. He had a full beard and was looking up into the dark sky. According to the Genesis account, Jacob enshrined Bethel with the words, "Surely the Lord is in this place, and I did not know it. . . . This is none other than the house of God, and this is the gate of heaven."

The next day I walked north toward Shechem, on the route close to that which presumably Jesus used in his many north-south trips. I was running out of time, so I cheated by hitching a ride to Shechem with a baker. There I marveled at Jacob's Well, where Jesus talked to the Samaritan woman. The well is deep, and they will pull up for you a pailful of sweet cool water, deeply refreshing in August in desert country.

I swam in Lake Galilee, the source of the Jordan River, and brought back bottles of Jordan water, which I then used in New Hampshire baptisms. Phillips Brooks, legendary Boston preacher of the nineteenth century, after a visit to the Holy Land wrote

"O Little Town of Bethlehem." He is also known for an often quoted homily comparing Lake Galilee, full of fish and surrounded by green growth, with the Dead Sea, no life. The reason for the difference, he said, is that Galilee is outgoing and pours its being out beyond itself, whereas the Dead Sea only receives, giving out nothing. Of course I was there a hundred years after Brooks, but I saw a zillion minnows swimming in the Dead Sea. All the same, it is still a good story.

From the Dead Sea I looked up to the clifftops where I could see the Caves of Qmran where the famous Dead Sea Scrolls were discovered. Later at the Claremont School of Theology I was to work with the Scrolls' first translator, John Trever, helping him with public presentations.

One of my vivid mental pictures of the Israeli countryside is of how skillfully young boys, ten to twelve years, wearing nothing more than a stick, had total control, moving great numbers of sheep and goats from place to place.

When I arrived in Nazareth, the Franciscans had just completed building a beautiful gleaming Church of the Annunciation. (The Franciscans have responsibility for Christian holy places in Israel.) On the upper sanctuary level a section of the flooring is cut away and replaced with heavy transparent blocks. A guide takes visitors over to look down into a cave below where it is said that the Angel Gabriel told Mary she would be the Mother of God. "This is where the incarnation began," he says.

The buses were Israeli based, and we were not allowed to stop in Palestinian territory on the West Bank, where sometimes, even then, rocks were thrown. The Israeli tour guides were good at explaining both Old and New Testament stories at the various places, accepting quite literally the Biblical accounts.

The Muslims, as well as the Jews and the Christians, see Jerusalem as their Holy City. Their revered mosque, the Dome of the Rock, rests on Mount Moriah where Abraham, a figure embraced by all three religions, was tested and ultimately not required to sacrifice his son Isaac. Many Christians say the Second Coming cannot happen as long as those people hold that rock. A basic cause of the seemingly unsolvable, fratricidal riddle of the Middle East is the claim of different groups that God promised them the same land.

The Garden Tomb in Jerusalem looks more like the way we think of Jesus' burial place from the scriptural accounts, but the Church of the Holy Sepulcher, with additional garish memorials a few blocks away, is thought to be more authentic.

The Franciscans every Friday lead a public retracing of the original route believed to be followed by Jesus on his last day, between the spot where Pontius Pilate released him to the executioners and the place he was crucified. Along the way they highlight their Stations of the Cross. This experience was a factor in my putting together both in New Hampshire and in California a Way of the Cross, a participatory reenactment every Good Friday of Christ's last half mile.

There are those who prefer not to visit the Holy Land and rather to keep their own thoughts about how all those places look. But I would recommend that for any one dealing with biblical subjects—preachers, professors, Sunday School teachers or whatever—it is invaluable to be able to visualize what the road to Jericho looks like, or the Mount of Olives, or the Garden of Gethsamane. There is some advantage in see-hear-feel-touch.

Country Churches

Back in New England, shipping and oil magnate Aristotle Onassis moved to establish a refinery on the bay back of Durham, the seat of the University of New Hampshire. The bay is connected to the Atlantic Ocean, and tankers could easily enter. Agents surreptitiously bought up parcels of wooded land, claiming they were acting for an elderly gentleman who wished to establish a hunting lodge. When the true facts began to emerge, the area was plunged into a swivet. Outraged citizens demanded and got a hearing on public television. Onassis sent his top people to explain their objective, including how clean was modern oil refining. The hearings went on day after day, and the local public television station fed the highlights to the commercial networks.

I worked up some brilliant stuff that I might say, as a country preacher in Lee and Madbury, the "back eighty" and "back forty" of Durham. I planned to recall Will Rogers's comment when he was a luncheon guest in San Francisco of executives of the Standard Oil Company of California. Asked to speak, as he always was, Rogers said, "When I was a boy, I asked my father one day what was all that commotion going on in the barn?" He said, "Son, that's the neighbor's bull servicing our cow."

"Gentlemen," Will is said to have concluded, "Looks to me like the Standard Oil Company is servicing the entire state of California."

I suspected NBC might pick up this kind of material from the local outlet. I was almost at the head of the line at the microphone when I chickened out. I had to return a motion picture reel to somebody in the afternoon, and it was a convenient excuse.

In Lee and Madbury our communicants were salt-of-the-earth farmers, artisans, and schoolteachers. At first very few people came. I had fantasized that when the word got around about this spellbinding new preacher, people would flood in. They did not. Even if a stemwinder should show up, New Englanders are good at keeping their enthusiasm under control. However, by the time we left, the Sunday attendance at Lee was around sixty, and a new education/fellowship hall had been built.

One new member who entered in with some enthusiasm was Deborah Fahnestock, a University of Pennsylvania graduate who came north to pursue a career in psychological counseling. I met her in a diner on Highway 125 where she had stopped for coffee on the way to an antique sale in Concord. In the sixties students of means like her on both coasts left the universities to acquire property to the north and pursue their back-to-the-land, counterculture lifestyle. Deborah's late father was a race car enthusiast and her mother was Frances Jeffery Fahnestock, a cultural icon in Boston, who chaired the Boston Symphony Orchestra.

Mrs. Fahnestock's living quarters occupied an upper floor of a Beacon Hill town house. She knew everybody who was anybody and was a gracious hostess. One evening she invited Mary Louise and me to have dinner with her at her home before going on to the Pops concert, where she wanted us to meet the orchestra's patriarch, Arthur Fiedler. "Arthur is dying to meet you," she said. Skeptical, I surmised that the only way that could be true would be if she had told him something like, "If you're not nice to these friends, I'll kill you." Our hostess had two other dinner guests that evening. Having long been imbued with John Collins Bossidy's famous rhyme:

> And this is good old Boston,
> The home of the bean and the cod,
> Where the Lowells talk to the Cabots,
> And the Cabots talk only to God.

we were astounded when the only other guests turned out to be a Mrs. Lowell and a Mr. Cabot!

Frances died in 1997. Deborah and her sister asked me to come back from California to conduct the service, which was held, appropriately enough, in Boston's Symphony Hall, from the stage seen by millions on TV. A special message came from Japan where Conductor Seijo Ozawa was on assignment.

Back in New Hampshire Lee and Madbury were where some of the university people lived, an easy distance from work. In the 1970s our two small churches were a little rural for their tastes, and on Sundays they were apt to stick with their weekday friends in the more academic setting of the Durham church, which offered variety in the way of music and extras.

Exceptions were Guy and Margaret Angell. They were a handsome gray couple, he being the retired head of the dairy department at the University's agricultural school. He thought people should support the church in the town where they lived. Originally from Vermont, his broad accent carried granite strength and farm friendliness. The Lee and Madbury churches looked to Guy as their elder statesman, and he chaired the joint search committee that retained me in July 1970. Before we left six years later, he was generously giving me credit for a turn-around in new life and attendance.

After we left, with the growth of the two small towns as bedroom communities, it became respectable for professional and academic types to attend the Lee church, which grew quite dramatically. The Lee and Madbury churches later dissolved their "yoke," and again became independent of each other.

The Lee parsonage where we lived was a square structure with four rooms on each of the two floors. The one bathroom was downstairs. We turned one of the upstairs rooms into a study, where I worked with my pre-computer standard typewriter. The church folks cared for the place, and kept coming around to give it tender loving care and also to grace us with vegetables like zucchini. When our Bob died, they brought casseroles.

The Madbury church was smaller than the one at Lee, and perhaps a bit more old line. They called themselves the Union Congregational Church of Madbury, and they were one of the churches whose predecessors were generated by the Great

Awakening of New England in the eighteenth century. The church building was next door to the park and across the street from the Town Hall.

One of our Madbury deacons, Fred Mudgett, was a member of the New Hampshire legislature. He invited me to open the sessions of the two Houses in the Capitol with prayer on June 16, 1971. Fred was getting on in years, and he had been a member of the House for a long time. The New Hampshire legislature is the third largest parliamentary body in the English speaking world, with twenty-four members in the Senate and four hundred in the House. Fred told me the large size was a good thing—it was too expensive for anybody to corrupt that many people! I gathered that the members take turns asking one of their constituents to deliver the opening invocation each day. Fred was proud to have his minister do this, and his minister was proud to be asked to do it. There are two prayers, one for each chamber. The Governor and his cabinet come into each, one after the other, stand facing the legislators and bow their heads. Everyone is quiet and listens. One of my phrases appeared in the press; I prayed that the legislators might "disagree without being disagreeable."

For some reason the Madbury church became a refuge for a few families who were dissatisfied with their own church. Polly Webster, the wife of retired UNH English Professor Robert Webster, used to slip in at the beginning of the service and slip out before she had to talk to anyone. She was a published writer and she and her husband and I had some good times together around their kitchen table in Durham. They were sad when advancing years made them give up their summer antiques shop in Kennebunkport. Their daughter Dudley Webster, who, when she married attorney Thomas Dudley, generated the bumper-sticker name of Dudley Dudley, was a power in the Democratic party, a member of the Governor's Council, and a candidate for Congress.

Especially memorable was the steady support of Donald Babcock, retired Professor of Philosophy and Religion at the University and unofficial Poet Laureate of the New Hampshire tidelands, with his more recent volumes of poetry published while we were there. He tried us out in Madbury, liked what he heard, and recommended us to others. When he shook my hand at the end of his first visit, he said, "Now lettest thou thy servant depart in peace. I didn't know there was preaching like this going on anywhere."

Later he moved to California where he lived with his son in Orange County until he was over one hundred years old. I used to visit him every month. "You are our pastor," he would say.

New England Center

Mary Louise continued to commute daily the five miles between Lee and Durham to her office at the New England Center. Her two brothers, both business types, were concerned about their aging mother in Indianapolis still driving an automobile and persuaded her to give her car to her commuting daughter, which worked out well for us. I used our green Volkswagen "bug," which I had bought from a seminary classmate.

All the time we were in New England, Gordon E. Michalson, President of the Claremont School of Theology, my boss when I worked there in the spring of 1970, was asking me to return to his staff. He and his wife Louise invited us down from New Hampshire to New York to talk about it. Louise Michalson was always a delight, with a sense of humor that wouldn't quit. She had a habit of telling us that of all the new people who had come aboard at the School of Theology, we Hunters were her favorites. At length I said to her, "O, come off it, Louise, you say that to all the folks."

"No, no," she protested, "Maybe once in a while to a trustee, but then that's a matter of dollars and cents."

Dr. Michalson said I had done things at the School that had not been done before, and he had been unable to find anyone who could do the same.

My response was that although I appreciated the honor, I had done that and was now into another phase. However, after six years in our country churches, and having completed work at the seminary for two Master's degrees, I felt I had done all I could in New England and finally decided to go back west. For four years from 1976 to 1980, I again served the Claremont School of Theology as Assistant to the President for Communications. There was a switch of bosses. Michalson retired in 1977, and the last three years I worked for his successor, Richard Cain. In October 1980 I became a free-lance speaker and writer.

Preaching to Beat All

Back in California I was sometimes asked to be interim pastor at small churches. Especially significant were the Moreno Valley Congregational Church east of Riverside for three years, and the Faith United Church of Christ in Garden Grove for six months.

From the former, Dick Dale, an avocado grower in a town then called Sunnymead, later Moreno Valley, telephoned one night to say they needed an interim leader for a month or so. I agreed—and stayed three years, to March 1985. The church was one of the town's oldest institutions, dating from 1892. In spite of the fact that it was in the heart of the fastest growing area in California, church growth was a struggle. The most successful device was telemarketing, a team going to the phone and making personal invitations. We received great assistance from the Congregational Church in Riverside in the persons of Finley and Betty Bown, who made Moreno Valley their church during the interim period.

During those three years I was a "weekend warrior," and showed up on Sunday mornings, with added weekday visits for funerals, weddings, and other special events.

A special friend was Myrtle Eagle, one of our congregation's genuine "Okies," who came to California during the dust storms of the Depression and lived in Moreno Valley forty-five years. She had enough Indian in her to qualify for Cherokee tribal benefits, and intermittently returned to the old reservation in Oklahoma for medical support and eyeglasses. I made a point of stopping to see her even after my Moreno Valley assignment was over. She was born in 1896 and lived to be ninety-nine. Near the end she wrote asking that I say a thousand words at her funeral. It was a deeply heart-warming request. When the day arrived and she was laid out in the church, I was ready. Nobody counted my words, but I came close.

Schuller Country

Early in 1986 I received a telephone call from a woman who said they needed preaching help at their church in Garden Grove. The only thing "Garden Grove" meant to me at that point was Robert Schuller's massive Crystal Cathedral in Orange County near the Anaheim baseball stadium. For a moment I had the fleeting incredible notion that I was being asked by someone on Schuller's staff for some sidebar preaching assistance. Fleeting is right. The lady identified herself as Barbara Rayburn, moderator of the Garden Grove United Church of Christ (later Faith United Church of Christ) four miles west of Schuller. Their pastor had resigned, and they needed a supply preacher to tide them over for a few months until they called a new one. Also they wanted someone not only to preach but also to make calls on defectors from the fold, to entice them back. I accepted the invitation and went down there every Thursday through Sunday for the rest of 1988. They were a lively group, and it was a rewarding experience for me.

A pleasing compliment on my preaching came from a lady pillar of the Garden Grove church who had carried much of the load there for many years. She said that before I came, she spent the sermon time with her pencil filling in the "O's" on her worship bulletin. After I came, she stopped that and listened.

For another dozen years after I left the members put up a valiant struggle; but at the end of the century they believed they simply had to close the church down. The closest I came to Dr. Schuller was at a Garden Grove Prayer Breakfast where he was the speaker and I the invocator.

The Preacher as Communicator

I always enjoyed preaching. I think I was better at that than at other aspects of church life. Being a wordsmith by nature, I had told friends back when I was bogged down in college administration, I really needed to get into a spot where I could speak and write. Much of this of course is ego, but it also represents the need for exercising one's capacity for expression. I may be one of those covered by the saying, impression without expression leads to depression. A preacher has the obligation, and privilege, of addressing an assemblage for twenty minutes at least once a week.

A seminary professor thought I tended to use too many illustrations. This could be due to my experience with Frank Buchman, who counseled speakers to give a little truth and then an example, then more truth, followed by a story, and so on.

A parishioner in Madbury said I was their "explainer." I felt the need to give the historical background of any proposition. I always spoke without notes, as I believed that eye contact was important. A deacon in southern California said she appreciated me coming out in front and "just talking to us." I always tried to get away from the pulpit. You wouldn't want to propose marriage or try to sell a car with a pile of wood between you and your intended. As indicated in the "How to" section of the Appendix, it may look like "just talking to us," but extemporaneous speaking generally is possible only as a result of thorough preparation.

-20-

RHETORIC IS NOT A DIRTY WORD

The aim of forensic oratory is to teach, to delight, to move.
—Cicero, 106-43 B.C.

In recent times, there has been breast-beating about the decline of oratory. Some blame television for the reduction of public speaking to chitchat around the microphone and the eight-second sound bite. These have apparently replaced the compelling presentation, one that tries to persuade somebody with an argument that has a beginning, a middle, and an end. John D. Tierney wrote in the *Wall Street Journal*, "The decline of eloquence has many roots. Because orators no longer write their own material, they do not fully believe it."

The decay of the word "rhetoric" is sad. For 2,500 years the term has meant persuasive speech. In the Middle Ages, rhetoric was canonized as one of the liberal arts. At theological schools today, there are chairs in "Sacred Rhetoric." Yet now, commentators often use the word to describe "phony baloney." They imply that on the one hand there is the rhetoric, and on the other, the truth.

One of my purposes in public speaking, besides enjoying it and hoping the message will be helpful to someone, has been to encourage a revival of oratory, especially among young people—to get people excited about speaking a solid piece without notes, persuasively, and with eye contact.

It is hard to discern what the effect has been. People tend to regard me as someone having a special style and a good memory, someone who sounds off in his own way. I do have a good memory. But many people tend to tell themselves, fearfully and falsely, that their memory is not good enough. Most people who believe in something, and are familiar with their subject, could talk about it persuasively, without notes, if they took the trouble. A fellow student found he could talk for twenty minutes about his project interestingly with friends during a nighttime automobile ride. The experience convinced him he could make other talks that way. A city councilwoman, formerly mayor, has recently taken to leaving her notes behind and has found the pattern both more effective with her audiences and more satisfying to herself.

The rise or fall of oratory will be determined, as in so many areas of human activity, by the Zeitgeist, the spirit of the times.

After the war, on a return visit to Carleton, I discovered that public speech activity had been virtually abandoned. It was not liberal arts, they said. Carleton doesn't do "how to." Besides, Harvard doesn't do it. Later I found that there has been a move at Harvard starting in the 1990s to revive their Boylston Professorship of Rhetoric and Oratory, once held by John Quincy Adams, which over the years has been co-opted by the English literature people.[1]

Carleton College has received a major gift, in this direction, the Burnham and Nina W. Enersen Endowed Fund for the Teaching of Rhetoric. Mr. Enersen, a prominent San Francisco attorney and an alumnus of the Cochran debate era in the 1920s, says his college experience helped convince him that rhetoric, *the art of persuasion through language,* "was the key component" of his Carleton education.

---

[1]Jay Heinrichs, "How Harvard Destroyed Rhetoric," *Harvard Magazine*, July-August 1995.

Guinness and Me

To some, the name Guinness means a stout ale at a favorite pub. To many it means world-class Alec, stepping to Colonel Bogey's March in the 1957 Academy Award winning film, The Bridge on the River Kwai. But to millions of others, Guinness is The Book of World Records—the ultimate referee of backyard arguments. My picture appears in the 1984 and 1985 editions. The reason is that on July 2-3, 1982, I stood in Independence Square, Philadelphia, and delivered a Fourth of July oration that continued for two days and a night—thirty-four hours and eight minutes.

In 1977, I had started the annual Independence Day oratory program in Claremont, California. The hot dogs, popcorn, balloons, parades, and fireworks were unquestionably essential to the survival of the Republic. But it seemed to me that, in addition, folks ought to get up somewhere in the park, talk about the Declaration of Independence and American values, and say something about why we were taking the day off. We enlisted a number of speakers, but nobody paid much attention. I had heard that, in the old days, following a reading of the Declaration, a leather-lunged senator would mount the courthouse steps and, for a couple of hours, point with pride and view with alarm.

It occurred to me that in this chopped-up age, length might gain some attention. So, on July 4, 1979, I spoke for three hours in Claremont's Memorial Park. The next day, the speech, with photo, was featured on the front page of the Los Angeles Times. Apparently people would pay attention to oratory if delivered in an interesting manner.

Whenever one deals in length, people start talking Guinness, and Claremont's mayor, Richard Newton, wrote to the book's American headquarters in New York. On February 26, 1982,

Ms. Cyd Smith, assistant to the editor, wrote that a speech from 7:00 A.M. one day to 5:00 P.M. the next "would qualify for a world record."

It seemed an encompassable assignment. The record for a Senate filibuster was just over twenty-four hours. In 1981, I felt relatively fresh after speaking for six hours at the waterfront park in Petoskey, Michigan. Besides, unlike Lindbergh during his thirty-three-and-a-half-hour trans-Atlantic flight, I could stop and get off at any time.

I considered the possibility of a spot in the nation's heartland and talked to the people at Chicago's Grant Park. In the end, the Philadelphia shrine where the Declaration of Independence was adopted 206 years earlier seemed the appropriate site for a major Fourth of July oration. Hobart Cawood, superintendent of the national park at Independence Hall, was a friend. I had spoken there the year before. He sped up the construction of a platform on the south side of the Hall, which he was going to use later, so that I could start Friday morning, July 2, 1982.

Since my effort was to take about the same length of time as Lindbergh's flight to Paris, I decided to start my oration at 6:52 A.M., which is the moment, standard time, at which he took off from Long Island. Maybe some of the magic might rub off.

The platform was not in place until ten in the morning, so I began the speech by walking up and down the concrete plaza with my cordless microphone and body-pack in place. During this time, I was interviewed by Marguerite Del Giudice, an attractive and witty feature writer for the *Philadelphia Inquirer*. To draw me out, she played a word-association game, procuring my quick responses to the names of a dozen prominent figures.

Jane Pauley and the crew of NBC's *Today Show* were in Philadelphia that morning, covering the 300th anniversary of the founding of the City of Brotherly Love. She told her millions of viewers that some of the *Today* crew were at Independence

Hall, looking for the man who was trying to break the record, but could not find him! The probable reason was that the platform was not yet ready, and the camera people probably did not realize that the character pacing the flagstones was actually making a speech.

At two o'clock the first day, Dora Reyner of the *Philadelphia Daily News* came by for an interview. Then there was Seena Gressin of United Press International, whose item on the wires was seen on the West Coast the next day.

The Guinness requirements for authenticating endurance events include periodic signing of a logbook by impartial observers and newspaper accounts of the event. As I was speaking in a national park, rangers on duty sometimes signed my log, giving it an official look. The rules allow a five-minute break every hour. Recess time could be accumulated, so once during the night I spoke for two hours, and then rested for ten minutes. Since the nearest restroom was more than a five-minute round trip away, I took to reciting the Gettysburg Address going and coming. On the rostrum table I had a small timer that kept me honest through the night. It still sits on a shelf in my study.

I thought that after midnight I would be talking only to the night air. But Independence Square is a busy place, and many people walk vigorously through it all night. There were only some twenty-five minutes, during the entire thirty-four hours, when no one was present.

Three radio outlets reported the event. Camera crews came regularly from at least three television stations, with running reports to their viewers. One station carried me, live, on three evening news shows. Fifteen miles away, a couple saw one of the segments on their screen and drove into the city, spending the rest of the evening in the live audience. Four days later, in a downtown gas station, the black attendant said, "Aren't you the man who was speaking on television?"

People ask, "What did you talk about for thirty-four hours?" I answer that I had a series of subjects, starting with the Declaration of Independence, and going on through topics like the Great Awakening that preceded the self-government movement, the giants of the Revolution, the symbols of liberty (flag, bell, songs), Franklin and the Constitutional Convention, Lincoln as the prophet of the American dream, women and the Revolution, Will Rogers, Charles Lindbergh, and Martin Luther King's "I Have a Dream" speech, which was based on the Declaration of Independence. As no sales are allowed in Independence Park, audience members were offered a free bound copy of the prepared material, entitled "We Mutually Pledge."

All this, including diversions, and spoken without notes, took about seven hours to deliver. After that, it was recycling. I had a flip chart bearing the titles of all sections, and people would tell me the topics about which they would like me to speak. Favorites were Patrick Henry and Will Rogers. I had been delivering long Fourth of July orations every year since my two-hour speech in Madbury, New Hampshire, in 1975. So I was familiar with the material.

Passersby were enlisted to take pictures with my camera. At some point between clicks the camera was stolen, but not until some dramatic shots were recorded to send to Guinness. About four o'clock in the morning, five University of Pennsylvania students stopped to listen. From the flip chart they chose Will Rogers, and I spoke about him for an hour, after which they said, "Thanks a lot," and disappeared into the night.

Just before sunrise, I began to feel faint and as though I might pass out. I thought this might be "it." The only way I could keep going was to lean back on a rail for support, half sitting and half standing. But when the sun came up, I was infused with new energy, and the rest of the day was OK. At noon of that second day, the weather closed in and for the last five hours I spoke in the rain.

Since the previous record was just over thirty-three hours, I decided to go beyond it by one hour and then quit, even though I could have gone longer. One reason was that I had agreed to deliver another Fourth of July oration in Chicago the next day at the convention of the National Speakers Association.

So, at the end of the second day, standing with Rick Lyman, another *Philadelphia Inquirer* reporter, we looked up at the Independence Hall clock. It said 5:00 P.M. I decided to hang it up. Jim Merrell, nephew, brought my beat-up Volkswagen van from the parking lot, loaded the cordless microphone, the amplifiers, and other paraphernalia, and we were off to his parents' home in suburban Radnor. There I had a soaking hot bath and nine hours' sleep, before taking the plane for Chicago at dawn on the Fourth of July, where I addressed the National Speakers Association on Patrick Henry.

I was sixty-six years old.

I sent the log to the Guinness office in New York, along with the photos and press clippings. They were sent to London. Then a glitch developed. The headquarters there wrote that I did not qualify. You can imagine my dismay. They said that *eight months* before I even opened my mouth in Philadelphia, one A. H. Neville Ajith, a Sri Lanka legislator, speaking in Colombo, October 30–31, 1981, had talked continuously for thirty-seven hours and forty-five minutes! I had surpassed Marvin Eakman's Minneapolis record of thirty-three hours and five minutes, which the New York office had told me was still standing. But London's information was different. What a downer!

At once, I asked the New York office why they had told me that the record I had to break was thirty-three hours when in fact is was nearly thirty-eight hours, and that the latter had been set eight months before I began speaking in Philadelphia?

Their answer: "The London office does not always keep us up to date with their information."

And thereby hangs a tale.

What happened, although I did not realize it until later, was that I was caught in the crossfire of internecine warfare within the Guinness organization.

The *Guinness Book of World Records* was begun after World War II by British identical twins, Norris and Ross McWhirter, who started a small, fact-finding business, serving encyclopedias and advertisers. The brothers became known also for carrying a remarkable mass of records in their heads.

Britain's Guinness family in 1759 acquired the Dublin brewery that produced the ale that came to be known as Guinness Extra Stout. In the 1940s, the managing director of the Guinness Brewing Company, Sir Hugh Beaver, heard about the McWhirters and hired them to produce a book of records which could settle barroom disputes in the United Kingdom's 81,400 pubs. The twins brought out their first book in 1955, and they called it *Guinness Superlatives Limited*. Today they sell more copies worldwide than any other copyrighted book. (The Bible is not copyrighted.)

Two years later, in 1957, the energetic young manager of Sterling Publishing Company in New York, David A. Boehm, saw a copy of the British book and at once perceived its potential. He made a deal with the McWhirters to publish an edition in the United States, under a contract running to 2016.

When I hove into view, Boehm's American version was running twenty-five million copies annually. By now, Norris McWhirter was trying to break Boehm's hold on the lucrative American market. Norris's strategy was to withhold information from Boehm. In this way, he could reduce the accuracy, and consequently the marketability, of the American edition. This is why the New York office did not know what the speaking record was when responding to my inquiries in the spring of 1982.

McWhirter went so far as to tell Boehm his contract was unilaterally terminated. He accused the New Yorker of technical, financial irregularities, and said he would receive no more information. A federal judge held for Boehm, accusing the parent firm of "blatantly unreasonable cupidity." The opponents settled their differences out of court. Boehm and the Sterling Publishing company kept their American franchise, but were forced to hand over nine believe-it-or-not type Guinness museums around the United States.

The Los Angeles County Fair promoters wanted me to go for the record again, during their annual, two-week exposition in September 1983. The publicity department planned to set me up on a central platform and to organize a bivouac of Boy Scouts to assist me with logistical and refreshment support through the night.

I declined. The Guinness people had shown their speaking categories to be in disarray. They could change the rules in midstream. There was no assurance that all that effort would pay off on another try. Norris McWhirter himself wrote to me August 25, 1983, that the rules had changed:

> At our editorial discussion it was resolved that we are in future going to allow the absolute talking record to be a lecture or a political speech if this latter is conducted inside an elective assembly. . . . This means that the political category is now only accessible to elected representatives inside an elective assembly.

So much for citizen oratory.

Then a really nice thing happened. David Boehm, backed by his associate Cyd Smith, realizing the injustice of the situation, proposed something better. He said he was allowed to add certain American records to the U.S. edition, independent of the British book. He asked me for a photograph of myself speaking in a patriotic setting. I sent him one from the front page of the *Los Angeles Times* July 5, 1979—microphone in front, flag behind, hands clasping lapels. He ran it for two years, in the 1984 and 1985 editions. Instead of the usual line of type or two, here was a photo and caption.

After David Boehm's departure, the publication underwent a change. The American *Guinness* was published briefly by *Facts on File Newsletter*, but the New York records office has been shut down and the personnel returned to their London headquarters. The only address on the book is an e-mail destination. The publication has been gussied up with color photos and has dropped the public speaking categories, even the long-included Senate filibuster. (Strom Thurmond, 1957, twenty-four hours, eighteen minutes). The only salute to eloquence in a recent issue is recognition of a female gray parrot from Uganda said to have a vocabulary of nearly eight hundred words, and rated the best talker at the British Bird Show for twelve consecutive years.

A Lifetime of Words

> *An orator is a good man who is skilled in speaking.*
> —Cato the Elder, 234-149 B.C.[1]

I have been a public speaker and a student of public speaking all my life. When I was nine, my mother had me recite William Wordsworth's "Daffodils" ("I wandered lonely as a cloud") for the women's circle of her church. Introducing me, she said, "I don't have talent myself, but I have a wonderful family."

My father was a good speaker and, in addition to his teaching and preaching, he was in some demand as a lecturer, high school commencement speaker, and funeral eulogist. I may have picked

---

[1]Cato was the orator in the 150s who added to every speech he made in the Roman Senate the words, "Carthage must be destroyed." Eventually it was.

up some of this from him.

In high school, I resolved to get into it. My first speech before the school assembly was an absolute terror. I can still hear my knees knocking that day. But I was determined. Northfield High School sent me to the regional oratorical contest in Cannon Falls on a wintry night in February. Cannon Falls boasts a monument commemorating a 1924 campaign speech by President Calvin Coolidge in their park. My subject in the contest was the ominous impact of the movies on national life. That was 1931.

The traditional Memorial Day observance in Northfield, in preparation for the folks going out to decorate graves in the Protestant and Catholic cemeteries, was held in the Grand Theater. It had been built as an opera house, and was then the town's movie house. The pattern was for a high school student to deliver the Gettysburg Address, followed by a distinguished name speaker. In 1931, as a high school junior, I was tapped to recite Lincoln's words. (Five years later, my brother Stuart had the honor.) The orator of my day was Roy L. Smith, a prominent Methodist minister from Minneapolis, who was soon to move to Los Angeles, where in 1935 he was an officiant at the funeral service at the Franklin Avenue church for Will Rogers.

Ever since that day in Northfield, I have delivered the Gettysburg Address at some gathering at least once a year, often more frequently. Bob Rivera, La Verne University debate coach, heard me give it at the Claremont University Club and he invited me to address a regional conference of Toastmasters International in Los Angeles, and to include a recitation of the Gettysburg Address in my remarks.

I cannot say enough good things about Toastmasters, which has provided weekly opportunities to thousands of men and women to break free form all sorts of shackles. Highlights of the meetings are chances to speak to a sympathetic group and then be evaluated by one's peers.

I have delivered other historic speeches on occasion in addition to my own, such as Patrick Henry's "Give Me Liberty," Benjamin Franklin's plea for divine guidance at the Constitutional Convention, Lincoln's Second Inaugural, and Martin Luther King's "I Have a Dream." Replicating these via the spoken word is important, I think, because the originals were spoken to an audience, and they are not nearly so meaningful if only read in a classroom from a printed page.

My senior year in high school was 1932, the bicentennial of George Washington's birth. I found a good oration about him, complete with the story of the Washington monument, which had been planned in the centennial year, 1832, and dedicated in 1885. My mother was active in the Daughters of the American Revolution, and one of their projects that year was to plant Washington elm trees all over the country. These were slips taken from the, at that time, still spreading elm tree in Cambridge, Massachusetts, under which General Washington took command of the Continental Armies on July 3, 1775.

Mother was in charge of the planting event in Northfield, which was to take place on the lawn of the Carnegie Library on Division Street. She gathered a distinguished group for the occasion, the mayor and everybody. It was a big deal, maybe a dozen people. She had me make the speech of the day with an oration on George Washington.

In a few weeks the poor little tree died. It could not stand all that hot air. So they sent back to Cambridge for another, which was replanted, this time without the oratory. It lasted some fifty years, until the area was needed for a new library wing.

In college, I was at it again. Carleton had long had a distinguished record in forensics, which is defined as "the study or practice of formal debate: argumentation." Our coach was the eminent I. M. Cochran, who at that time was president of the Interstate Oratorical Association. As mentioned in an earlier chapter, for two years I was the college orator, representing Carleton in the Minnesota and regional contests.

There was then quite a gap in my speaking career. In law school there was not much opportunity. But speaking was, incidentally, the best thing I did there. I got better marks for the argument of cases in moot court, the Ames competition, than I did in classroom work.

During my years as a Moral Re-Armament operative, Frank Buchman did not cotton to my style, so occasions were limited. Later, when I was in college administration, my role tended to involve paperwork behind the scenes.

In 1970, I broke out and began to get back into gear. I have not stopped speaking since.

Fourth of July

In Claremont we have developed a unique pattern where every Fourth of July, during the community's small-town-type celebration, some twenty speakers mount the rostrum in Memorial Park and say their piece. One reason for the program's success is that presenters are absolutely free. They are not required to make the eagle scream or beat the flag. They can express appreciation, or they can point out what needs to be improved.

On the Fourth of July in 1984 I set up a soapbox at the Speakers Corner in Hyde Park and spoke for six hours through the long London twilight, from 3:00 to 9:00 P.M. My college roommate Don Raish was planning to go from Austin, Texas, to join me in London for the event, and booked passage. But in the end the doctors told him he was too sick, and he died the next year of lung cancer.

My theme for the oration was the relation of American independence to Great Britain. I was greatly helped by the words of a British statesman in London earlier that summer. Lord Hailsham, British Lord Chancellor, also known as Quintin Hogg when a member of the House of Commons, had addressed the ceremonies dedicating the Diplomatic Gates, commemorating the Peace between the United Kingdom and the United States at the close of the American War of Independence. He graciously forwarded to me a copy of that speech. In it he made the case that, even for the British, American Independence had been a good thing: (1) the release of its energy, and its strength-building immigration made it possible that "twice in our lifetime the new world has come to the rescue of the old"; and (2) it taught the British to work out independence for all their other colonies by negotiation and not bloodshed.

In addition to the passing tourists, I soon attracted at least four "professional" hecklers. There seems to be a special breed that keep an eye on the Corner to make sure no one gets away with anything. I got rid of one of the most strident and disruptive hecklers, partly by offering to trade places with him. The other three, starting out rather belligerently anti-American, stuck around. When they saw I was not a Yankee jingoist, but was speaking in terms of genuine teamwork between our countries, they entered into the spirit and provided a helpful dialogue. It came to be more like a Socratic conversation in the marketplace than a speech. When we closed down at nine o'clock, two of them said how really glad they were that I came.

Some of the most satisfying speaking experiences have been frequent appearances at the Will Rogers Memorial at Claremore, Oklahoma, and at the Charles A. Lindbergh boyhood home in Little Falls, Minnesota. I was asked to return a number of times at both places.

I was a sometime keynoter at Will Rogers Days. There I made friends with people like western rider and roper Montie

Montana; Laurence J. Peter, who said his career in conveying serious ideas by the use of humor had been inspired by Rogers; and Patty Ziegfeld Stephenson, the daughter of Billie Burke and Florenz Ziegfeld, Rogers' Broadway producer. Each year Claremore staged a long parade, and one time they put me in the number two car, after son Jimmie Rogers, with large letters on the side saying ORATOR.

At a Claremore reception one evening I was able to catch Will Rogers Jr. in a corner by the buffet. I had first met him in Washington back in the days when he was a member of Congress. He looked a lot like his father. I asked him about his father's famous saying, "I never met a man I didn't like." I said it made me feel guilty. How is it possible that a person can live up to something like that? He said it made him feel the same way. Also, he added, the saying spun off its own jokes—he never met Howard Cosell—Elizabeth Taylor never met a man she didn't like. But he thought the key word was *met*. He never *met* a man he didn't like. He figured that up to the moment of meeting he could give the other person the benefit of the doubt, see his or her potential, take the positive view. That helped me a lot. Yet his older brother Jimmie disagreed. He wished the old man had never said it, because they were always being asked about it. But unlike his brother, he thought his father meant it just the way he said it. After a speech in Bakersfield, where I gave Will Jr.'s interpretation, Jimmie came up to me and asked whether I had obtained a "Supreme Court ruling" on the meaning of the word "met." Jimmie, a lifetime rancher in Bakersfield, and the last of the Rogers family, died not long after I saw him and his new wife as fellow guests of Ben Bollinger and the Candlelight Pavilion in Claremont at their presentation of the Broadway musical *Will Rogers Follies*.

Montie Montana acted less like a celebrity than almost any other celebrity I have known. I met him in November 1979

during the Will Rogers hundredth birthday weekend in Claremore, Oklahoma. He was there as a part of a historical
reminiscing panel of people who knew Rogers, people like
Montana, Peter, Ziegfeld and the Rogers brothers; actors Joel
McCrea and Evelyn Venable; plus Emil Sandmeier, who for
years was the faithful steward of the Rogers ranch in Santa
Monica Canyon. (Shirley Temple was overseas and sent her
regrets). Montie was a sort of successor to Will Rogers as the
world's best western roper, and he was the stand-in roper for the
big star in the movie, *The Will Rogers Story.* I was in Claremore
as an aide to Joel McCrea and his wife Frances Dee. I had just
written for him a memoir article for *Modern Maturity,* "I
Remember Will Rogers."

Montie and I ran into each other at a Claremore reception
near the punch and cookies, and I was surprised that he wanted
to know who I was and what I did. We kept up a casual friendship for the rest of his life. He liked the column I wrote about
him, or at least he said he did. On a Los Angeles County
Sheriff's Posse outing, he autographed for me his autobiography,
Montie Montana: Not Without My Horse. Nearly every year, I
would go out to his ranch around Rose Parade time and have a
visit. His base was in Agua Dulce, on the other side of the
mountains north of Los Angeles. There he kept a mixed array of
stage coaches and other western gear that he rented to
producers of western movies. He first rode in the Rose Parade
back in 1933 when he was a young member of the Sheriff's
Posse, and for sixty consecutive parades, through 1994, he was
on his horse in the lineup. One year I told him I would be
watching from the Colorado Boulevard sidewalk with a group of
Carleton alumni. He said, "Put up a sign and I'll stop and
salute." I did, and he did. It made a great picture in the alumni
magazine.

The Little Falls appearances arose out of activity with the Charles A. and Anne Morrow Lindbergh Foundation, advancing the balance between science and nature. I had known the aviator and wrote an inner-man biography of him. Charles' father was a congressman from Minnesota, and his son grew up half the year in Washington and half the year on the family farm in Little Falls, Minnesota. The small town in central Minnesota has been the recurring site of conferences sponsored by the Foundation. The family donated their 110-acre farm there to Minnesota authorities, and it is now a state park.

Los Angeles Bicentennial

In 1981, the city of Los Angeles celebrated its two hundredth birthday. El Pueblo de la Reina de Los Angeles, City of the Queen of the Angels, was founded by settlers (*Los Pobladores*) recruited in Mexico by California's first governor, Don Felipe de Neve. They were brought up through the missions at San Diego and San Juan Capistrano, and equipped and oriented at Mission San Gabriel. From there, they trekked the nine miles to what is now the Los Angeles River and, on September 4, 1781, they established the city.

At the time of the Los Angeles Bicentennial, I was serving as Assistant to the President of the Claremont School of Theology, and was appointed to the education wing of the planning committee. It occurred to me it might be educational to link the history of Los Angeles with that of the rest of the country. I proposed a speaking tour that would cover the nation's great historic sites, with emphasis on what was happening at them during the period when Los Angeles was being established.

The Bicentennial's executive director, Jane Pisano, said there was no money for such a project, but if I made the trip, they would be pleased if I brought greetings from Los Angeles to each community along the way.

So I launched forth in my beat-up 1972 Volkswagen van. Trip statistics: 20,000 miles (the circuit was traversed twice, once to line it up and once to deliver), 20 weeks, 61 speeches in 28 cities and 15 states. The trip itinerary is included among the appendices to this book. Financial contributions, including one from the University Club of Claremont, pieced out what I was able to produce from my personal savings.

The first speech was at Boston's Old North Church on Patriots' Day, April 19, 1981. The last was before the downtown Los Angeles Rotary Club on the Bicentennial day itself, September 4. The last topic: "A City's Promise of Renewal." This audience was kind enough to close the trip with a standing ovation.

In between were addresses at the Statue of Liberty; the Capitol steps in Washington; the harbor in Saint Augustine; the railroad depot in Springfield, Illinois; the military cemetery at Gettysburg; the Dexter Avenue King Memorial Baptist Church, Montgomery, Alabama; the Alamo; Mission San Juan Capistrano; and other honored sites from our nation's history. At Gettysburg the National Park Service had me deliver Lincoln's address five times, standing on the original spot.

Early in the morning after Old North Church, I was privileged on Patriots' Day to join the Minute Men of Lincoln, Massachusetts (twelve miles southwest of Boston) in their colonial uniforms for the six-mile march on Concord. Back in 1775, on April 19 before dawn, Paul Revere having been captured in Lincoln by the British the night before, the militia of the surrounding towns moved to join the battle at Concord, the Lincoln unit being the first to arrive. All this is reenacted every year, the same day as the Boston Marathon. When we arrived at the "rude bridge that arched the flood" I peeled off and, videotaped by the Park Rangers, delivered Ralph Waldo

Emerson's famous "Concord Hymn" several times to visitors from the spot where it was first given in 1837 by the poet himself at the dedication of the Battle Monument. The first verse closes with the familiar words:

> Here once the embattled farmers stood
> And fired the shot heard round the world.

Sometimes during the 1981 journey I found family or friends with whom to stay. Mostly I pulled into roadside rest stops or shopping-mall parking lots and slept in the van. I carried two loudspeakers and a cordless microphone for situations where there was no sound system in place. Many of the addresses were delivered in the open air.

Near the close of the tour, our friend and neighbor, Jo Hartley, gave a welcome-home party in Claremont. In her introduction, she said, "This is the kind of person one hesitates to call on to say a few words."

Somebody said I have addressed the University Club of Claremont more times than any other speaker. In addition, in 2001-02 they put me on at the beginning of each Tuesday's program to give a "Word for the Day."

Teaching

In the 1980s, I accepted an invitation from nearby La Verne University to teach public speaking for a semester at the Women's Prison at Chino, California. The textbook was Dale Carnegie's *How to Develop Self-Confidence and Influence People by Public Speaking*. It is, bar none, the best book on public speaking yet published, in my opinion.

The women I taught were a pretty tough group; some were in for murder and other violent crimes. I felt we developed a good rapport during the semester. However, I tended to give them higher grades than were warranted, as a kind of mild insurance against reprisal!

Rhetoric as Gateway

Seminarian Roy Pearson, one of the classic preachers of the twentieth century, used to say to his students:

> If you wonder whether history can be influenced by the spoken word, remember two names: Adolf Hitler and Winston Churchill.

Churchill, with some experience in the field, speaking before inclusive language, is quoted by commentator David Gergen:

> Of all talents bestowed upon men, none is so precious as the gift of oratory. He who enjoys it is an independent force in the world.

Shakespeare as usual had a word:

> Beauty itself doth of itself persuade
> The eyes of men without an orator.

But if you don't have all that beauty, then you have to fall back on oratory. My college president, Donald J. Cowling, came to a year-end dinner our undergraduate debate teams put together in Margaret Evans Hall on campus. An accomplished speaker himself (I never saw him use a note) he prefaced his remarks with the opinion that public speaking could get a person farther with less ability than any other pursuit. It certainly is the avenue to many things—confidence and social mobility, as well as persuasive communication.

I trust more young people will avail themselves of the opportunity.

IT IS WRITTEN

I was first conscious that I could write when I was a sophomore in Northfield High School. We had a caring English teacher with a great Norwegian name, Emma Overvaag. I think she was the first person who told me that I had writing ability. Naturally I was pleased, and I have never forgotten her encouraging words.

Don Bailey and I had vied with each other in her class as to how screwily we could ham up our essays. The resulting grades reflected this attitude. Then, for some reason, I decided to quit the horseplay and to tell the stories straight. The results were not only better grades, but also more personal satisfaction.

From there, I went on to become the editor of the *Periscope*, our high-school biweekly newspaper. I wrote most of the stories myself, and did all the layout and make-up on the pressroom stones at the *Northfield Independent*. As I have said, what I learned there about typefaces and point-sizes I've remembered all my life.

I have turned out hundreds of articles, editorials, columns, pamphlets, and brochures. But one does not reach "author" status until one produces a hardcover book. I have been able to produce two, the most recent, before this one, being *The Spirit of Charles Lindbergh* (Lanham, MD: Madison Books, 1993). The other was *The Tax Climate for Philanthropy* (Washington, DC: Council for the Advancement and Support of Education, 1968).

The Spirit of Charles Lindbergh

The *Lindbergh* book grew from a maze of roots. My interest in the aviator, along with millions of others, dates from May 1927. The *Minneapolis Journal*, which I was delivering at age eleven on a route to Northfield customers, was carrying daily features on the Minnesota farm boy, turned airmail pilot, who was waiting on Long Island for the rain to stop so he could take off for Paris. When Lindbergh landed in France, all of us were caught up in the worldwide explosion of enthusiasm. As described in an earlier chapter, my father packed us into our Model T Ford and drove the forty miles to the Wold Chamberlain field to see the pilot at one of the eighty-two stops on his forty-eight state welcome-home tour.

I met Lindbergh several times over the years, in Washington and in Florida. This came about because I knew so well Jim Newton of Fort Myers Beach, who was the aviator's closest friend for thirty-six years. The first time was at Captiva Island, off the southwest coast of Florida, where Anne Morrow Lindbergh found the seashells that inspired her classic *Gift from the Sea*. Mary Louise and I were vacationing in a nearby motel, the Gulf View Inn, owned by her uncle Roy Wedekind,[1] when one afternoon we received a call from Jim and Ellie Newton, would we like to come over and meet the Lindberghs. When we arrived, we found that they were playing a quiz-game found in the daily paper. Lindbergh turned to me and asked, "Why are flies able to walk on the ceiling?"

I said that I had thought that when they rubbed their legs behind their "ears," they picked up a sticky substance that made their feet adhere to the ceiling. Without saying whether this was

---

[1] The site was later occupied by the Mucky Duck Restaurant.

the approved solution, he commented, "Very observant!"[2]

Charles was best man at Jim and Ellie's 1953 wedding in a home in northwest Washington, and Jim assigned me to be his friend's chauffeur through the capital city streets on the occasion. After the ceremony I drove him back to his quarters in the Army-Navy Club.

In the 1980s, I began a series of assignments with the churches of the Hana Coast at the eastern tip of Maui. While there I conducted for the Minnesota Historical Society an oral history project, involving personal interviews with a dozen people who had come to know the Lindberghs through their hideaway home in Kipahulu 1968-74. Accordingly, I became an authority on Lindbergh in Hawaii and gave lectures at places like the Lindbergh Historic Site at Little Falls, Minnesota.

At the same time, I became active in what is now the Charles A. and Anne Morrow Lindbergh Foundation, which promotes that couple's dedication to the balance between technology and the environment. Former Minnesota Governor Elmer L. Andersen was the foundation's president in the 1980s. He increasingly stressed the spiritual legacy of Charles Lindbergh, especially as set forth in the aviator's postwar testament of faith, *Of Flight and Life* (New York: Scribner's, 1948). I began to pick up on this theme. When the Lindbergh statue was installed at the state capitol in Saint Paul, three quotations were inscribed at the base. They were fine, expressing sentiments about science and the air. But I felt that was not the full dimension of what Lindbergh had to say to posterity. So I began to agitate with state officials to add new quotations, expressing this wider dimension.

---

[2] "(The housefly) clings to ceilings by means of the two little pads below the claws, which are covered with hairs that excrete at the tips a sticky fluid." Anna Bothford Comstock, *Handbook of Nature-Study* (Ithaca: Comstock Publishing Co., 1950).

I secured approval for a new set from Anne Lindbergh. But I completely struck out with Minnesota officialdom. Each bureau told me of another agency I should see.

However, Reeve Lindbergh, youngest of Charles and Anne's six children, spoke to me one snowy morning, following a foundation event the evening before. I was driving her to an early plane at the Minneapolis-Saint Paul airport. She said, "Whenever I hear Elmer speak, and you talk, about this idea, I keep thinking there must be a book in there." I didn't give it much thought, figuring she might be contemplating a list of sayings—a sort of "wit and wisdom of Charles Lindbergh."

The next summer, in 1988, I was the closing speaker at a Lindbergh symposium in Little Falls on the subject "The Three Goals of Charles A. Lindbergh." Reeve was present and came up to me afterwards, saying, "That's the first chapter of the book!" Fortunately, I did not say, "What book?" But it did start me thinking seriously about a broader treatment of the inner man, his motivations, his character influences, and his basic message. People knew something about the *Spirit of St. Louis*. Perhaps they might profit from knowing something more about the spirit of Charles Lindbergh.

While pulling notes together, I sent out a dozen "query letters" to publishers with a record of interest in history and biography. Most of them returned rejection slips, but Madison Books in Lanham, Maryland, a Washington suburb, replied they would like to see the manuscript, and, later, that they would publish it, provided I revise it along the lines indicated by one of their editorial critics. For this, I hired a professional editor based in Orange County, Claudia Suzanne. We met every Wednesday morning at a halfway point, a Denny's restaurant at the intersection of the Orange Freeway and Imperial Boulevard, and completed the project. This editorial investment and my personal travel and promotion cost me several thousand dollars. Royalties returned only a portion of that. But it was all in such a great cause.

As to travel, I have many friends around the country, some of them in the media, and I was able to line up radio, TV, and newspaper interviews as well as author-signing engagements in bookstores. Most of the appearances were in the Middle West, but some on the West Coast. The most successful bookstore showings were in my hometown, at the Chancery Lane in Claremont, California; the Book Case in Wayzata, Minnesota; and Hasegawa General Store in Hana, Maui.

I was particularly proud of the endorsements the book engendered. Perhaps the most outstanding was from M. Scott Peck, whose *The Road Less Traveled* was on the *New York Times* bestseller list for a dozen years. Since my book deals with values, I took a chance sending Dr. Peck a manuscript. He replied,

> As you might imagine, I am deluged with manuscripts and get to look at only about one in ten and write a comment for only about ten percent of those. Somehow, your manuscript properly found its way up through the screens, and I found it fascinating. I very much sense in Mr. Lindbergh a kindred spirit, and while I do not have the problem in the same magnitude that he had, I deeply empathize with some of the difficulties of fame, and particularly the difficulties he had with the media. Anyway, please feel free to use the following quote in any way you desire for promotional purposes:
> "A fascinating account of the spiritual odyssey of a most fascinating man—one whom I admire and with whom I deeply empathize."

The following year, in Lexington, Kentucky, I attended one of Dr. Peck's seminars, and was able to thank him personally.

Madison Books had announced in *Publishers Weekly* in both January and February 1993, that the book would be out in April. With friends in Minneapolis I lined up a book-launching event for May 21 under the replica of the *Spirit of St. Louis* which hangs in the Lindbergh Terminal of the Minneapolis-Saint Paul

Airport. Minnesota was Lindbergh's home state, and May 21st was the sixty-sixth anniversary of his trans-Atlantic flight. Round-the-world flyer Richard G. "Dick" Rutan, who had enthusiastically endorsed the book, agreed to be the speaker. In 1986 Rutan and co-pilot Jeana Yeager had circled the globe non-stop in nine days in their *Voyageur* without refueling. The flight had similarities to Lindbergh's sixty years earlier, among them being the absence of government help and a flying speed of around a hundred miles an hour.

The book-launching plan fell through, however, because of a printing glitch that delayed the book's availability for a month. The airport event and other planned announcement affairs around the Middle West had to be canceled.

One of the most interesting of the book-signing events took place in the summer of 1993 in the Authors' Corner at the famous international fly-in sponsored by the Experimental Aircraft Association (EAA) at Oshkosh, Wisconsin. Each summer some 12,000 planes and 800,000 people converge on this eastern Wisconsin town, forty miles west of Lake Michigan. I hitched a ride to the event with my friend Don Moore of Upland, California, who flew his own Piper Cherokee. For eight nights we slept on the ground of a parking pasture in a pup tent under a wing.

The publisher did not send as many copies as the EAA store ordered, so we ran out about two-thirds of the way through. My friend Verne Jobst, retired from United Airlines, and the official pilot of EAA's replica of the *Spirit of St. Louis*, was director of the fly-in's air show. He introduced me to Patty Wagstaff, world aerobatics champion, to whom I presented an autographed copy of the book. She spoke of flying over Lindbergh's grave on Maui.

Before leaving Oshkosh, Don Moore filled up with gasoline, calculated to fly for five hours, enough for the four hours to a lunch stop at Sioux City, Iowa. For some reason, perhaps the carburetor, we ran out of gas seven miles short of the Sioux City airport. We spotted a lonely gravel road just off Interstate 20, and Don made a skillful dead stick landing, coasting to the top of a rise. We were glad there was no truck coming from the other direction. He had radioed our situation to the airport tower, and soon an ambulance, sheriff squad cars, TV, radio, and newspaper personnel appeared from nowhere. We were on the evening news that night and on the front page the next morning. Without further fuel problems, we made it home to southern California comfortably in two more days.

The publisher printed a modest original run of *The Spirit of Charles Lindbergh*, and it sold out. A second printing rolled off the presses in 2002, a Lindbergh anniversary year—the 100th of his birth and the 75th of his famous flight.

The Tax Climate for Philanthropy

At Macalester College, in the 1950s, I had produced a major booklet, *Underwriting America's Future by Giving to Education*. The idea of philanthropy as a part of estate planning, with planned giving to encourage the life-income type of gift, was beginning to take hold nationally. The booklet had a complete glossary of terms in the back, something that had not been done before. The publication was well received.

My first hardcover book, *The Tax Climate for Philanthropy*, grew out of my conviction that the nation needed a new attitude towards taxation, a change from today's almost universal negative approach to a constructive appreciation for what tax money provides for us. This conviction led me to take a sabbatical to research the idea with the movers and shakers of America's tax policy, as described in the next chapter.

Did the book do any good? The *Wall Street Journal* featured the findings at the top of page one. Lammot DuPont Copeland, chairman of the giant chemical company, called it "the best organized piece of research in the field I have seen in my long experience with philanthropic causes."

World Changing Through Life Changing

One of my objectives at Andover Newton seminary was to write up in as objective a manner as possible, for one as involved at the heart of it as I was, an eyewitness account of one of the dynamic seminal forces of our time. I had given eighteen years of my life full time to MRA. And to a writer, as Anne Morrow Lindbergh once said, an experience is not complete until it is written about. Also I thought that a graduate school setting would be a good place to write such a dissertation, where I would have the advantage of the discipline and oversight of sharp academic minds. In fact I stayed longer as a student at Andover Newton than I had originally planned just so this could happen. I started out under the supervision of church historian Gerald Cragg. But unfortunately he died before I finished, and my chairman then became Roger Hazelton. In the oral examination another member of the committee, Earl Thompson, said he found my thesis so fascinating that he stayed up through the night reading it. Hazelton urged I seek publication. I did, but the thirty editors I sent it to did not respond as Thompson did, and it is still unpublished. A friend in Illinois offered to pay for publication, but I have been involved in other things and kept thinking it needed de-theologizing for a public market. Interested inquirers have looked up the work in the library of Andover Newton Theological School, 210 Herrick Road, Newton Centre, Massachusetts 02159. It is entitled *World Changing Through Life Changing: The Story of Frank Buchman and Moral Re-Armament*, a thesis for a Master's degree by T. Willard Hunter, 1977.

This thesis has been cited in a number of other works. One observer who was rather critical of MRA was warmly appreciative of how I treated both the plus and minus elements. Garth Lean, the authoritative Buchman biographer (*On the Tail of a*

Comet), although he did not entirely agree with my conclusions ("That's your opinion," he said) more than once referred to it in his pages.

Columns

For a good deal of my life, I have been a columnist. During the MRA years, I wrote a monthly page for *New World News* called "Washington Report." In those days I spent much time on Capitol Hill, and reported on personalities and tides, emphasizing positive background trends in the news. The editor of *Newsweek* told David Carey, *New World News* editor, he wished he could find writers of that quality.

In the 1960s, Rajmohan Gandhi founded a weekly newsmagazine in Bombay called *Himmat* [Courage].[3] He asked me to write on events in the United States. This I did until the late 1970s, when unfortunately Gandhi had to shut down, partly for political and partly for financial reasons. Russi Lala, the editor, had sent along one of the most encouraging messages I have ever received:

> Your articles we value beyond measure. I feel God may mean you to have a major role in interpreting America to the world through *Himmat* weekly. [He then mentioned the libraries in the U.S. and Russia that received it and certain statesmen known to read it.] There are few men I know in the United States, even among the top professional journalists, who in their excellence can equal the material you send us.

Moreno Valley, California, an amalgamation of three towns east of Riverside, on the road to Indio and Palm Springs, was during the 1980s the fastest growing community in California.

---

[3]Gandhi, a former Senator in India and currently a lecturer on Asian history in American universities, is the son of Devadas Gandhi, New Delhi news editor, and grandson of Mahatma Gandhi.

Orange County residents to the south, who found their land and rent values squeezing them, discovered they could live more cheaply in Moreno Valley. And they came in droves.

One evening during the time that I was serving the Moreno Valley Congregational Church as a weekend preacher, the head deacon and his wife, Dick and Kris Dale, invited me for dinner along with Jim Lewis, editor and publisher of the *Butterfield Express*. The *Express* was a colorful, down-home, country weekly named after the stagecoach that once ran through town from the desert to Los Angeles. Jim, a one-man-show, green-eye-shade newspaperman, said he had not been able to induce any of the preachers in town to write for the paper. I offered to, and continued for sixteen years. The paper was later bought by the Donrey Media group, which changed its name to *Moreno Valley Times*, but they kept my column on the opinion page.

Before that, Joe Gendron, editor of the Pomona *Progress-Bulletin*, had run a report I wrote on the swallows returning to the Mission San Juan Capistrano. He encouraged me to submit other items. It resulted in a regular column which James Fulton, Joe's successor, continued. He liked my focus on national events and anniversaries, saying he was dissatisfied with what he received from wire services. So the column ran in the *Progress-Bulletin* for seven years. But when Donrey purchased the paper and merged it with the Ontario *Daily Report*, the new editors dropped the column.

During the same period, the column came to the attention of the *Galesburg Post*, a western Illinois weekly. Bill Foley, owner of a photography shop and loyal Knox College alumnus, invited me to address the Galesburg Rotary club due to my being a great grandson of a prominent Galesburg pioneer, Silas Willard.

Learning of my column, Foley's store sponsored it for an

introductory six months in the local paper, which then decided to stay with it. That was in 1983, and it ran there continuously from that time to July 1999, both in the *Post* and in its sister paper, the *Knoxville Journal*, which serves another Knox County town nine miles away.

Alcoholics Anonymous

I have written and spoken so much about AA that some have wondered whether I am a recoverer myself. The answer is no. I have my share of problems, but for some reason that was never one of them. I know something about the origins of the movement because I came into the Oxford Group experience about the same time as the co-founders, Bill Wilson in New York, and Bob Smith in Akron. I did not know them, but I did know Sam Shoemaker, the New York Episcopal rector, Buchman lieutenant, a leader of the Oxford Group who was Bill Wilson's spiritual mentor.

I also knew rubber tire mold inventor T. Henry Williams and his wife Clarace, in whose Akron home the first AA meetings were held. In New York I was acquainted with Rowland Hazard, the Rhode Island businessman and an alcoholic, whom C. G. Jung in his Swiss clinic told a transforming spiritual experience was his only hope. Rowland found that experience in the Oxford Group, passed it on to his friend Ebby Thatcher, who passed it on to Bill Wilson.

Mel B. in *New Wine: The Spiritual Roots of the Twelve Step Miracle*, (Center City, MN: Hazelden, 1991), was kind enough to write that it was "largely" through my efforts that "publishers are now beginning to acknowledge the role of Frank Buchman in the ever-growing mutual, spiritual self-help movements."

In 1978, the 100th anniversary year of Frank Buchman, in the first small step that had been taken in forty years to build a bridge between the parent and AA, I proposed to the AA General Service Headquarters in New York that they run an article in their monthly magazine, *Grapevine*, about the initiator of the Oxford Group, since Wilson always credited the movement with the ideas for the Twelve Steps. They thought it was a good idea, and assigned Mel B., (AAs do not use last names in public) an industrial public relations man from Toledo, to work with me on it. We wrote a good piece, but a change of editors resulted in a change of policy. Although the article never appeared in *Grapevine*, the AA leadership arranged for it to be reproduced and made available to inquirers under the title *AA's Roots in the Oxford Group*.

The origins of Alcoholics Anonymous go back to Switzerland in the 1930s. Rowland Hazard, who came from a substantial Rhode Island chemical and textile family, was tall, handsome, and always had about him a sophisticated, cosmopolitan, shrewd businessman air. Formerly he had been a hopeless alcoholic, but still hopeful enough to keep on a world-wide search for a cure. Being a person of means, he could go anywhere and at length spent a year with C. G. Jung in the latter's psychiatric clinic in Zurich. At the end of that time Jung said he and science could do nothing more for him, but he had heard that some severe cases had responded to a spiritually oriented experience. Hazard soon found the Oxford Group, and his life was transformed. He never took another drink, and immediately went into action with a former drinking buddy, Ebby Thatcher, who transmitted the recovery experience to Bill Wilson, a New York stockbroker, who with an Akron doctor, Bob Smith, started Alcoholics Anonymous.

Whether Hazard found his renewal through the Swiss Oxford Group or the New York Oxford Group is not clear. But the Swiss group was near Jung, included a prominent Jungian in its number, and at the time was a dynamic force which counted among its active promoters some rather unusual leaders, including best-selling psychological writer Paul Tournier, who credited Frank Buchman with his choice of profession and counseling style[4]; theologian Emil Brunner; Immanuel DeTrey, eminent dental inventor; and his son-in-law Philippe Mottu, Swiss diplomat, who was to play a central role in establishing the global Moral Re-Armament center at Caux-sur-Montreux above Lake Geneva. Brother Roger, who later founded the international caring community at Taizé, France, was also associated with this group in Switzerland in those days, and was to speak of Frank Buchman as one of the "lights of our time."

In 1994, Dick Ruffin, MRA chief executive, told me he was receiving so many inquiries on the links between MRA and AA that he would like me to draft a new publication on the subject.

The result was *It Started Right There: the Story Behind the Twelve Steps and the Self-Help Movement* (Saint Paul: Grosvenor Books, 1995). The title came from a conversation I once had with T. Henry Williams (see page 126).

Foreword to a Romance

I have written the foreword to only one book, but that one was an honor I deeply cherish. My friend Jim Angell called one day and asked for my help on what turned out to be his last book. The Reverend James W. Angell was a popular preacher and author (*How To Spell Presbyterian*) and had served as minister of the Claremont Presbyterian Church for nearly two decades. He also authored a national church magazine column and a number of books. There were distant family links. While a seminary student, he had been an intern preacher under my

---

[4] In 1978, Tournier wrote to me in his own hand, "Frank Buchman is the man who most influenced my life."

cousin John A. Lampe at a church in Illinois. Before that he had sought counseling from my uncle, M. Willard Lampe, at the University of Iowa when he was switching from the law to a ministerial career.

When he called me, Jim was dying of cancer, and he wanted to wind up his last publication, which he hoped would be helpful to young preachers. He said he liked things of mine he had read, and he hoped I could help him. Within minutes I was in his study. In due course the work was published posthumously in 1995 by CSS Publishing Co., Lima, Ohio. During its production I had the privilege of working with Jim and then with his daughter, Ann V. Angell, on the editing. He had accepted my suggestion for the title, *The Romance of Preaching*.

-22-

TAXES AND PATRIOTISM

Taxes are what we pay for a civilized society.
Oliver Wendell Holmes, Jr.

It's a great country but you can't live in it for nothing.
Will Rogers

Ever since the 1960s, the role of taxes in our national life has been big in my attention span. Two concerns have provided a focus for me:
(1) *deductibility*
(2) *public attitude*

Benjamin Franklin wrote to a friend, "In this world nothing can be said to be certain, except death and taxes." Both are cordially hated. But death is now seen by many as a friend. And paying taxes is basically an act of patriotism.

My concern about deductibility started with uneasiness over widespread misunderstanding of its role in the tax laws. There was a danger of people losing sight of its purpose. Government policy has long encouraged voluntarism through allowing citizens to reduce their taxable incomes by the amounts of which they decide to deprive themselves in the public interest. Charitable contributions are a way people voluntarily tax themselves. An additional, involuntary, tax piled on would be double taxation.

Deductibility has been one way America fulfills the image described after an 1831-32 visit to the United States by the twenty-six-year-old French writer, Alexis de Tocqueville. He wrote of "the extreme skill with which the inhabitants of the United States succeed in proposing a common object to the exertions of a great many men, and inducing them voluntarily to pursue it."

Yet candidates for public office were seeking mileage on the stump by claiming that all this was somehow a "loophole," used by many, including the wealthy, to avoid public responsibility. In the view of those of us trying to advance education and other causes, the opposite appeared to be true. The American Association of Colleges, in their magazine *Liberal Education*, in May 1966 printed my article, "Education Is Not A Loophole."

The other aspect of the tax question I have tried to address is the generally negative attitude about the role of taxation in national life. Somehow we have fallen into a ditch. Paying taxes is no longer an avenue for patriotism, like jury duty or service in uniform, but rather a monster that has been dreamed up by an enemy who is to be defeated by any means available. Candidates who ask us to pay our fair share are defeated and those who tell us we do not have to pay so much are rewarded. All of this drains and depresses the federal government, and probably the economy.

Meanwhile the repressive national debt continues to explode—at least five trillion (spelled with a "t") and counting.

The first concern, deductibility, resulted in the book *The Tax Climate for Philanthropy*, which arose out of my year, 1966-67, as a Guest Scholar at the Brookings Institution in Washington, D.C.

When I entered the field of college fund-raising in 1956, there was a growing, worrisome attack on the deductibility of gifts to charitable institutions—colleges, hospitals, churches, museums. To the uninitiated, deductions could be made to appear as a way of getting out of paying taxes, because the giver is allowed to reduce the taxable part of his income by the amount of the gift.

True, the deduction meant that the gift did not cost the giver the full amount of the gift, but if he did not make the gift at all, the amount would remain as discretionary income for him to spend on himself or his family. There was still some self-denial.

Out of the thirty-five members of the tax-writing committees of the House and Senate with whom I talked in Washington during my tax-climate study, twenty-five said deductions simply encourage a different kind of responsibility and should not be regarded as avoidance.

I decided to see if I could take a "sabbatical" leave and study the subject. College professors' contracts call for a furlough every few years to pursue special study. The idea is rooted in the Shabbat principle, through which one day in seven is treated specially. Administration types do not normally enjoy such breaks. So when, as Coordinator of Development at the Claremont University Center and Graduate School, I worked one out for myself, my counterparts in other colleges were impressed. I obtained a year's leave of absence for 1966-67 and found enough donors interested in the project to cover my salary. The American College Public Relations Association (ACPRA, now the Council for the Advancement and Support of Education) budgeted $10,000 for expenses of travel and publication. The ACPRA Executive Director, John Leslie, provided constant backup throughout. His office was only a few blocks from Brookings.

Mary Louise and I rented a house in the Chevy Chase area of the District of Columbia, and enrolled our youngest son Bob in the Alice Deal Junior High School, reputed to be Washington's best. The other two boys were at college in New England. Mary Louise secured a secretarial position at the National Science Foundation.

Washington is one of the most fascinating cities in the world, and we tried to take advantage of some of its opportunities. One Saturday morning Bob and I joined an environmental group which was sponsoring a walk to gain attention for restoring the deteriorated Chesapeake and Ohio Canal, a nineteenth century conduit for eastern coal that ran 185 miles inland to Cumberland, Maryland. For several miles that day twenty of us walked along with Supreme Court Justice William O. Douglas and his young wife, Cathleen. Known as an avid outdoorsman, Douglas is credited with saving the canal from becoming a paved parkway and providing the impetus that led in 1971 to making the waterway a National Historic Park. There is still an annual walk there in his memory. Another highlight for us was season tickets for the *National Geographic* illustrated programs in Constitution Hall.

Joseph B. Platt, founding president of Harvey Mudd College, obtained for me an appointment as Guest Scholar at the Brookings Institution through his friend, Kermit Gordon, who was president at the time. My inquiry was not an official Brookings study, but each year the prestigious think tank provides space for visitors who are pursuing ends of consequence. I was afforded a small office on the seventh floor of the Institution's impressive building at 1775 Massachusetts Avenue. My cubicle had a window looking out to the north. Like the Smithsonian, Brookings is an "institution," not an "institute."

Brookings' reputation was of course a great help in making appointments on Capitol Hill and elsewhere in Washington. At the same time, I was always scrupulous in making it clear that mine was not an official Brookings study.

The study was divided into two parts. The first aimed to discover from major donors how much the tax factor motivated their gifts. From the office of the American Association of Fund-Raising Counsel, I obtained news clippings of reports on donors who made philanthropic gifts of one million dollars or more to something in 1965. Developing a list of forty persons, I was able to track thirty for individual interviews. In three instances, I had to settle for talking to financial agents, but in each case they were thoroughly familiar with their principals' motivations. Interviews were held in New York City and Rochester in New York; Delray Beach, Fort Lauderdale, Sebastian, and Hobe Sound in Florida; Toledo and Youngstown in Ohio; Compton and Santa Monica in California; Rutherford, New Jersey; Portland, Oregon; Wilmington; Pittsburgh; Dallas; Chicago; Ann Arbor; and Washington, D.C.

The results made the front page of the *Wall Street Journal* in August 1967. The basic summary was that the big donors do not give for tax reasons. Taxes came out as fifth in a list of donor motivations. Most of the persons I talked with were close to the causes they supported, such as being a trustee. They were quite clear, however, that if their gifts were not deductible, those gifts would be far less. The difference would go to the government.

Among the people I talked with were W. Van Alan Clark, Avon Company; Harold F. Johnson, New York attorney, who gave six million dollars to found Hampshire College, Massachusetts; Nicholas H. Noyes, Eli Lily Company; Edwin W. Pauley, petroleum; Joseph C. Wilson, chairman, Xerox Corporation; and Lammot DuPont Copeland, chairman, E. I. du Pont de Nemours and Company.

The other half of the study involved canvassing those in Washington who make decisions on tax policy, particularly where the deductibility factor is concerned. For this, I concentrated on members of the House Ways and Means Committee, which initiates tax legislation, and its Senate counterpart, the Finance Committee. Secondarily, I talked with key figures in the Treasury Department, the people whose interpretive rulings on Congressional tax language become a part of operative tax law.

One of the most memorable interviews I had on Capitol Hill was with Wilbur D. Mills.[1]

Growing up in a small town in Arkansas, Mills made his way to the Harvard Law School, and soon ran for the U.S. House of Representatives, where he served from 1938 to 1974. He was appointed to the Ways and Means Committee in 1942, four years after he arrived in the House. He headed Ways and Means, the powerful chairman of the most powerful committee of the House from 1957 to 1974, presiding over four revisions of the tax code and the creation of Medicare. It is said he knew the tax code from memory. He was regarded as totally thorough and completely fair. Laurence N. Woodworth, chief of staff of the Joint Committee on Taxation, told me, "The other members of his committee have come to trust his judgment implicitly. In fact many trust his judgment more than they do their own."

This was the main source of the man's power and why most of the Mills legislation traveled so expeditiously, not only through his committee and the Joint House-Senate conference committee, but also through both houses of Congress. If Mills thought it was OK, it was OK.

On the tax survey interview, which took about forty minutes, his first question was, "Is this for attribution?" I assured him that none of the respondents would be quoted. It was obvious better answers would be forthcoming.

Mills's counterpart in the Senate was Russell B. Long of Louisiana, chairman of the Senate Finance Committee. This unit and Ways and Means are the tax writing committees of Congress. Mills and Long, from adjacent southern states, shared their tenure as chairmen for nine years, proving a productive association.

---

[1] A *Bicentennial History of the Committee on Ways and Means* stated, "The Arkansas Democrat was one of the most influential leaders in congressional history."

Russell B. Long, son of Huey Pierce "Kingfish" Long, was elected to the Senate at age thirty, minimum age for a Senator, and retired nearly forty years later, in 1987. He became at once a no-nonsense legislator, who, while always loyal to his father, showed none of the flamboyance. His votes were generally favorable to the oil interests of his native state, but he was also credited with assistance in major social legislation, such as Social Security and Medicare. Frustrated, as are most legislators, with irresponsible tax attitudes, he liked to cite the line,

> Don't tax my brother, don't tax me,
> Go tax the other man behind that tree.

My appointment with Russell Long was for after lunch in his office, and as I waited for him to come in and take off his hat and coat, it was right away not a cold call. His family and ours have been summer neighbors for decades near Petoskey, Michigan. Huey's older sister Charlotte Long Davis and her lumberman husband, Robert Davis, and offspring have come there each year for most of the century.

Another Senator I remember was Thruston Morton of Kentucky. He and his brother, Rogers Morton, were fairly bright stars at the time, both having served as Chairman of the Republican National Committee. Thruston was familiar with big-time philanthropy in Kentucky, and he liked what I was talking about. He wanted to be sure I sent him the results of the study. (Everyone interviewed received a copy of the book *The Tax Climate for Philanthropy* as soon as it was published.)

Morton at the same time was concerned that there might be instances where the donor can work the tax laws in such a way that he personally benefits from making the gift. "All philanthropy should involve some pain," he said.

Hale Boggs of Louisiana had high seniority on Ways and Means. Also in the Democratic party, as he soon became

Majority Leader in the House. I had visited with him and his wife at a lawn party a few years earlier when we lived in Washington. During our tax interview, he was busy and preoccupied, and it did not last as long as some others. Five years later, in 1972, he died tragically in a plane crash in Alaska. His wife succeeded him in the House for many years, and his daughter, Cokie Roberts, became a radio and television commentator.

Back on the Senate side, I had interesting conversations with George A. Smathers of Florida, with whom I had traveled to a parliamentary conference in Switzerland in 1948; Carl T. Curtis of Nebraska; Wallace F. Bennett of Utah; and one of the all-time legends of the Senate, Everett McKinley Dirksen of Illinois.

Another memorable visit was with George H. W. Bush in his congressional office, for nearly an hour. He had received a good word about me from his friend Richard Cornuelle, author of *Reclaiming the American Dream*. Bush had just been elected from Houston for the first of two terms in Congress in 1966, and was appointed to the House Ways and Means Committee in January 1967.

I found him unusually interested in my project, and coming from a family that had a history of active philanthropy, he quickly grasped the central issue.

My basic conclusions from the study were that the big donors made the big gifts not from a tax motive, but because of personal involvement with the philanthropy. The tax laws enabled them to give much more, and they believed that ending deductibility would not hurt them personally, but would hurt the institutions involved by reducing the amount of the gift that actually reached its object.

As to the Washington decision-makers, I found a more favorable reaction to deductibility than I expected. Nevertheless, there has been steady erosion since then, under the pressure of making the tax laws simpler.

The book giving the results of the study, *The Tax Climate for Philanthropy* was published by the American College Public Relations Association. The writing was done in two months in the summer of 1967 at Mary Louise's family's summer place in Petoskey, Michigan. Each morning I sat down to the typewriter from seven to eleven o'clock. After a two-hour break, I chained the seat of the pants to the seat of the chair from one until five. It made a neat eight-hour day.

The ACPRA office retained an editor to finalize the copy for publication at a printer in Baltimore. Since by now I was back at work on the west coast, this process took some time, and the book finally came out in 1968, with the foremost media announcement appearing on the front page of the *Wall Street Journal.*

There were no reports that the book was a hot seller at supermarket check-out counters, but ACPRA sent a copy to each of their 800 members in college and university development offices across the country, offering a second copy free upon request. For some time people would tell me they kept the book on their office shelves for reference, and newcomers to the profession were warmly urged to read it. The *Saturday Review* wrote it up as "one of the broadest surveys yet made of the very large donors." Blake-More Godwin of the Toledo Museum of Art commented, "The most interesting and encouraging, and I believe authoritative, statement on the subject that I have yet to meet."

The Secretary of the Rockefeller Foundation told me he gave an early copy, with the injunction it was a must-read, to Peter G. Peterson, at that time President of Bell & Howell, and in 1969 about to take on the chairmanship of a national commission on foundations, philanthropy, and volunteerism. Peterson, who was Secretary of Commerce in the 1970s, was later to join Senators Warren Rudman and Walter Tsongas as President of the budget-balancing activist organization, the Concord Coalition.

After the "sabbatical" at Brookings was over, Mary Louise, Bob, and I returned to our home in Claremont, California. During this time I was still active in the national tax communication fraternity and was made founding chairman of the "501-C-3 Group," consisting of representatives of organizations, gifts to which were tax-deductible under Section 501-C-3 of the tax code. The guiding genius behind the group was New York lawyer Conrad Teitell, and we met every three months in Washington to keep abreast of developments in the tax law affecting philanthropy. Usually we met with a tax policy-maker, from Capitol Hill or from the Treasury Department or IRS. Of all the experts who met with us, Laurence N. Woodworth, Chief of Staff of the Congressional Joint Committee on Taxation, was most helpful.

At one point, when we were especially concerned that Congress would act detrimentally, I was asked to spend full time in Washington for six weeks, on a leave of absence from ICSC, and financed by the American Association of Fundraising Counsel in New York. In retrospect, I was not nearly aggressive or vocal enough when I had a chance with people like George Romney, Secretary of Health and Welfare, and Senator Walter Mondale of Minnesota. But we were able to mobilize our college constituencies across the country and defeat Senator Ted Kennedy's proposal to repeal the deductibility at its fair-market value of appreciated property.

On this assignment I again met Wilbur Mills, several years after our first encounter. I was struck by what he remembered from before. Although his administrative assistant told us it was a terrible afternoon for his boss, and we might get three minutes if we were lucky, Mills graciously sat down in his conference room off the floor of the House and talked with our committee for forty-five minutes.

My last visit with Mills was in the 1970s, when he was an ex-

Congressman practicing tax law in the District. He asked me to meet him at a restaurant on the Virginia side. He had been forced to resign from Congress in 1974 because of a drinking problem, and had then achieved sobriety through Alcoholics Anonymous. I hoped he could come in 1978 and speak in Allentown, Pennsylvania, on the occasion of the centennial of Frank Buchman's birth. We were trying to gather persons who could speak out of experience with outgrowths of Buchman's work. Again, Mills was the southern gentleman all the way through, but explained that on the day in question, he had agreed to speak at an AA meeting in Florida.[2]

Public Attitudes

The other side of the tax question that has concerned me has been the negative attitudes toward taxation. Increasingly these have resulted in fiscal strangulation at all levels of government, whereas taxpaying deserves to be regarded as a patriotic undertaking. One problem is the huge tax-advice industry that has an enormous stake in encouraging anti-tax emotions. A few years ago, one of the big Los Angeles savings and loan companies promoted a television commercial explaining how they could reduce one's income tax, and featuring Bob Hope mailing his return while a gloved Uncle Sam arm swings out at him, causing Hope to exclaim, "What do you want, blood?"

I protested to the company that depicting the government as an enemy was hardly helpful in these days, and particularly

---

[2]When a bust of Buchman was dedicated at Muhlenberg College in 1991, I invited Mills, not long before he died, to send a message for the printed program. He sent these words: "I am grateful to be a beneficiary of this great man's work. . . . His pioneering has resulted in millions finding a new life, including myself. . . . If we could get the leaders of the world to think along these steps and terms, there would be no threat of nuclear war."

coming from Bob Hope, who had done so much for those who laid their blood on the line for their country. A vice president of the S & L responded, "Similar comments led us to withdraw the Bob Hope commercial."

A metropolitan daily ran a tax-wise series of columns by economic writer Sylvia Porter. All helpful material, but across the top of each installment was a headline, "Beating the Tax Man," accompanied by a drawing depicting Uncle Sam as a glowering antagonist whom the citizen is encouraged to overthrow. The heading was dropped the next year.

An alarming movement is growing in California, and if there, soon elsewhere, namely popular referendum on how much taxes one wishes to pay. Public officials are elected to grapple with public services, figure out what they cost, and ask the taxpayer to cover. When we go to a football game, we are not asked how much we wish to pay for beer, pizza, or tickets to the game. We pay the price. No one asks letter-writers whether they wish to pay more for each letter. We are told it is going to cost so much to keep delivering the mail. The present philosophy, pioneered by California's late Howard Jarvis, is: if you don't give the bastards any money, they can't spend it. So the disaster worsens. Like the indulgent parent of a spoiled brat, we are now asking Joe and Jane Citizen, "You don't want to pay any more taxes, do you?" The answer is predictable. So the schools and universities deteriorate, libraries disappear, human services suffer, and bridges crumble—and the generation-crushing national debt zooms as the atomic-size threat of the future.

Advertising Council

It occurred to me that if the public attitude is the problem, then the public attitude can be changed. The national Advertising Council has produced extraordinary results in raising the public's consciousness on many issues. For example, their "Smokey the Bear" campaign for nearly fifty years is said to have reduced forest fires by fifty percent. Through this Council, the top brains of Madison Avenue contribute their skills to advance public interest causes. What more in the public interest than to help people see taxes in terms of patriotism?

My first step was an interview in Hollywood with the late Richard Dwan, vice president of the Advertising Council, January 3, 1985. He explained that the creative aspects of the campaigns are contributed, but the sponsoring organization needs to come up with two hundred and fifty to five hundred thousand dollars a year to pay for tapes, materials, and mailing to the newspapers and broadcast stations—16,000 media outlets. Dwan liked my idea a lot and said, "Who could be against such a proposal?"

For a sponsor, it looked as though the U.S. Treasury would be the best bet. The Ad Council had successfully promoted their campaigns for buying war bonds, and they should be interested in people paying their taxes. However, they were counting on an upcoming tax "reform" bill in Congress which they hoped would make the structure fairer, and they held, naively I thought, that if people believed the system was fair, they would happily pay up everything due.

I tried to see Senator Robert Dole of Kansas, elected in January 1985 Majority Leader, thinking he might encourage the Ad Council. He had just issued a report that the government loses $100 billion a year in taxpayer non-compliance. Translation: cheating. Certainly an attitude problem. Recovering this amount would cut the annual deficit in half. Bill Rhatican, of the Ad Council in the Washington office, sent me to Dole's aide Jo Anne Coe, as he was sure the senator would respond to my proposal. I've usually been pretty good at penetrating the fortresses of Capitol Hill, but although I talked with half a dozen of his aides, their final defense line was adequate to the challenge, and I never got through, even to Jo Anne.

In New York, the ladies running the Ad Council office, particularly Elenore Hangley, Vice President, were most cooperative, and apparently positive about the tax project, but of course still said we needed a sponsor before they could submit the idea to the board. Having failed to find a sponsor in the public sector, I turned to the *Reader's Digest*, usually to be counted on for all things bright and beautiful. I had known the founding publisher, DeWitt Wallace, who died in 1981, in the Macalester College days, and had kept up with business manager Al Cole and vice president for public relations, John Allen. Allen arranged a luncheon with himself and a colleague, Terry Kirkpatrick, at the Guest House in Chappaqua, but at the end of the afternoon the problem remained: the *Digest* would continue their stance that people should pay a lot less taxes than they do.

Robert K. Gray, public relations virtuoso and a fellow Carleton alumnus who had been on Eisenhower's staff, wrote me in his own hand, "I will see if I can nudge your notion along."

Much progress was made in the 1990s, when the Congress and the president bit the bullet and balanced the federal budget, actually producing surpluses—however short-lived. For the first time in living memory there was even serious talk bout paying down the national debt.

The claim is made that the surpluses belong to the people, to whom the money should be sent back in tax cuts. Not so, in my opinion. The surpluses belong to the creditors, those to whom the government owes over five trillion dollars. Federal Reserve Chairman Alan Greenspan says debt reduction should come before other "stimulus"schemes.

The public is inching this way. Polls are suggesting that tax reduction, which politicians believed was a sure thing at the ballot box, does not have the appeal it once did. In some of them debt reduction has crept above tax reduction.

Although resistance to taxes will remain alive and well, there is hope for a more patriotic posture.

-23-

HAWAII

I was chatting in a Houston hallway with Anne Lindbergh. It was 1984, and we were between sessions of an annual meeting of the Charles A. and Anne Morrow Lindbergh Foundation. The purpose of the foundation is to advance the balance between science and nature, between technology and the environment—a long held concern of the famous couple. I had just come from Maui where I had been interviewing friends of the Lindberghs on the Hana Coast in an oral history project for the Minnesota Historical Society.[1]

The Lindberghs had been introduced to Hawaiian living by Samuel F. Pryor, Jr., with whom Charles had worked for decades in the development of Pan American World Airways. As a result the Lindberghs had built in the 1960s a primitive A-frame cabin near the Pryors in Kipahulu, eleven miles south of Hana on the eastern Maui coast. They occupied this hideaway a few weeks at a time in the late sixties and early seventies. In New York in 1974 the lymphatic cancer which had plagued the aviator for over two years was closing him down, and he asked to be taken back to Hawaii to die. He told his doctors, "I would rather spend one day on Maui than thirty days in the hospital."

When I talked to Mrs. Lindbergh in Houston I asked about her husband's grave, which people were visiting in some

---

[1]The recordings of these interviews are on file at the Lindbergh Park, Little Falls, Minnesota. They are mentioned by A. Scott Berg, *Lindbergh* (New York: Putnam, 1998), 567.

numbers, whether the Bible verse chiseled in the stone was his idea or hers. Diplomatically she replied, "We worked all that out together."[2]

I wondered to her also whether the placement of the initials "C.A.L." on the stone under the lines from scripture, might lead some visitors to think that the stonecutter believed her husband was the author of those words. Her initials, "A.M.L.," are also cut in the stone, and she went on to cite a report from the "stone cutter," by which she meant Charles's great Hawaiian friend, Joseph "Tevi" Kahaleuahi, who actually was the one who dug the grave. He had informed her that the burial vault allowed for *two* places. "I suppose he was suggesting the other space was for me," she said. "But I don't know about that. I think I'm going to get burned up. There are enough graves already." When her daughter Reeve was reminded that the Pryors and the Lindberghs had drawn up the plan for the church burial of the two couples, she said, "The *men* made the plan." Actually the whole Hawaiian thing was Charles's idea, and Anne went with it only as long as he lived. He died in Hawaii in 1974 at seventy-two; she in Vermont in 2001 at ninety-four. Her ashes have been scattered throughout the world in places she loved, including Maui.

Tevi was a tall, likeable, athletic, skilled Hawaiian artisan who was reputed to be able to do just abut anything. He and Lindbergh went together on many an outdoor venture like skinny lobster fishing. Tevi was the one chosen to build a writing cottage for Anne, up the hill from their place on the shore. I had a visit with him at the 1980 Christmas luau put on each year in Kipahulu by Sam Pryor. I asked Tevi how come he was the one

[2]The verse: "If I take the wings of the morning and dwell in the uttermost parts of the sea. . ." Psalm 139. Anne Lindbergh's writings carry an unusual number of Biblical allusions.

to do all these things for and with Lindbergh. His big ebony face burst into a wreath of smiles as he replied, "Because he was my friend."

When death came to his friend, it was Tevi who lovingly dressed his body and carried it from Ed and Jeannie Pechin's Pu'uiki guest cottage to a pickup truck, tied the homemade, heavy eucalyptus coffin down with a tarp, and drove past the Seven Pools to the church in Kipahulu. Bystanders had no idea what was passing through.

I was privileged to be a denizen of the Hawaiian Islands off and on for thirty years. The first visit Mary Louise and I made was in 1969, when we accompanied great friends, an older Minneapolis couple, Ralph and Theone Beal, as house-sitters at a home in Kailua on the leeward side of Oahu. We were there in July when Neil Armstrong and Buzz Alldrin first set foot on the moon. That day we attended the Sunday service in Honolulu's downtown Kauaihao Church, built by the first missionary to the Islands, Hiram Bingham, in 1820. That morning the moon landing was expected, and the Rev. Abraham Akaka, popular native Hawaiian *kahu* (shepherd), set up television sets all over the sanctuary so the parishioners would not miss it. As it turned out the historic event took place a few hours later.

Subsequent island visits arose out of a coincidence of two circumstances. The first was church assignments at the Wananalua Congregational Church in Hana, where I was minister in residence in December 1980 and again in December 1990. The second was the Lindbergh/Pryor presence on the Hana Coast. Sam Pryor, both a friend and a business associate of the aviator, attended the Hana Church every Sunday, sometimes with one of his beloved gibbon apes, and we became good friends.

Pryor, Lindbergh's associate in New York and host in Hawaii, had been Executive Vice President for Pan Am for twenty-eight years. He was also a sometime power in national politics and supervised the arrangements for the 1940 Republican convention in Philadelphia that nominated Wendell Willkie.

Retiring to Kipahulu, Sam persuaded Lindbergh to come and see him. One visit did it. The flyer bought five of Pryor's acres and built a simple A-frame cabin that had no electricity.

Sam was the soul of hospitality and welcomed one and all to his home and the nearby church. He was a shameless name-dropper but one tended to make allowances as he really did know everybody who was anybody throughout industry and government.

The Congregational church in Kipahulu where Lindbergh is buried carries the Hawaiian name *Palapala Ho'omau* (the Eternal Word). Because of population shifts in the 1920s, the church had been abandoned, and the building was falling down when Sam obtained permission from church headquarters in Honolulu to restore it. Since that time, there have been worship services there for extended periods, highlighted each year by a popular community Thanksgiving gathering. I have been a recurrent guest speaker.

I came to know Sam pretty well in December 1980 and went down from Hana to Kipahulu every afternoon to join him at three o'clock for his ritual ringing of the church bell, which he had imported from Connecticut. He would then say the "Our Father" with whomever was there, and go out to Lindbergh's grave to talk with pilots and other visitors who came that day. He wanted them to know what came before and after the Bible verse on the grave, so he would read in a loud voice the 139th Psalm. Some of the visitors he would invite to his house, which was not far away, for tea and camaraderie.

In those days he was in a row with the neighbors about access to Lindbergh's grave. He felt that any one who wanted to should be able to walk through the gate at the main road and pay his or her respects to his friend and national hero. He insisted the gate be kept open. Some neighbors were equally passionate about keeping the gate closed and were upset by the tourist noise and traffic. Confrontations on the road became ugly, sometimes highlighted by bitter profanity and spray-paint attack guns. Reports of all this were most disturbing to Anne and her family on the mainland. The last thing they wanted was to disturb the natural environment or the community. At one time they even considered the possibility of removing the remains, but concluded the publicity might make things worse.

At one of our 3:00 P.M. Lord's-Prayer sessions around the bell rope in the Kipahulu church, I talked to Sam, a devout Episcopalian, about the line in the New Testament that insists that one be "reconciled to your brother" before doing anything else, like making a gift. As we talked he began to believe he should make amends. One antagonist was Peter Frelinghuysen, a Congressman from New Jersey 1956-74, who with his wife Bea, a Procter & Gamble heiress, owned a beautiful bluff home next door, some acreage around the church, and the access road down to it. Sam agreed he should apologize to these neighbors, not for his convictions but for his bitterness. He was about to do so when his family talked him out of it on account of a matter that was then in court. From then on, however, Sam showed quite a different attitude with the neighbors. The Lindberghs' son Land in Montana told their family friend Jim Newton that it looked as though the controversy had died down.

The Kipahulu church is owned by the Hawaii Conference of the United Church of Christ based in Honolulu. When Sam Pryor decided he wanted to restore the dilapidated building, he obtained permission from the Honolulu office to do so. When Lindbergh expressed interest in being buried there, Sam introduced him to the same authorities, who leased a burial spot to the family. Upon the flyer's death, the Lindbergh Foundation took over the lease, and for several years I provided informal liaison between them and the church headquarters.[3] Anne Lindbergh made additional contributions for the church, designating part for maintenance and part for "program."

In 1995 I was able to persuade the board of directors of the Lindbergh Foundation, who were then still taking responsibility for maintenance of the burial area, to hold one of their regular meetings on the Hana Coast in order to understand the situation on the ground.[4]

My first serious visit to eastern Maui, known as "the last Hawaiian place" because of its lack of development, came in 1980 in response to a plan adopted by the Wananalua Congregational Church in Hana, the mother church of the one in Kipahulu. They were having difficulty finding a permanent pastor, and they discovered they could bring some one from the mainland for a one-month hitch. It proved to be an attractive assignment for preachers, and a waiting list soon developed. Although the scheme had the obvious problem of lack of

---

[3]A number of these tiny missionary churches, sometimes established only five miles apart, went out of business for reasons like improved transportation, consolidation, or population shifts. In such cases, their property reverted to church headquarters in Honolulu. Many of these churches were Congregational, now known as the United Church of Christ, because the first operatives, who came from New England in the early 1800s were Congregational. These missionaries were invited to Hawaii by a group of native Hawaiians, headed by Henry Opukahaia, to help them rid the Islands of internecine slaughter and to promote educational, social, and spiritual development.

[4]Not long after the 1995 meeting in Hana, the Foundation terminated its lease and turned over the maintenance to local church officials, the family having provided endowment funds for the purpose.

continuity, Roselle Howell, the Hana coast doctor's wife who dreamed up the idea, said it had its advantages. "If the minister is a good one," she was fond of saying, "you have the person for a month. If not, it's only a month."

The stipend doesn't cover the air fare, but a house and a car for the month are provided the guest. I had two of these appointments, the first in December 1980, and then again exactly ten years later in December 1990. I heard about the opportunity in 1977 when one day I was passing through Palm Desert, and called at the church office of a friend of mine only to discover he was on a preaching assignment in Hawaii. "Hawaii!" I exclaimed, "How do you get an appointment like that?" His secretary said they were looking for people, gave me the address, and I wrote. They put my name on a list, and three years later they called me. There have been many return trips.

We knew we were in Hawaii the first morning in December 1980 when we discovered that a parishioner was backing his pickup to the rear door of the *hale kahu* (house of the shepherd) and was hanging a big bunch of bananas on a string. They had to be hung, he said, or our friendly neighborhood mongoose would get them before we did. Another Hawaiian reminder the first day came from the lava rocks at the base of the church, some of them with flowers growing straight out of the stone. In my album I titled this picture "The Story of Hawaii." The whole of the islands were once lava rock, and seeds dropped by wind and birds on the bare boulders gave Hawaii's lush flora its original impetus.

One of the friends for life we made in Hawaii in 1980 was Frayn Utley. She and her husband, Clifton Utley, prominent Midwest broadcast commentator who in Chicago bridged the transition from radio to television, had retired to Hana and had a nice house high on the bluff south of town overlooking the

Pacific. Someone erected a street sign on the road by their house that said, "Fifth Avenue." Clifton, whom Mary Louise's family had known in Indianapolis when her mother invited him more than once to address the Indiana League of Women Voters, had died before we reached Hana, and she continued to be a force in the community. She was particularly anxious to provide cultural vitamins for folks who lived there and held a monthly soiree at her house, where she would play records of classical music and opera, introducing each number with her own spoken program notes. She claimed to be of the Unitarian persuasion, yet active in the Wananalua Congregational Church, the only Protestant aggregation in town. One of her contributions to the church was a new set of hymn books in memory of her husband.

It may have been a reflection on the quality of the previous month's guru plus the fact that she did not yet know me at all, but early in my first week, she paid me what I chose to regard as a compliment when she said, "I'd even go to a prayer meeting if it were conducted by you."

Frayn later retired again to a residence virtually across the street from us in Claremont, where until her death we enjoyed happy visits. Her son Garrick Utley, a Carleton College alumnus and trustee, followed in the commentating footsteps of his parents with various outlets including NBC and CNN. He frequently visited his mother in Claremont.

In the fall of 1989 when I finished an assignment in Hawaii, I made my first and only visit to Asia. Since I was half way across the Pacific already, I assumed I could continue west from Honolulu. Not so, I had to fly back to Los Angeles and then launch forth across the Pacific, leaving from Portland, where I had seen that flying trans-Pacific Clipper Ship fifty-nine years earlier.

An old friend, Ambassador Yu-tang Daniel Lew, veteran of

wide-ranging appointments with the Chinese Nationalist Government's foreign service, invited me to attend in Taipei what he billed the first international conference on Abraham Lincoln. He had become an admirer and a promoter of America's Civil War president and had established Lincoln Clubs in places like Taipei and Seattle. He was editing a foreign affairs magazine *Sino-American Relations*, in which he carried a Lincoln article by me. We who were delegates to his conference were put up in the magnificent Grand Hotel, owned at the time by Mme. Chiang Kai-shek, then ninety-one. She lived a mile away.

When I asked Yu-tang why the interest in Lincoln? He would only speak of things like strength. But two impressions emerged in conversations:

(1) Sun Yat-sen, the hero of the Chinese uprising of 1911, which threw off centuries of domination by the Manchu dynasty, based his revolution on the Gettysburg Address—of, by, and for the people. (Chinese high-school students still enter national Gettysburg Address contests.)

(2) In addition, listening between the lines, I concluded that Lew and his colleagues responded to the parallel—America divided then and China divided now—with Lincoln prepared to go to war to preserve the oneness of his nation. Both Taipei and Beijing agree that there is but one China. They do not agree which. There was no question that from what we saw and what we heard in 1989, including the bristling armaments at Quemoy, the Republic of China was still contemplating war as a solution.

Before the conference, I had a few days free and was able to visit Beijing and Japan, traverse the tourist section of the China Wall, the only man-made structure seeable from the moon, walk through the Forbidden City, the Hall of the People, and Tiananmen Square—five months after the massacre. In Japan I took the Shinkansen, high speed bullet train, from Kyoto to Hiroshima and saw the horror of the 1945 atomic devastation.

In 1993 *The Spirit of Charles Lindbergh: Another Dimension* came out, and my friend Harry Hasegawa in Hana Maui set me up to sign books in front of his legendary emporium, Hasegawa General Store. This is a fabulous four-generation establishment immortalized in a popular song. Lisa Kristofferson, who lived with her husband Kris and children in nearby Nahiku, made my day. She purchased two copies and gave me a big hug. Maybe it was because my leg was in a cast for a knee injury suffered on a local hike.

One of the most rewarding friendships in Hawaii was with Harry Mitchell, the most Hawaiian man with a non-Hawaiian name I met. Known as "Uncle Harry," he was a patriarch of the north Maui coast, operating a Hawaiian fruit and crafts stand on the Hana highway. He also worked indefatigably at preserving the Hawaiian language and culture. We heard that barely a thousand people are left who can still speak Hawaiian. (The tourist industry strenuously preserves a few phrases.) Harry was often called to teach at the University of Hawaii. His daughter, Pearl "Lei" Pahukoa, was a beloved teacher and lay minister in the taro patch town of Keanae, half way between the Maui airport (Kahalui) and Hana. The Pahukoas were our best Hawaiian friends.

One of Uncle Harry's sons, Pearl's brother Kimo Mitchell, was a Hawaiian activist, and apparently gave his life for the cause of preserving the island of Kaho'olawe, which had been devastated under target bombing by the U.S. Navy ever since they took it over in 1941, World War II. One night in 1977 Kimo and a friend drowned in the Alalakeiki channel between Kaho'olawe and Maui under circumstances that were never explained. A friend of the family suspected foul play, saying "He grew up in the water—he didn't know how to drown."

Kimo's native reclamation movement, though, has made progress. In 1990 President George H. W. Bush ordered the target bombing stopped. In 1993 the Congress made the cessation permanent and voted to return the island's title back to the State of Hawaii. The Navy has cleared ten thousand acres of surface ordnance and have eradicated the plant-destroying goats.

Kimo's father was sympathetic to his son's aims, but was concerned that his boy may have fallen in with the wrong crowd. "Who goes with evil dies with evil," he told me.

It was a moving experience to attend Harry's funeral at his family's missionary church in Keanae—a traditional two-hour outpouring of love, flowers, Hawaiian music, and everybody going up more than once to the coffin at the altar to pay their respects. Then we all proceeded outdoors to the freshly dug grave where the music continued and hundreds of flowers were flung to smother the descending casket.

Harry's legacy to me—and perhaps to all of us—comes in his timeless words:

"You take care of nature; nature take care of you."

-24-

HISTORY COMING ALIVE

Many a meaningful observance that enriches our lives consists in a reenactment of an historic event. The Christian communion is a reenactment of Jesus' last supper in Jerusalem, which in turn was held in observance of the Hebrew Passover, a reenactment of the escape from Egyptian slavery. Each Muslim hopes to make one lifetime pilgrimage to Mecca, reenacting the flight of Mohammed. When we blast off fireworks on the Fourth of July, we replicate the rockets' red glare that gave proof through the night that our flag was still there.

I have been privileged to develop the reenactment of three historic milestones in which many people of all ages and backgrounds have taken part.

They are:
- Fourth of July oratory
- Good Friday Way of the Cross
- Trek of the Los Angeles Settlers

Fourth of July

On American Independence Day I used to develop an uneasy feeling that something was missing. I had read that in the old days something was made of the Declaration of Independence, whose adoption was being feted. Notable speakers expounded on its significance. On July 4, 1937, I accompanied my uncle, M. Willard Lampe, Dean of the School of Religion at the University of Iowa, to Washington, Iowa, where in the town square he was the featured speaker. People gathered around and listened.

But for forty years after that I did not hear anybody say anything on the Fourth of July. There were the Tiny Tot Bathing Beauty contests and the hot dogs. All agreed the parades and the fireworks were essential to the survival of the Republic. After all, John Adams, one of the five members of the committee that drafted the Declaration, wrote to his wife Abigail the week it was approved:

> The day will be the most memorable epoch in the history of America. I am apt to believe that it will be celebrated by succeeding generations as the great anniversary festival. It ought to be commemorated as the day of deliverance by solemn acts of devotion to God Almighty. It ought to be solemnized with pomp and parade, with shows, games, sports, guns, bells, bonfires, and illuminations, from one end of this continent to the other, from this time forward forever more.

In addition to all this, it seemed to me, someone ought to get up in a corner of the park and talk about why we are doing these things, why we are taking the day off, and what the Declaration of Independence has meant and is still destined to mean for the world.

And so in Madbury, New Hampshire, on the Fourth of July 1975, I persuaded the town fathers and mothers to add oratory to the lemonade. The old-fashioned celebration took place in the park next to the Union Congregational Church. Somebody had contributed the largest American flag in New Hampshire, and a farmer provided a wagon with bales of hay on which to stand. I decided to speak for two hours. People came and went; nobody was locked into the audience. And they seemed to think it added something to the celebrations. On a return visit there years later, a woman recalled to me the occasion.

By mid-1976, the American Bicentennial year, our family had moved from New Hampshire back to California. On July fourth I was committed to an engagement in Eagle Mountain, the

Kaiser iron mine community. But the following year I approached Judy Kern, General Chairperson of Claremont's Fourth of July Committee, and proposed setting up a speakers' platform for the day. Judy is a positive person and quickly agreed.

We had lived in Claremont before, and I recalled that on a Fourth of July in the early 1960s, the festivities were held on the Claremont McKenna College football field. The opening ceremonies at ten o'clock consisted of thirty-second greetings by Mayor Ed Dittmer, State Assemblyman Houston Flournoy, and Claremont McKenna President George C. S. Benson. None of them was about to say anything more than opening pleasantries. But Benson concluded with a rifle shot that landed in my gizzard, and I have never been able to shake it. He said, "The Fourth of July reminds us that there are principles that are worth dying for." Then it was off to the fun and games.

The assertion set up in me a chain of thoughts. I said under my breath, "OK, George, *what* principles? And *why* don't we *talk* about them—*particularly* on the Fourth of July?"

By July 4, 1977, the idea began to get going. For two years we had a few speakers talk near the band shell. But nobody seemed to be paying much heed. I wondered whether length might draw some attention.

So in 1979 I announced I would speak for three hours in the park. The Metro editor of the *Los Angeles Times* sent a writer and a photographer, and the result was a feature with a photo on the big daily's front page. Apparently people would pay attention if the activity were done in an interesting manner.

The idea took hold, and recently each year on the one day more than twenty people have spoken on the Claremont oratory platform. In 1995, I received a flattering commendation, all gussied up in scroll-fashion the way they do those things, from Governor Pete Wilson of California, and the Claremont Committee voted to name the annual feature, the "T. Willard Hunter Oratory" program. They imbedded the words on a small plaque in the sidewalk by the speaker's stand in the park. I felt as though I'd made the Hollywood Walk of Fame. The event has since been renamed "Speakers Corner" (like Hyde Park).

On some Fourths, Hank Maxwell, genial chairman of the local American Bicentennial committee, gave a lively spoof of old-fashioned oratory, with full flourish and hyperbole. The crowd swelled when he came on. One of his recommendations was that T. Willard's face be carved on Mount Baldy north of town. But Gutzon Borglum was gone by that time, and nothing came of it. The sidewalk plaque is better.

As far as I know, the custom of the Independence Day citizen's oratory is unique to Claremont. There was talk, unmaterialized, of writing a manual for the guidance of other communities. The city of Boston has an unbroken tradition since 1776 of featuring a Fourth of July oration in Faneuil Hall, "the Cradle of Liberty." The orator of the day is usually a prominent citizen, no doubt sometimes selected as a reward for civic service. I have spoken there three times on Independence Day afternoons at the invitation of the Park Rangers, but there is no general provision for citizen participation.

Way of the Cross

The initiative for the Way of the Cross also came out of restlessness. On Good Friday each year many Protestant churches conduct three-hour worship services from twelve to three. It is generally an ecumenical effort by all the community's denominations, with seven segments and seven preachers explaining the seven last words of Christ. Many people find these services meaningful, and they are well attended. I have often turned up, and have on occasion been invited to give one of the messages.

But after sitting through such a service, I found myself wanting to find some undeveloped desert terrain around Claremont, with its Mediterranean climate, and try to get the feel of what the original day must have been like. It was fine to enjoy cool pews, sing sad songs out of hymn books plucked from the racks, and hear someone in a robe give his or her idea about the event's meaning. But it seemed to me that it might also be helpful to give people on Good Friday a chance to sweat in the hot sun. I saw the Pope on television carrying a cross through the streets of Jerusalem, and I said to myself, "Wouldn't it be great if every Christian could have the chance of carrying a cross on Good Friday?" And feel the heavy weight eat into his or her shoulders?

So I started in 1980. I found a location in Claremont that looked promising, on a hillside between the golf course and a local church. Not far from the hilltop, winter rains had eroded a cave-like escarpment that proved ideal for a simulated "tomb." The land is owned by The Claremont Colleges, and they readily gave permission for using the area, and also mowed paths for the participants through the tall grass.

The idea was to make the experience as visual and sensual as possible. At the first stop, a simulated Pilate's Pavement, we provide a basin where people can wash their hands of the whole thing. Everybody is issued a script that contains a consolidated modern language version of the Biblical account. The public is invited to arrive any time between nine and eleven-thirty. Those arriving receive an orientation on the purposes of the occasion. They generally form themselves into groups of ten to fifteen, and are led through the thirty-minute sequence by a docent. Participants are encouraged to trade off reading parts of the story from the script. It is suggested that the different ones think of themselves in the role of one of the originals—a soldier, a merchant, a zealot, one of the women, an out-of-town visitor.

We encourage people to look back from the slope to the chapel at the School of Theology, as representing the temple in the original story. At the top of the slope, persons insert the cross into a socket in the ground, stand in a circle with the script, and meditate on Christ's last hours. At this station, those who wish can pound nails into a four by four, roll dice for Christ's robe, and taste vinegar by sucking on a small sponge. During this time a white sheet, representing Christ's body, is draped over the cross before being taken down to the "tomb." One year the rising breeze unwound the sheet, and the newspaper picture made it look like a laundry line. After that we showed each docent a picture of the way the shroud is folded on the cross at the Oberammergau Passion Play.

Because of the visual effects, the newspapers have most years sent reporters and photographers, and occasionally there has been television coverage.

Walk to Los Angeles

The annual Labor Day Walk to Los Angeles grew in its first twenty years from one to hundreds of enthusiastic walkers, sometimes filling streets on their way through San Gabriel, Alhambra, and Los Angeles. The event takes place Labor Day, a holiday close to the birthday of Los Angeles, September 4th.

The city of Los Angeles celebrated its Bicentennial in 1981. The year before, I was appointed to be an education member of the planning committee. Claremont lies at the eastern edge of Los Angeles County, and the officials were including the entire county in the plans.

The history of Los Angeles is rooted in the progress of Spanish colonial interests in North America. In 1542 an explorer named Juan Rodriguez Cabrillo landed in San Diego and claimed the entire area of the Californias, plus the lands beyond, for the King of Spain. Not a bad day's work. In those days any European could land anywhere in the world, plant a stick in the ground, and say, "All of this, seen and unseen, belongs to us and our boss back home." (That is, unless another European had arrived first. Then there might be a war.) Having staked out the territory, however, the California area was difficult to get to—hot sands by land or shipwrecking storms by sea. Consequently the Spanish did nothing with it for two hundred years.

There was then a change, namely the Russians were coming, the Russians were coming. They were pushing their fur trade down from the north and were operating as far south as the Farallon Islands off San Francisco. In addition, the British began to look like a threat from the east. Soon after Cabrillo, Sir Francis Drake had claimed the West Coast area as the New Albion for the first Elizabeth and "all her heirs and assigns forever." (When Britain's Queen Elizabeth II addressed the Los Angeles City Council, she assured them, "I did not come here today to press that claim.")

The Spaniards finally decided they had better nail down their holdings. To do so, they settled on a thrust that was both religious and secular, now known as the Spanish missions. Priests and soldiers moved in and established a thriving colony of agriculture and trade, converting and training the native peoples. Separation of church and state was unknown. To give added support to the missions, the authorities decided a larger commercial anchor was needed. And that is when they decided to found Los Angeles.

Felipe de Neve, the first governor of the Californias, north and south, was commissioned to accomplish this. He recruited a cadre of settlers from Mexico, brought them up through the Missions at San Diego and San Juan Capistrano, and outfitted and oriented them at Mission San Gabriel, which by then was ten years old. The first week in September 1781 they were ready.

At my first meeting of the Bicentennial planning committee, a huge lunch at California State University at Los Angeles, we saw a film on the dynamism of Los Angeles history. The first scene was a dramatic shot of a cross above the Mission San Gabriel, seen against the brightening daybreak sky. Creaking oxcarts were rolling out down below, toward the trail that would take them nine miles to the Los Angeles River. There on September 4, 1781, we were told, forty-four Mexican nationals in eleven families, plus four soldiers, founded El Pueblo de La Reina de Los Angeles, the City of the Queen of the Angels. The founders have been called *Los Pobladores*, town settlers. They created that day a tiny community on the river that in two centuries became the most influential metropolitan center in the world.

When I saw those exciting screen images of people at dawn moving out to the trail, I said to myself, "I'd like to do that." On the Bicentennial day itself, September 4, 1981, I was the speaker of the day at the noontime meeting at the Statler Hilton Hotel of the Los Angeles Rotary Club, the fifth oldest. My topic was "A City's Promise of Renewal." The night before, I had made a speech at the Mission Plaza in San Gabriel, which I entitled "The Womb of Los Angeles." The next day, to get into the mood for the occasion I decided that before the noon meeting, I would walk that original trail from San Gabriel to Los Angeles. A Pomona doctor decided to come along. While on the trail I thought others might also like to do this. After all, some 75,000 people walk across the Mackinac Bridge in northern Michigan every Labor Day. So I cast around for support.

I had worked with the San Gabriel Historical Society, and they said the logical group to back such a commemoration would be a new organization, formed during the Bicentennial. These were direct descendants of the original founders. Marie Northrop had just published a genealogy of the settlers, and many living Americans learned for the first time they were descendants. Marie and her husband, Joseph Northrop, organized the group and called them Los Pobladores 200, signifying their founding in the bicentennial year of the city.

I met with them several times, and they liked the idea of the walk. But organizational problems kept them out of the picture until 1984. I made the walk by myself in 1982 and 1983. After that the descendants group began to participate, and from 1984 on, the project grew.

We had a public relations problem for a while in that the press apparently thought it was a better story if they treated all walkers as descendants. I was concerned that the general public might stay away if they thought the exercise was only a family reunion. But the descendants themselves from the beginning were encouraging new walkers, and with the growth in numbers, it became clear that the descendants, prominent in the walk and proudly wearing their identifying orange sashes, were being happily joined by a broad representation of modern Los Angeles's cultural diversity.

At the Los Angeles Bicentennial in 1981, Jean Bruce Poole, British born historian at El Pueblo Park, was in charge of the city's birthday celebrations, and continued for many years. I first met her on a call to find out about reports that Mexico was making a birthday gift to the city of Felipe de Neve's bones for preservation under his statue in the Los Angeles Plaza. This interesting project never materialized, partly because of authenticating problems. Apparently some of the remains were chicken bones. Jean has been a wonderful friend, and I have always enjoyed the many meetings we have attended together over more than twenty years. We had friendly disagreements over the contribution of Father Junipero Serra to California. She takes a dim view, while I have always been a fan.

At first Jean was opposed to the Walk, pointing out that it is too hot in early September, and besides the settlers had not all made the San Gabriel to Los Angeles trip on the same day. She felt all of us going at the same time might confirm what she believed was not true. She became reconciled, however; we always walked early in the morning when it is cool, and our modern walk is seen as symbolic and not accurate in every detail.

Jean was the main architect of the city's birthday program in the Plaza on the date itself, September 4. However, to make it possible for more people to participate in the Walk, we began holding it on Labor Day. Soon the whole celebration was being held on the holiday.

Now the celebration is under the aegis of a city agency, El Pueblo de Los Angeles Historical Monument Commission, which supervises Olvera Street, the Plaza, and downtown historical events. In recent years Nick Pacheco, the LA City Councilman in whose district the Plaza lies, has made the Walk and from his office has supplied staff services. Tom Labonge, another Councilman, elected in 2001, has long been an enthusiastic backer and walker starting when he was aide to then Mayor Richard Riordan.

San Gabriel is ten years older than Los Angeles, its Mission having been founded in 1771, and the Walk each year is a tale of two cities. A stirring 6:00 A.M. ceremony at the Mission tells this tale. San Gabriel officials help in the advance planning and publicity.[1]

At the close of the San Gabriel welcoming ceremonies, the Mission's senior padre sends the walkers on their way with his blessing.

---

[1]Outstanding from the beginning has been Mary Cammarano, council person and mayor when it's her turn. Likewise, Councilman Harry Baldwin, also sometime mayor. In recent years Cynthia A. Smith, the city's special projects manager, has brought her considerable public relations gifts.

Some participating families say they have learned history by doing history.

When the Swallows Come Back to Capistrano

There is another reenactment that has been an annual focus for me during the last quarter century—not a people reenactment, but a centuries-old nature reenactment. For on Saint Joseph's Day, two days before the vernal equinox, the swallows come back to the Mission San Juan Capistrano.

The legend gives everybody a welcome lift two days before the vernal equinox and buoys us all with the happy promise of spring. The media treats it with some amusement.

I became aware of press notices, attributed to the most reputable of news sources, the Associated Press, that the swallows arrived at the mission on March 19 at 7:19 or at 8:23 or some other precise time. I asked myself, how can they do that? I decided to go and see.

In 1979 I drove my Volkswagen van down to San Juan Capistrano, a burgeoning community on the seacoast halfway between Los Angeles and San Diego, where the Franciscans built a mission in 1776. I wanted to be there in plenty of time in case the swallows arrived before dawn. It was raining, and I put my sleeping bag out under a freight car parked at the quaint railroad station. The next morning, March 19, Saint Joseph's Day, I was among the first at the entrance turnstile. I asked the lady when they expected the swallows She replied that last year it was around eight o'clock, but because of the rain, they thought there might be a couple of hours' delay. So I joined the other visitors in the courtyard and waited. Rain fell intermittently.

There was a television crew and a radio announcer and assorted folks from around the U.S. and Canada—all wondering, all expectant. About ten o'clock, a muffled shout erupted, everyone looked up, and there came a flock of around fifty swallows flying inland about a hundred feet above us. At once old Paul Arbiso, official bell ringer at the mission for forty years, trotted down the path and rang the bells.

It made a believer out of me. I was there on Saint Joseph's Day, and I saw the swallows.

In the years following, it did become a joke. It will never be the same. The Swallows Festival, complete with city parade, began drawing larger crowds. The public relations experts in the mission's tourism office began announcing a swallow arrival time according to what suited their day's agenda. If Paul Arbiso had to be at a church function at 9:00 A.M., then the swallows would simply have to arrive at 8:30!

I wrote many columns on the phenomenon over the years, so each time I could start my visit to Capistrano in the press room —"mission control," they called it—with sweet rolls and coffee. I never saw a public relations person look out and see whether any swallows had actually come. By this time, it was irrelevant. "We're perpetuating a myth," one of them said. I suggested to the Rev. Paul Martin, the parish priest, who had me speak at the Mission in the summer of 1981, that they bring in people from the Audubon Society to tell the visitors what happens and restore credibility.

But today nobody really cares. There are so few swallows. In recent years I've seen only two or three. Orange County is so paved and roofed over that the swallows cannot find their necessities—insects for food, mud for nests. So they go else-where. Also the Chamber of Commerce prefers that the swallows come on a weekend for the larger crowds. So now it is mostly a commercial festival, and the swallows are mostly a memory.

The ornithologists take a dim view of the swallow legend. I went out to interview Dr. Henry E. Childs, Jr., the "Bird man" of Chaffey College in Upland. He objected to the precise-day theory, saying the swallows come in over a two-week period. He also said there are no such birds as "scouts," which is the name the Mission gives to swallows that arrive before March 19. He said that of course hundreds of thousands of swallows are invol-ved in the annual migration, and only a few choose the Mission.

The legend of the tiny fliers is kept very much alive by the popular song, "When the Swallows Come Back to Capistrano." Leon René wrote it on March 19, 1939, when he was listening in his Los Angeles home to swallows reports on the radio. The song was an immediate hit, introduced by Fred Waring and recorded by a dozen artists including Bing Crosby, Kate Smith, and Guy Lombardo. In 1940 it landed at the top of the Hit Parade on national radio. We got to be pretty good friends, Leon and his wife Irma and his son Rafael. He wrote out permission for me to use his song, waiving claims of royalties.

Just before Leon René died in 1982, he was my guest on a swallows presentation in Hollywood. It was covered by the Voice of America. It was the last time he recorded his work. In my talk that day I said that Leon had done for the swallows what Henry Wadsworth Longfellow did for Paul Revere. I concluded with the thought that many myths, while not always physically true, are often psychologically and spiritually true. They help sustain us on our journey.

The miracle of the swallows may be not so much the time of their arrival but the fact that they make that long trip, seven thousand miles—from Goya, Argentina, with very little rest, not needing older birds to guide them, and land close to the vernal equinox. Then in the fall they make the return trip, all apparently because of some wondrous guidance system in their gizzards. Do human beings have an equivalent?

In conclusion I noted that every state and every Greek god has its bird. We are even willing to let the ornithologists have

-25-

PILGRIMS' LATTER DAY PROGRESS

The Golden Years have been kind to Mary Louise and me. I stopped receiving salary checks at age sixty-five in 1980, but she kept on another ten years, making her ongoing Social Security ducats bigger than mine, a disparity of which she is happy to remind me. My last job was as assistant to the president of the Claremont School of Theology. Hers was as a personnel administrator at The Claremont Colleges.

Since then she has been active in the League of Women Voters, observing the operations of the Claremont City Council for the League; our local church; and serving twelve years on the Personnel Committee of the Pomona Inland Valley Council of Churches.

During this time I have written a book on Charles Lindbergh and another on yours truly, which you are now reading, filed a weekly column for sixteen years with three newspapers (I am told that if there are two, they qualify the writer as a "syndicated" columnist), continued the "History Alive" reenactments in Claremont, San Gabriel, and Los Angeles, addressed a modest number of service clubs (including a weekly "Word for the Day" at the University Club of Claremont), and promoted family reunions with cousins across the country.

On the Fourth of July in 1987 Mary Louise and I rode down Indian Hill Avenue in a top-down convertible. It was Claremont's one hundredth year, and I had been named Grand Marshal of the Centennial Parade. The City later installed my name on that sidewalk plaque in the park by the Speakers Corner.

In 1991 I persuaded the City Council to change the date on the municipal logo from 1907, the date of incorporation, to 1887, the date of founding. Ginger Elliott, Executive Director of Claremont Heritage, sometimes refers to me as "1887."

In local politics in the late nineties I was local chairman of the drive to stop a state ballot measure designed by the Howard Jarvis anti-tax forces to make it even more difficult for schools and other local agencies to develop financing. We won in Claremont but lost statewide. In the 2001 City Council election there were seven candidates for two seats. I was honorary chairman of one campaign where we lost and a committeeman on another where we won, installing Llewellyn Miller, the city's first African-American council person.

Bay View

Bay View, Michigan, which has been a summer family focus on Mary Louise's side for over a century, was the location of our wedding reception in 1945 (the wedding itself was held in the First Presbyterian Church of Petoskey). Mary Louise's grandfather, Adam Vogt, a second generation German jeweler and real estate developer from Louisville, had visited the area by lake steamer in 1898. Later a relative's miraculous cure from asthma after a few days in the northern Michigan air persuaded him that if it was that good for the sick, it must be good for the well. He brought his wife Louise Wedekind Vogt and children (one of them would become my mother-in-law) to temporary dwellings there and then in 1911 built the house that the family still occupies. The environment he chose was the Bay View Association, related to the United Methodist Church, founded as a Camp Meeting in 1875. It is located thirty-five miles south of the Straits of Mackinac bridge and one mile north of Petoskey on Lake Michigan's Little Traverse Bay. It is the only area in the world where is found the ancient fossil known as the Petoskey Stone, designated as Michigan's state stone. Bay View has developed through the years as a Chautauqua center, with notable preaching, concerts, music education, and lectures— plus family activities, boys' and girls' clubs, and a waterfront agenda. In the 1980s I was a recurrent Sunday morning preacher and weekday lecturer. Our tribe has now been at it long enough to make us a six-generation Bay View family.

As others have found, a summer focus like this becomes a long-range stabilizing force for the family. Through war, peace, depression, career changes, relocations, and age advances, the different generations come back year after year to find quiet re-assurance. The Victorian architecture too does not change, and in 1987 it attracted Stacy Keach and a television crew who came to shoot a segment of a TV biography of Ernest Hemingway, filmed there because Hemingway grew up summers on nearby Walloon Lake ten miles to the south. For a wedding scene they needed the Bay View turn-of-the-twentieth-century look.

In our later years, along with millions of other "elders," we have profited by participation in the Elderhostel program. Mary Louise was in on its inception when in the seventies she was administrative assistant to Harry Day, Executive Director of the New England Center for Continuing Education in Durham, New Hampshire. The Elderhostel movement was hatched in that office in 1975, and she was on the ground floor. This popular program where persons fifty-five and over can take educational mini-courses in interesting places, while living in reasonable accommodations almost anywhere in the world, was started by Marty Knowlton, a social activist and former educator, who got the idea from the European youth hostels, especially those in Scandinavia where he found folk schools handing down traditions. Back in New Hampshire he floated the idea with Harry Day and the continuing education department that Mary

Louise was serving. The conversations resulted in a pilot program in the colleges of New Hampshire, and it was an instant success. Today the summary of the worldwide Elderhostel offerings makes up a huge newsprint catalog.

Mary Louise and I have been fortunate to participate in interesting Elderhostel programs in Minnesota, New England, the Carolinas, Athens and the Greek Islands, and Turkey. In the 1990s Elderhostel introduced Service Programs, an early one of which we helped with in Jamaica, a "mini-peace-corps" setting where we both taught in the Happy Grove High School in the Province of Portland, on the eastern tip of the island.

While in Durham and managing the Continuing Education office, Mary Louise found time also to study at the University of New Hampshire, earning a Master's degree in guidance and counseling. Back in Claremont she did telephone crisis advising and facilitated support groups for returning women students at nearby community colleges. For a dozen years she was a full time professional providing employee services in the personnel office of The Claremont Colleges.

And oh, yes, beyond all I have said so far in this account, she was the lead player in raising three remarkable sons.

Mary Louise and I enjoy a broad-based happy life in our latter day community known as Pilgrim Place. We already were old-line Claremonters, having lived in the town most of the time since 1959. So it was for us a shift of only a few familiar blocks down the street. Pilgrim Place is a "retirement" community, it says here. But the residents have spent the days of their years in all out efforts to change the world—and when they arrive here they don't quit. They enthusiastically do myriad chores on their own campus, and in addition they swarm out to southern California agencies—political, social, and religious—to lend their hands to a hundred good works. It is indeed a lively place in which to live and move and have one's being.

Pilgrim Place was founded in 1915 by the Congregationalists of Pomona College, led by their president James A. Blaisdell, to give a break to veterans of the foreign mission field, many of whom in those pre-pension, pre-Social Security days, concluded their life's service penniless. Blaisdell, who later was to mastermind the creation of The Claremont Colleges group plan, was ever the practical visionary. Not only did he provide a home for the retired missionaries but he also enlisted them to deliver lectures to his students on the countries they knew so well. As to denominational origins, a majority of today's residents still come from the Congregational background (now called United Church of Christ), but nearly half are identified with almost twenty other denominations, Protestant and Catholic.

The grounds were first located where Scripps College now is, and in the 1920s moved to a larger space in artesian wetlands west of the campuses. It now occupies thirty-three acres and serves 330 retirees. It is a unique community in that admission requires a person or couple to have served twenty years in professional Christian work—missionary, minister, director of YWCA or YMCA, or professor of religion or theology. Also a prospective resident must be at least sixty-five and not over seventy-five—making for a more charged community energy level. Another distinctive feature: there is no financial means test.

We were turned down when we first applied in 1970. Although I had been for ten years an ordained minister serving churches and a seminary, the other ten years to make up my twenty proved problematical. Apparently the full time evangelistic work we had done for eighteen years with the Oxford Group/Moral Re-Armament (later known as "Initiatives of Change") did not at the time appear main-line enough. A decade later, however, Wilbur Simmons, a church veteran from

Montana and New Zealand, urged us to try again, and this time the new committee recognized our earlier service. In 1986 we moved into a nice house just inside the Berkeley/Sixth Street gate, and have found the living great and the fellowship greater. As in other retirement centers, there are at least two dozen committees in place to help people keep the ball rolling. Mary Louise has served on the Human Resources and the Health and Welfare Committees. I have been a recurring member and chairman of the Communications Committee, have been president of the Andiron Club (all-campus personal and theological discussion group), and throughout 1997 was the Moderator of Town Meeting, which is like being president of the student body.

The annual Pilgrim Place Festival is an event that has to be seen to be believed. For two November days, before Thanksgiving, most of the residents don Pilgrim costumes and market the arts and crafts they have been making all year. In addition they sell thousands of dollars worth of fine used goods and pre-owned books donated by friends from far and near. The venture is a combination of a county fair, theme park, flea market, thrift shop, kiddy rides and glue-in, and about everything else you can think of. It is a widely anticipated community event that brings 10,000 visitors from surrounding towns. Over a thousand volunteers of all ages turn up from everywhere to make it go. The net currently is over $150,000 a year, which goes into a fund to support residents who may have run out of money. Approximately ten percent of the residents receive subsidy assistance. Pilgrim Place does not assure life care, but no resident has yet been turned out for lack of funds. This of course puts a little motivational overtime steam into making the Festival a fundraising success!

The flagship experience for visitors to the Festival is the stage play "The Pilgrim Story," a one-hour outdoor dramatization of the original Pilgrims' seventeenth century trek from England , to Holland, and on to the New World. About the time we joined the community the play was being tightened and improved by Robert Dewey, retired chaplain at Kalamazoo College who has a lifelong background in drama. I helped change the show's title from "Pilgrims Triumphant" to" "The Pilgrim Story." On stage I was given the role of Chief Massasoit of the Wampanoag Indians, which sensitized me to the role of the Native Americans. We strengthened the contribution of the Indians in the treaty scene, and I wrote a speech for the Chief spelling out what the Indians wanted out of the agreement, with ideas borrowed from the famous Chief Seattle speech about the land. We also created an all-Indian opening scene, putting first the Native Americans, who were here first.

I have also played Squanto, the English-speaking aborigine that saved the Pilgrims from extinction by teaching them how to survive in the wilderness. After the performances cast members accommodate camera-toting parents looking for photo ops for their kids. Being a paleface, my make-up was obvious. One bright young girl came up and asked me, "Are you happy being a fake Indian?"

In 1992, the five hundredth anniversary of the arrival of Christopher Columbus, I was asked to present at the close of the play a commentary on today's ongoing challenges arising from the impact of European civilization on North American life.

The Executive Director of Pilgrim Place since 1998 has been William R. Cunitz, who happened to be a classmate of mine at Andover Newton Theological School. The community is going through a long-range Strategic Planning process to ensure that the fellowship meets the challenges of the twenty-first century as successfully as it has those of the twentieth.

-26-

AND IN CONCLUSION . . . .

In childhood I adopted the traditional orthodox beliefs of my parents, and the world was secure. In teenage years I fell away from this personal concept of God. I thought there was probably something behind the sunset and the stars, but whatever it was had nothing to do with me and my life. There were no imperatives except what I wanted to do.

This changed radically when as a student I was attracted to the Oxford Group and what looked to me like impressive evidence of God's intervention, when sought, in personal and national affairs. I conducted a thorough moral inventory and made restitution where indicated. The result was that something came into my life that dynamically resembled what I had heard about God. It felt as though, at least in my case, moral clean-up was a key to God becoming real. I thought this could be an explanation of the Apostle Paul's statement that "the law was our schoolmaster" leading to a life-changing experience. (Galatians 3:24) After that experience, he wrote, "we are no longer under a schoolmaster." I understood this to mean that morality is then no longer imposed but issues from something that has happened inside oneself.

This experience led to surrendering my future to the God who had now become such a felt reality in my life. This God apparently had many of my own characteristics. He had a plan and a will (Martin Luther King: "I just want to do God's will."). This God spoke to people, listened to them, had a personality that was loving and sometimes got upset, liked to be praised, meted out punishment to wrongdoers and rewarded good deeds, forgave those who were sorry, provided guidance at forks in the road, and at all times was, in Gershwin's words, "some one to watch over me."

There was a covenant idea behind it all. If I gave myself over to God's plan, he in turn would bless me and mine and protect us from harm. Abraham of old was promised—you go my way, and I'll give you land, lots of Middle East land, plus numerous descendants. A problem arose when different ones believed they were promised the same territory. They have been fighting over it ever since.

It was to this God that had a plan for my life that in college under the influence of Walter Judd I made the turning-point decision that was to direct my days. His challenge, against the background of my family upbringing, led me to make an unconditional commitment to "God's plan." In spite of the vicissitudes and the later doubts, I would probably do the same all over again. I believe that from the beginning I was programmed in that direction by some Reality somewhere, however different the image of that Reality might appear at different times.

The nature of God is explained in various ways. For example, in response to the question as to where was God on September 11, 2001, Billy Graham seemed to hold that God could have stopped the disaster if so inclined, and confessed at a memorial service in the National Cathedral that he had no idea why these things are allowed to happen. The Process Theology people say God is not all-powerful and cannot prevent evil events, but does suffer with us in our pain. At the same time some of them say that evil will not have the last word, and they quote ground-breaking Process thinker, Alfred North Whitehead: "The kingdom of heaven is not the isolation of good from evil. It is the overcoming of evil by good."

Will we ever know answers to all these questions? Do we

have to leave it as entirely a mystery? Will Paul's promise come true—that although we now "see through a glass darkly," we will some day see "face to face"? I frequently quote Robert Hamerton-Kelly, former Scripps College professor:

> If I could understand or explain what God is up to, my worst fears would be realized, namely that the human mind is the greatest force in the universe.

There probably is nothing wrong about a person having a different kind of faith at various stages of life—rising at times and falling at times. The world changes; times change; and perspectives change. Older people, as they near the end of the road, often find a deeper, more intense, faith. As of this writing, mine is still evolving.

One cannot ignore the great minds of the past who have followed what they believed was God's leading. Of course the idea also has done great mischief. My college president, Dr. Cowling, a lifelong dedicated churchman, said on occasion that he believed that over all, religion may have done more harm than good. But even if one accepts that contention, it is also true that the column of progress has been created by God-fearing devotees with an others-centered motivation. Saint Augustine claimed we are made in such a way that we are incomplete without God. George Buttrick, the New York preacher, told me at his summer home in Charlevoix, Michigan, that man is not only a tool-building animal but he is also an altar-building animal. The implication is that there must then be Something out there to which the altar is built.

Benjamin Franklin told the U. S. Constitutional Convention he believed "God governs" in human affairs. Abraham Lincoln said, "I am satisfied that when the Almighty wants me to do or not to do a particular thing, he finds a way of letting me know it." C. G. Jung, psychiatry pioneer, said his scientific observations led him to "know" of God's existence because those with faith lived more fulfilled lives.

Whatever may be the character of the transcendental forces that may or may not be guiding us. I think most could probably subscribe to the sentiment expressed by Winston Churchill in a 1941 address to the United States Congress shortly after Pearl Harbor:

> He must indeed have a blind soul who cannot see that some great purpose and design is being worked out here below, of which we have the honor to be the faithful servants.

With another century already well under way, the question is, will we live any better in the new era? A wag advises, "Live every millennium as though it were your last." So far, in terms of justice, we seem to have been making progress. But is there chaos ahead? A friend comments, "Every generation believes the world is going down the tubes. Only this time it really is." The man with the sandwich board proclaiming, "The end is near," says people don't laugh any more.

British historian Arnold J. Toynbee wrote that of the more than twenty civilizations that have arisen and disappeared, only ours remains. Will we be any different? Nations as well as individuals are apparently subject to a universal cycle. People—and systems—are born, they live, and they die. This happens even in the heavens according to the late astronomer Carl Sagan, who said that galaxies go through stages of "coming into being, evolving, and perishing."

Will our planet perish? If so, will it be from overpopulation? sustainability failure? climate changes? meteor collision? fossil fuel depletion? atomic waste? armed conflict?

If human nature is the problem, can it change in time? Alcoholics Anonymous has dramatically demonstrated that human beings can change completely around. There are also illustrations in American history of whole peoples finding a new orientation.

The Great Awakening of New England in the mid-eighteenth century was a people's firestorm that swept the colonies and transformed large numbers of persons and their communities. Some say that it was this spiritual revolution that made possible the Independence movement. Harvard's Alan Heimert wrote, "In the Great Awakening the will of the people began its steady march to eventual supremacy."

The Second Great Awakening—a hundred years later— produced another gale-force outbreak that swept from upstate New York through the Middle West. In an important by-product it established a hundred small colleges while their communities were dedicated to renewal. Most importantly its crusade generated much of the moral fervor that ended slavery.

Is there an equivalent today? If so, is it something we create or does it just happen to us? We are told there is a difference between the Greek and the Judeo-Christian views of history. The one holds that the world goes around and around in endless repetition (like the busdrivers), and the other that it all began sometime, it has gone through a long process, and someday it will come to an end.

This could take a long time, and each of us is called to do our part.

Loren Eisley's famous starfish story, so popular at the turn of the century, is always fresh.

A young man was picking up objects off the beach and tossing them out into the sea. A second man approached him and saw that the objects were starfish. "Why in the world are you throwing starfish into the water?" he asked.

"If the starfish are still on the beach when the tide goes out and the sun rises high in the sky, they will die," replied the young man.

"That is ridiculous. There are miles of beach and millions of starfish. You can't really believe that what you're doing could possibly make any difference!"

The young man picked up another starfish, paused, and as he tossed it out into the waves, he said, "I'm making a difference to this one."

APPENDIX A

HOW TO WRITE A SPEECH
(At Least These Steps Have Worked for Me)

1. Put down in one sentence what you want your speech to say.

2. Formulate from that sentence an attractive title (not too cute).This can be postponed until your message is clearer.

3. On a sheet of paper or pad, start one-third of the way down and record a free association of every idea you can think of relating to the topic. Save the top third for a later step. On the bottom two thirds, record in free association the following:
   a. Everything you can brainstorm on your subject.
   b. Number each idea, one idea to a line
   c. A quotation to be looked up
   d. An illustration or joke
   e. A recalled incident
   f. Notes or text you may have written previously on a related theme

4. Then go to reference sources for more ideas—keep numbering them—one idea to each line. The following may prove useful:
   a. Internet
   b. *Bartlett's Familiar Quotations*—its index often turns up an apt quotation or line of poetry
   c. *World Almanac and Book of Facts*
   d. *American Book of Days*
   e. *Roget's Thesaurus*—if your computer's thesaurus fails
   f. *Collegiate Dictionary*
   g. Encyclopedias—electronic—*Columbia*—*Britannica*
   h. *Webster's Biographical Dictionary*
   i. *Reader's Encyclopedia of American Literature*
   j. *The Oxford Companion to English Literature*

5. If you run out of work-sheet space (bottom two-thirds), scotch-tape a second sheet extending out to the right—these additional ideas need to be seeable and flat without flipping sheets.

6. When you have recorded all the ideas you can think of, see whether the ideas listed are starting to fall into two or three general categories.

7. Now go back to the blank top third of your work sheet—
   a. On the left hand margin write Roman numerals I-V, one below the other
   b. Assign the least space to "I" and "V"—they are for intro and conclusion. Referring to "6" above, give a sub-head to each of the three categories that have emerged, writing that sub-head next to each of "II", "III", and "IV"—these may prove to be your speech's three main points. You may have less or more than three points, but three has a modified magic about it. People tend to remember three points. What's more, the speaker can remember three points!

8. Roman numeral I is devoted to your gripping opener. Numeral V is for your power-closing illustration, poem, quotation, or appeal.

9. Now is the time to take the ideas you have recorded on the bottom two-thirds of the work sheet, and group them above under the "chapter " headings in the top third—II-III-IV—by taking the Arabic numerals you have assigned to the brain-stormed points and placing them in the top third of the sheet alongside the Roman numeral where they logically fit.

Now you are ready to write

10. To prime the pump, it sometimes helps just to **do something!** Starting with a blank screen or paper. In the upper right hand corner write the date the speech is to be delivered. Under that write the occasion of the speech; then the name of the sponsor; and under that, your name. Then in capital letters in the center of the page, write:

THE TITLE OF THE SPEECH

11. Start writing.
    a. If your compelling opening has come to you, start right in with it.

   b. If not, you can leave that until your main text is clearer.

   c. A good joke often relaxes both the audience and you, but it should be germane to your theme, the occasion, or your audience.

12. Write every word.

   a. You will not deliver it all. Modifications will suggest themselves when on your feet.

   b. However, writing generates confidence and fluency; phrases come back.

   c. A neat script, interestingly, is helpful, even though you leave it behind. You are not memorizing, but somehow a messy text back on your desk affects your subconscious at the podium.

13. Rewrite

   a. Polish for grammar, syntax, rhythm, sequence, flow.

   b. Keep asking, is this written for the ear?

14. Copies

If you make copies for the media, your sponsors, or others, photocopying two-sided saves bulk. Filing your speeches according to date or topic helps. You may speak on the same subject again, and you will not have to reinvent the wheel. Of course you will have fresh ideas for the new occasion, but the old ones may be starters for you.

HOW TO DELIVER A SPEECH
WITHOUT NOTES

Believe

1. Enthusiasm is all-important. Another word: passion. Winston Churchill said, "Before he can move their tears, his own must flow."

Manuscript

2. The first step toward good delivery is to write the speech out.

3. The second is to get it into one's head.

4. To do this, read the manuscript out loud all the way through once.

5. Leaving the script behind, take a walk and say the speech through—with gestures—as much as you can remember. Having talked it through once, turn around and repeat the process all the way back.

6. Go back to the script and see whether on your walk you made important omissions. Unimportant ones may prove dispensable. Think over the important ones.

Re-Outline

7. On a 5x7 card, write in a list one word for each paragraph of the speech, each word a boil-down of that paragraph, preferably with felt pen in block letters, so they make a strong visual impression. This helps set in your mind the flow of ideas.

8. On the back of the card, type out the speech's main quotes, the only part of the talk that should be memorized.

Rehearse

9. Dale Carnegie, grandfather of modern public speaking, recommends a half dozen rehearsals. Driving to the speech site usually allows for another two out-loud run-throughs.

Dress
10. It is important that your clothes do not compete with your words for attention.

Notes
11. Speaking without notes is highly recommended. Carnegie says notes cut people's interest in a talk in half. Notes are a circuit-breaker. They subvert eye-contact and make the speaker pre-occupied with what he or she had prepared rather than with what the audience needs at the moment.

12. People who say, "I can't do that," have probably talked on more than one occasion for an hour at a time without notes on a subject they were interested in—family, sports, special project.

13. It is not a matter of **memory**. It is reconstructing on your feet what you have already constructed at your desk In fact memorization is not helpful because it shifts your mind off the audience onto yourself, makes you concentrate on what was in the script instead of what is in the audience in front of you.

14. "If you do not use a manuscript, why write it out in the first place?" Three reasons:
    i. It provides girders for your talk—a beginning, a middle and an end;
    ii. It improves fluency—many of the phrases you have written out will surface when you are on your feet;
    iii. It heightens your confidence; you know you are well prepared.

Platform
15. TV personality Art Linkletter says it's better to speak without a lectern, people have more confidence, you are not hiding anything. If you were proposing marriage or selling a Buick, you would not speak to the person from behind a pile of wood. Exception: courtesy may suggest fitting in to the platform customs of the sponsoring organization.

16. Microphone: Cordless, body-pack is probably best, lavaliere next. The hand-held mike is least effective, OK for chairman's announcements, but it is bad for a speaker, interferes with body language, cuts gesturing in half, and hides expressive parts of the face. Leave this all-day-sucker to Vegas entertainers who are nervous about what to do with their hands.

Humor

17. Humor at the outset is a rapport builder, increases audience interest in what comes next and oils up the speaker, but needs to be related to the situation or the subject matter. A goodie saved for later in the speech is not a bad idea—to keep people interested. Occasional humorous treatment of your material may be as effective as punch-line jokes.

Pauses

18. A pause is one of the world's best ways of riveting attention. It almost has the effect of a rifle shot. Many speakers are terrified of silence and rush in with words to fill what they are afraid will be dead air, when they could bind their listeners to them with a moment of silence. Pauses also help one avoid monotonous delivery. After a pause it is natural to speak at a different volume and pace.

Gestures

19. The best gestures punctuate what your words are saying; they come out of your body's natural urge to back up what your voice is saying. It is best to start with one's hands hanging naturally at one's sides, although this takes some doing in view of our natural inclinations. Hamlet admonished his players, "Do not saw the air too much with your hand thus, but use all gently."

Close

20. This is the second most important part of your speech, the opening being the most important. The close is designed to leave the listeners with a life-changing challenge. A line from a poem is often effective, or a classic quotation from a Lincoln, a Churchill, or a Shakespeare.

21. After you finish, hold the audience with your eyes for a few moments and let the message sink in. Then say some appropriate sign-off. I like "God bless us, every one!" from the *Christmas Carol*. Never say "Thank you" or "Thank you very much." This is nervous garbage that only can mean, "I'm through now." It is the speaker, not the audience, who has provided the service, and it is demeaning for him or her to thank them.

22. It is helpful to record the speech on your own inconspicuous recorder. Listening on the way home, you can give yourself a self-critique which may prove useful in the future.

23. Rhetoric changes things. The classic meaning of the word *rhetoric* is "the art of oratory, especially persuasive language to influence the thought and actions of listeners." If you wonder what impact the spoken word can make on history, remember two names— Adolf Hitler and Winston Churchill. Your speech can make a difference.

APPENDIX C

I TALKED MY WAY ACROSS THE COUNTRY
FOR THE LOS ANGELES BICENTENNIAL

From April 19, 1981, at the Old North Church in Boston, to the following September 4th in downtown Los Angeles, I conducted an oratorical salute to the Los Angeles Bicentennial. Its theme, according to Los Angles Mayor Tom Bradley was "to honor the past, celebrate the present, and shape the future." It was a private initiative on my part, but Jane Pisano, Executive Director, wrote me a request that on the trip I would "salute the 200th anniversary of Los Angeles."

Transportation on my transcontinental tour was mostly by an old 1972 Volkswagen van, which I drove 20,000 miles. Mike Colton, executive director of the LA Chamber of Commerce, paved the way for me by writing to the Chamber of Commerce in every city on my itinerary. In 20 weeks I delivered 61 addresses in 28 cities (15 states). The last one was on the Bicentennial day itself, September 4, 1981. The hearers at the finale were gathered as the downtown Los Angeles Rotary Club. What they heard was: "A City's Promise of Renewal."

The following speeches were made:

April 19 Sun   Old North Church, Boston, 8:00 P.M.—annual Lantern Service
April 20 Mon   Concord Bridge, noon— "Dare to Die" the Concord Hymn
April 21 Tue   Boston Common, noon—"Swim or Sink - Survive or Perish"
April 23 Thu   Provincetown, noon—Mayflower Compact monument
               "Covenant and Combine Ourselves"
April 24 Fri   New York Harbor Statue of Liberty, noon—"I Lift My Lamp"
               Manhattan visit Nathan Hale Plaque, 4-5:00 P.M.—"But One Life"
April 26 Sun   Yorktown Bicentennial Center, 1:30 P.M.—
               "Yorktown's Declaration of Independence"
April 27 Mon   Washington Capitol steps, noon—Lincoln's 2nd Inaugural
               "To See the Right"
April 28 Tue   Richmond Capitol Square, noon—"Give Me Patrick Henry"
               St. John's Church, 5:00 P.M.—"Give Me Liberty or Give Me Death"
May 2   Sat   St. Augustine waterfront band shell, 12-3:00 P.M.—
               "St. Augustine & LA"
               Jacksonville Wesley Manor, 5:45 P.M.—"Founding Parallels"
May 3   Sun   Jacksonville Church of Our Saviour, 10:00 A.M.—
               "A Great Awakening"

May 4   Mon   St. Augustine Rotary, noon—"Roots East and West"

May 5   Tue   St. Augustine Kiwanis

May 11   Mon   Bartlesville, OK Rotary YWCA, noon—
               "The Impact of Will Rogers"

May 12   Tue   Claremore Rotary 1st United Methodist Church, noon—
               "The Impact of Will Rogers"

May 13   Wed   St. Louis Old Court House, noon—"The Spirit of Lewis & Clark"

May 14   Thu   St. Louis Jefferson Memorial Auditorium Forest Park, 4 P.M.—
               "The Spirit of Charles Lindbergh"

May 18   Mon   Springfield, IL Old State Capitol, noon—"A House Divided"

May 19   Tue   Springfield Lincoln Farewell Depot, 8 A.M.—
               "With That Assistance"

May 21   Thu   Vincennes George Rogers Clark Memorial, 6:30 P.M.—
               "A Few Well Conducted"

May 25   Mon   Pennsburg, PA following Memorial Day Parade—
               "That That Nation Might Live"

May 26   Tue   Philadelphia Independence Hall, noon—
               "Our Lives Our Fortunes & Our Sacred Honor"

May 30   Sat   Gettysburg National Military Cemetery, noon—
               "The Last Full Measure of Devotion"
               Repeated the Gettysburg Address five times that afternoon,
               Memorial Day, on original site

June 5   Fri   Galesburg, IL, Exchange Club, Elks Club—
               "Hold My Coat While I Stone Stephen"

June 6   Sat   Galesburg, IL, Railroad Days, 8:30 A.M.—presentation at opening
               Historical Society Browning House, 2 P.M.—"Rails on the Prairie"
               Dinner program, Knox College Class of 1931

June 7   Sun   Galesburg, IL, Central Congregational Church, 10:30 A.M.—
               "The Answer is Blowin' in the Wind"
               Historical Society, 2 P.M.—"Lincoln & Douglas at Galesburg"

June 13   Sat   Little Falls, MN, Lindbergh Interpretive Center, 1:30 P.M.—
               "Lindbergh and Hawaii"

June 20   Sat   Northfield, MN, Scriver Bank Raid Bldg, 10:30 A.M.—
               "The Fascination of Jesse James"

July 4   Sat   Petoskey, MI, Bay Park, 11-5 P.M., Independence Day Oration—
               "More Than Self"

July 5   Sun   Bay View, MI, Assembly, 10:45 A.M.—"What's Fair"

July 6   Mon   Bay View, MI, Assembly, 10 A.M.—
               "The Faith of George Washington"

July 7   Tue   Bay View, MI, Assembly, 10 A.M.—
               "The Faith of Benjamin Franklin"

July 8   Wed   Bay View, MI, Assembly, 10 A.M.—
               "The Faith of Abraham Lincoln"

July 9   Thu   Bay View, MI, Assembly, 10 A.M.—
                 "The Faith of Will Rogers"
July 10   Fri   Bay View, MI, Assembly, 10 A.M.—
                 "The Faith of Charles Lindbergh"
July 19   Sun   Montgomery, AL, Dexter Ave King Meml Baptist Ch, 11 A.M.—
                 "The Power to Change"
July 21   Tue   San Antonio, TX, Kelly Lackland Air Bases Rotary Club, noon
July 22   Wed   San Antonio, TX, Alamo Park Plaza, noon—
                 "Why We Remember the Alamo"
Aug 23   Sun   Claremont, CA, evening, hometown welcoming reception
Aug 27   Thu   Mission San Juan Capistrano, noon—
                 "Bicentennial Mission & Bicentennial City"
Sept 3   Thu   Mission San Gabriel Arcangel Plaza Park, 7 P.M.—
                 "The Womb of Los Angeles"
Sept 4   Fri   Los Angeles Hilton Hotel, LA Rotary, noon—
                 "A City's Promise of Renewal"

The New York Times

THE NEW YORK TIMES, SATURDAY, APRIL 25, 1981

Notes on People

Orator to Talk His Way Across Country

The patriotic orator may be an increasingly endangered species, with a platform hard to find beyond the small-town Fourth of July celebration, but **T. Willard Hunter** firmly believes that "America is worth talking about." Yesterday at the Statue of Liberty he did just that, making a 35-minute speech, "I Lift My Lamp," to tourists in the flagpole area.

Although it was hardly a patch on his lifetime record of three hours, the speech was the second in a transcontinental series at historic sites scheduled by Mr. Hunter, a 63 year-old minister and educational fundraiser, who is now assistant to the Theology School president at the Claremont (Calif.) Colleges. The tour began on Patriots' Day at Boston's Old North Church and will end at the Los Angeles Bicentennial Sept. 4.

Traveling in his '72 Volkswagen van, the Idaho-born orator plans to make 40 speeches with 40 different titles from the Capitol steps in Washington and the Gettysburg National Cemetery to the Alamo and the Spanish missions in California.

Although Mr. Hunter attended Harvard Law School and served at a New Hampshire church for six years, the Statue of Liberty was new to him. "I went to the top; I have to go to the top of everything," he said. "But what I liked most was the way the lady's right heel comes up from the ground. Nothing flat-footed, she's ready to go."

APPENDIX D

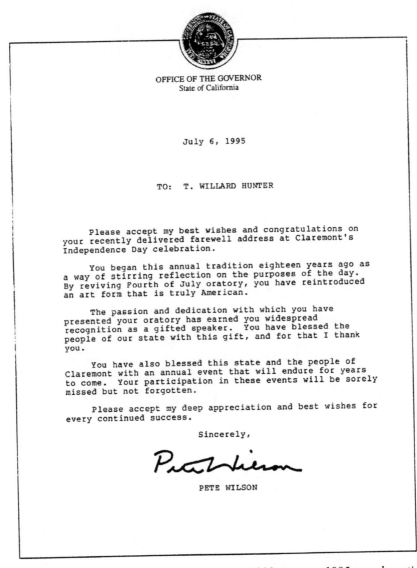

OFFICE OF THE GOVERNOR
State of California

July 6, 1995

TO: T. WILLARD HUNTER

Please accept my best wishes and congratulations on your recently delivered farewell address at Claremont's Independence Day celebration.

You began this annual tradition eighteen years ago as a way of stirring reflection on the purposes of the day. By reviving Fourth of July oratory, you have reintroduced an art form that is truly American.

The passion and dedication with which you have presented your oratory has earned you widespread recognition as a gifted speaker. You have blessed the people of our state with this gift, and for that I thank you.

You have also blessed this state and the people of Claremont with an annual event that will endure for years to come. Your participation in these events will be sorely missed but not forgotten.

Please accept my deep appreciation and best wishes for every continued success.

Sincerely,

PETE WILSON

Pete Wilson, governor of California, 1991-1999, sent a 1995 proclamation commending the Fourth of July oratory program in Claremont, saying, "You have also blessed this state and the people of Claremont with an annual event that will endure for years to come."

APPENDIX E

STATE OF NEW HAMPSHIRE

Wednesday
16 Jun 71

The Senate met at 1 o'clock.

A quorum was present.

Prayer was offered by Guest Chaplain, Rev. T. Willard Hunter of the Union Congregational Church, Madbury, New Hampshire.

O God of ages, maker and breaker of mighty nations, we come before you this afternoon in the humble knowledge that all our human wisdom has thus far failed to stem the tide of the destruction and decay we see all around us. Pour into our souls the concrete of character that will help make us more nearly adequate to the assignment has been handed to us.

We pray that towering conflicts within our state may be healed. We pray for Walter Peterson. We pray for William Loeb. We pray for teamwork. We would that New Hampshire might be not only first in the nation with a presidential primary election but also first as a pattern of reconciliation that might launch a wave of national unity throughout our country.

Give us wisdom and insight above and beyond our poor powers in the decisions we must make in this room this day, and give us not only our daily bread but also the peace that passes all understanding, both at home and abroad, starting with ourselves.

We pray today not only for our state leadership but for our national leadership as well. We pray especially for your servants Richard Nixon, Henry Kissinger, and all those who have the awe-ful decisions to make affecting peace and war. Uphold them in their fearful moments. Reprove them when tempted with lesser motives. Encourage them to follow your ways. And give us all a just peace at last, in Jesus' name. Amen.

Pledge of Allegiance was led by Sen. Poulsen.

Guest Chaplain at State Senate, New Hampshire, 16 June 1971.

Wednesday, 16 Jun 71

HOUSE
JOURNAL

STATE OF NEW HAMPSHIRE

The House met at 1:30 o'clock.

JOINT CONVENTION

Prayer was offered by Guest Chaplain Rev. T. Willard Hunter, Union Congregational Church, Madbury.

Our Father and our God, we meet here again in this historic hall, in the hope that we can help order our society and the relationships among the men and women of this great commonwealth. Oftentimes the problems look simply too great for human wisdom to handle. And so we turn to you at the opening of this session in the prayer that you will give us wisdom from on high. In that wisdom we pray that we can somehow create here in New Hampshire a level of teamwork and compassion that will be like a beacon set on a hill. Remove from us, we pray, all desire to continue or inflate factionalism. Teach us how to disagree without being disagreeable. Help us to decide the issues before us on the basis not of who's right but what's right. May we seek the good of all and not of any one interest. These things we ask in the name of Him in whose service is perfect freedom, Jesus Christ our Lord. Amen.

Rep. Ralph Wilson led the pledge of Allegiance.

HOUSE
LEAVES OF ABSENCE

Rep. Webber, today and tomorrow, illness.

Rep. Ackerson, the week, important business.

Rep. Whittemore, the day, important business.

Guest Chaplain at State House, New Hampshire, 16 June 1971.

APPENDIX G

City of Los Angeles

COMMENDATION

T. Willard Hunter

WHEREAS, T. WILLARD HUNTER, A NOTED SPEAKER AND AUTHOR, FORMER ADMINISTRATOR AT THE CLAREMONT COLLEGES AND EXECUTIVE VICE PRESIDENT OF THE INDEPENDENT COLLEGES OF SOUTHERN CALIFORNIA, BELIEVED THAT REENACTMENT OF HISTORIC EVENTS WAS A GOOD WAY FOR FAMILIES TO SUSTAIN THEIR CULTURAL HERITAGE, AND, WHILE SERVING ON THE BICENTENNIAL COMMITTEE OF THE CITY OF LOS ANGELES IN 1981 CONCEIVED OF THE IDEA OF AN HISTORIC WALK RETRACING THE ROUTE TAKEN BY THE ORIGINAL SETTLERS FROM SAN GABRIEL MISSION TO FOUND EL PUEBLO DE LA REINA DE LOS ANGELES OVER THE SUMMER OF 1781, AND

WHEREAS, IN 1981, ON SEPTEMBER 4TH, THE DAY CELEBRATED AS THE CITY'S BIRTHDAY, HE WALKED ALL NINE MILES FROM SAN GABRIEL MISSION TO THE OLD PLAZA AND ENCOURAGED THE DESCENDANTS OF THE ORIGINAL SETTLERS TO JOIN IN THE WALK AS WELL AS ANYONE ELSE INTERESTED IN THIS SYMBOLIC REENACTMENT; AND

WHEREAS, NOW THAT THE HISTORIC WALK HAS BECOME AN INTEGRAL PART OF THE CELEBRATION OF THE CITY'S BIRTHDAY AND IS A TRADITIONAL EVENT, WILLARD HUNTER IS THE ONLY PERSON TO HAVE MADE ALL FIFTEEN HISTORIC WALKS FROM 1981 TO 1995;

NOW, THEREFORE, I, RICHARD J. RIORDAN, MAYOR OF THE CITY OF LOS ANGELES, ON BEHALF OF ITS RESIDENTS, DO HEREBY COMMEND T. WILLARD HUNTER FOR HIS CREATIVE ROLE IN PLANNING AND PROMOTING THIS SYMBOLIC REENACTMENT OF THE FOUNDING OF LOS ANGELES AND THANK HIM FOR THE INSPIRATION HE HAS PROVIDED FOR THE MANY POBLADORES DESCENDANTS AND ALL THOSE INTERESTED IN CELEBRATING THE FOUNDING OF THE CITY OF LOS ANGELES.

SEPTEMBER 4, 1995

MAYOR

Richard Riordan, Mayor of Los Angeles, 1993-2001, sent a 1995 proclamation saluting the annual Walk to Los Angeles which each year reenacts the founding of the City, September 4, 1781.

gene perret

1485 Westhaven Road
San Marino, CA 91108
(213) 793-4716

12/17/82

Dear T. Willard,

I really like what you're doing with Words.

I especially liked the issue on Will Rogers. I have it bound for preservation.

Keep it up

Sincerely,

Gene.

+ Happy Holidays

Gene Perret comments on the communications newsletter Words. He has written for Bob Hope since 1969 and for the last decade was the comedian's head writer.

APPENDIX I

WALTER H. JUDD
3083 ORDWAY STREET, N.W.
WASHINGTON, D. C. 20008

9/83

Dear Willard,

Just today, while riding our subway, I read your August "WORDS". After reading with approval your telling the story of how the various "anonymous" movements emerged from Buchman's vision and dedication and understanding of man — with God, I came to page four and your report on a certain "Orator-Statesman". My surprise was followed by a glow of appreciation greater than from any appraisal of my work and witness anyone has ever written or said. Not because of the eloquent tribute to myself but because you perceived what the crusading was all about, you've been doing it yourself too, these many decades — which is why you understand.

Thanks so very much for what you wrote, and still more for what you are.

With my love and deep appreciation

Walter.

Walter H. Judd, medical missionary to China and U.S. Congressman from Minnesota, responds to an item I wrote in the newsletter Words.

INLAND VALLEY

Daily Bulletin
July 8, 2001

The Speakers Corner is a wonderful tradition for Claremont. It began many years ago after Hunter heard George C. S. Benson, founding president of Claremont McKenna College, give a short July Fourth speech to the effect that the holiday reminds us that there are principles worth dying for.

I said afterward, "What are those principles, and why don't we talk about them on the Fourth of July," Hunter recalled Wednesday. "The hotdogs are great, the fireworks are great, the parade is tremendous, but we ought to spend some time talking about those principles."

Hunter is an orator of note. An 86-year-old who reckons he began his public speaking at age 9, he has delivered Lincoln's Gettysburg Address at the Civil War battlefield itself on five occasions. He was in the Guinness Book of Records for a couple of years in the 1980s after he spoke nonstop for 34 hours and eight minutes in front of Philadelphia's Independence Hall in 1982.

In Claremont on July 4 he delivered the day's final and lengthiest oration as usual, among other things reciting from memory "Casey at the Bat," the Gettysburg Address and Martin Luther King's "I Have a Dream" speech.

He exhorted his audience, as an act of patriotism and moral obligation, to send the upcoming tax rebate back to Washington to pay down the national debt. It was hard to tell how many takers he had in the crowd for that idea.

Claremont owes Hunter its gratitude for beginning and maintaining a tradition that speaks to the highest ideals of the Fourth of July.

—*Mike Brossart, editor*

INDEX